IMPACT

IMPACT

The History of
Germany's V-Weapons
in World War II

**BENJAMIN KING &
TIMOTHY J. KUTTA**

SARPEDON
Rockville Centre, NY

Published by
SARPEDON
49 Front Street
Rockville Centre, NY 11570

© 1998 by Benjamin King and Timothy J. Kutta

ISBN 1-885119-51-8

Cataloging-in-publication data is available from the
Library of Congress.

Published in the UK by Spellmount Ltd,
Staplehurst, Kent, ISBN 1-86227-024-4.

10 9 8 7 6 5 4 3 2 1

MANUFACTURED IN THE UNITED STATES OF AMERICA

Contents

This Book is Respectfully Dedicated
to the Memory of
RICHARD C. BIGGS
Dick was a retired Army colonel and a combat veteran
of World War II. The authors owe him a great deal.
He was able to find rare reference material when we were
just getting started and continued to help with research
and editing. Throughout, his comments and suggestions
were laced with good sense and wry humor. Even after
he became terminally ill, he continued to assist us.
We will miss you, Dick.

Authors' Preface

For more than three years, the authors discussed weapons development in World War II and found there were a number of unanswered questions about the German V-weapons. The most commonly held belief was that even though the weapons killed and injured thousands of civilians in London, they had no effect on the course of the war. We wondered how thousands of flying bombs and ballistic missiles could be launched against a city like London with no effect on the war and began research to answer the question. What we found was that the V-weapons had an incredible impact on operations and war plans and we decided to tell the story.

No book like this can be written without a great deal of assistance. The authors would like to thank the following: Mr. Richard Biggs, to whom the book is dedicated; Dr. Robert Browning, Historian of the Coast Guard, for his assistance in tracking down merchant ships damaged during the V-weapon assault on Antwerp; Mr. David Ross of the U.S. Army Air Defense Musum at Fort Bliss, Texas, who assisted with information on the S.C.R. 584 radar and the air defense of Antwerp; Ms. Barbara Bower, director of the U.S. Army Transportation Museum at Fort Eustis, VA, and Ms. Carolyn Wright who maintains the photo collection of the museum, for helping us find photos of Antwerp taken during the period; Mr. Richard Baker and Ms. Louise Arnold-Friend of the Military History Institute Library at Carlisle Barracks, PA; and last but not least Ms. Marion Knihncki, head of the U.S. Army Transportation Library at Fort Eustis. Ms. Knihncki and her staff, Valerie Fashion, Diane Forbes and Michelle Masias made available original records of the Transportation Corps during World War II and assisted us with uncounted inter-library loans. If there is anyone who we have forgotten to thank, we sincerely apologize. The authors take full responsibility for any errors of omission or commission within these covers.

Benjamin King
Timothy J. Kutta
1998

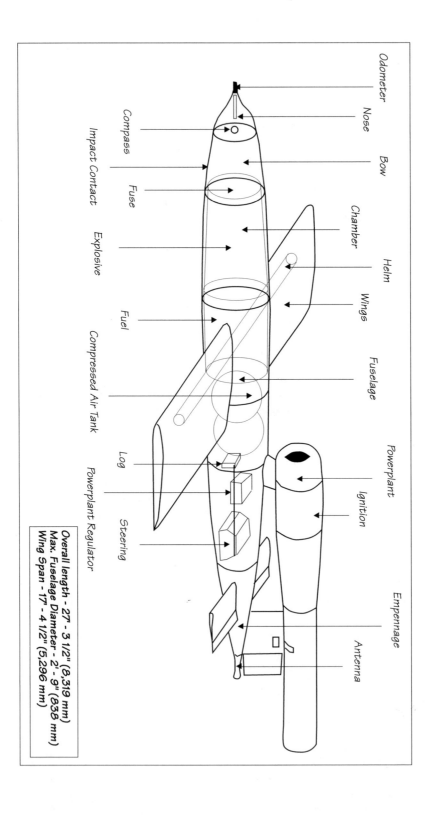

Odometer

Nose

Compass

Bow

Impact Contact

Fuse

Chamber

Helm

Explosive

Wings

Fuel

Fuselage

Compressed Air Tank

Log

Powerplant

Steering

Ignition

Powerplant Regulator

Empennage

Antenna

Overall length - 27' - 3 1/2" (8,319 mm)
Max. Fuselage Diameter - 2' - 9" (838 mm)
Wing Span - 17' - 4 1/2" (5,296 mm)

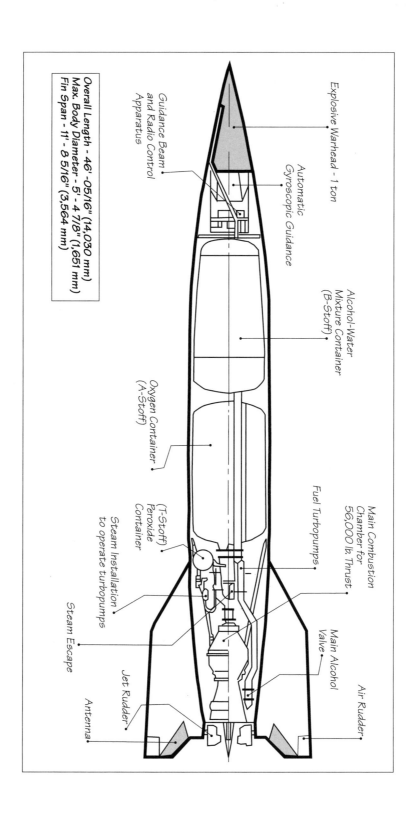

Explosive Warhead - 1 ton

Automatic
Gyroscopic Guidance

Guidance Beam
and Radio Control
Apparatus

Alcohol-Water
Mixture Container
(B-Stoff)

Oxygen Container
(A-Stoff)

Main Combustion
Chamber for
56,000 lb. Thrust

Fuel Turbopumps

(T-Stoff)
Peroxide
Container

Steam Installation
to operate turbopumps

Main Alcohol
Valve

Air Rudder

Steam Escape

Jet Rudder

Antenna

Overall Length - 46' -05/16" (14,030 mm)
Max. Body Diameter - 5' - 4 7/8" (1,651 mm)
Fin Span - 11' - 8 5/16" (3,564 mm)

Introduction

Shortly after 4:00 A.M. on June 13, 1944, observers E.E. Woodland and A.M. Wraight at Observer Post Mike 2 at Dymchurch, England spotted a flying object spurting flames from its tail and making a noise like a Model T. The first V-1 "flying bomb" to be fired at England passed by the observers and overflew a series of towns until its engine stopped some five minutes later and it dove to earth to explode in an open field. The second V-1 to appear from across the Channel landed in a potato field, but the third reached Bethnal Green, destroying a railroad bridge and two houses, killing six people and injuring another thirty. Among the dead were a young mother and her eight-month-old baby. This tragedy initiated a new era in warfare.

Until that moment in World War II, the aerial bombardment of cities and production centers had been carried out by flying machines crewed by human beings, operating their aircraft through opposing fighters and antiaircraft fire. No matter how high or how fast the bombers flew, or the seriousness of the damage they caused, there was still a small comfort that the enemy was flesh and blood and could themselves be killed or turned back. Photographs of downed enemy planes, captured pilots and dead aircrew populated the newspapers, magazines and news film of every nation to show just how vulnerable and human the enemy really was.

The V-1 changed that. Today, in an age when ballistic missiles and television-guided cruise missiles are everyday realities, it is difficult to imagine just what the V-1 meant to the people of England in that weary summer of 1944. For the first time, a population was faced with a weapon so devoid of humanity that it and the later V-2 left more and deeper psychological scars than the Battle of Britain or the subsequent

1

Blitz. Perhaps the best way to communicate the feelings of those in the target area can be summed up in a line from the 1984 science fiction film *Terminator*, about an indestructible robot, when a character says, "It can't be reasoned with; it doesn't feel pity or remorse or fear. It absolutely will not stop."

For those launching the missiles that rained on England and Belgium from the summer of 1944 until the end of the war, it was a way to hit back against the enemy at small cost in terms of human life and materiel. Compared to the cost of a manned bomber and its crew, the V-1 was cheap and easy to produce. If the defenses shot down the majority of them, some still made it through to wreak havoc on the civilian population in the target area. And the cost to the Allies in human resources and materiel to maintain their defense against the robots became enormous.

The flying bomb's distant cousin was a different story. Still cheaper than a manned bomber, the V-2 was hideously complex and difficult to make. Fueled by liquid oxygen and alcohol derived from the potato, which was a staple of the German diet in the last years of the war, it traveled at more than three times the speed of sound and exploded before people in the target area could even hear it coming. Against the V-2 there was no defense. The people of London were tough and made every attempt to laugh off the dangers they faced, even giving the V-1 the nickname "Doodlebug." For the V-2, there was no nickname, and only the end of the war brought relief from this archetype "terminator."

Despite their chilling ability to get through to the target, the V-weapons were not war winners. By the time they were deployed, the Soviet Army was in Poland and the Western Allies had landed in Normandy. The Third Reich was merely staving off defeat. No single weapon or series of so-called "wonder weapons" could delay the inevitable for very long, and in less than ten months after the V-1 had been fired at England the war was over. Had they been deployed six months earlier, as originally planned, they might have done more, but they could not have turned the tide of war in Germany's favor. In the final analysis, the name Josef Goebbels designated for the weapons was accurate: "Vergeltungswaffe," or "vengeance."

Since the V-weapons did not win the war, as Adolf Hitler had boasted they would, they have been dismissed in postwar histories as the useless gestures of a desperate lunatic. In countless books and articles, the weaknesses of the V-weapons have been magnified to support this premise. The V-1 was easy to shoot down, at least in clear weather, and the V-2 was overly complex; further, neither missile was accurate. While these statements are true, it is a mistake to assess a weapons system out of context and it is a grievous error to do so with the V-weapons. In their short operational life they had a tremendous influence on the course of World War II on both operational and strategic levels.

The Allied commitment to stopping these weapons was nothing short of overwhelming. All British fighters except for the British Second Tactical Air Command were removed from the Continent to deal with the V-1. In England, the "Diver Belt," the massive antiaircraft defense against the V-1 created by Lt. General Sir Frederick Pile, absorbed a quarter of a million men and women to operate, and supported 2,500 guns and 200 radar installations. On the Continent, Allied logisticians were forced to bring ammunition into France and haul it 200 miles to the front rather than risk a V-1 or V-2 hitting an ammunition ship in the harbor of Antwerp. On the strategic level, the massive Allied airborne assault to capture a bridge across the Rhine in September 1944 was switched from Wesel, Germany to Arnhem in Holland in order to capture V-2 launch sites along the way. Because the Allies went "a bridge too far," the operation failed and thus prolonged the war. Diversion of Allied air resources to counter V-targets amounted to tens of thousands of sorties and the effect of the V-weapons on the port of Antwerp was staggering.

Here, for the first time, the V-weapons have been evaluated in context, from their evolution to their commitment as an integral part of Nazi Germany's war effort. The book documents how neither side fully grasped the implications of guided missiles at the time, and how misconceptions about the V-1 and V-2—weapons that inaugurated the modern age of warfare—continue to this day.

1

Rockets, Guidance and Pulse Jets

In its basic form a rocket is little more than a tube sealed at one end. Its forward motion is produced by a reaction to the rearward ejection of hot gases at a very high velocity. Invented by the Chinese in the 13th century, the rocket was quickly transformed from a ceremonial device to a weapon of war. One of the earliest historical references to the rocket was at the siege of K'ai Feng in 1232, in which the Chinese defenders used "arrows of flying fire" against the attacking Mongols. It quickly caught on. The Arabs reportedly used rockets in the Iberian Peninsula in the middle of the 13th century, while in Italy the Paduans and Venetians used them in the 14th. While it was simple to build and easy to use, the rocket was wildly inaccurate and the firer had little or no control over detonating the small warhead. Nevertheless, when fired en masse, rockets could be very effective in panicking soldiers and horses who were not used to them, even if the casualties they caused were minimal.

For the first six centuries of its use, the rocket remained as the Chinese invented it: a cardboard or leather tube with a small bursting charge in the nose. Although there were several proposals during the Renaissance to make it more effective, little of a practical nature was done while artillery science meanwhile advanced as a specialty form of warfare. The rocket became increasingly eclipsed by the cannon, which progressed rapidly from the huge stone-throwing bombard of the 15th century to the mobile field guns of the 18th.

The first major improvement in the rocket occurred in India under Hyder Ali, the ruler of Mysore, who made them out of hammered sheet iron instead of paper or leather. These iron rockets, which could stand much higher pressures and carry heavier payloads, weighed between 6 and 12 pounds and had a range of around 1,000 yards. Ali's son, Tippu Sultan, increased the size of his father's rocket corps from 1,200 men to 5,000 and used them with some effect against the British at the siege of the Seringapatam in 1792.

The first European to improve and systematize rockets was British Colonel William Congreve, who began experimenting with them in 1801. Despite many statements to the contrary, Congreve had never been to India so could not have seen Tippu Sultan's rockets in action. He most likely got his ideas about rockets from *A Narrative of the Military Operations on the Coromandel Coast, Etc., Etc.* by Innes Munroe, which was published in London in 1789. Congreve bought up large quantities of fireworks skyrockets and fired them to determine their maximum range, which he found was between 500 and 600 yards. He then went to the authorities with his idea for a system of rockets. No doubt aided by his father, Lieutenant General Sir William Congreve, who was comptroller of the Royal Laboratory at Woolwich, he obtained permission to use both the laboratories and firing ranges at that establishment. The rocket system that now bears his name consisted of fifteen rockets with changeable heads. They could be used to carry an exploding shell or a combustible casing.

At first Congreve's rockets were made of paper, but later of sheet metal. Like all previous rockets, they were stabilized by a single stick and the maximum range was about 2,000 yards. The British first used Congreve's rockets in a raid on Boulogne, France in 1805. Whether the rockets were damaged by bad weather or mishandled by inexperienced crews is not clear, but only a few hundred were fired and they caused very little damage to the town. Nevertheless, the British were encouraged and the next year they returned to Boulogne and did much more damage to the town. In the British attack on Copenhagen in 1807 the "greater part of Copenhagen was burned to the ground, set aflame by a mass expenditure of about 25,000 rockets."[1] In 1813, Congreve rockets set part of the city of Danzig on fire and burned its food stores, forcing it to surrender. Perhaps the most famous tribute to Congreve's system is the line in the "Star Spangled Banner," the U.S. national anthem, which refers to the "rockets' red glare" during the British attack on Baltimore in the War of 1812.

Congreve rockets were economical when fired en masse; however, they seem to have been much more successful at sea than on land and several ships were specially modified to launch them. Congreve continued to improve his invention throughout the Napoleonic wars and was convinced rockets would eventually replace conventional artillery. There was certainly little to choose in the way of accuracy, and rockets were definitely cheaper than conventional ammunition as Congreve took great pains to explain in his book, *The Details of the Rocket System,* published in 1814. Despite difficulties in manufacture, he wrote, "there is an actual saving in the 32-pounder Rocket carcass which contains more composition than the 10-inch spherical carcass [mortar shell], without allowing anything for the difference of expense of the Rocket apparatus, and that of the mortar, mortar beds, platforms, &c. which, together with the difficulty of transport, constitute the greatest expense of common carcass."[2] Congreve's influence on military rockets was enormous. After the Napoleonic wars, many armies adopted the Congreve system, while others experimented with it.

A major drawback of the system was the long guidance stick, which took up a lot of room and weight when the user was firing tens of thousands of rockets at a time. A number of ideas were tried to make it perform some other function besides stabilization, such as carrying propellant or some of the bursting charge, but none of them were practical. In the 1830s, a British engineer named William Hale did away with the stick entirely by designing his rockets with three slightly bent metal vanes in the nozzle. The gases escaping at an angle caused the rocket to spin and stabilize itself without a stick. The Hale rocket consisted of a steel tube with a cast-iron head and was a fairly successful design. It was used by the United States Army in the attack on Vera Cruz, Mexico in 1847 and by the Austrians in both Hungary and Italy. The Russians also used rockets with some success in their long-drawn-out attempt to subdue Turkestan.

But the day of the rocket as a weapon of war was on the wane as the nineteenth-century revolution in artillery began. New techniques in metallurgy, hydraulics and chemistry produced increasingly more sophisticated weapons. In 1897, the French Army adopted the Model 1897 75mm gun manufactured by Schneider. With a hydro-pneumatic recoil mechanism and fixed ammunition made to exacting specifications, the Model 1897 was capable of performance that no rocket, even employed in mass, could match. And so the rocket as a weapon fell out of favor. It was retained as a signaling device well into the 20th century, but World War I was an artillery war and the rocket saw limited use. The Germans used rockets to carry grappling hooks across no-man's-land to hook enemy barbed wire, while the French used incendiary anti-balloon and anti-zeppelin rockets fired from both the ground and aircraft. In 1916, ground rockets mounted on a truck brought down at least one zeppelin, the LZ 773. Rockets mounted on aircraft brought down a considerable number of German observation balloons in the same year, but they quickly fell into disuse as better incendiary ammunition became available. The conditions at the front in World War I were not suitable to the employment of rockets. Despite sheet-metal casings and spin stabilization, the rocket was still powered by black powder, which was extremely hygroscopic. In addition to its propensity to absorb water, the powder was grainy and would not burn uniformly, so the firer had no control over the time of burn, nor the time or place the warhead would explode—something that could easily be done with artillery shells.

World War I posed tactical, range and accuracy problems hitherto unimagined. Instead of one or two lines of soldiers arrayed on the battlefield to a depth of about a mile, as was customary in the 19th century, the support structure of each side extended miles beyond the trenches that eventually formed the forward edge of the battle area. It was not only necessary to attack the combat troops in their fighting positions, but it became essential to attack targets deeper and deeper in the enemy rear. The first and most logical target was the enemy's supporting artillery, so counter battery fire became a priority. After the supporting artillery, logistical and other support functions also came under attack. If enemy troops in their trenches could be cut off from food, ammunition and friendly artillery support, they could be defeated more easily.

The Germans reached the limit of conventional artillery with the "Kaiser Wilhelm Geschütz," or Paris Gun, which was the inspiration of a Dr. Eberhardt, an Austrian engineer who worked for Krupp. He theorized that a projectile launched at sufficient velocity would enter the stratosphere where it would be less affected by air resistance, thereby gaining a significant increase in range. In 1916 Eberhardt took his proposal to his chief, Prof. Rauschenberger, who took it to Admiral Rogge of the Naval Ordnance Department because the Navy had more experience with heavy guns.[3] The result was a modified naval gun of 210mm caliber mounted on a railway carriage. Emplaced in Bois Gobain in March 1918, it fired some 300 very light shells at Paris, 68 miles away, causing 876 casualties.[4] Everything worked, but the high velocity of the projectile caused rapid erosion of the gun's barrel and the attempt was never repeated.

Even though artillery was capable of reaching targets deep in enemy territory, it was almost impossible to hit anything when results of the fire could not be seen by a forward observer. The balloon and the aircraft went a long way to solving these problems, and early in the war aircraft were roaming the skies photographing everything the aerial observer could see. In modern war, information is a weapon as deadly as artillery shells and it was not long before attempts to prevent the gathering of intelligence brought on the first air war. Gradually, aircraft evolved from general-purpose machines to specialized fighters, observation planes and bombers—the latter being a logical extension of the artillery. They had the ability to strike deep into the enemy's rear accurately, with bombs heavier than most artillery shells. Initially, single aircraft could be used for raids, but as the air war became more sophisticated, early-warning systems and patrols organized to counter such an action became commonplace. The patrols had to be overcome by escorts for the attacking formations, and the air war escalated.

By 1916, both sides developed sophisticated aircraft big enough to carry a heavy bomb load hundreds of miles. The Germans built a fleet of heavy bombers to strike London and other key enemy cities. Slow and unwieldy by later standards, the Zeppelins, and then Gotha bombers, of the German air force were able to reach the British capital, drop tons of bombs and return to their bases—a terrifying portent of future air campaigns. The British were forced to defend themselves and by 1918 had stationed 16 front-line fighter squadrons in Britain and built a defensive line of searchlights and antiaircraft artillery manned by 25,000 men. With the air routes thus defended, losses rose and the Germans switched to night bombing, which was far less accurate. Nevertheless, the attacks caused considerable damage and tied down British forces which were desperately needed on the Western Front. By the end of the war the German bombers had carried out 27 raids, dropped 150 tons of bombs, and caused 3,000 casualties and more than $5 million in property damage. Over the course of the war the defenders shot down 27 of the monsters. While this is a ridiculously small number by World War II standards, it must be remembered that the entire German bomber force during the first war numbered slightly more than one hundred and that seldom were more than a handful operational at any one time.

The heavy losses were a drain on German resources and the High Command looked to the scientific and industrial community to find a stand-off weapon that would allow the bombers to attack heavily defended targets from a distance. Within a few months the Zeppelin Company developed a wire-guided flying bomb. The bomb mounted small stub wings that gave it better aerodynamic characteristics and was controlled by a wire connected to the rear of the bomb and controlled from the bomber. The war ended before the bomb could be used operationally, but many of the men who worked on the project and much of the research data survived the war to become the basis of the cruise missile and other German stand-off weapons of World War II.

While the Germans concentrated on wire-guided bombs, the Allies experimented with unmanned, self-guided aircraft. The idea of an unmanned aircraft surfaced in magazine articles in Britain, the United States and France even before World War I. The theory was that gyroscopes mounted in these "aerial torpedoes" or "flying bombs" would control their approach to the target, but no one did any practical work with one. Such an aircraft had considerable advantages. It could be made smaller and lighter since it did not have to accommodate a pilot, and it needed only half the fuel because it only flew one way. With the space and weight savings it could carry a much larger bomb load on a smaller air frame. The only way such an aircraft could be shot down or diverted from its course was by direct damage to the engine or control surfaces, since there was no pilot who could be turned back due to injuries, fear or bad weather.

The English were the first to practically consider a guided aircraft carrying a bomb. Shortly after the beginning of World War I, the War Office asked professor A.M. Low to develop a range finder for coastal artillery and it quickly turned into a project to develop a radio-controlled flying bomb to attack both ground targets and zeppelins. In

March 1917, Low exhibited his device to an expectant crowd. The first device crashed on take-off. The second flew for a time, then dove on the crowd and crashed a few feet from Low and the controls. A new airframe was designed by H.P. Folland, designer of the SE-5 fighter plane, and built at the Royal Aircraft Factory. It was less successful than the first. The British continued their research but had little success until the 1920s.

In the United States work on flying bombs began even before that country became involved in hostilities in Europe. In 1915, Peter C. Hewitt, inventor of the mercury vapor lamp, conceived a practical gyroscopically guided, pilotless flying bomb. He brought the idea to Elmer A. Sperry, head of the Sperry Gyroscope Company, who enthusiastically supported the idea. Sperry and Hewitt designed the guidance system and tested it in existing aircraft with results that showed the system had definite potential. They decided to demonstrate the device to the Army and wrote to Lieutenant Colonel George O. Squier of the U.S. Army Signal Corps, the proponent for aircraft. The Army didn't answer the letter, but Sperry and Hewitt were not the kind of men to be deterred by unimaginative officials. They wrote further letters and planned more demonstrations, but these had to be canceled because of mechanical failures.

In November 1916, they invited William "Billy" Mitchell, soon to be one of the most famous aviators in U.S. history, but Mitchell failed to make an appearance. Sperry and Hewitt were more successful in appealing to the Navy and arranged an official demonstration of the device in September 1916. Sperry's son Lawrence flew the test aircraft with Navy Lieutenant T.W. Wilkinson as the observer. The seaplane took off, climbed to the necessary altitude at which point the device took over, flew a prescribed course, then began a dive that was canceled by the pilot. Wilkinson's critique of the device indicated that the flying bomb had a longer range than guns and would certainly be more difficult to shoot down, but felt that it was of "doubtful military value on account of the difficulty of striking at any desired point rather than at random within the limits of the city or fortress."[5] This lack of precision made the Navy decide against the device until war was declared against Germany a few short months later, in April 1917.

Little more than a week after the declaration of war, the Naval Consulting Board recommended that $50,000 be allotted to Sperry's 'flying' bomb project."[6] Secretary of the Navy Josephus Daniels agreed and formed a commission that recommended support of the project. Daniels then approved $200,000 for the development of a flying bomb. Along with the money, the Navy supplied five Curtiss N-9 seaplanes and bought six sets of Sperry controls. The tests, which began in September 1917, followed the pattern of the original Sperry and Hewitt tests. The pilot of the test aircraft took it off, monitored the guidance system and as soon as the plane began to dive on its target, interrupted the control device and flew the aircraft home. Unfortunately, the inventors were soon to discover that a completely unmanned aircraft was a totally different kettle of fish.

In the next stage of development, Curtiss designed an aircraft specifically as an unmanned flying bomb and built five prototypes that were delivered ahead of schedule with great expectations. Unfortunately, Sperry, Hewitt, Curtiss and the Navy were to be greatly disappointed. They literally could not get the aircraft off the ground. In twelve tests the aircraft worked only once for a range of little more than a 1,000 yards, because the catapult used to launch the vehicle upset the guidance controls. Manned flights were resumed and it was found that the Sperry guidance control did not work correctly for the Curtiss flying bomb because it was far more sensitive to control changes than the N-9. The Curtiss aircraft also had stability problems and the fuselage had to be lengthened.

The U.S. experiments continued, including more with the N-9. One of the N-9 tests provided the longest test flight of any of the attempts, but it could hardly be considered a success. The control mechanism of a pilotless N-9 malfunctioned and the aircraft was last seen flying due east over the Atlantic Ocean. The experiments continued, but a practical flying bomb never emerged. The project was finally canceled in 1922.

The war also convinced the Army to reconsider its position on the flying bomb. After watching one of the successful manned N-9 flights, Squier, now a major general and chief signal officer, recommended development of a flying bomb to the Aircraft Board, which approved Squier's recommendation. As directed by Secretary of War Newton D. Baker, experimental work began. Eventually a cost plus contract was awarded to Charles F. Kettering, inventor of the automobile self-starter. Kettering formed a team that included Elmer Sperry, Orville

Wright, C.H. Wills (one of Henry Ford's top engineers) and S.E. Votey of Aeolian Player Piano for pneumatic controls. The resulting aircraft had a dihedral wing and was officially dubbed the "Liberty Eagle," although it was more commonly known as the Kettering "Bug." The first successful piloted flight did not occur until July 1917 and then only for six minutes. Once again piloted flights worked, but the guided flights, for the most part, did not. While the Army "Bug" used a dolly rather than a catapult, the shock of take-off still affected the control device. There were some hopeful incidents, such as a machine remaining aloft for 45 minutes flying in unprogrammed circles, but the Army's project proved no more successful than the Navy's. After costing the taxpayers $275,000, the project was finally dropped in March 1920.

All those gifted men were unable to produce a workable flying bomb because their concepts could not be accommodated by the technology of the day. Guidance systems were constantly thrown off by the impact of take-off. Not enough was known about aerodynamics and whenever one of the flimsy test aircraft crashed (which was almost always) there was not enough left to make a proper analysis. Except for a few experiments with radio-controlled aircraft as target planes, little was done about the flying bomb until World War II.

Like the rocket and the flying bomb, the pulse-jet engine, which powered the V-1 cruise missile of World War II, was an idea that predated the Great War. On April 10, 1907, French inventor Victor de Karavodine was granted a patent for a pulse jet that used a low-pressure supercharger to pump the fuel mixture into a combustion chamber where it was ignited by a spark plug. Prophetically, Karavodine's idea was to use his pulse jet to power a flying bomb. Georges Marconnet, a Belgian engineer, was also granted a French patent for a pulse-jet type device in 1910. But neither device went beyond the laboratory stage. The theoretical foundations for developing a stand-off weapon with inertial guidance were in place by World War I.

The scientific and military communities recognized the validity of the concepts, but the technology needed to turn the ideas into workable weapons still did not exist, and the end of World War I brought a halt to the experiments. The victors saw little reason to proceed with experiments since the application of conventional weapons had brought Germany to her knees. There was little need for expensive and temperamental devices when airplanes, tanks and artillery supporting the infantry had done the job very well. With little to gain, the victorious Allies relegated rockets, flying bombs and experimental engines to the realm of unfunded scientific experimentation.

On the other hand, the First World War ended in disaster for Imperial Germany, shattering it politically and socially. The German Empire that went to war in 1914 was not a truly single country but a federation of states established in 1871 with the Kaiser as its unifying element. Far from a homogenous state, it had Prussian, Bavarian, Saxon and Württemberg armies under control of the Imperial (actually Prussian) General Staff. Fortunately, there was only one navy, but during the war three air forces were created. When the Kaiser abdicated and fled to Holland, Germany became a parliamentary democracy known as the Weimar Republic. The new government was forced to agree to the harsh terms of the Treaty of Versailles, by which Germany lost territory, transatlantic cables, colonies and control over its own rivers. Stigmatized by its acceptance of the treaty—which became known among Germans as the "Diktat," or decree—the Weimar government was a fragile creature that had to cope with an undeclared war between Germany and the new nation of Poland, fought not by the German Army but by groups of ex-soldiers in what they called the "Freikorps" who would eventually pose a danger to the German government itself. Internally, separatists and revolutionaries attempted to divide the country or seize power. The inability of the Weimar government to prevent the 1922 French occupation of the Ruhr and the execution by firing squad of Germans who resisted the occupation made it even less popular. In the short run it was able to form an uneasy alliance with the Army to save the nation, while Germany and the rest of Europe settled into the exhausted, uneasy peace of the 1920s.

Ignored by the victors, the revolutionary ideas of the rocket, pulse jet and inertial guidance were seeds upon the wind that found fertile soil in Weimar Germany, where the vanquished carefully nurtured them. At first, only a group of highly intelligent enthusiasts, determined to reach outer space in rocket-propelled vehicles, began the initial experiments. The pulse jet was seen as an inexpensive way of producing faster aircraft and it, too, underwent years of experimentation.

The men who laid the foundation of rocket science comprised a motley crew of scientists and dreamers who had no idea that one day the resources of the state would contribute to the fulfillment of their ideas. Ultimately their concepts flourished, but the results became death and destruction as the idea of rocket propulsion became harnessed by a tyrannical regime seeking to avenge itself against its enemies.

2

The Woman in the Moon and the Ordnance Office

Although warfare is an excellent catalyst for technological progress, other motivations can be equally compelling. Throughout history, as human beings conquered distance and terrain on their own world, they have looked beyond to the largest objects in the skies. Even before astronomers realized that the sun and the moon were celestial bodies, people longed to visit them, and if they couldn't reach them in reality they went in their imaginations. Tales of trips to the moon abound in the world's literature, most of them flights of fancy in which the hero or heroine travels by bird or, in the case of Baron von Munchausen, by cannonball to find strange and wonderful beings.

In the 19th century the fancy ended. The 19th was the first engineering century. Previous centuries witnessed great advances in science, but the inventors of the 19th were the first to put them to practical use on a grand scale. The term "industrial revolution" is a pale expression that does not come close to describing the effect the engineering revolution had on the world. The sole purpose of engineers was to solve problems, and even their imaginations were grounded in practicality. From the engineering perspective anything was possible if one had the right tools and materials, and that attitude changed the globe. When Jules Verne wrote *The First Men to the Moon*, baskets pulled by swans and barons riding cannonballs were no longer acceptable. There had to be a practical engineering solution to get the explorers to their destination. Many of Verne's ideas were misguided (the men in his hollow projectile would have been killed instantly), but in one aspect of his tale he was absolutely correct. In order to transport men to the moon it would take a well-planned project using some of the best minds on earth and lots of money. The effort would also need sophisticated rocket technology.

In the wake of the revolutionary turmoil that followed the end of World War I, Germany settled down to the first real peace it had seen in nearly a decade and the citizens of the Weimar Republic returned to their livelihoods and cultural interests. In 1923, the publishing house of R. Oldenbourg in Munich produced *Die Rakete zu den Planeten Raum* (The Rocket into Planetary Space) by Prof. Hermann Oberth, a small paperback of 92 pages. Since no one knew who Oberth was, the professor had to pay a substantial part of the printing costs himself. The premise of the work was that spaceflight was practical and that men could build rockets to escape the earth's gravity and carry people into space. It also suggested that under the right conditions space flight might be profitable.

In three parts, *Die Rakete zu den Planeten Raum* discussed the physics of a rocket fueled by liquid propellant; proposed an instrument-carrying rocket; and finally discussed one that would carry people. The book was not a hit among scientists, but it was non-technical to enough to appeal to a large, receptive audience in Weimar Germany, a social and political hodgepodge ranging from the old Prussian aristocracy on the right to the Communists on the left. Between the two extremes were the industrialists, the universities, the Social Democrats and the middle class. These cultural and economic crosscurrents created an intellectual freedom hitherto unknown in Germany and with it came an enthusiasm for new ideas and concepts. Space travel was a new idea and Oberth's book gave it form and substance. Enough copies of the book sold to warrant a second edition in 1925. In that same year Oldenbourg also published *Die Erreichbarkeit der Himmels Körper* (Reaching the Heavenly Bodies) by Dr. Walther Hohmann, of Essen, a discussion of the mathematical basis of rocket travel.

At this point the popularity of space travel stalled despite the curiosity of newspaper publishers and the general public. Only a mathematician could understand Hohmann's work and Oberth, who had no media sense, delivered boring lectures to interviewers. Fortunately, the cause was taken up by Max Valier, an author, showman and sensationalist who wrote scientific articles for popular magazines. Caught up in the craze, he wrote *Der Vorstoss in Weltraum* (The Drive to Outer Space), published by Oldenbourg in 1924. It was supposed to be a popularization of Oberth's book, but contained many errors that irritated the purists. Despite the errors, laymen found it so much more informative and exciting than Oberth's and Hohmann's pedantic works that it went through five printings from 1925 to 1929 and in 1930 was revised and retitled *Raketenfahrt* (Rocket Travel).

Valier's book was followed in 1926 by *Die Fahrt ins Weltall* (Voyage to Space) by Willi Ley, who was destined to become one of the most prolific popular writers on the subjects of rockets and spaceflight in the 20th century. Ley's book had no formulae and was error-free, but he was unable to capture the public's imagination the way Valier had because the latter was first and foremost a showman who did dangerous stunts in rocket-powered cars. While Valier was fascinating the public with his derring-do, serious aficionados organized the "Verein für Raumschiffahrt" (Society for Space Travel), better known by its German initials "VfR."

Established in Breslau in 1927 with Johannes Winkler, an aeronautical engineer, as its president, Oberth and Hohmann were among its first members. In compliance with German law, the VfR had to register with the court as an organization doing business, but when the club's officers arrived at the Breslau court to apply for its registration, there was a minor snag. There was no definition for "Raumschiffahrt" (space travel) and there was a legal necessity to have one if the public were to understand the purpose of the group. At first the court suggested a change of name, but the VfR adamantly refused. Perhaps unwilling to pass up the registration fee, the court allowed the group to define "Raumschiffahrt" on the registration document. One of the society's goals was experimentation with rockets, but it did little more than meet and publish a monthly magazine called *Die Rakete* (The Rocket). Nevertheless, it was a popular club and its membership grew rapidly to more than 800.

The popularity of space travel spread to the German entertainment industry and soon Fritz Lang, the German director who made the classic film *Metropolis*, announced he was working on a film about space travel and had hired Oberth himself as technical advisor.

As an advertising stunt, he also announced that Oberth would build a liquid-fueled rocket which the scientist would launch on or about the day the film debuted. The entire project was to be financed by the studio. On the surface the idea had merit, but Oberth's efforts, which came to nil, were a preview of the difficulties the German rocket program was going to face in the not-so-distant future.

Despite his theoretical brilliance, Oberth was from a small German enclave in Transylvania, where the pace of life was not only slower, but much different than that of the thriving city of Berlin. Not only was he in unfamiliar surroundings, he had difficulty understanding the rapid cosmopolitan dialect spoken in the German capital, and he had even more trouble in the film studio where a number of foreign languages were frequently spoken. Having no managerial experience, he decided to build the rocket his way, with assistants of his own choosing. Instead of looking for qualified assistants at employment agencies or societies specializing in engineers, Oberth ran ads in newspapers. One of his first applicants was Rudolf Nebel, a former fighter ace and diploma engineer whom Oberth hired on the spot. Unfortunately, Nebel was not what he appeared to be. Graduated from the university early so he could enter pilot training, he never practiced his profession and, before joining Oberth, worked part-time selling kitchen gadgets. He was also an opportunist.

For his second assistant Oberth sought out Aleksander Borissovitch Shershevsky, a Russian aviation student, whose articles Oberth had read. A revolutionary Communist, Shershevsky had overstayed his visa and was afraid to return to the Soviet Union. Incredibly lazy and slovenly, he barely eked out a living writing articles. It isn't surprising that this mismatched trio failed to build a liquid-fueled rocket and nearly blew themselves up in the process. What is surprising is that they made a very important discovery.

Theorists objected to Oberth's proposal for a large rocket fueled by gasoline, or by alcohol and liquid oxygen, claiming the concept was impossible because the two liquids would explode as soon as they were mixed. Since one of the theorists was a man who had considerable experience with liquid gases, Oberth proceeded cautiously, using liquid air, which is less dangerous than pure liquid oxygen. He and his assistants poured the liquid air into a bowl, into which they sprayed a fine mist of gasoline and ignited it. The resulting explosion, which did minor damage to the workshop, appeared to confirm his critics' theories, but Oberth persisted. The next time he tried the experiment he observed that the droplets of gasoline were torn apart and consumed "much faster than had been assumed,"[1] which meant much larger amounts of fuel could be burned in a given space in a given time. Liquid-fuel rocket motors were not only possible but practical.

Unfortunately the rest of Oberth's efforts were not only unsuccessful, but dangerous. Shortly after his observation of the disintegrating droplets of fuel, an explosion did considerable damage to the workshop and injured Oberth to the point where he was bedridden for several days and thought he might lose the sight of one eye. As soon as he recovered, Oberth designed a motor for the rocket. It had a conical nozzle and combustion chamber and he named it "Kegeldüse" (roughly, conical nozzle). The rocket, based on the instrumented model in Oberth's book, was to be torpedo-shaped, about six feet long and made of an aluminum alloy. After reaching its maximum height, it was supposed to fall gently back to earth by parachute.

When the movie studio announced the rocket would be launched from Greifwalder Oie, a small island in the Baltic, the authorities denied permission, citing possible danger to the lighthouse there, so the proposed launching place was moved to the nearby resort of Horst. With only a few weeks left and no plans for pumping fuel into the combustion chamber and igniting it, Oberth abruptly changed his plans in favor of a rocket fueled by a carbon-based core surrounded by liquid oxygen with the exhaust nozzles in the nose to save weight. But it was too late. *Frau in Mond* (Woman in the Moon) by Fritz Lang premiered in Berlin on October 15, 1929. The studio announced it was too late in the season to safely launch a rocket and the public quickly forgot it.

The members of VfR were heartbroken at the turn of events. Not only had Oberth failed to build a working rocket but *Frau in Mond* didn't do as well as expected because it was silent and had to compete with recently released talkies. Thanks to the worsening economy, the club had to suspend publication of *Die Rakete*. Winkler resigned as president and Oberth succeeded him, with Willy Ley as vice president. Erich Wurm, one of the Berlin members, allowed the VfR to use his office for meetings, and his mimeograph machine to publish newsletters and bulletins as a substitute for the magazine.

Disappointment soon gave way to renewed determination to produce a liquid-fueled rocket, however, and club membership climbed to a total of 870 in 1929.[2] One of the new members was none other than Rudolf Nebel, Oberth's erstwhile assistant, who was brought into the organization by Ley. Nebel and Oberth had obviously had a falling out because the new VfR president and the new member glared at each other at their first meeting since the end of their ill-fated project. While Wurm acted as peacemaker, the membership decided to go forward with rocket research and be the first to launch a liquid fueled rocket, unaware Robert Goddard had already done it in the United States in 1926.[3] The VfR had tried to correspond with Goddard after reading a translation of one of his articles, but the American scientist was extremely secretive and the world would not learn of his experiments until after World War II.

Newly dedicated, the membership wanted to retrieve Oberth's equipment, which was gathering dust in studio warehouses and contractors' workshops. This took considerable effort to accomplish, but they managed to get all of Oberth's equipment, including the iron launching rack, which they later put to good use. Oberth and his fellow members decided the film rocket was useless and wanted to build a new one. Nebel suggested they launch a reliable black powder rocket to get publicity, but the other members wanted none of that kind of flimflam.

Despite his limited scientific background and certain flaws in his character, Nebel was an asset to the organization, however. He was a "wheeler-dealer" who could scrounge material that wasn't needed by the VfR and trade it for goods or services that were. He also had a practical streak and proposed a small rocket that was affordable and would work. Christened the MIRAK for "Minimum Rakete" (smallest rocket), it met with the approval of the membership but not Oberth, who objected to a liquid-fuel rocket that could not surpass the performance of a powder rocket. While Nebel drew preliminary sketches, the society tried to get funding from foundations and societies that gave grants for research, but money was not available. The best the group could do was accept an offer from the Chemische-Technische Reichsanstalt (Chemical and Technical Institute) to observe the rocket motor in operation and certify it.

The demonstration was scheduled for July 23, 1930, and everyone was looking forward to it. While the VfR held lectures to gain publicity, and Nebel with Klaus Riedel worked diligently to complete the MIRAK, tragedy struck. On May 17, while preparing for one of his stunts in a rocket-powered car, Max Valier was killed. Many of the amateur rocket community objected to the sensational way he promoted rockets and himself, but it was a close-knit community and they mourned one of their own pioneers who was, at worst, a charming scoundrel.

Valier's death, and one of a teenage boy who was building a model rocket, prompted the Reichstag to consider a bill to ban rockets, but it was voted down. The test of Oberth's Kegeldüse rocket motor at the Chemische-Technische Reichsanstalt, which went off smoothly despite abysmal weather, did much to defeat the Reichstag bill. The certificate issued stated that the rocket motor ran for 90 seconds, consumed 7 kilograms of fuel and produced a thrust of 7 kilograms without mishap.[4] Nevertheless, rocket experiments were highly unpopular after Valier's death and, not wishing to draw unwanted attention to their efforts, Nebel and Riedel retired to a farm in Saxony owned by Riedel's grandparents to test MIRAK. The detailed reports of their progress, punctuated by minor mishaps, were distributed by the VfR to the membership via mimeographed newsletters. Despite the eventual destruction of MIRAK by explosion, the reports were exciting and loosened the purse strings of some of the wealthier members.

The move of MIRAK to Saxony made it evident that the VfR needed a home of its own. It was Nebel who found it and it was too good to be true. The parcel of land had been a former military installation complete with access road and concrete buildings. The terms and conditions for leasing it were extensive, but at $4 a year it was an incredible bargain. The VfR accepted its good fortune without question, taking possession on September 30, 1930. Even a man as astute as Willi Ley assumed the price was low because the property was a "white elephant." Most likely Nebel got the property in a deal with Lieutenant Colonel Karl Emil Becker, head of the Reichswehr's Waffenprüfamt (Weapons Testing Bureau), who was interested in rockets but had no funds to do his own testing. Nebel's dealings with Becker would soon result in army control of large rocket research. Nebel continued to work on MIRAK II, which exploded with depressing regularity, and the others proceeded with the development of a rocket motor, the prototypes of which also had a tendency to explode.

1931, however, was a year of great progress for the enthusiasts. In a solo effort, Johannes Winkler managed to get a liquid-fueled rocket off the ground, as did the VfR a few months later. Their final series of rockets were named "Repulsor," from a popular science-fiction novel by Kurd Lassewitz, and Repulsor 3 managed to reach an altitude of 1,500 feet. The day of the amateur, however, was rapidly drawing to a close.

The depression in the winter of 1931–32 devastated the membership of VfR, which fell to barely 300 members. Before the society closed its doors, in 1934, internal strife also took its toll when von Dickhuth-Harrach and Ley, the president and vice president, officially accused Nebel of embezzling funds and evicted him from the organization. As the ranks of the VfR thinned, its place in the forefront of rocket research was gradually assumed by the German Army. Uncoordinated efforts to launch rockets continued until the Army had all non-military research stopped. By the time the Nazis gained control of the country, the Army was firmly committed to rocket research and had gathered those it deemed worthy into its circle. Others, like Ley, who recognized the Nazis for what they were, left the country.

Despite the VfR's admirable goal of developing a liquid-fuel rocket, and the enthusiasm of the members for reaching that goal, the organization had three glaring weaknesses. It never set parameters for any of the rockets it tried to develop, so there was no way to measure progress or lack thereof. There was no conscious attempt to objectively document the lessons gained from early rockets and incorporate them into later ones. Instead, they relied on personal and institutional memory. The most serious shortcoming of the organization was the want of positive leadership in the experiments, which contributed to the lack of focus and direction. Rather than scientific or engineering pioneers, they were an idealistic group of amateur enthusiasts cheerfully going nowhere. Manpower and resources were frittered away on competing projects and the members were unable to cope with the major technical problems inherent in liquid-fuel rocket motor development.

The new technology presented a formidable array of interrelated problems. The most pressing was getting fuel and oxidizer to the ignition chamber, mixing the two in the right proportions and igniting them at the proper time. After ignition, a nozzle of the proper shape had to be maintained at a low enough temperature to prevent "hot spots," created by an accumulation of burning fuel in one part of the motor. A hot spot could melt through the wall of the nozzle and let gas escape out the side, destroying the stability of the rocket or causing the motor to explode—a common occurrence with VfR experiments. A problem which the VfR enthusiasts totally failed to address was a stabilization or guidance system. Perhaps most surprising is that for all their efforts nothing was documented in a scientific fashion. "It was not, for instance, possible before the middle of 1932 to obtain from the Raketenflugplatz in Berlin any sort of records showing performance and fuel consumption during experiments."[5]

The decision of the German Army to involve itself in rocket research stemmed from its desire to circumvent the Versailles Treaty and rebuild after its defeat in World War I. At the end of the war, the Army was in a frightful condition. It had been bled white after four years of fighting, and although it loyally came home with flags flying and bands playing (unlike the Navy, which had mutinied), it was not popular. To distance themselves from the disasters of 1914–18, politicians blamed the war on "the militarists," and the Weimar government looked on its own army with justified skepticism and suspicion. Under the provisions of the Versailles Treaty, military aircraft were forbidden and the Navy, once the third largest in the world, was reduced to a small coastal defense force manning obsolete ships. The German Army, or Reichswehr, was limited to 100,000 men with no tanks, and its artillery was limited to 105mm, which, by late Great War standards, was light artillery.

Stung by its defeat, and chafing under the restrictions of the treaty, the German Army, with ineffective and obsolete weapons, was tasked with defending a diplomatically isolated nation surrounded by enemies. To the west was France, the traditional enemy of the past 250 years; to the east was the new nation of Poland, carved partially out of former German territory; and to the southeast was the new nation of Czechoslovakia, a staunch ally of France. All of these nations were well armed and could easily invade Germany with little opposition, as France demonstrated when it seized the Ruhr in 1922. It is not surprising, then, that the Germans embraced any expedient that would enable them to escape political isolation and overcome the armament limitations of the Treaty of Versailles.

Even before the treaty was signed, the German Army and Navy looked for ways to circumvent the repercussions of the "Diktat." Airplanes were disassembled and plans for new weapons were hidden from the armistice inspectors. Other conventional weapons research was concealed in academia. The proscription against heavy artillery was felt most keenly by the Army, because thousands of heavy guns had been needed in every battle in World War I. In the final German offensive of 1918, approximately 6,000 guns were used to fire tens of thousands of shells in a sustained five-hour bombardment prior to the attack.[6] In the technology of the era, only artillery could accurately deliver that amount of ordnance in such a short time. Bombing aircraft were in their infancy and carried light loads. Artillery could also fire in bad weather conditions that grounded most aircraft.

Militarily, the Paris Gun had made a significant impression. On one hand it was a logical extension of the traditional doctrine of siege artillery, and on the other it allowed the ground commander to reach deep into the enemy's rear without the use of aircraft. The type of research that produced the Paris Gun was essential if the Army were to stay ahead of its potential enemies. It was kept alive under the Weimar Republic by transferring the Prussian army's artillery laboratory to the Technical University of Berlin, as an institute of applied physics, in order to prevent its dissolution.[7]

The Reichswehr of the Weimar Republic had the mission of providing its ground troops with the maximum amount of firepower and reaching as deeply into the enemy rear as it could. The artillery officers of the Reichswehr were responsible for developing weapons and doctrine to fulfill that mission, but the influence of those artillery officers went far beyond the management of firepower on the battlefield. As a defeated army, the Reichswehr became a revolutionary army in the same way the French Army became one after the Seven Years War (1756–63). Despite the traditional conservatism of senior army officers, there were no sacred cows and no "tradition of victory" to get in the way of examining in the harsh light of reality what had happened in the war. Equally important, there was no large inventory of obsolete equipment left over from the previous war to hinder the development of new materiel to suit new doctrine.

The higher-ranking officers of the armies that served Imperial Germany in World War I were drawn mostly from the aristocracy, and while they served diligently and with great courage, one of their glaring faults was their lack of technical expertise. They were mostly apathetic and sometimes contemptuous about technological and tactical changes. This was one of the reasons Germany went to war with a light field piece significantly inferior to the legendary French "75" in weight of projectile, range and reliability.[8] The junior officers of the artillery, engineers and air corps—the most technical branches—were primarily well-educated men from the middle class who had to cope with constant changes in technology during the war. The overwhelming number of officers selected to remain in the small postwar Reichswehr were from this group and they were determined to see a better educated, more technologically astute officer corps in the new army.

Typical of this attitude was the Ballistics and Munitions Branch of the Army Weapons Department, headed by Lieutenant Colonel Karl Emil Becker and his assistant, Captain von Horstig. Assigned to the branch were three veteran captains, Walter Dornberger, Leo Zanssen and Erich Schneider, who received Master of Engineering degrees from the Institute of Applied Technology that had once been the Prussian Army Artillery Laboratory. Both Dornberger and Zanssen would become key figures in the German guided-missile program.

From the mid-1920s the Germans, in cooperation with Soviet Russia—the other pariah of Europe—began experimenting with weapons such as tanks and airplanes that were forbidden by the Treaty of Versailles. To bypass treaty restrictions on conventional artillery, Becker and his subordinates explored other technologies for possible artillery applications. They found the rocket promising because it was an undeveloped technology not forbidden by the treaty. With the economy in decline and the value of the Reichsmark falling daily due to a severe depression, however, Becker was unable to do little more than solicit commercial firms and self-styled experts for information on rockets.

In 1931, Becker found enough money to award a research contract to Paul Heylandt, who had been Valier's collaborator in rocket-powered cars. Heylandt produced a workable engine of 20kg thrust under the first contract and one for a 60kg thrust motor six months later. Both the engines worked, but by 1932 the Army's rocket program was gaining momentum and, along with higher performance goals, it had gained a passion for secrecy. The single event that turned the Army to its own devices for development involved none other than Rudolf Nebel, who offered to build a rocket for the Army.

Becker signed a contract to pay Nebel 1,367 Reichsmarks (RM) if the rocket performed to specification, and nothing if it failed. The demonstration was held in secret on June 22, 1932, at a firing range on the Army's proving ground at Kummersdorf, 25 miles southeast of Berlin. At the site, military authorities had set up photo-theodolites and ballistic cameras to measure the performance of Nebel's "one stick repulsor." Nebel set up the rocket and launched it, but it performed erratically and failed to reach the specified altitude. Becker, who had been frustrated with Nebel for years, refused to pay him and finally bid him good riddance. Nebel did not take the rejection of his rocket lying down and visited the Army Ordnance Office more than once to argue over the outcome and get the money he felt was owed him. Nebel's ability to survive was nothing short of miraculous, and he continued to be a pest for years, writing articles and proposing wild schemes; but from that day at Kummersdorf he faded from the scene as far as serious rocket research was concerned.

Despite Nebel's failure to impress the German Army, a development with far-reaching consequences emerged from the attempt when Colonel Becker made the acquaintance of one of Nebel's assistants, a young VfR enthusiast named Wernher von Braun. Whether this was the first time Becker had met von Braun is not clear, but, impressed with the young man's intelligence and enthusiasm, he offered him a position. This marked the beginning of the Army's determined quest for a long-range missile and the end of amateur rocket research.

It is a tribute to Becker's judgment that the first civilian he hired for the Army's rocket program was the 20-year-old von Braun, whose name would become indelibly linked with guided missiles and spaceflight for the rest of his life. Born in Wirtsitz, Germany in 1912 to well-to-do aristocratic parents, von Braun was authorized to use the title of Freiherr (baron), but he seldom did. For Confirmation, his mother gave him a small telescope, which sparked an interest in astronomy but not in any academic discipline, and he did poorly in mathematics and science. When Oberth's *Die Rakete zu den Planeten*

Raum appeared, the young von Braun sent for it. Opening it, he was appalled to find the book full of mathematical equations he was unable to decipher. When he asked his teacher what he could do to understand them, he was told to study mathematics and physics, which were his two worst subjects. Von Braun redoubled his efforts and his grades improved.

In 1928 he was sent to the Hermann Lietz School on an island in the North Sea, where he was soon far ahead of his classmates. It was here that the young von Braun first exhibited the traits of enthusiasm, charm, affability and persuasion that would be his trademarks in every organization he joined. No longer satisfied with the small telescope his mother gave him, he convinced his school to purchase a five-inch refracting telescope and he then organized the students to build an observatory. Graduating a year early, von Braun enrolled at the Charlottenburg Institute of Technology, a practical school that required its students to be apprenticed to a machine shop. When von Braun found himself apprenticed to the Borsig Works factory, he was outraged when his first assignment was to make a perfect cube from a piece of iron the size of a child's head with a vise and a file. The mustachioed foreman was unforgiving and the cube that finally won his approval was the size of a walnut. The young technical student went on to master the lathe and the shaper and then worked for an additional three months at the founding and forging plant. Finally, he worked at the locomotive assembly shop as a card-carrying member of the metal workers' union. The future engineer later admitted that his apprenticeship "gave him more insight into practical engineering problems than any semester at the university."[9] Von Braun was only twenty when he graduated.

It is interesting to speculate whether the brilliant student met Captain Dornberger while at the Charlottenburg Institute. If von Braun was already a known quantity, it might explain Becker's willingness to hire him so quickly. The hiring of von Braun meant that, for the first time, rocket research would be systematically organized with the goal of producing a viable weapon. The project also provided a fertile ground in which genius flourished in pursuit of that goal. It was an opportunity not to be missed. Von Braun put it succinctly: "Our feelings toward the Army resembled those of the early aviation pioneers, who, in most countries, tried to milk the military purse for their own ends and who felt little moral scruples as to the possible future use of their own brainchild. The issue in these discussions was merely how the golden cow could be milked most successfully."[10]

It would have been surprising, indeed, if von Braun had turned down the opportunity to get paid for working on his lifelong dream with the added incentive that he was performing a patriotic deed for his country. There are those who claim that he sold the VfR out to the Nazis, but the charge is groundless. Von Braun went to work for the Army before the Nazis took over the country and it was the Army, intent on keeping rocket research secret, that closed down the Raketenflugplatz and other groups. When the Nazis came to power, they only continued the suppression of private rocket research and any contact with rocket groups outside Germany.

The Army did not limit its recruitment of rocket experts to the VfR, Heylandt and Nebel. They searched from one end of Germany to the other to find knowledgeable people and working rockets; however the results were disappointing. An engineer named Wilhelm Belz from Cologne claimed to have a working liquid-fuel rocket, but it turned out to be an excellent quality powder rocket. Needless to say, the Army had nothing more to do with him. Alfons Pietsch, a former employee of Heylandt, offered to build a liquid-fueled rocket with a 650-pound thrust and a burn time of 60 seconds. After getting an advance and a few subsidies, Pietsch disappeared with most of the money, leaving his assistant Arthur Rudolph, another former Heylandt employee, to complete the project.

Rudolph duly demonstrated his design, which met the specifications submitted by Pietsch. The Army didn't buy the rocket, but it did hire Rudolph. Captain Dornberger also visited Albert Püllenberg, an enthusiastic amateur working in Hannover with very limited funds, and realized that Püllenberg was on the wrong track. However, Dornberger was favorably impressed with the man's eagerness and advised him to get an engineering degree and join the Army project. Püllenberg took the advice to heart and, after getting his degree, joined the German Army's secret development project at Peenemünde.

At the Army proving ground at Kummersdorf, the beginning of research on the liquid-fuel rocket was a voyage into the unknown. Except for Oberth's observation of burning fuel droplets, not one of the dreamers of the VfR or the Raketenflugplatz had solved a concrete problem. The first goal was development of a reliable rocket motor that would develop 650 pounds of thrust, and the Army committed some of its limited funds to the renovation of an existing powder rocket facility in the western part of Kummersdorf. They built two additional buildings to hold administrative offices, a design area, a measurement room, a dark room and a small workshop with a lathe and other tools. The test stand, the first of its kind, was eighteen feet square surrounded on three sides by concrete walls twelve feet high and metal doors on the other. The tar-paper roof slid back and forth by means of a hand crank. It was "fully equipped with all available resources of measurement techniques."[11]

This is not to say the surroundings were luxurious or that money was readily available. The project was scrutinized carefully by the Bureau of the Budget, which allowed them to order experimental equipment but not office equipment or machine tools. However, the bureaucrats were fighting a losing battle as the dedicated engineers of the Army Weapons Department found ways around the red tape. "We learned in a hard school how to get everything we wanted," Dornberger, who was a member of Becker's staff at the time, reported. "We acquired things 'as per sample.' For instance, even the keenest Budget Bureau official could not suspect that 'Appliance for milling wooden dowels up to 10 millimeters in diameter, as per sample' meant a pencil sharpener; or that 'Instrument for recording test data with rotating roller as per sample' meant a typewriter. The whole secret was circumlocution. And if there was nothing else to do, we entrenched ourselves behind the magic word 'secret'."[12]

From the time von Braun joined the Kummersdorf facility on October 1, 1932, work went on ceaselessly. The small staff worked long hours at design tables, the lathe and at calculations. After constant delays, the first test of the 650-pound thrust motor took place on December 21. It was fueled with alcohol and liquid oxygen, fed into the combustion chamber by nitrogen. Despite Dornberger's assurances that the test stand was "fully equipped," the rocket had to be ignited by hand, and shortly thereafter the motor blew up, wrecking the test stand. Fortunately no one was hurt. The age of the liquid-fuel rocket in Germany had begun with a bang and it was not reassuring.

Undeterred, von Braun and the small staff took a giant step and designed their first rocket, "Aggregate 1" (A-1), as a test vehicle. The admission that they couldn't jump from experimental motor to deployable missile says much for the realistic attitude of the men at Kummersdorf. Had they tried to leap forward they would have made their task even more difficult. By developing test vehicles, they were not only advancing the technology in small, relatively easy to accomplish steps, but they were skillfully playing the bureaucratic game. Nothing opens purse strings like success, and Dornberger and von Braun were the ones defining "success."

The A-1 was about four and a half feet long and a foot in diameter with a take-off weight of 330 pounds. Its engine, which developed 650 pounds of thrust for 16 seconds, was built into the fuel tank at the rear of the rocket and for the first time stabilization was a design factor. In conventional artillery and powder rockets, spinning was used to stabilize the projectile, and it was this experience Dornberger and von Braun hoped to build on with A-1. Since spinning would upset the liquid fuel system, only the nose of the rocket spun, acting as a gyroscope. Before launch it was run up to 9,000 RPM by electric motor and left to run down in flight.

The test stand built for smaller motors, which were still being tested, was inadequate for A-1 and a new test stand was constructed. The engineers at Kummersdorf rapidly learned that what applied for a small rocket did not necessarily apply to a larger one. Before A-1 was tested, design work began on the A-2, its successor, and Dornberger departed to command a conventional rocket battery, his last assignment before returning to the Army Ordnance Office permanently. After six months of hard work, the first A-1 blew up on the launch pad and a little later the A-1 number two shared the same fate. The motor of the third A-1 ignited successfully, but a failure of the liquid oxygen tank destroyed the rocket before it could take off.

Outwardly similar to A-1 and with the same 650-pound-thrust engine, A-2 was an entirely different beast and the first true ancestor of the modern guided missile. The fuel and liquid-oxygen tanks were separated to prevent explosions from leaking tanks. A gyroscope was placed between the tanks close to the center of gravity of the rocket that allowed better control in the early stages of flight. The combustion chamber was elongated to give the fuel more time to burn and the engine was again placed inside the fuel tank for cooling. As in A-1, nitrogen was used to pressurize the tanks. The A-2 also required assistance from outside the Army, and the Zarges Company of Stuttgart was contracted to do special welding for aluminum and other "exotic" metals in the rocket.

The A-2 could not be fired at Kummersdorf because of safety and security considerations. By the time the Army was ready to launch A-2, rocket research was secret and, with the Nazis in power, it was able to suppress amateur rocket experimentation and most publications. The subject was so secret that when von Braun earned a Ph.D. in June 1934, the diploma stated it was for "Combustion Experiments." If the rocket went awry in Kummersdorf it might not only reveal the existence of such a revolutionary development but could possibly cause considerable damage, so the island of Borkum in the North Sea was selected as the launch point.

In December 1934 two A-2 rockets named "Max" and "Moritz," after the mischievous characters in the German version of the comic strip "The Katzenjammer Kids," were shipped to Borkum with all their support equipment—which included a forty-foot-tall launch platform. After several delays "Max" was launched on December 19, 1934, and "Moritz" the following day. Unlike their namesakes both rockets performed well, reaching an altitude of 1.4 miles and falling by parachute approximately 800 meters from the launch point. Everyone was delighted and some Army officials wanted to know if A-2 could be made into a weapon. Von Braun admitted it could, but talked them out of it because the range would be comparable to conventional artillery with a similar payload.

One tragedy of note occurred in liquid-fuel rocket research during 1934. In March, Dr. Kurt Wahmke, who was assigned to the Army Ordnance Department to conduct experiments on liquid fuels separately from von Braun's group, was investigating the possibility of using ninety-percent hydrogen peroxide as an oxidizer instead of liquid oxygen because it appeared to be easier to handle. During one point in the experiment Wahmke decided to mix alcohol and hydrogen peroxide, feed them into a combustion chamber and ignite the mixture. Realizing the risk, he asked his assistants to leave, but they stayed. The ignition traveled from the combustion chamber to the fuel tank, the test stand exploded and Dr. Wahmke and his assistants were killed. The accident not only ended experimentation with hydrogen peroxide as an oxidizer but it also ended separate liquid-fuel rocket experimentation and concentrated everything to do with the subject in von Braun's group. As of 1934 his was the only rocket research organization in the Army.

March 16, 1935 marked a turning point in rocket development—as well as the history of mankind—when Adolf Hitler, undisputed Führer of the newly announced Third Reich, repudiated the Treaty of Versailles. German rearmament, which had been going on slowly and carefully for several years, speeded up to a frantic pace. The Nazi government opened its coffers and money poured forth to clothe, train and equip the new German Army. The massive expansion created enormous problems, but amid the sudden largesse the confusion went largely unnoticed. The Army authorized additional funds for the rocket development section of the Ordnance Office at Kummersdorf, which helped immensely.

In his memoirs, Dornberger constantly carped about shortages of funds—the hallmark of the modern project manager—but in those early days he had no cause for complaint. The facilities at Kummersdorf were upgraded and expanded and given the title "Experimental Station West," which reflected their geographical location in the proving ground. The elements that marked 1935 as a watershed year for missile development were the design of A-3, already on the drawing board when A-2 launches were conducted from Borkum, and a cooperative effort with the nascent Luftwaffe that led to the development center at Peenemünde.

Like its predecessor, the A-3 was simultaneously the next step in the evolution of the guided missile and a revolutionary technological leap forward. Considerably larger than its forebears, it was 21 feet 8 inches long, 2 feet 4 inches in diameter and had a take-off weight of 1,650 pounds. Internally, too, it was entirely different. In the nose was a telemetry package designed to measure heat and pressure in flight. Directly behind the nose was a new guidance system designed to control the attitude of the missile. The liquid-oxygen tank in which the nitrogen reservoir was located also took up nearly a quarter of the rocket, and behind it was the container for the parachute. In the rear, encased in the alcohol tank for cooling, was a 6-foot-long motor designed to develop a ton and a half of thrust. For stability in flight there were four large fins as well as molybdenum alloy jet vanes, which were inserted into the nozzle to provide more positive control in the initial stages of flight, and also when the fins could not provide stability in the thin upper atmosphere.

Von Braun estimated A-3 would take about a year to build, but it took nearly two. One of the reasons was the new guidance system. It was one thing to install a gyroscope in a rocket to keep it vertical for a few seconds, and quite another to control the yaw and pitch of a rocket approaching the speed of sound. With no experience in any form of three-dimensional control, Dornberger and von Braun were forced to turn to those who did. Based on a Navy recommendation they contacted Aerogeodetic, a Dutch company that the German Navy purchased in the 1920s and used as a front to conduct navigation and fire-control research. The technical director of the company was Johannes Maria Boykow, a former Austrian naval officer and inventor, who was considered the Navy's top gyrocompass expert. Boykow received von Braun's proposal enthusiastically and threw himself wholeheartedly into the task of building the world's first three-dimensional guidance system. In doing so he drew on not only his naval experience, but also considerable experience with autopilots for aircraft.

Boykow's one weakness was that he was an "idea man," who left engineering details to his subordinates, and they occasionally produced something other than what he had in mind. That might not have been a problem had Boykow not died suddenly in 1935. Nevertheless, the company, which soon dropped its Dutch front and changed its name to Kreiselgeraete GmbH, completed the world's first guidance platform, the Sg 33, which was designed to keep A-3 vertical. Four gyroscopes spinning at 20,000 RPM controlled the yaw and pitch of the rocket. When the rocket tipped, the corresponding gyro would precess to bring the platform level. Accelerometers that resembled little wagons on rails sensed the movement and sent signals to the fins and jet vanes to keep the rocket vertical.

Completed in 1936, the Sg 33 was installed in the four A-3 rockets built for testing and shipped to the island of Greifswalder Oie, ironically the same small island selected by the UfA film studio for the launch of Oberth's rocket in 1929. This time the authorities did not object and a large crew of technicians with their equipment landed at the island in November 1937. The island, 1,100 yards long by 300 wide, had no roads and no buildings except for the lighthouse and small farmhouse-cum-inn run by the island's lessee, Herr Halliger, who tended to the crew's every need "with inexhaustible good humor." In fact, the arrival of over one hundred off-season guests comprised a windfall for the innkeeper.

Fortunately, the narrow-gauge railroad used for the erection of the lighthouse had been left in place and was put to good use by the enthusiastic construction and firing crews. Army engineers dredged the harbor, built a wharf with harbor equipment, then built a concrete launch pad and a bunker at the launch site. Finally came storage tents for the rockets. The engineers' enthusiasm was a godsend to the project because the weather consisted of heavy rain, high winds and bitter cold. At the end of the month the rockets arrived in huge crates that Dornberger called "giants' coffins" and the technicians went to work; but the weather got worse and delayed the launch. As if the weather weren't enough, the local rodent population developed a taste for the insulation on the electrical cables and the tar-paper roofs of the bunkers and storage buildings. Finally the weather cleared and on December 4, the feast day of Saint Barbara, patron saint of artillerists, the first A-3—patriotically christened "Deutschland"—was prepared for launch.

For three seconds the rocket rose vertically, then everything went wrong. The parachute popped out of its container and was consumed by the exhaust as it trailed behind the rocket, which turned into the wind. The engine cut off as the rocket tipped too far over, and twenty seconds after it left the launch pad "Deutschland" crashed, about 330 yards away. With eyewitness accounts contradictory, no modifications were made to the second A-3, which was launched on December 6 with similar results. The malfunctioning parachute was replaced with a flare for the launch on December 8, but the flare was ejected after four seconds of flight and the rocket headed into the wind, crashing into the sea a mile and quarter away. The last launch, on December 11, was little different.

The results were crushing. "The result of our years of labor was complete failure," wrote Dornberger later,[13] but von Braun was not one to be stopped by a few crashing rockets. Methodically, the engineers eliminated every possibility until they concluded, after months of analysis of the films taken of the launches, and static bench tests, that the rocket, aerodynamically very stable, inherently headed into the wind and the Sg 33 guidance system was powerless to prevent this. In addition, the Sg 33 was incapable of correcting any pitch or yaw beyond 30 degrees, the limit of its range. When it reached this limit, the platform tumbled and sent the signal that the rocket was turning over, which released the parachute. The platform also lacked the ability to sense roll and, even if it did, the servo systems controlling the jet vanes were powerless to overcome the innate tendency of the rocket to turn into the wind. Since none of the A-3s burned or exploded in flight, it appeared that some things had gone right. With the A-4 designation already reserved for the military rocket, the engineers decided to design another rocket as a pure test vehicle. Christened A-5, it was smaller and cheaper than A-4 and allowed the rocket group to further test most of the new concepts before they were included in the larger version.

When Dornberger set the parameters of A-4, he conceived of the missile as a tactical artillery weapon, rather than as a replacement or complement to long-range aircraft. Even the crude Dornier Do23, available to the emerging Luftwaffe in 1935, had a range of 745 miles and carried a metric ton of bombs. Only in the artillery context were the developmental parameters for A-4 logical. Later criticisms that Dornberger and Becker had no strategic vision, while accurate, are totally irrelevant because they are made from a perspective of the second half of the twentieth century, when short, medium and long-range guided missiles with nuclear warheads were commonplace.

In 1935 the armies of the world lay in the shadow of World War I with the tank still an infantry support weapon and the fighter bomber in the future. The deepest a commander could reach into the enemy rear without relying on aircraft was with his artillery. Railroad guns offered the longest ranges and the heaviest punch, but they were slow-firing and tied to the rail system. Heavy railroad guns lacked a traversing mechanism, and in order to traverse one the crew had to locate curved track or have a railroad construction battalion build a special curved spur for the weapon.

The Paris Gun, with its 68-mile range, was the ultimate railroad gun, and had the longest range of any conventional artillery piece prior to the invention of rocket-assisted projectiles. That was its only advantage. Its major drawbacks were the short tube life, slow rate of fire and light projectile. Dornberger wanted his missile to have all of the advantages of the Paris Gun and none of its disadvantages. "My idea of a first big rocket was something that would send a ton of explosive over 160 miles—that is, double the range of the Paris Gun. When I compared the enormous weight of the Paris Gun and the difficulties of rail transport and bringing the gun into firing position with the insignificant weight of the equipment necessary for launching large rockets, when I considered the quantity of high explosive and the consequent increase in efficiency, it was clear to me that the military prospects of the rocket were extremely bright, provided it could be given even greater accuracy than the shells from the Paris Gun."[14] Dornberger also limited the size of A-4 so that it could be transported by road or railroad, a further indication that it was intended to be used in a field army environment.

As a purely experimental platform, the A-5 underwent more changes than any of the previous rockets, and laid the foundation for the A-4 and many other missiles—some of which would be deployed long after the war. Begun as a logical upgrade of the A-3, it provided substance to the theoretical changes that had been in progress since the Army took over the rocket program. As the design of A-4 moved closer to reality, every aspect had to be examined to insure this revolutionary weapon would work properly. Unlike A-2, A-3 and A-5, the A-4 would travel at supersonic speeds. Army ballisticians doubted that fins could stabilize a body traveling in excess of the speed of sound since they were familiar only with spin-stabilized projectiles. The aerodynamic shape of A-5, and later A-4, was based on the standard bullet shape, but there the similarity ended. As early as 1935 the A-3 was tested in a wind tunnel in Göttingen at speeds around Mach 1, but the effort to obtain the best body and fin shape for supersonic flight did not begin until 1936.

With the Sg 33 guidance platform unable to control a missile as small and as slow as A-3, Dornberger and von Braun began to look at firms other than Kreiselgeräte. Most of the contractors dealing with gyroscopic and autopilot controls were already straining to keep up with the demand for conventional controls brought about by the armament increase for the expansion of the Army, Navy and Luftwaffe. While Kreiselgeräte worked on an improved guidance platform, Dornberger and von Braun held top-secret discussions on November 9, 1937, with the aviation instruments division of Siemens, the huge electrical firm. Since conventional autopilots were attached to the aircraft and not based on a platform that could move freely in three dimensions, in 1938 Siemens produced the D13, a guidance system in which the gyroscopes were attached to the body of the rocket. It was not as accurate as a platform because a lateral shift of the rocket would throw everything off, but it was much cheaper than a platform and it was felt that the short period of guided flight would not result in large errors. The Siemens system relied on hydraulic power to send signals to the fins and jet vanes.

Karl Fieber, one of Siemens' employees proposed using two specialized control gyroscopes and a clockwork mechanism to tilt the platform to make the rocket nose over on its trajectory. One of the gyroscopes, the "Horizont," controlled pitch while the "Vertikant" controlled roll and yaw and sent the signals that tilted the rocket. Kreiselgeräte produced a more robust and simplified successor to Sg 33. Designated Sg 52, the new platform had a third gyro for roll, but all the gyroscopes were inertial rather than electrical and the little wagon accelerometers were eliminated. In their place were three rate gyros which were not on the platform that measured the rate of pitch, roll or yaw. The fins and jet vanes were mechanically controlled. None of these systems was in itself completely satisfactory, although they allowed research to continue with the A-5.

The most revolutionary breakthrough of the period was the redesign of the rocket motor, and the man primarily responsible was Dr. Walter Thiel, a brilliant but irascible man who offended a great many of his contemporaries and subordinates. Thiel came to the rocket group with a doctorate in chemistry and considerable experience in rocket engines and fuels. Wahmke's replacement, he had experimented with hydrogen peroxide as an oxidizer and had supervised a graduate student working on one of the small Heylandt motors. His interests also ran to exotic propellants like liquid hydrogen—a concept far ahead of its time. While he wanted to cooperate with academic institutions on a large scale, the Army's insistence on secrecy kept him confined to Kummersdorf.

The problem facing Thiel was that the motor of the A-3/A-5 was functional but nowhere near as efficient as it should have been. Taking up nearly a quarter of the length of the rocket, a scaled-up version installed in the A-4 would be unwieldy. First, Thiel changed the method of mixing the fuel and liquid oxygen. The A-3/A-5 engine used a version of the Heylandt system in which the fuel was sprayed upward toward liquid-oxygen nozzles. At a suggestion from Dornberger, he designed small centrifugal injectors that atomized the fuel droplets more completely and mixed them more evenly. By fitting these nozzles to an A-3/A-5 motor he got an immediate 12 percent increase in efficiency. By mid 1937, Thiel had refined the injector idea and created a prechamber system in which the fuel and oxidizer were mixed in their own small cups before injection into the combustion chamber. This produced even better mixing, kept the flame away from the injection nozzles and reduced the chance of the flame burning through the side of the motor.

Thiel also solved the problem of motor length when he discovered that it was the volume of the combustion chamber and not its length that was critical. Shortening the engine by increasing its cross section and making it nearly spherical also reduced power fluctuations due to uneven burning. Last of all, Thiel changed the shape of the exhaust nozzle. Though the initial design of A-5, a 10- to 12-degree opening had been considered the most efficient, but Thiel demonstrated that an angle of 30 degrees was nearly ideal in that it reduced friction of the exhaust gases and allowed the nozzle to be shortened.

By the end of 1938, the exhaust velocity of the A-3/A-5 engine had jumped from roughly 5,700 feet per second to nearly 7,000—just short of the theoretical maximum of 7,500. Despite the design changes successfully tested in A-5, and incorporated in the plans of the larger rocket, however, A-4 was still a long way from becoming a reality. In order to build and test the large rocket, they needed expanded facilities, additional labor and a lot more money. For this, Dornberger was fortunate that nearly all of Germany's commanding generals were artillery officers, who supported him wholeheartedly.

3

Army Installation Peenemünde

While Walter Dornberger, Wernher von Braun and their associates were making great strides in rocket technology, Germany changed under Nazi rule. The Weimar state was a parliamentary democracy strongly influenced by the nation's aristocratic past, its military traditions and the results of the Treaty of Versailles. Economic deprivation at the end of World War I made the government fiscally conservative. Having signed the Versailles Treaty it was not a popular government, and political turmoil following the war forced the Weimar Republic to defend itself constantly against attacks by separatists and radicals. With the support of the Army it survived until the Nazis, who never received a majority of the vote, were able to subvert the parliamentary process and seize control.

Wary of moving too quickly, the Nazis consolidated their power over the Army and the state over a period of years. Nazi rule rested in the hands of Adolf Hitler, a ruthless demagogue whose philosophy of rule was the "Führerprinzip," or leader principle. Under this system the Führer appointed his subordinate leaders and they appointed their subordinates, in total disregard of democratic process. Nazi ideology was a combination of racial superiority based on the mythic ancient German race, or "Volk," and a form of socialism. In the Nazi state the individual subordinated himself to the will of the Volk and worked at the occupation that most benefited the nation. Because the Nazis rapidly expanded the military and put a vast majority of the population back to work after years of economic privation, the average German was more than willing to support them and look the other way while Jews and other enemies, according to Nazi ideology, were sent to concentration camps, driven underground or forced out of the country.

The Nazi state was far from the social and political monolith it pretended to be. The extraordinary powers of efficiency attributed to Hitler and other Nazi leaders never existed. Organizationally, it bordered on chaos, with several political and economic centers constantly vying for power, funds and influence. This was the perfect situation for Hitler, who played his subordinates against one another to make sure none of them grew too powerful. The ultimate decision on any important matter was reserved for the Führer. Neither was Nazi Germany a revolutionary state. While the party contained many socialist elements who demanded an end to both the Weimar regime and the last vestiges of Imperial Germany, in the end it merely took over existing social, labor and academic organizations. The Nazis removed Jews and other "undesirables," placed a swastika over the organizations' existing insignia and letterheads and let them continue under Nazi control.

Labor unions, which were anathema to the Nazis, were disbanded and replaced by the Deutsche Arbeitsfront, or DAF (German Labor Front), after the Nazis seized the property and real estate of the unions. This process went on until every society and organization was Nazified or replaced—a necessary step because the leaders of the Nazi party and subsequently the Nazi state were neither politicians, businessmen nor manufacturers. Loyalty to Hitler was the most valued characteristic of a Nazi functionary and the smallest matters of day-to-day operation of even a local government were foreign to most of these men. Neither were the Nazis scientists, engineers or technocrats. To make matters worse, most were either anti-intellectual, like Martin Bormann, or pseudo-intellectual like Heinrich Himmler. Despite the slogan of a "thousand year Reich," none of them were futurists, nor could they grasp the potential of scientific developments.

Hitler, the leader of the nation, was the ultimate dilettante. According to Albert Speer, the Führer's personal architect and later Armaments Minister, Hitler "had never learned a profession and basically had always remained an outsider to all fields of endeavor. Like many self-taught people, he had no idea what specialized knowledge meant."[1] In addition he demonstrated an appalling ignorance of the effect of technology on warfare. Hitler insisted: "strategy does not change, at least through tactical interventions. . . . Has anything changed since Cannae? Did the invention of gunpowder change the laws of strategy? I am skeptical as to the value of technical inventions. No technical novelty has ever permanently revolutionized warfare. Each technical advance is followed by another which cancels out its effects."[2] Hitler covered the gaps in his technical education by memorizing the details of weapons systems and by reciting ranges, rates of fire and projectile velocities as if he knew his subject. His closest cronies, the party Gauleiters, were more concerned with maintaining their power and lining their pockets than the welfare of their Gaus (regions) or the nation as a whole. Invariably the work done in existing industries in the Third Reich was accomplished by those who had done it all along. The industrialists ran their own factories and shipyards while the Reichsbahn (the German Railroad) continued under the remaining managers once the social and political undesirables were removed.

In addition to their lack of technical expertise, the leaders of the Third Reich were incapable of giving the German state anything that resembled a rational government. The ponderous German governmental bureaucracy continued to function as it had under the Kaiser and the Weimar Republic, its cumbersome procedures legendary in a Europe rife with awkward bureaucracies. Instead of streamlining governmental functions, the Nazis made the situation worse by adding the party bureaucracy to the picture. Hitler was the head of the party and the government and his Gauleiters were both local government and local party leaders. The question of which should administer day-to-day policies was never satisfactorily solved.

The first step toward Nazi control of the economy was a law passed in 1933 that cartelized the economy but left considerable independence at the local level. Government control was increased a year later when Hjalmar Schacht, the Minister of Economics and President of the Reichsbank, was empowered to reorganize and control economic life, by decree, if necessary. Under the law of 1934 all economic associations and chambers of commerce were brought under central control and every businessman was required to belong to one of the organizations. Schacht's powers were increased in 1935, but he was a realist and Hitler, whose requirements for economic expansion were mixed up with the social and political objectives put forth in his book, *Mein Kampf*, was dissatisfied with Schacht's policies. Hitler's obsession was the recreation of a strong German armed forces, which meant the economy had to be placed on a war footing immediately. There was to be no stockpiling of materials or creation of surpluses for later use. Everything was done to provide an immediate supply of weapons, ammunition and equipment. Worse, he instructed, "no attention should be paid to gold reserves or balance of payments deficits as such, but rather all means should be used to purchase essential resources unavailable in Germany; whenever possible, essential materials should be produced at home no matter how uneconomical such production might be . . ."[3] Since Schacht could hardly be expected to subscribe to this kind of radical thinking, Hitler turned to Hermann Goering, head of the Luftwaffe and a dedicated Nazi, to provide the necessary control for a four-year economic plan.

As with most Nazi programs, the Four-Year Plan was a failure. Goering lacked the necessary expertise and bureaucracy to carry it off. In many ways Goering's responsibilities overlapped Schacht's and a power struggle ensued in which the economist lost his positions as Plenipotentiary of the Military Economy and President of the Reichsbank. This should have cleared the way for Goering, but as soon as he appointed subordinates they began establishing their own domains at his expense. Walter Funk, whom Goering appointed Minister of Economics, and who should have been Goering's ally, immediately carved out his own empire without regard to satisfying the requirements of Goering's plan. Throughout the Byzantine struggles for power in the Third Reich, Funk remained Propaganda Minister Joseph Goebbels' ally while strengthening his personal position. In the long run Hitler refused to support Goering, who eventually lost his power to the Ministry of Armaments and Munitions under Dr. Fritz Todt, and later Albert Speer; but Hitler made no attempt to eliminate Goering's weakened Four-Year Plan and get rid of the superfluous offices and positions he had created.

Initially, Hitler left the details of organizing, equipping and leading the new army to the generals, but the number of men in the military became one of Hitler's most pressing concerns. As part of the Weimar Republic's second five-year plan, of 1933, the General Staff intended to expand the Reichswehr to twice the size allowed by the

Treaty of Versailles. With only 4,000 officers available, including doctors and veterinarians, they were stretching the envelope, but considered the task achievable in a peacetime environment, which allowed for gradual expansion over the full five-year period. To Hitler and his cronies, who did not consult with the General Staff on the issue of expansion, only numbers mattered. Hitler's initial directive on expansion brought the Army immediately to a strength of 450,000, two and a half times the planned number. Officers and noncommissioned officers had to be culled from the police, border guards and veterans, who had not seen active service since 1918. To further distance itself from the Weimar Republic, in 1935 the Nazi regime changed the name of the Reichswehr to the Wehrmacht.

To parade watchers in Berlin the Wehrmacht had all the outward appearance of a fully modern force, but what the public and foreign observers saw was a well-contrived facade. Equipment was as severe a problem as leaders, because the economy could not equip a massive new military force and simultaneously meet the nation's demand for consumer goods. The issue was one of guns or butter, and German industry could not supply both. The Mauser Kar 98, a bolt-action rifle designed before World War I, was the Army's standard shoulder weapon, but rifles such as the Gewehr 98, a longer, more cumbersome weapon, were used until the end of the war. The MG 34 was the Army's standard modern machine gun, but older models, some dating back to World War I, were used until 1942. Throughout World War II the Germans used captured equipment to an extraordinary degree to make up for their shortages. Very few divisions were motorized or mechanized. On the day the war started, the 86 non-motorized divisions needed 445,000 horses to pull their guns and transport wagons into action. By the end of the war the Wehrmacht used 2,700,000 horses, nearly twice the number needed for World War I.[4]

The Nazi government literally poured money into the military with little regard for organization or duplication. In the economic chaos that typified the Third Reich, there was such fierce competition for funds and labor that each activity needed a bureaucracy to demonstrate its progress, protect its interests and garner funds. It was essential to grab as many resources and as much money as one could from the avalanche of Reichsmarks available to military projects. Otherwise an agency was liable to be squeezed out of the process.

The rocket program, which also needed raw materials, money and labor, was no exception. One of the first concerns of the program under the Nazi regime was to find a new location. If the A-2 could not be fired from Kummersdorf, then A-3, which theoretically had a longer range, definitely could not be launched from there, while having to travel to the Baltic for launchings was also costly in time and labor. An additional consideration influenced the move from Kummersdorf and that was the philosophy of keeping all the research and development, as well as a limited production facility with housing for the scientists and workers, at a single installation. Patterned after the army post or military "Caserne," such a site would allow for economy of resources and unity of purpose with maximum security at minimal cost. It was merely to be the first of many secret developmental installations, from Bletchley Park to Los Alamos. Concentrating all the expertise in a government-run establishment also kept out commercial interests that might want to profit from technology developed at the taxpayer's expense. For the rocket scientists this was a particularly sensitive subject and was addressed by von Braun in a position paper in 1935.

In a 1936 reorganization of the Army Ordnance Department, von Braun's rocket group was designated "Weapons Testing Branch 11," which the army shortened to "Wa Prüf 11." In March 1936, now-Major Walter Dornberger returned from his assignment as a rocket battery commander to become the head of Wa Prüf 11. Remaining as the project head and driving force until the end of World War II, Dornberger attempted to gain the highest possible priorities for the project, at the same time protecting it from both political and commercial encroachments. He achieved the latter with varying degrees of success.

As the proponent for liquid-fueled rockets, Dornberger's section suddenly found that one of its fiercest competitors for resources had become an ally. In the era before radar and the turbojet, air war strategists saw the need for an aircraft that could climb to intercept an enemy bomber formation with little or no warning, and the Luftwaffe became interested in rocket-powered aircraft because of their potentially high speeds. In 1935, Lieutenant Colonel Wolfram von Richthofen, a cousin of the famous "Red Baron" and head of the Air Ministry Technical Office, visited Kummersdorf to watch a rocket launch in order to see if the Army's work could be adapted to Luftwaffe needs. Three months later Captain Leo Zanssen, Wernher von Braun and Dr. Adolf Busemann, an academic aerodynamicist, accompanied Dr. Willy Messerschmitt, the famous aircraft designer, and Air Ministry officials to see the work of Paul Schmidt, an independent inventor. Schmidt had experimented with the pulse jet and developed a new valve system that was a major step toward an operational pulse jet engine. Both manned aircraft and guided bombs were discussed for the application, but the engine was not ready to be placed on an aircraft. Schmidt was ultimately unsuccessful and the technology was later used by the Argus Aircraft Engine Company to develop the Fi 103 cruise missile, better known as the V-1.

Unwilling to fund its own project, the Luftwaffe proposed a joint venture with the Army. In April 1936, General Albert Kesselring, Chief of the Luftwaffe General Staff, and Lt. Colonel von Richthofen met with General Karl Becker, head of the Army Ordnance office, Major Dornberger and Wernher von Braun to establish a joint installation in which resources would be shared by the two services but which would be run by the Army. In June, the Army's Captain von Horstig and the Luftwaffe's von Richthofen worked on a detailed layout of the installation that included laboratory space, housing and security. An absolute necessity was a long-distance firing range, which meant a coastal region since Germany was too densely populated for a cross-country missile range several hundred miles long. No one knew what the future would bring, so "to avoid being disturbed by further building for some time [the Luftwaffe and Army] had to plan the laboratories, workshops, and test stands so they would need no additions for a number of years."[5] The planners, in fact, designed the installation several orders of magnitude larger than their current needs and their foresight paid off handsomely.

A significant part of the agreement arranged by Dornberger assigned construction to the Luftwaffe because new Luftwaffe buildings were designed in the neoclassical style, which meant they were unornamented square buildings that were light, airy and roomy, in contrast to what Dornberger referred to as "Unit Model 78, Old Type," built by Army construction engineers. The only detail remaining was the construction site.

Von Braun had already looked for a suitable site along the Baltic coast and in December 1935 decided that the island of Rügen would be appropriate for what they had in mind. Unfortunately, this island had been claimed by the German Labor Front as a "Strength Through Joy" recreation area. Since neither the Luftwaffe nor the Army Ordnance Department could match the political clout of the Labor Front, the young engineer had to look for a site elsewhere. He found it during his Christmas holiday.

While visiting his family farm at Anklam, von Braun mentioned his search to his parents, and his mother suggested the village of Peenemünde, on Usedom Island at the mouth of the Peene River, where her father used to go duck hunting. It was the perfect place. The area had been bypassed by the prosperity of other parts of the Baltic Coast which catered to the tourist trade. Consisting of tree-covered dunes inhabited by wild life, the island was distant from large towns, major roads and the railroad. Just to the north was Greifswalder Oie, the tiny island from which the A-2 had been launched in December 1934.

Dealing with the Luftwaffe, a young service without an entrenched bureaucracy and a penchant for getting things done, resulted in another benefit. As soon as Kesselring agreed to the selection of the site, an official of the Air Ministry was "immediately sent to Wolgast in a high powered car to buy the desired area from the city which owned it."[6] In 1936 construction crews began turning the sparsely forested dunes of Peenemünde into the most modern research development center in the world. More land was purchased in 1938 for the proposed production center and its employees. By May 1937 most of the staff at Kummersdorf were able to move there. However, the test stands were not ready and Dr. Thiel and the engine development group remained at Kummersdorf until 1940.

Peenemünde was in the northern part of Usedom. The island is a thumb-shaped piece of land, roughly 100 km long and 45 km wide at its broadest point, bordering the Peene River on the west and the Baltic Sea on the north and east. In the northwest corner was a section about 20 km by 25 km which contained an airfield and the Luftwaffe research facility that was the birthplace of the V-1 cruise missile. The remainder of the land was occupied by "Heeres Anstalt Peenemünde" (Army Installation Peenemünde). Its position offered a clear 300 km firing range due east. The facilities were literally built from scratch and included two small harbors, a power plant and sewage processing. The installation was concentrated on the eastern shore of the island. In the north were most of the test stands and just south of these were the administrative offices, workshops and research departments. Farther south were a planned production facility, housing for Peenemünde employees and their families, as well as barracks for both compulsory laborers and German Labor Front personnel. A railroad transported the employees of Peenemünde from their homes to their places of work and back. Two aspects of "Heeres Anstalt Peenemünde" were quite extraordinary and demonstrate Dornberger's prescience. The first was the establishment of a supersonic wind tunnel and the other was the attempt to construct a small production facility for the new rocket.

Since the A-4 would be traveling at roughly four times the speed of sound—a velocity unknown for contemporary aircraft and approached by very few artillery projectiles—it was necessary to gather as much data as possible on the shape of the rocket before it was built. Army ballisticians didn't believe a fin-stabilized projectile could travel at supersonic speeds and were of little help. Thus, Dornberger and von Braun turned to the Luftwaffe, which put them in contact with Dr. Rudolf Hermann at the Technical University of Aachen.

In January 1936 Hermann began tests with models of A-3 in the tunnel that could reach a velocity of Mach 3.3. The cross section of the tunnel was a square only 10 cm (roughly four inches) on a side and the models were extremely small. The results of the test were disappointing because A-3 was aerodynamically too stable and would automatically head into the wind. Hermann also discovered that the fins had to be enlarged if the rocket were to operate at extremely high altitudes and that they had to be kept away from the exhaust, which would expand as the air pressure decreased. Otherwise they would burn up. To make matters worse, the results were not available until July 1936. This was too slow for von Braun and he pressed Dornberger to get a supersonic wind tunnel built at Peenemünde. Dornberger said, ". . . the cost frightened me; the estimate was 300,000 marks."[7]

It's difficult to imagine this archetype project manager worrying about a few hundred thousand marks after he had already spent over 10 million, and he certainly didn't seem reticent when he went to

Becker for the money. The Chief of Ordnance wasn't overly enthusiastic about building a wind tunnel, but told Dornberger he could have
it if he could get another division of the Army Weapons Department
to agree to use it. Despite Dornberger's assertions that tests in the tunnel would result in more efficient artillery shells, all turned him down
except the antiaircraft division—but that was enough. In November
1936, the order was issued to build the wind tunnel. As a bonus,
Hermann came with it. At 40 cm by 40 cm, the resulting tunnel was
much larger than the one at Aachen, but it was not fully operational
until 1942. Prior to that date the maximum speed was less than Mach
3. Thereafter, the tunnel produced speeds of Mach 4.4, a world record
not exceeded until after World War II.

Dornberger surfaced the idea of a small production facility at
Peenemünde in a discussion he had with von Braun and Arthur Rudolf
during the launches from Greifswalder Oie in December 1937. It was
a logical outgrowth of the original concept of the missile as an artillery
weapon and the small numbers required. Both civilian engineers were
opposed to the idea, however, and insisted they were only concerned
with pure research. At times the debate grew heated. The discussion
ended with Dornberger pulling rank and insisting on the production
facility to the point of threatening to have Rudolf, who was head of
the development section, put under a project manager and forced to
design the production plant.

While Dornberger has been roundly criticized for this decision, it
was a good one and shows his ability to deal realistically with every
aspect of the development of the long-range missile. His initial concept
was that the missile was an artillery weapon as opposed to a weapon
of mass destruction, so that thousands were not needed. The other
part of the problem concerned the change from experimental prototype to production model. In the German aircraft industry, one man-
ufacturer normally developed an aircraft and produced it. This meant
that the transition from experimental prototype to production model
was a gradual process during which the tools, dies, patterns, templates
and jigs required for production were already available. If the aircraft
were to be manufactured under license, the tools, etc., could be readily copied.

For a device as complex as A-4, building the production facility
next to the development facility was only good sense. The aerody-

namic shape of the missile, the fuel and motor system and the guidance and control system were the three new major technologies (along with thousands of minor ones) necessary to turn the A-4 into reality. These required unique skills that would demand highly trained specialists. The only people who could train and supervise these specialists were the scientists who developed the A-4. If the production facility was close to the scientists, problems could be quickly solved and production kept on a smooth, even footing. While tests continued on A-5, the design team at Peenemünde gradually finalized the conception of A-4. To Dornberger, meanwhile, A-4 was merely an interim step to A-10, a giant missile with a ten-ton warhead.

The shape of the missile was the work of Dr. Hermann Kurzweg, an aerodynamicist from the University of Leipzig, whom Rudolf Hermann lured to Peenemünde. Initially Kurzweg had no wind tunnel with which to work, so he carved an A-3 rocket body out of pine and made three sets of fins for the model. Attaching the model to a wire affixed to a car, Kurzweg drove down the autobahn at 100 km/h and found that the smallest set of fins didn't work. Further tests determined the correct size and shape of the fins and that the body of the rocket appeared to be adequate.

In actual flight, A-5 oscillated as it approached Mach 1 and the vibration prevented it from exceeding the speed of sound. The leading edges of the fins were radically swept back and the angle at the nozzle widened even more. The aerodynamic shape of the A-5 and later the A-4 were not a sure thing. Tests continued at the wind tunnel at Aachen and launches of A-5 began in the summer of 1938. Subscale A-5s powered by reusable hydrogen peroxide motors were used to test different fin shapes. There were even drop tests of iron models from a bomber flying at more than 20,000 feet. With the data from these tests, the A-4 fuselage took shape.

The A-4 motor was the work of Dr. Thiel, who continued the process of widening the nozzle and shortening the combustion chamber. The new motor was only 5 ft. 8 in. long and 3 ft. 1 in. in diameter. Had Thiel not made his revolutionary discoveries, and the A-3/A-5 type motor development continued, the A-4 motor would have been approximately 12 feet long, and taken up so much space that the A-4 would have had to be changed considerably. The fuel and oxidizer were mixed in eighteen cups arranged in two concentric circles of six and twelve on top of the combustion chamber. The fuel and oxidizer were funneled into the cups by an elaborate system of pipes and valves that made the feed system a plumber's nightmare, but it worked. The motor itself was cooled by alcohol that seeped into the interior of the motor from four rows of holes and formed a film which prevented hot spots that allowed ignited fuel to burn through the wall of the combustion chamber and destroy the rocket. The fuel pressurization requirement was solved by slight pressurization with nitrogen and with a turbo pump powered by steam, produced from the reaction of hydrogen peroxide and sodium permanganate.

The guidance system was essentially a compromise. None of the manufacturers were able to fill orders for Peenemünde because of wartime demands of the other services. Kreiselgeräte produced a new version of its guidance system, the Sg 66, but only a few reached the development center. Although it was the best, it was the most intricate and the most expensive. Siemens and Askania/Möller also built workable guidance systems that were neither as elaborate nor expensive as the Sg 66, nor were they as effective. A sensible solution that combined the three systems was proposed by Dr. Karl Fieber, who worked in the aviation instruments division of Siemens.

His system had two gyroscopes, one which controlled pitch and another the roll and yaw. It was simple, reliable and accurate. The missile and guidance platforms were oriented on the target with a theodolite prior to launch and the number-one fin became the orienting fin for the rocket in flight. Deviations to the flight path were "sensed" as the gyroscopes precessed when pushed away from the correct course, and sent a correcting signal through amplifiers to the servomotors controlling the jet vanes in the exhaust and the small aero vanes on the fins.

In the production missile all controls were hydraulic, for these were far superior to the electric ones tried earlier. The expensive molybdenum jet vanes of A-3/A-5 were replaced with graphite vanes in A-4. They did the job as well and were much cheaper. One of the most innovative aspects of the guidance system was a signal "mixing device" that prevented the controls from overcompensating for errors. Originally devised by Helmut Hölzer for a beam guidance system, it was adapted for inertial guidance controls. The final component necessary for the missile to hit the target was the fuel-cutoff mechanism.

Initially both radio control and inertial controls were used, the latter gaining acceptance as it proved more reliable.

As research, experimentation and development of A-4 proceeded, the outside world impinged on the heady world of Dornberger and his engineers. Quite naturally, the military authorities who provided the money wanted results, and others were waiting in the wings to see if Dornberger's efforts would succeed. In March 1936, General Werner Freiherr von Fritsch, Commander-in-Chief of the Army, visited Wa Prüf 11 at Kummersdorf and, after attending several lectures, observed the test firing of the A-1, A-2 and A-3 rocket engines. Impressed, the general offered his full support as long as Wa Prüf 11 produced a viable weapon. Money was not an object.

Fritsch, a victim of Nazi allegations that he was a homosexual, was subsequently forced to resign in February 1938, and was replaced as army Commander-in-Chief by Walter von Brauchitsch, who had received the grand tour of Kummersdorf on November 21, two years earlier. Deeply impressed, he considered the military rocket vital to Germany's growing arsenal and commanded that the development of the A-4 proceed at full speed. He also agreed that a production facility was necessary and authorized the construction of a small factory to produce 500 rockets a year. The planned completion date for all this was the end of 1942.

Since both Fritsch and von Brauchitsch were artillery officers with combat service in World War I, they understandably concurred with Dornberger's concept of the rocket. In their experience, the need to strike deeper and deeper into the enemy's rear in the Great War meant either airplanes, which were not controlled by the ground commander, or huge railroad guns, which were. The rocket envisioned by Dornberger would have twice the range of the Paris Gun, the largest railroad gun used in World War I, ten times the warhead and the mobility and ease of concealment of a medium field howitzer. This was the long-range weapon of which ground commanders and artillerists dreamed.

With plenty of monetary support and command emphasis on the project, Dornberger established Gruppe (Group) IV of Wa Prüf 11 in Berlin under the direction of Godomar Schubert to plan and construct the factory. In keeping with Dornberger's policy of building everything several orders of magnitude larger than that immediately needed, the facility was designed to ultimately produce A-10, Dornberger's 100-ton rocket with a 10-ton warhead.

On March 23, 1939, a cloudy day with the ground still wet after a rain, Adolf Hitler arrived with Field Marshal von Brauchitsch and General Becker to tour the rocket test facility at Kummersdorf. Dornberger, now a colonel, personally conducted the tour, during which the Führer of the German Volk witnessed, unmoved, the firing of an A-1 and A-3 engine. After the firings Dornberger briefed him on the rocket development program with a cutaway model of the A-3, and von Braun explained what was being done at Peenemünde. Without comment they proceeded to a classified briefing about A-4 and then to lunch. During the meal, Hitler chatted with Becker, and asked Dornberger how long it would take to develop A-4. The head of Wa Prüf 11 explained that under the current peacetime development schedule, the missile would not be ready until the end of 1942. Acknowledging Dornberger's estimate with a nod, Hitler asked if the aluminum in the rocket could be replaced with steel. Dornberger assured him it could, but it would delay development. The tour ended and Hitler commented, *"Es war doch gewaltig"* ("It was grand") politely and without enthusiasm.

As he was leaving, Hitler mentioned to Dornberger that he had known Max Valier in Munich and considered him a dreamer, which in the Führer's vocabulary was not a compliment. Dornberger tried to explain that the rocket project was only the beginning of a long period of development and cited the airplane and airship as examples of other technologies that took years to mature. Hitler expressed his distrust of airships, then departed, leaving the colonel to ponder what had transpired. The head of Wa Prüf 11 was certainly baffled and later wrote, "In all the years I had been working on rocket development this was the first time that anyone had witnessed the massive output of gas at enormous speed, in luminous colors, from a rocket exhaust, and heard the thunderous rumble of power thus released, without being enraptured, thrilled, and carried away by the spectacle . . . I simply could not understand why this man, who always showed the greatest interest in all new weapons . . . could not take in the true significance of our rockets . . ."[8]

The reasons Hitler didn't show more interest in the rocket program can be derived from later decisions he made. Hitler's notion of technical progress was that "bigger" was better—whether in quantity or in the actual size of the weapons. He supported absurd projects like the Maus tank, which was too heavy for most bridges, and the E.100, which was even larger. On the other hand he chose not to equip the Luftwaffe with heavy bombers because a far larger number of medium craft could be manufactured. It was also difficult for him to understand any complex developmental process, while on the other hand he constantly referred to the few instances when he had made correct decisions about weapons to demonstrate his infallibility. His order to put a high-velocity 50mm gun on the PzKw III tank rather than a low-velocity gun was one of his favorite examples. However, Hitler's correct decisions regarding weapons development were few, while his mistakes were legion. One need go no further than his decision to convert the world's first operational jet fighter into a bomber to understand the depth of his technical ineptitude.

Another reason for Hitler's lukewarm reaction to the rockets was that in March 1939 he was already planning for war in which panzer-Luftwaffe cooperation—blitzkrieg—would win swift victories. Poland would in fact fall in twenty days, France in six weeks and most of the other nations in Europe by 1941. A complex weapon that couldn't even be fired for another three years held little interest for him. His question concerning aluminum was certainly valid and a concern for someone who knew that such a valuable commodity was more important for existing weapons such as aircraft than for something that had not been proven. The visit to Kummersdorf undoubtedly settled Hitler's ambivalent attitude toward the rocket and was responsible for the ups and downs the project would suffer once war was declared.

In the spring of 1939, Thiel and his team were still at Kummersdorf, where they made the first test runs of the A-4 motor; but the days of Wa Prüf 11's independent control and self-paced experimentation were rapidly coming to an end.

On September 1, 1939, Germany invaded Poland and two days later France and England belatedly honored their obligation to their ally and declared war on Germany. On September 4, the Reich declared full mobilization of the economy and on the fifth, von Brauchitsch once again declared Peenemünde necessary to the defense of the nation and signed an order to exempt vital personnel from call-up. In fact, he transferred approximately 3,500 technically qualified troops to Peenemünde to bolster the project. The deployment date of the missile was moved up to September 1941. Only two days later, however, Hitler reduced the priority of every project not immediately vital to the war, which meant that Peenemünde would have to accept a lower priority for labor and raw materials than that to which it was accustomed. To Dornberger, the situation was unacceptable and, as the war progressed, his primary objective was to maintain priority status for the A-4 project.

Although Goebbels' Propaganda Ministry declared full economic mobilization, there was nothing of the sort. Germany was still operating under Goering's failed Four-Year Plan, which had no established system of priorities for the allocation of raw materials or the production of vital weapons or ammunition. General Georg Thomas, head of the Economics Office of Oberkommando der Wehrmacht (OKW) imagined that the Army would have the same control over the economy it had in 1918, but found instead the same free-for-all competition for resources that existed in peacetime. When he tried to get some sort of plan, he was bullied by Goering, head of the Four-Year Plan, and had to back down. Even Thomas' superior, Wilhelm Keitel, nominal head of the armed forces, was unwilling to lock horns with the second most powerful man in the Reich. Thomas did get Goering to sign a priority for construction for all three services in October 1939.

Peenemünde was on the top of the Army's list but it meant little as the services continued to compete. Speer explained that because of "sudden shifts of program, the factories had hitherto tried to assure themselves of four or five different contracts simultaneously, and if possible, from different branches of the services, so that they could shift to alternative contracts in case of sudden cancellations. Moreover, the Wehrmacht frequently assigned contracts only for a limited time. Thus, for example, before 1942, the manufacture of ammunition was checked or increased depending on consumption, which came in sudden bursts because of the blitz campaigns."[9] It was this confusion that caused the ammunition shortage of early 1940 and would not be completely fixed until February 1942, when Hitler appointed Albert Speer to succeed Fritz Todt as armaments minister and divorced armaments from the Four-Year Plan.

Along with the confusion over priorities, the scheduled deployment date for A-4 was moved up to the end of May 1941. On November 21, 1939, after a meeting with Becker on the rocket program, Hitler clarified the situation regarding Peenemünde. The development project was to continue at full allocation of materials and labor, but the production facility would not be supported due to shortages. In December, the Army's allocation for steel was reduced by nearly two-thirds so that, even with a high priority, Peenemünde found its steel allocation severely cut back.

Dornberger tried to paint a rosy picture despite the cutbacks, reporting that Peenemünde would be able to produce 18 A-4s per month by September 1941,[10] with increasing production figures every month thereafter. Emphasizing the decisive nature of the missile, his main concern was for the production facility. He voiced misgivings that if construction were not continued, critical personnel would be withdrawn and distributed throughout the war effort, making it even harder to build A-4 later. He ended with the warning that at that point Germany had a lead over other nations in missile technology but that enemy nations would catch up by 1942. This was purely an estimate, but for the time was remarkably accurate considering he had no current intelligence data.

Peenemünde began the new year with a slowdown because of the shortage of steel, and received mixed news in February when Speer, General Building Inspector for the Capital of the Reich—the area in which Peenemünde was located—confirmed that A-4 development would continue at Priority I but the production facility would no longer be maintained at a high priority. In March 1940 the steel allocation was reduced further.

As the German armed forces prepared for the attack that would knock France out of the war and make Germany master of Western Europe, development of A-4, despite all the bureaucratic and construction setbacks, proceeded at an accelerated pace. The guidance system neared its final form and during the summer von Braun decided to use the steam-powered turbo pump to pressurize the fuel system. In April, the older members of Wa Prüf 11 felt a special loss when General Karl Becker, the man who started the Army's rocket program and who encouraged both Dornberger and von Braun, committed suicide. Unable to endure attacks on his personal life made by industrialists who were trying to saddle him with sole blame for the ammunition shortage that developed early in the war, he shot himself. Fortunately, his successor, General Emil Leeb, was also an artillery officer who wholeheartedly supported the rocket program.

After the smashing victory over France and the isolation of England, many German leaders felt victory was within sight and the need for a weapon requiring a long period of development didn't seem vital. Accordingly, A-4 was removed from the October 1939 priority list in July 1940 and, as a security precaution, all foreign workers were removed from the installation. The situation was retrieved by von Brauchitsch, who assured Heereswaffenamt (the Armaments Ministry) that he would have the most important weapons under development at Peenemünde classified as urgently needed weapons, which made them eligible for top priority. The A-4 was given the code name "Rauch-Spur-Gerät II" (Smoke Trail Apparatus II) and as a result of this successful subterfuge, von Brauchitsch ordered Dornberger to keep his workers.

On August 15, 1940 the Heereswaffenamt received the news that Albert Speer was taking charge of all construction at Peenemünde. The young architect, a favorite of Hitler, had been quite taken with the project since 1939 and admitted, "The work . . . exerted a strange fascination upon me. It was like the planning of a miracle. I was impressed anew by these technicians with their fantastic visions, these mathematical romantics. Whenever I visited Peenemünde I also felt, quite spontaneously, somehow akin to them."[11] Speer's sympathies had already proven beneficial to the program in 1939, when he allowed construction at the site to continue despite Hitler's order to cancel any and all new work. His continued interest in the A-4 would prove invaluable during the future bureaucratic battles over the rocket program.

The ups and downs of Peenemünde's priority battle continued for the rest of the year and in many ways reflected Germany's fortunes at war. In August the development project was raised to "Sondersufe S" (Special Rank S) which was now higher than Priority I and II because it was fourth on the Reich's list of urgently needed weapons. The production facility was placed in Priority I, which led to more confusion because the priority was further divided into Ia and Ib. At the end of September the confusion was ended when the production facility was classified Ib. While this sounds impressive it actually meant that the project was allowed to continue but had to scrape by as best it could because most of Germany's resources were consumed by projects in the first two priorities. Furthermore, even with the higher priority for the development project, the project had to contend with the low steel quota established in January 1940.

The Luftwaffe's lack of success in the Battle of Britain once again increased Hitler's interest in the long-range rocket and on November 9, 1940 he authorized Priority Ia for the production facility, but once again refused to increase the steel allocation. Dornberger complained to von Brauchitsch, but this time it did no good. The general let both priorities stand. In early 1941, priority classifications were further complicated by the introduction of a new "Sonderstufe SS," which was a higher priority than "S." Instead of leading to better control, however, it created another scramble for top priority and in a few months the only meaningful priorities were "SS" and "S." In March 1941, A-4 development was rated "SS" and the production facility "S," but this changed little as steel rationing was still in effect. In April Dornberger reported that he had difficulty getting machine tools for the production facility. He once again attempted to get the priority raised but von Brauchitsch stood firm on Hitler's latest order, undoubtedly due to "Operation Barbarossa," the invasion of Russia, which began on June 22, 1941 and consumed men and materiel at incredible rates.

Frustrated by the inability to get a high priority for production, Dornberger faced a new threat from Dr. Fritz Todt, Minister for Armaments and Munitions. Due to hard work and unswerving loyalty to the Nazi party, Todt gained control of most German technical functions, which included armaments and construction. Determined to see both workers and materiel used efficiently, he ruthlessly cut back projects he thought unnecessary. The Peenemünde production facility was one of these, and in mid-July 1941 Todt cut over 8.5 million RM from its budget. This was not something Dornberger was going to take lying down. Responding in a lecture, the head of Wa Prüf 11 changed the concept of deployment for the long-range rocket forever. He referred to the weakening of the Luftwaffe and the missile's ability to bombard a target day and night regardless of the weather.

Dornberger's concept was nothing short of visionary. By making the leap from an artillery weapon slated for limited use on the battlefield to a weapon of mass destruction that could substitute for the much weakened Luftwaffe, the head of Wa Prüf 11 was looking far into the future. Neither his superiors nor the much vaunted Speer were able to make this step; Dornberger had to lead them. There was also a cynical side to the change. A weapon of mass destruction would garner more support than a parochial artillery weapon. The speech also warned against further cuts, but before anyone could react Todt reduced the construction budget again in August.

On August 20, 1941 Dornberger managed to get an audience with Hitler in the company of Field Marshal Keitel and General Friedrich Fromm, Commander of the Reserve Army, and gave the Führer an impressive briefing which included a film. Hitler appreciated the presentation but would still not authorize a production facility until the rocket was ready for employment. Nevertheless, Dornberger must have impressed Hitler because on August 28 the latter ordered that all contracts for Peenemünde be ranked priority "SS" and the entire project, which included both the development center and the production facility, was now included in "Heeres Versuchsstellung (Army Experimental Station) Peenemünde" (HVP). Along with the order came a restoration of Peenemünde's steel allocation. The fly in the ointment was Todt's refusal to increase the construction budget limit for Peenemünde above 21 million RM. The armaments minister derisively referred to the project as a "worker's paradise" because of the installation's excellent working and living conditions. Although he agreed to keep funding the project, he threatened to turn the matter over to Hitler if his restrictions were not observed.

Despite Todt's sincere desire to optimize German labor and resources, his control was limited to a very narrow range of activities and Hitler and his Gauleiters pretty well did as they pleased with both funds and labor. In September, Berlin let contracts for 30 million RM for stone from the major quarries in Europe for the rebuilding of Hitler's capital on a grand scale after the war. In addition to the order for stone, a "fleet" was planned to transport the stone from all over Europe to Berlin. These were absolutely unnecessary expenditures in wartime and the funds could easily have made up the difference needed for Peenemünde.

Dornberger realized that in addition to having Hitler's approval he needed to use his considerable powers of persuasion to convince Todt that the A-4 was a worthy project and would someday be a decisive weapon. The Minister of Armaments was finally swayed and agreed to fully support Peenemünde if Heereswaffenamt placed it under his control. The Army declined his gracious offer, but the bid should have put Leeb and Dornberger on their guard. This was the first attempt by an outside agency to take over a project in which the Führer was now showing interest. Compared to later attempts, it was extremely polite.

1941 drew to a close on a less than happy note for Peenemünde. In November, Dornberger sternly rebuked his staff for their failure to maintain control over crucial tests of the A-4 and A-5. The ups and downs of the priority battles had adversely affected the morale of the top engineers and scientists, and in order to escape the frustration they concentrated their efforts on computations for space travel while assistants with far less knowledge and experience carried out important experiments. This may partially explain why A-4 engines continued to explode during tests. Suitably chastened, they returned to work. On December 4, Heereswaffenamt and HVP formed a working staff divided into nine working teams to prepare for mass production. Under the overall control of Dornberger, the teams were tasked to determine what materials were needed in order to produce an initial run of six hundred missiles, as well as the time needed to complete the run. As part of the project they also had to finalize the working drawings and look for ways to simplify the design for production.

On February 8, 1942, Fritz Todt's aircraft developed engine trouble and crashed, killing everyone on board. The following day Hitler appointed his architect Albert Speer to replace Todt as Armaments Minister. To demonstrate his confidence in the 36-year-old, he removed armaments and munitions from Goering's Four-Year Plan. The Reich Marshal was rapidly losing influence in the higher echelons of the party due to his failed economic policy and the loss of prestige of his once vaunted Luftwaffe. As a result he once again became addicted to morphine, which further reduced his influence and effectiveness.

Speer meanwhile took to his new task with a creative will and used a democratic approach to management that flew in the face of the "Führerprinzip." His methods increased Germany's arms production more than fifty percent in six months. Although he thought very highly of the staff at Peenemünde, he was now responsible for the entire Reich instead of merely the Berlin area and one of his first acts was to compel Leeb to cut his construction budget back 2 million RM. Within a few days the new minister also proposed a study to determine the consumption of hydrogen peroxide based on a use rate of 3,000 rockets a month. Hydrogen peroxide, of sufficient concentration to be used for test rockets and turbo pumps for the A-4, was expensive to make and if sufficient amounts could not be made the A-4 would have to be dropped and the chemical given to the Navy, which was the Reich's largest user.

If that news was not bad enough, the first completely assembled A-4 blew up during a static test on March 18, 1942—a failure that prompted the Luftwaffe to offer Hitler a "study" of the rocket. The Luftwaffe's negative assessment of A-4 was already so transparent that Hitler declined the offer.

On March 24, Dornberger further outlined his concept of the employment of A-4 to the Economic Office of OKW. Continuing with the philosophy he had framed in July of the previous year, he indicated that with a planned production of approximately 5,000 missiles a year A-4 would be launched against "profitable targets such as London, industrial areas seaports, etc."[12] He emphasized that the targets could be attacked day and night regardless of the weather, and the enemy would be unable to use any countermeasures. In his presentation Dornberger also stressed the psychological effect of A-4 and mentioned that such a bombardment would relieve pressure on the Luftwaffe.

By including London as a target, Dornberger was undoubtedly playing to Hitler's determination to bomb the British capital, regardless of cost. Before he could forward a proposal to Hitler, the Royal Air Force struck a devastating blow at the ancient city of Lübeck on March 28, causing extremely heavy damage. Enraged, Hitler demanded retaliation with a 5,000-rocket salvo against London and the manufacture of 50,000 rockets a year. While this demand clearly demonstrated the Führer's inability to grasp the technical and material problems involved with rocket production, at least it proved that he was now eagerly anticipating the weapon.

Dornberger, a realist, soberly calculated that 5,000 rockets a year would be possible, albeit a severe strain on Germany's economy. The following month Hitler received Dornberger's memo concerning his ideas for employment and once again the RAF punctuated Dornberger's point when the first 1,000-plane raid bombed Cologne on the night of May 30, 1942. Just two weeks later Speer promised Peenemünde a priority "SS DE," the new highest priority, with production planned for the spring of 1943. The schedule was to begin with 50 units in January, rising to 1,000 in December. However, Hitler still refused to give the A-4 production facility the highest priority.

In April, a command with the mission of testing and evaluating field handling equipment—developing doctrine and tables of organization as well as a three-part training program for potential crew members—was set up within Versuchskommando Nord (Experimental Unit North). The first, or introductory, part of the of the training would last eight days and give the potential crew member an overview of the A-4. The second part would consist of two parallel seven-week courses. One was for electronics and the other was for the other technical aspects of the rocket. After the first two phases, trainees would be given both written and oral exams. If they passed these tests, they would be selected for further training at Peenemünde. If they failed the exams, they would be removed from the program.[13]

On October 3, 1942, A-4 number four was prepared for launch at Test Stand VII at Peenemünde. The overall attitude was expectant and tense because A-4 rocket number two had exploded during its static test, as had number one, and A-4 rocket three exploded during its attempted launch on August 16. At noon on a cool, cloudless day, Dornberger gave the order "Rocket Away." The technicians made their final checks, and condensation from the liquid oxygen circled the monster as it stood firmly on its massive fins. It was 46 feet 11 inches tall and 5 feet 5 inches in diameter. The distance across the fins was 11 feet 8 inches. Fully fueled it weighed 28,229 pounds. The countdown indicated three minutes to ignition. The test stands were withdrawn and the missile automatically sealed. With less than 10 seconds to go, green smoke was fired from a signal pistol, followed quickly by the report "Ignition."

After three seconds of burn the last cables attached to the rocket released and it rose slowly, barely covering its own length in the first few seconds. As engine thrust rose to 25 tons, the rocket accelerated skyward with a thunderous noise. Forty seconds after launch the speed exceeded Mach 2, the engine cut off and the rocket tilted toward the target. At slightly less than five minutes from lift-off, A-4 number four impacted on its target 125 miles away.

Dornberger and his engineers had realized their hopes and dreams. Their concept worked, but it was only one rocket, and the following thirteen launches were failures. Despite the failures, the single success proved A-4 would work if only the rocket program received sufficient support. Dornberger tried to get more backing for the program but Hitler remained skeptical, even while he fantasized a 5,000-rocket salvo on London.

One reason Hitler was unable to give the A-4 more consideration in November 1942 was that his attention was taken up by the uniformly bad news on all fronts. On November 4, Rommel's Afrika Korps was forced to retreat from El Alamein with the loss of over 50,000 men plus a thousand tanks, guns and vehicles. Four days later the Allies landed in North Africa and on the nineteenth, the Soviet Army launched its counteroffensive against the German Sixth Army at Stalingrad. In those dark days, Albert Speer realized that the Allies were starting to overwhelm the forces of the Reich and that a new, advanced weapon might help restore the military balance. He saw A-4 as that weapon and became its champion. On November 22, the Armaments Minister presented Hitler with a memo repeating Dornberger's idea of using the rocket against England. Although it would take another month for Hitler to sign the order giving A-4 top priority, the Führer decided to begin the construction of huge concrete bunkers from which to fire them.

On December 11, 1942, only a few weeks after the first successful flight of an A-4, Reichsführer Heinrich Himmler, head of the Gestapo and the SS, arrived alone at Peenemünde for a low-key visit. Looking around, he liked what he saw and decided it should be a project controlled by the SS. Sensing that the SS might help him get an audience with Hitler, Dornberger had the Chief of Development, Lt. Colonel Gerhard Stegmaier, an ardent Nazi, ask for assistance from his old friend SS-Gruppenführer Gottlob Berger, who worked in the Reichssicherheitshauptamt (Central Security Office) of the SS. Berger dutifully informed Himmler, who tried to arrange a meeting, but Hitler declined. Nevertheless, the SS had its foot in the door. Now that Dornberger had produced a working guided missile, others would take it away from him in far less time than it took to develop.

The Führer finally signed the order for mass production of the rocket on December 22, 1942. That same day, Speer ordered the normal production practice for A-4 in which he "set up development commissions in which army officers met with the best designers in industry. These commissions were to supervise new products, suggest improvements in manufacturing techniques, even during the design stage, and call a halt to any unnecessary projects."[14] Speer appointed Gerhard Degenkolb head of the Special A-4 Committee.

Degenkolb was a dedicated Nazi and a ruthless technocrat who had changed German locomotive production from a craft industry to mass production. It was Degenkolb who had roundly criticized the Heereswaffenamt for the ammunition shortage and was one of those who heaped personal abuse on Karl Becker before his suicide. Degenkolb refused to pamper the engineers and technicians at Peenemünde and offended nearly all of them. This was obviously not the man Dornberger wanted as the midwife for his brainchild, but times had changed. Degenkolb was Speer's hatchet man and he was determined to get things done. Initially he underestimated the complexity of putting the A-4 into production but he was ready to use any means, including bypassing normal army channels, to get the job done. Dornberger finally achieved his development goal, but in personal terms it became a hollow victory.

In January 1943, the only good news on the military front was in Africa, where there was a stalemate. In Russia the news was grim as Soviet forces surrounded Field Marshal Friedrich von Paulus' Sixth Army and gradually destroyed it. Hitler refused to let it break out and attempts to supply it by air were to no avail. The strategic initiative passed to the Allies. Amid the news of Nazi defeats, Dornberger, who was having difficulty getting electrical equipment, once again asked Speer for priority "SS DE," but the Minister for Armaments could not give it to him.

However, events were in the works that would change the priority of the rocket program. The first was the increasing interest in the program by the SS. On January 23, 1943, Himmler asked Hitler for control of the A-4 program. The Führer refused, but the interest regenerated a spark of enthusiasm in Hitler's mind. Perhaps the rocket program could be put to use to reverse the tide of defeat. In early February Hitler created the "Entwicklungskommission für Fernschiessen," the

Development Commission for Long-Range Bombardment. The commission was chaired by Waldemar Petersen, a former director of the electrical firm AEG. The objective of this new commission was to organize and control every aspect of the A-4 and its stablemate, the Fiesler 103 cruise missile, and prepare both weapons for production. How this bureaucracy—set on top of the A-4 Special Committee, the Heereswaffenamt, HAP and the Luftwaffe—was to "organize" anything is beyond comprehension.

On February 3, Dornberger was summoned to an urgent meeting at the Ministry of Munitions in Berlin with Prof. Karl Hettlage, the financial troubleshooter for the Ministry and one of Speer's most able assistants. Attending the meeting were Heinze Kunze, Degenkolb's managerial assistant, and a Herr Mackels, a ministry representative for Stettin. The head of Wa Prüf 11 sat thunderstruck as Hettlage explained that they were there to discuss the best way to turn Heeres Anstalt Peenemünde into a private stock company. This was what von Braun's position paper in 1935 had warned against and was precisely why the military installation at Peenemünde was created.

Dornberger was even more angry when Hettlage informed him that this was being done at Degenkolb's suggestion. The plan was to "make a cut in capital and declare assets of between one and two millions and let the rest go," Hettlage explained.[15] He continued by declaring that Peenemünde was not run in accordance with good business practices and that the specialists and technicians were not adequately employed. At that point Mackels tried to intimidate Dornberger with unfounded allegations of mismanagement and impropriety. Losing his temper, the colonel asked who would run the place. Hettlage replied that the directors would come from a trustee firm. Dornberger explained in no uncertain terms that Peenemünde was an army installation and there was no way they could turn an army command into a private stock company. He concluded, "Do you believe that after years of labor, with success just around the corner, I shall agree voluntarily to the change you plan and leave my closest associates, who were laughed to scorn for years, in the lurch? Never!"[16]

This was Dornberger at his finest, defending his personnel and his project, but he was approaching the limit of his influence. If Hitler was interested in the A-4, then so was everyone else. In the bizarre world of the Third Reich, controlling a program in which Hitler was interested meant power, and if getting that power meant ruining the program and swindling the German taxpayer, the end justified the means. Dornberger was soon to realize that the A-4 project had become a target for other power-hungry leaders of the Third Reich.

In March 1943 the Reichsführer SS, Heinrich Himmler, made his first overt attempt to seize the project when he tried to disgrace Colonel Leo Zanssen, the Commander of Peenemünde. Zanssen's subordinate, Lt. Colonel Gerhard Stegmaier, was an ardent Nazi who was not above using his influence with his old friend Gotlob Berger, a subordinate of Himmler's who specialized in security, to get ahead. Since Himmler was looking for a way to get a toehold in Peenemünde, Stegmaier denounced Zanssen as an alcoholic and a member of the resistance group "Catholic Action."[17] Zanssen was irascible, excitable and not very popular, but the charges were so patently false that the SS quickly backed down without an apology and bad blood remained between Zanssen and Stegmaier for the remainder of Peenemünde's existence. Dornberger was able to win these two battles to protect the A-4 program from encroachment.

While the design of A-4 was finalized, the Special A-4 Committee conducted its initial meeting February 3–6, 1943. With Degenkolb as director and Heinz Kunze, a representative of Speer, in charge of management, the committee was organized into twenty-one subcommittees to cover the entire spectrum of production of the 20,000 components that made up the A-4. The committee had four basic goals: the completion of a single design; production sites; production goals; and the procurement of a large enough labor force to meet those goals. During those first meetings of the A-4 Committee, Peenemünde and the Zeppelin Works at Friedrichshafen were chosen as sites for the mass production of the A-4.

In April 1943, the Rax works of the Henschell Company in Wiener-Neustadt was selected as an additional site. Detmar Stahlknecht, Director of Production Planning for the A-4 Special Committee, intended for production to begin in May 1943 with ten units and thereafter increase to one hundred in October, two hundred in April 1944, finally reaching six hundred monthly from September to December 1944, for a total of more than five thousand rockets. As things turned out this was a fairly realistic assessment of what German industry could do. In order to impress Hitler, later versions of the plan showed increased production rates and earlier delivery dates, but they were meaningless.

In an April meeting the recommendation for using prisoners for labor was approved and the committee turned to Fritz Sauckel, the Third Reich's Plenipotentiary for Labor Allocation. Starting with a decree from Hitler dated March 21, 1942, Sauckel began mobilizing both German and foreign workers. At first the foreign workers were treated with consideration, but as the need for labor grew and resistance to Nazi domination stiffened, Sauckel's subordinates resorted to harsher measures until he was operating a brutal slave syndicate. Caring little for anything but numbers, he often impressed workers from foreign factories producing armaments for Germany. By war's end over five million people had been caught up in his cruel web. On May 13, Dornberger and Stahlknecht demonstrated an A-4 at Peenemünde to put Sauckel in an amenable mood for supplying workers. Two weeks later, on May 26, 1943, the Entwicklungskommission für Fernschiessen arranged a comparison firing of the A-4 and the Fi 103. While this was touted as a competition, it was really nothing more than a demonstration to reach a consensus to produce both weapons. On June 9, Peenemünde was finally awarded the SS DE priority, but the good mood engendered by the news was dashed on June 22 when the RAF bombed and destroyed the Zeppelin Works at Friedrichshafen because of its production of radar components.

At Hitler's request, Speer invited Dornberger and von Braun to visit the Führer 's headquarters on July 7, 1943, where they gave Hitler a rather substantial presentation. Dornberger admittedly "packed everything—the film, the model of the big firing bunker on the Channel coast, the little wooden models, the colored sectional drawings, the organizational plans, the manual for field units, the trajectory curves."[18] This was the first time Dornberger had seen Hitler in a while and he remarked that the Führer looked old and careworn. Nevertheless the presentation excited Hitler and the star of the show was the film of the successful A-4 launch in October 1942.

After a moment the Führer looked at the models more closely and questioned Dornberger and von Braun, who summed up the current state of development. Using models, they also demonstrated firing procedure from a proposed bunker and from mobile launchers. When Dornberger mentioned again that A-4 was an interim step to A-10,

Hitler wanted the larger rocket built immediately. Dornberger carefully explained why A-10 wasn't feasible at that time and Hitler accepted his reasoning. In an extraordinary gesture, Hitler apologized to Dornberger for not believing in him in 1939 and promoted him two steps in rank, to major general. Then, at Speer's behest, he personally signed the certificate making von Braun a professor—quite an honor for a 31-year-old engineer. Once again the subject of the firing bunkers came up. Dornberger was opposed to them but, unknown to him, Hitler had already made up his mind. Searches for sites in France had already begun. Cordially, Hitler bade the new general and the new professor goodbye.

Much is made by Dornberger of this meeting, and for him and von Braun it was certainly a great personal triumph, but the presentation was actually made for the benefit of Albert Speer. From Speer's meeting with Hitler on November 22, 1942, it is evident that Speer played a greater role in the development and deployment of the rocket than he ever admitted. It was Speer who brought Hitler Dornberger's concept of the A-4 as a weapon of mass destruction and a substitute for the Luftwaffe, and convinced the Führer it was feasible. To reinforce his position, Speer brought Dornberger and von Braun with their models and film to the Führer's headquarters. Since the decision to produce and deploy the weapon had already been made, there was no controversy and Hitler enjoyed the presentation. Unfortunately, he came away from it with a number of misconceptions, not the least of which was that A-4 was the decisive weapon of the war. By not agreeing to the small production facility at Peenemünde, he had caused a critical delay to production. He admonished Speer to give it the highest priority and insisted that no one but Germans be allowed to work on production.

As a result of the meeting with Hitler, A-4 training was upgraded and orders were issued to begin finding qualified personnel. Lehr und Versuchs Batterie 444 (Training and Experimental Battery 444) was activated at Peenemünde in mid-July. Composed primarily of military personnel from Versuchskommando Nord, it was commanded by Oberst Gerhard Stegmaier. Lehr und Versuchs Batterie 444 had the mission of developing firing procedures for the A-4 in the field, training firing crews and evaluating the A-4 as a weapon system prior to fielding.

At this time there were two schools of thought about deployment. The scientists and engineers were of the opinion that only technicians could successfully fire the A-4 and they needed a massive support structure like a bunker that could house the crews, store the fuel and contain all the necessary test and maintenance equipment. The military favored mobile firing batteries manned by military personnel operating in a field environment like any other artillery weapon. In keeping with Hitler's decision to build the large bunkers in France, two batteries were organized for field use and a fourth as a bunker-based unit.

Later in the month, Paul Figge, Director of Delivery of the A-4 Special Committee, discovered the Wirtschaftliche Forschungsgemeinschaft (Wifo) underground depots at Niedersachswerfen near Nordhausen in the Harz Mountains. Convinced that the former gypsum mine would make an excellent underground production facility, he went to the Army, and with the help of the Heereswaffenamt persuaded Hitler to order Wifo to turn it over to the A-4 Special Committee for production. It was a timely move, because a series of devastating Allied air raids began in late July and carried on through the rest of the year. Three of them directly affected the A-4 program. Five major raids from July 24 to August 2, 1943 devastated Hamburg and caused tens of thousands of casualties. On August 13 the Rax Works were bombed and heavily damaged. During daylight on August 17 the Americans conducted massive raids on the ball-bearing factories at Schweinfurt. And that night the RAF bombed Peenemünde.

"Operation Hydra," as the raid on Peenemünde was codenamed by the British, comprised 596 heavy bombers with approximately 4,000 crew who were told they were bombing an installation that was developing radiolocation equipment which would limit the effectiveness of Bomber Command if it weren't destroyed. They were ordered specifically to bomb the workshops and the factory and kill the irreplaceable scientists and technical experts at the installation. Before the actual raid a squadron of Mosquitoes spread "Window," strips of aluminum foil, through the air to confuse German radar and then made a mock bombing attack on Berlin to draw German night fighters away.

The plan worked brilliantly and shortly after midnight on August 17 the pathfinders' flares marked the target and the bombers began their runs with no interruption from German fighters. Due to technical problems, some of the markers were more than two miles from the target, which proved a blessing for the rocket development program. Dornberger was awakened by the sound of Peenemünde's anti-aircraft guns firing, followed by the shock of bombs exploding. Communications went out and firefighting plans fell apart. Von Braun and a secretary saved priceless records from burning buildings while others put out fires with fire extinguishers and anything else that could be found.

By the time the third wave of bombers reached the target German nightfighters from the Berlin vicinity had arrived on the scene, and by the time the raid ended 40 British aircraft had been downed. However, the bombers left 732 dead and over 800 injured, many of them forced laborers from whom the British were getting valuable intelligence. The most important casualties were Walther, a chief engineer, and Dr. Thiel and his family. Perhaps Thiel alone was worth the cost of the raid since no one of his caliber could subsequently be found to replace him. The housing area was badly hit, but physical damage to the experimental installations, though serious, was not crippling. The test stands, measurement house and wind tunnel received no damage at all. Dornberger estimated that the raid only put the center back four to six weeks, but these were critical weeks and time was running short.

The morning following the raid, SS Obergruppenführer Ernst Kaltenbrunner, Himmler's head of security, visited the damaged installation, ostensibly to determine how the British had learned about Peenemünde, but his real intention was to insert the SS into the situation. He reported the results of his visit to Himmler and the following day the Reichsführer SS recommended to Hitler that A-4 training be moved to Poland under SS supervision. He also recommended that the missile be built by slave laborers who had no contact with the outside world. Hitler approved the idea and this gave Himmler the lever he wanted because the SS controlled concentration camp labor.

Moving swiftly, Himmler summoned Speer and Saur on the following morning and announced his coup. Neither of the men liked what was happening but they had little choice. Himmler appointed as his deputy SS Brigadeführer Hans Kammler, an engineer who had been one of the designers of the extermination camps. Dornberger described him as having the slim figure of a cavalryman, with brown eyes and a mouth that "indicated brutality, derision, disdain, and overweening pride."[19] In addition, Kammler was sensitive, jealous, arrogant and cruel—perfect qualifications for a high-ranking SS officer. He was also well connected. He was a good friend of SS-Oberführer Hermann Fegelein, who was married to Gretl Braun, the sister of Hitler's mistress.

Less than a week later, Kammler announced his plans for the "Mittelwerk," as the production plant at Nordhausen was to be called. On August 26 the first prisoners arrived at Camp Dora from Buchenwald Concentration Camp, and by September there were 3,000 working in the galleries in appalling conditions. Eventually 60,000 prisoners would be sent to Dora and 20,000 of them would die.

Shortly before the raid on Peenemünde, Dornberger submitted a proposal for a headquarters to control A-4 operations with the recommendation that he be relieved as Chief of Wa Prüf 11 so that he could command the new organization. His recommendation was accepted, and on September 1 Dornberger was removed from Heereswaffenamt and assigned by General Fromm as "Beauftragter zur besonderen Verwendung Heer" (Commissioner for Special Duties–Army, or B.z.b.V. Heer for short) and Höhere–Artillerie Kommandeur (Mot) 191 (Superior Artillery Commander, motorized, 191) or simply HARKO 191. His duties consisted of expediting development of a deployable A-4; establishing a supply system for procuring the necessary raw materials; raising and training firing crews; conducting field trials; and preparing sites in France for the active employment of A-4. Establishing his headquarters at Schwedt/Oder he organized his staff into command, engineer and supply sections. The establishment of the new headquarters left Peenemünde with two missions: development work, which could be carried on until threatened by the advancing Soviet Army, and the simplification of the A-4 design so it could be more easily manufactured. Production was the responsibility of Mittelwerk.

The first A-4 firing unit, Artillerie Abteilung 836 (Mot) (Motorized Artillery Section 836), was activated in October and Artillerie Abteilung 485 (Mot) was activated a month later. Each of the units was the equivalent of a conventional artillery battalion with a headquarters battery, three firing batteries and a service battery. In addition to commanding the Lehr und Versuchs Batterie, Oberst Stegmaier also assumed the duties of commandant of the Long-Range Rocket School and Artillerie Ersatz Abteilung 271 (Artillery Replacement Section 231), which was to provide replacements for the firing units once they were in combat. Instead of the lectures of the early three-part training program, the trainees of Artillerie Abteilungen 836 and 485 were taught with mockups of the actual equipment. Training was further divided into an officer course and those who were qualified engineers, and one for those who were not assigned to command or technical positions. The latter course lasted six weeks and included the subjects of guidance, propulsion, power supplies, fuels and the radio guidance apparatus for manual control of fuel shut-off.

When the units reached the point where they were ready to fire live A-4s, the Army had to find someplace other than Peenemünde to fire the rockets. All the rockets fired from that installation landed in the Baltic. Although the warheads contained green dye to retrieve them, there was no way to tell precisely where the warhead landed, and that was the sort of information the Army needed to develop firing tables and flight data. This could only be done over land, so the Army began searching for an adequate location. Helpfully, Himmler offered the SS training ground at Heidelager near Blizna, Poland. The impact area was in the Pripet Marshes, 200 miles to the northeast of the training area. The Army was reluctant to accept because of possible liability claims in the cases of A-4 gone awry, but the Reichsführer SS assured them that he would be responsible for liability outside Heidelager while the Army would be responsible for safety within the training area. The army accepted. During the next two months a training and barracks complex was constructed, along with a rail spur connecting Heidelager with the Krakow–Lemberg rail line.

Degenkolb appointed the operations staff headed by Dr. Kühl on November 8, 1943, but complained to Speer that development of A-4 had not been completed as von Braun had reported in September. It had in fact been completed, but final drawings were not delivered to Mittelwerk until December 5. The operations staff also found that the original Heereswaffenamt cost estimates for A-4 could not be met and the new cost would be 750 million RM for 12,000 rockets, or 62,500 RM per missile. The new production facility at Mittelwerk was completed at a cost of 42.9 million RM and thousands of lives, but the hurried construction and use of slave labor did not produce the desired production results. At Blizna, rocket crews in training reported only one rocket in eight worked while the others failed due to faulty components. An additional problem arose with premature air bursts, all due to the precipitous move of A-4 production to Mittelwerk. Regardless of the results, Heinrich Himmler was happy. He had a firm grip on the A-4, and the SS now controlled its production and deployment training.

4

The Luftwaffe Gets a Missile

In the spring of 1942, the Luftwaffe was in serious trouble. After three years of war, deficiencies in materiel, training and leadership, in addition to combat losses, were taking their toll. The Luftwaffe performed well enough in Poland and France, where it was able to gain air superiority from the outset. Without a respite, however, it was thrown into the Battle of Britain, a strategic operation for which it was singularly unsuited. Following its failure over England, it was committed successively in North Africa, the Balkans and then in Russia without a chance to reorganize or to correct some of its most glaring problems. By March 1942 the Luftwaffe was fighting a two front war in Russia and the Mediterranean, with a third front opening in the sky over Germany as Allied bombers began pounding the industrial and population centers of the Reich. To make matters worse, aircraft production in German factories was still at single-shift, peacetime levels and Luftwaffe doctrine failed to address Germany's serious military crisis. The situation was a direct result of the poor leadership that had plagued the German air force from its inception.

Since an air force was forbidden by the Versailles Treaty, Hitler initially concealed it within the Reich Air Ministry. The Air Minister and head of the Luftwaffe was Hermann Goering, a former World War I fighter ace who was a ranking member of the Nazi party, the head of the secret police and a member of the Reichstag. Goering was a poor choice to lead the new service. He was neither a manager nor a strategist and even if he had been, his other offices would have kept him away from his rapidly expanding service. To fill the office of

Secretary to the Air Ministry, his direct subordinate, he chose Erhard Milch, a ruthless and ambitious man who had built Lufthansa into one of the world's finest airlines. Having curried favor with Hitler by providing him with an aircraft during the 1932 election, Milch was exactly the man Hitler and Goering wanted, and the fact that Milch's father was Jewish was not allowed to get in the way.[1] While Milch was an excellent manager, and undoubtedly did a great deal of good for the growth of the Luftwaffe, he was neither a pilot, a tactician nor a strategist. Hitler thought highly of Milch, however, and this factor, coupled with the Air Secretary's unbounded ambition, made Goering look upon him as a rival and relations between the two men were strained from the beginning.

Goering's choice for Head of the Air Ministry Office, the de facto Luftwaffe Chief of Staff, was Colonel Walther Wever, a promising Reichswehr officer whom General Staff officers considered a future commander-in-chief of the Army. Taking *Mein Kampf* as Hitler's strategic concept, Wever planned a balanced Luftwaffe with fighters, tactical bombers and a long-range strategic bomber force. Wever's untimely death in an air crash in 1936 left a void that was never filled. His immediate successor, General Albert Kesselring, a tactician and not a deep thinker, held the post of Luftwaffe Chief of Staff for little more than a year. Kesselring's successor, General Hans-Jürgen Stumpff, remained in the office less than a year and a half. Thus, the leadership of the nascent German air arm failed to provide stable and consistent doctrine and planning when it was needed most.

General Hans Jeschonnek was appointed Luftwaffe Chief of Staff on February 1, 1939. A man totally dedicated to his profession and personally above reproach, Jeschonnek was also the wrong man for the job. He firmly believed in Hitler's infallibility and did not consider a general European war possible. Using typical Nazi logic that what mattered most was numbers,[2] Goering canceled the long-range bomber program in 1937 because Germany could build two and a half medium bombers with the material of one long-range bomber. Jeschonnek voiced no objection to Goering's decision and shared General Ernst Udet's mania for dive bombing. He must also share much of the blame with Goering for the faulty disposition of the Luftwaffe during the Battle of Britain.

General Ernst Udet, the head of the Luftwaffe Technical Office, was another officer unsuited for his position. A famous pilot and an excellent caricaturist, Udet was carefree and undisciplined. Neither a strategist nor a technician, he thought only in terms of individual pilots and aircraft. Obsessed with dive bombing, he insisted that even multi-engine bombers like the Ju-88 be able to dive bomb, and deployment of the much-needed bomber was delayed because of all the modifications needed for diving. Having no management skills, Udet did not get along with Milch. He became increasingly depressed and in 1941 committed suicide after scrawling anti-Semitic references to Milch on the wall. Udet was only the first high-ranking Luftwaffe officer to take his own life. Jeschonnek gradually became Goering's whipping boy for Luftwaffe deficiencies, which were increasingly evident as the war progressed, and he was subjected to one verbal blast from the Reichsmarshall after another. Following a particularly severe tongue-lashing after the Allied bomber raids on Schweinfurt and Peenemünde in August 1942, Jeschonnek shot himself.

Air Ministry leadership also failed the Luftwaffe in the area of technological development. At the beginning of the war, the Luftwaffe possessed a fleet of the world's most up-to-date military aircraft, many of which had been combat tested in the Spanish Civil War. Basking in the glow of its victories in Poland and Western Europe, the Luftwaffe leadership was less concerned with quantum leaps in technology than with replacing losses and updating its aircraft and weapons. The Air Ministry spent the first two years of the war keeping the Luftwaffe supplied with conventional weapons, concentrating on producing more powerful piston engines, bigger-caliber aircraft guns and a host of other requirements dictated by the combat experience gained during the previous campaigns.

Goering did not consider the development of new technology vital. Carrying the Nazi obsession with numbers to a ridiculous extreme, he wanted nothing to get in the way of current production. On February 7, 1940, "Goering signed a decree which was to have catastrophic effects upon the Luftwaffe, an order to stop aircraft developmental work. This decision affected work on all equipment which could not be ready for employment at the front within the next year."[3] Goering no doubt believed, like his Führer, in a short war, but the decree meant that government-sponsored developmental work on turbine- and rocket-propelled aircraft, along with other advanced equipment, had to be suspended. To make matters worse, the decree was confirmed in September 1941 after Germany lost the Battle of Britain and after the Luftwaffe was committed in Russia. Aircraft firms continued to work on advanced designs, but they had to do it with their own resources and could not apply the funds and the personnel necessary to advance the projects quickly. From mid-1941 to mid-1942 Germany lost her technological edge in the air.

With the war going badly for the Luftwaffe, Goering gradually lapsed into drug addiction, became increasingly ineffectual and lost credibility with Hitler. Milch, who had worked with Wever, knew the Luftwaffe needed a long-range bomber to strike deep into enemy territory, but had gone along with Goering's decision to cancel the long-range bomber program in 1937 because it was politically expedient. After Jeschonnek's suicide, Milch made sweeping changes in the Technical Office and in the area of aircraft production. Factories went to double shift and Milch worked more closely with Armaments Minister Albert Speer, which put Milch further out of favor with Goering, who looked on Speer as a political rival.

Milch also looked for a way to restore the Luftwaffe in Hitler's eyes by striking back at the British. Knowing that it would take too long to develop and produce a manned long-range bomber at that point in the war, Milch turned to the flying bomb—an idea that had been around since before World War I. Significantly, the logic behind Milch's choice of the flying bomb was totally superficial. Unlike the A-4, which was developed to fill a specific operational role and later became a weapon of mass destruction because of its range and payload, the flying bomb was selected because Goering and Milch were afraid A-4 would eclipse the Luftwaffe and wanted to show the Führer that the German air force could still bomb England. Prestige is hardly a good reason for developing a weapon that will consume precious resources needed for aircraft production, but from a military perspective the decision was an excellent one.

Since before World War I it was evident that stand-off weapons such as unmanned flying bombs offered numerous advantages in the form of larger payloads on a given airframe and reduced risk to aircrew, unarguably the most costly component of any aircraft. Like the Allies, the Germans had also experimented with stand-off weapons during the earlier war, but took a direction different from that of Low,

Sperry and Kettering in England and the United States, who were trying to develop a pilotless aircraft. In October 1914, Dr. Wilhelm von Siemens suggested a wire-guided glide bomb to the German Navy. With experience in remote-controlled boats, Siemens' company could draw on considerable expertise. During the course of the war, Siemens-Schuckert Werke (SSW) developed a wire-guided bomb that could be dropped easily from zeppelins and with some difficulty from the Staaken R. IV bomber. When the conflict ended, the guided bomb was not ready for deployment, but SSW was working on a huge bomber, the R. VIII, to carry it.

The Allies naturally halted SSW's research on the guided bomb in December 1918, but research into such weapons continued secretly in Weimar Germany. The products of this research were the guided bombs Fritz-X and Hs 293 that were initially employed against Allied shipping in the Mediterranean in 1943. These technologically advanced weapons were guided to the target by a human controller who visually tracked the bomb and made course corrections to keep it on target as one might a radio-controlled aircraft. A weapon of this type posed relatively few problems compared to a pilotless aircraft that we know today as a cruise missile, which must have a self-correcting guidance apparatus to keep it on course as it flies over long distances to deliver its payload on a specific target.

Along with the wire-guided missile, the Germans also experimented, in World War I, with remote-controlled aircraft and put them to practical use as target drones for training antiaircraft artillery crews. Fritz Gosslau, a designer of radio-controlled target drones, saw the potential for a flying bomb in his creations, but the war ended before he could put any of his ideas into practice. Undeterred, Gosslau went to the Technical University of Berlin at Charlottenburg, where he received a degree in aeronautical engineering in 1926. Upon graduation, he worked in the aircraft engine department of Siemens.[4] In the fall of 1936, he went to work for the Argus Motoren Gesellschaft (Argus Engine Company), where his first creation was the Argus As 292, a small radio-controlled drone with a three-horsepower engine for training antiaircraft gun crews.

Although the As 292 was not a warplane and had less than a twelve-foot wingspan, it was an impressive device that fully demonstrated Gosslau's grasp of the principles of pilotless aircraft. The

Luftwaffe was impressed and ordered one hundred of them with the official designation FZG 43 (Flakzielgerät—anti-aircraft target apparatus 43). Argus made its first proposal for a pilotless combat aircraft to the Luftwaffe in 1939. In August of that year, Dr. Ernst Steinhoff, a director in the Luftwaffe Research Center at Peenemünde sent a memorandum to the Air Ministry recommending the development of radio-controlled, unmanned aircraft for use against enemy targets. Argus learned of the memorandum and in October 1939 proposed a "motorized airfoil long-range projectile."[5]

The Argus team of scientists concluded that they could build an expendable, remotely controlled pilotless aircraft capable of carrying a one-ton warhead to a maximum range of 310.7 miles. Control was provided by a piloted aircraft flying some distance behind the load-carrying aircraft. Code-named "Fernfeuer" (long-range fire), the project was presented to the Air Ministry on November 9, 1939. The concept, an enlarged and refined As 292, was a small, simple, unmanned aircraft that, Argus insisted, would provide the Luftwaffe with an effective stand-off weapon for use against heavily defended targets or in difficult situations.

The Air Ministry was interested in the project and in the next few months held a series of meetings with Argus to determine if "Fernfeuer" was the pilotless aircraft it wanted and whether or not the engineers at Argus could produce it. On February 22, 1940 Gosslau presented the plans for his version of "Fernfeuer" at a meeting with representatives of the Air Ministry.[6] The aircraft was a high-wing monoplane with a slender fuselage, a "T" tail configuration and a maximum weight of 5,956 pounds. Powered by the Argus As 410 piston engine, its top speed fully loaded was 280 mph and its maximum altitude 19,600 feet. According to Gosslau, "Fernfeuer" could carry a payload of 2,205 pounds of bombs to a range of 621.4 miles, at which point the chase plane would signal "Fernfeuer" to release its bomb load. The proposal also included a series of aircraft with a rudimentary guidance system to allow them to attack large area targets such as cities or major troop concentrations without a chase plane. Gosslau assured the Luftwaffe that, as its guidance system was refined, "Fernfeuer" would be able to hit pinpoint targets at long distances.

Argus and Gosslau were so excited at the prospect of building "Fernfeuer" that they didn't wait for Air Ministry approval to begin development, and even approached the Arado Company for the possibility of developing the airframe, and C. Lorenz about the prospect of subcontracting the remote controls when "Fernfeuer" went into mass production. Having done all the preliminary work, Argus asked the Air Ministry for approval to begin development, but the Luftwaffe was not convinced "Fernfeuer" could perform as specified.

Although there were several obvious uses for Gosslau's remote-controlled aircraft, there were a number of genuine concerns about the range and speed claimed for the device. Despite Gosslau's assurances that "Fernfeuer" could perform as specified, Staff Engineer Rudolph Bree, the head of the Air Ministry's guided weapons department, was not convinced. He considered the aircraft too slow and inaccurate to be of much military use. It might have applications in dropping naval mines in the North Sea or off the English coast, but the Luftwaffe already had manned aircraft to accomplish those tasks.

The major concern was "Fernfeuer's" speed. The aircraft was of little use if it could not evade enemy defenses, and in 1940 the British Spitfire was already ninety miles per hour faster than the pilotless aircraft and its chase plane. Unimpressed, Bree summed up his findings on May 31, 1940. The brief memorandum stated that the Air Ministry's official position was that unless circumstances in the war or the design of the aircraft changed radically, there was little chance of the remote-controlled aircraft being built. However, Argus and Gosslau were convinced that they had an important new weapon and refused to let the issue drop. Gosslau began the process of redesigning "Fernfeuer" while Dr. Heinrich Koppenberg, the head of Argus, used his political contacts in an attempt to reverse Bree's decision, personally visiting a number of Air Ministry officials, including meeting with Ernst Udet in January 1941.

Koppenberg attempted to impress Udet and the others with the need for "Fernfeuer," but to a man they remained unconvinced. In addition to Bree's doubts about performance and the tactical vulnerability of the chase plane, the fact that "Fernfeuer" was powered by a conventional piston engine was a definite drawback. A complex engine in an expendable aircraft was a dubious economy, especially to officials who thought they were winning the war. Koppenberg tried other avenues, but the Luftwaffe had made up its mind and the issue was dropped.

Unbeknownst to Koppenberg, Gosslau and the Air Ministry, developments in unconventional engine design were about to make the long-range pilotless aircraft both feasible and economical. By the middle of the 1930s it was obvious that the performance limits of conventional piston aircraft engines would soon be reached, and in 1939 the Luftwaffe asked German aircraft engine companies to explore technologies that had the potential to exceed the performance of conventional piston engines and produce working prototypes for future aircraft. If the Germans could build a fleet of workable aircraft that could greatly exceed the performance of conventional planes, it would put the Luftwaffe years ahead of any potential adversaries and guarantee the Third Reich's security for years to come. The Luftwaffe experimental center at Peenemünde worked on rocket-powered aircraft and produced the Me 163, the world's first and only operational rocket fighter. Junkers and BMW developed the turbine-powered engines that eventually powered the Me 262, Arado 234 and He 162A jet aircraft that appeared late in the war.

The Luftwaffe now tasked Argus to research the potential of the pulse jet engine, which theoretically offered great power and a maximum speed of roughly 430 miles per hour with simple construction and economic use of fuel. Unlike a rocket or jet engine, which is powered by the continuous force of its exhaust gasses, the pulse jet was a primitive jet engine that worked on the principle of forcing air through a narrow tube. The engine was composed of a long pipe that narrowed toward the rear. As air flowed down the pipe it crossed a series of fuel injectors which saturated the air with fuel. The air-fuel mixture continued to the rear, crossed a glow plug which ignited it and the resulting explosion drove hot gas out of the rear of the pipe and created the thrust necessary to propel the aircraft. The cyclic rate of ignition emitted a distinctive hum or pulse which gave the engine its name. The principle can be demonstrated by placing a few drops of fuel in a test tube, shaking the test tube and igniting its open end. Instead of burning continuously, the mixture will burn with rhythmic pulses.

The problem facing Gosslau and the engineers at Argus was to build a motor that created these pulses and developed enough thrust to power an aircraft. The task seemed straightforward and simple enough, so Gosslau and his engineers designed and built a tubular engine closed at the front. Since either the air or the fuel had to be fed to the engine in spurts in order to get the rhythmic pulse required, the engineers decided to control the fuel flow with a an atomizing nozzle located in a small chamber masked by a fuel sieve that operated like a Venetian blind. Air flowed into the side of the engine and the two were mixed in a chamber in front of a Borda mouth, a device designed to control pressure and prevent a return flow of the burning gases.

The first model of the engine was tested on November 13, 1939. Gosslau and his engineers "were surprised to observe an intermittent operation with pulsations of high frequency,"[7] due to poor regulation of the airflow. Unable to get the prototype to function correctly, Gosslau and his staff completely redesigned the pulse jet. In the second prototype the combustion chamber was spherical and the air entered from the front under pressure and was then deflected into the combustion chamber by way of an annular vortex. The fuel was still fed into the combustion chamber with a small aerosol nozzle masked by a fuel sieve. Gosslau reported that the "combustion of this model was excellent, and its pulsating operation was steady. We were surprised, however, by the fact that the apparatus continued working satisfactorily after we had switched off the ignition."[8]

Another unpleasant surprise. An engine that worked well but could not be turned off was of little practical use and Gosslau returned to the design board. In the third model, he did away with both the Borda mouth and the annular vortex and designed the engine with a spray nozzle for introducing fuel into a spherical mixing chamber. Air was forced into the chamber and cut off by a series of flat shutters— a reverse of the first two models. The air–fuel mixture was then forced through a constricted conduit into a spherical combustion chamber where it was ignited by a spark plug. The third model was tested in March 1940, but again air control was unsatisfactory because the shutters didn't work properly.

Argus reported the progress of the engine development and design difficulties to the Air Ministry, which began to look for other companies doing developmental work with the pulse jet. After a few weeks someone remembered Dr. Paul Schmidt, who worked for the Machine Building and Apparatus Construction Firm of Munich, and whom air Ministry officials had visited with Willi Messerschmitt and Wernher von Braun in 1935. Schmidt, a Munich professor, had built a working pulse jet engine as early as the 1920s, but it had an operational life measured in minutes. When he offered it to the Luftwaffe in the 1930s, that service could not find a use for it and the professor gave up on development in 1938. The design languished until the Luftwaffe became interested in the pulse jet a short time later. As soon as it could be arranged, Gosslau visited Schmidt in Munich to watch a demonstration of the professor's pulse jet. It was impressive, developing nearly a thousand pounds of thrust before destroying itself after only thirteen minutes of operation.

Schmidt's pulse jet engine was impractical save for his air valve system, the one component necessary to make the Gosslau pulse jet function reliably. Schmidt's valves were curved in a closed state and flat while opened, exactly the opposite of the valve recommended by Marconnet in one of the earliest designs of the pulse jet. It was this new shape that Argus adopted for its own valve design, and Gosslau quickly redesigned the pulse jet incorporating his own improvements with Schmidt's valve.

The new engine was revolutionary: powerful, simple and quite unlike anything the military or aircraft industry had seen. It was tubular with no internal constriction, Borda mouth or annular vortex. Air was forced in the front of the engine while fuel was sprayed into the combustion chamber with a nozzle and mixed with the air. A spark plug ignited the air–fuel mixture, which exploded, causing the air valve to close and forcing the expanding gases to the rear, generating thrust. As soon as the pressure fell, the process was repeated from fifty to 250 times a minute, thus providing the pulse. A major drawback was the fact that the engine would not work from a standing start. It had to have compressed air or a substantial forward velocity before there was a sufficient flow of air to enable it to operate on its own, so an airplane using the pulse jet needed a "forward push." The scientists calculated that this could be achieved by placing the plane on a trolley and launching it down a ramp to gain enough forward momentum for the engine to kick in. While scientifically sound, it was extremely impractical for an aircraft that had to take off and land on primitive airfields. However, that was a problem that could be put off until later. The immediate question was how it would do in the air.

Argus modified a Gotha Go 145 biplane to carry a single pulse jet engine beneath the fuselage on the center line. The pulse jet was carried up against the belly of the aircraft for take-offs and landings but was lowered in flight to keep the exhaust from damaging the airframe. After a number of static tests, the first flight test was carried out by Werner Staege on April 28, 1941 on the airfield of the Luftwaffe experimental facility at Peenemünde West.[9] The engine produced 264 pounds of thrust, but could only be operated for a period of five minutes because of weaknesses in the air valve. Several other test flights followed and a few months later the test program expanded.

In the summer of 1942 two pulse jet engines were mounted under the wings of the German Research Institute for Gliding's DFS 230A-1 assault glider. The glider was towed aloft, giving it sufficient airspeed to ignite the engines, and it was released to become the first aircraft to fly using only the propulsion of the pulse jet engine. Nevertheless, the engine caused a great deal of damage to the glider. In September, the engine was tested on a Messerschmitt Bf-110 twin-engine fighter. Mounted directly under the cockpit, the engine caused such severe vibrations that the aircraft suffered damage. Later tests were made with the engine mounted farther forward and this seemed to cut down the worst vibration. Another experiment was made with the engine mounted on top of the fuselage. While the engine worked to increase the speed of the aircraft in all cases, experiments with aircraft and gliders were abandoned when the pulse jet became the power source of the flying bomb.

While experiments with the pulse jet proceeded, the "Fernfeuer" concept was never far from Gosslau's mind. Since a major objection to "Fernfeuer" was its slow speed, Gosslau considered a larger piston engine, which would increase the speed of the pilotless aircraft but would also start a spiral of increasing the strength of the airframe to hold the larger engine that would increase the overall weight of the aircraft—requiring more power, hence, a larger engine. Increased engine size and weight meant a more intricate machine costing much more than an expendable aircraft should. Worse, a larger engine would have to compete with fighter or bomber engines for production space on the limited assembly lines in wartime Germany. Clearly a conventional piston engine was out of the question. If Dr. Gosslau could not use a piston engine, perhaps he could modify the pulse jet engine he was working on to fit the remote-controlled aircraft. Precisely when Gosslau and Argus realized that the pulse jet was just the type of simple and cheap engine necessary to produce a flying bomb is not clear, but it was certainly in late 1941 or early 1942. The next step in the development of the flying bomb was the design of the airframe, which occurred by coincidence.

Robert Lüsser, a technical director for Heinkel working on air-frame design for the turbine-powered He 280, left Heinkel to look for a new post after the He 280 project was canceled. He was interviewed on February 14, 1942 by Koppenberg, who offered him a position at Argus. Lüsser wanted to continue working on airframes and Argus only produced engines, so he accepted a position with Fieseler Flugzeug Werke. On February 27, 1942, he returned to Argus to thank Koppenberg for his kind offer and became involved in an informal dis-cussion that included Gosslau, who suggested that Fieseler and Argus collaborate on the development of a flying bomb.

Surprised but delighted with the concept, Lüsser offered to help. When Gosslau drew a freehand sketch of the flying bomb with a pulse jet under each wing similar to the pulse jet-powered DFS 230A-1 glid-er, Lüsser countered with a sketch of a monoplane with a single pulse jet on top of the fuselage. In exactly two months Lüsser completed the design for a flying bomb that could carry 1,102.5 pounds of explo-sives at a speed of 434 mph out to a range of 186 miles. In order to give the pulse jet sufficient air to activate and send the bomb on its way, it would be launched from an 82-foot-long catapult.[10] An Argus-contracted guidance system similar to an autopilot would guide it to its target. Accuracy was limited to area targets such as cities or enemy troop concentrations. The proposal also stated that if the speed of the flying bomb was too slow, a larger engine developing more power could easily be installed. The project was named Erfurt P35 and the design package was submitted to the Air Ministry on April 28, 1942. The timing was propitious.

Regardless of how the war was going elsewhere, Hitler demanded no letup of the bombing of London, causing a continued drain on air-crews and aircraft that were desperately needed on the Russian Front. This constant attrition forced the Air Ministry to look for new ideas to fulfill Hitler's demands without unnecessary losses. In addition, March 1942 was a bad month for the Luftwaffe in the constant scram-ble for power in the Third Reich. On the eighteenth, the first static test of the A-4 ended in failure when the rocket blew up, but it was nevertheless bad news for the Luftwaffe, which had regarded the Army's effort to build its long-range artillery weapon with amused disinterest. Despite the destruction of the first A-4, it was obvious the Army was making great strides.

As evidenced by numerous "successful" A-5 launchings, it was only a matter of time before the Army successfully launched a rocket and put it into production. This was the reason the Air Ministry submitted its infamous "study" of the rocket to the Führer. Another blast came with Dornberger's presentation to the OKW economic office in which he indicated that the A-4 could be used to bomb London in order to take pressure off the Luftwaffe. London had always been the domain of the Luftwaffe and the idea of the Army hitting it with long-range rockets meant that funds, resources and political influence would be diverted from the Luftwaffe. This was more than the Air Ministry leadership could tolerate, and the race for a long-range weapon became a matter of political survival.

The most devastating blow to the air arm's prestige was the massive RAF attack on Lübeck on March 28, 1942. With Hitler furiously demanding retaliation, Argus' proposal speedily went through the labyrinthine Luftwaffe bureaucracy that had evolved under Udet and Jeschonnek and reached the Technical Office on June 5. Objections to the Erfurt P35's lack of accuracy were dropped and two weeks later, on June 19, Milch met with representatives of Argus and Fieseler and accepted the proposal. The design package was made SS DE, Germany's highest priority for materials and labor, and was designated the Fi 103 since the airframe was designed by Fieseler. It was also given the military cover name Flakzielgerät 76 (FZG 76) in an attempt to make it appear another target drone. The construction of the Fi 103 avoided the use of scarce materials wherever possible. The aircraft itself was made of sheet steel and it was fueled with standard army gasoline.

In August, development of the Fi 103 was transferred to Peenemünde West, home of the Luftwaffe Test Establishment at Karlshagen and the only place with the necessary scientific equipment and controlled flight ranges to test the new flying bomb. A launch site was constructed on the northern end of Karlshagen so the missile would be launched out over the Baltic Sea and maintain a flight east and parallel to the German coastline.[11] With the assignment to Peenemünde, the

Fi 103 became part of the Luftwaffe's "Vulkanprogram" (Volcano Program), the planning authority for all of the air arm's missile and guided-bomb developments. In addition to the misleading designation FZG 76, it was given the official code name "Kirschkern" (cherry-stone). Development of the various components was assigned to contractors specializing in the area of expertise under which the component fell. The airframe was naturally assigned to the Fieseler design team headed by Lüsser. Development of the engine was the responsibility of an Argus team headed by Dr.-Ing. Fritz Gosslau and Dr.-Ing. Manfred Christian. The guidance system was developed by a team at Askania in Berlin consisting of Guido Wünsch, Dr.-Ing. Herman Pöschl and Kurt Wilde. The construction of the catapult was the responsibility of Rheinmetall-Borsig. Static test runs were assigned to Dr.-Ing. Günther Diedrich and flight tests remained the responsibility of Flugbaumeister Dpl.-Ing. Werner Staege, who had overseen the earlier tests of the pulse jet engine at Peenemünde West, and Flugbaumeister Dpl.-Ing. Max Mayer.

Overall coordination including liaison between industry and the Luftwaffe Research Facility was the responsibility of Dpl.-Ing. Heinrich Temme of the Deutsche Forschungsanstalt für Segelflug (DFS). Berthold Wöhle, Bree's subordinate, was in charge of the entire program. Significantly, neither Armaments Minister Albert Speer nor anyone in his organization was brought into the program, thanks to Goering's personal rivalry with the minister.

The first Fi 103 airframe was rapidly completed and arrived at Peenemünde on August 30, 1942, scarcely two and a half months after Milch's meeting with Argus and Fieseler. The design had already undergone some major changes. The twin tail was dropped and the engine was mounted on the single tail, which extended beneath the fuselage. One of the prototype pulse jet engines, test model number 9, was mounted on the airframe and the first static test run of the new weapon was conducted on September 1. The pulse jet did not perform as expected. The engine stalled at high speed and there was excessive vibration, which should not have been surprising considering previous tests of the engine in flight at less than full speed in September of the previous year. The engineers at Argus were forced to dismantle the engine to find out why it was stopping and why it would not reach full thrust. For the latter problem, a pulse jet engine was taken to the

Hermann Goering Wind Tunnel at the Braunschweig-Völkenrode Aeronautical Research Institute.

Unfortunately, nothing could be learned from the test because the results showed that as the speed increased the thrust of the engine decreased, so that at roughly 370 miles per hour the thrust was nearly zero—a patent impossibility. What was discovered later was that the vibration of the engine caused the area containing the instruments to resonate and distort the readings. Further impetus was given to the development of "Kirschkern" on October 3, when Dornberger launched the first successful A-4. On the opposite side of Peenemünde, Dornberger was concerned lest "Kirschkern" take assets away from A-4, and he assigned von Braun to look into it. The latter, in an objective report, indicated that the Fi 103 had considerable potential, an opinion that did nothing to calm his chief.

While the Argus team worked to correct the engine problem, the airframe, minus the engine, underwent a series of tests to determine its flight characteristics. It was carried aloft by a Focke-Wulf Fw-200 on October 28, 1942 to test the aerodynamic stability of the flying bomb. The airframe held together at high speed and the scientists felt that the Fi 103 was ready for a powered test flight. The basic design proved quite airworthy and after a few more tests the program advanced to the ground-launch phase. In September 1942, Rheinmetall-Borsig began construction of the first Fi 103 catapult at Peenemünde West, less than a mile from Test Stand VII, the launch pad for A-4. The ramp was an impressive concrete structure 262.4 feet long, a distance necessary to give Fi 103 its initial thrust.

The pilotless aircraft was placed on a sled powered by a booster rocket that generated 66,150 pounds of thrust. In order to keep the sled on the launch ramp it was mounted on steel rails attached to the top of the ramp.[12] Once it was attached to the sled, the booster rocket fired and the thrust took the Fi 103 from a standing start to several hundred miles an hour over a distance of 196.4 feet in a matter of seconds. The Fi 103, its own engine activated and still under the force of the initial acceleration, detached from the sled and began flying under its own power. The booster rocket, its fuel expended, used the remaining distance of the ramp to brake to a halt. The ramp and sled were first tested using metal cylinders roughly the same weight and diameter of Fi 103.

The first ground launch was conducted on December 24, 1942 and the Fi 103 reached a speed of 310.7 mph but flew for only sixty seconds. Despite the disappointing results, the test gave the project managers confidence that the concept was sound and that the program could move quickly to a fully armed and functional Fi 103. After the first catapult launch, the Luftwaffe established Arbeitsstab (Project Staff) FZG 76 to control the development and production of the Fi 103. The staff included Gosslau, Lüsser and others from the appropriate firms. Dr.-Ing. Karl Frytag was responsible for coordination and liaison between the companies and their subcontractors.

The staff met once a month and meetings were sometimes attended personally by Milch. They hoped to complete Fi 103 as a weapon and field it before the Army could finish A-4, but their hopes were premature and the program began experiencing one difficulty after another. To make matters worse, the Luftwaffe researchers committed a number of procedural errors that also set back the program. Between January and July 1943, a total of 68 test Fi 103s were launched from the ramp, but only 28, roughly 41percent, worked properly. The rest crashed shortly after launch or went out of control. This flew in the face of Fieseler's claim in June that 90 percent of the bombs would hit within a six-mile radius of a designated target.

The scientists, engineers and technicians working on the project were at a loss to explain the failures because all of the components theoretically worked. One of the problems, however, concerned their methodology. The individual components of the Fi 103 were not thoroughly tested individually before they were incorporated into the complete aircraft. This was in sharp contrast to the A-4, in which major components such as the engine and rocket were thoroughly tested prior to inclusion in the final rocket. Dornberger's engineers had even gone so far as to build the A-5 as a test bed for components and concepts that had to be tested in flight. The Fi 103, on the other hand, was assembled and flown before exhaustive ground or bench tests on the components were conducted.

Once the tests began, there were few attempts to recover fired test samples that fell into the sea, although some of the later test models were fitted with telemetry units that passed information on twelve different components to ground monitoring units. Dornberger and his engineers made every attempt to recover the remains of A-3, A-4 and

A-5 rockets that fell into the sea, using simple devices like parachutes and dyes to mark the sites where the rockets hit the water.

The Luftwaffe was, however, unwilling to capitalize on the six years of experience gained by the Army in its development of the A-4 just a short distance away. This clearly demonstrates the consequences of the Nazi philosophy of divide and rule. Even Hitler's vaunted "Entwicklungskommission für Fernschiessen" (Development Commission for Long-Range Bombardment), which was organized to insure knowledge, was shared and resources used economically had no effect. After much experimentation, the Luftwaffe's team of engineers traced the problem to the guidance system.

The guidance system of the Fi 103, like that of the A-4, posed unique problems for the German aeronautics industry in general and Askania in particular. A conventional autopilot had to hold an aircraft on its current course at its current altitude, a problem relatively simple to correct in spatial terms because all the autopilot had to do was sense and correct deviations from the set course and altitude, which also included corrections for roll. The Fi 103 guidance system had myriad tasks to perform after it recovered from a 22g launch. First, it had to climb to a programmed altitude between 990 and 8,250 feet. While gaining altitude, it had to allow for course changes up to 60 degrees right or left. Once at the proper course and altitude, the guidance system had to keep the Fi 103 there for approximately twenty-five minutes, while not allowing the aircraft to diverge from its course more than four percent.[13] At the end of a predetermined distance the guidance system had to signal the elevators and cause the aircraft to dive onto the target.

If this were not enough, the system had to be robust enough to stand rough handling in the field and be simple enough for launch crews who were not engineers to maintain, calibrate and set target data very easily. The final design of the Fi 103 guidance system included a displacement gyroscope for heading and roll, as well as a rate gyroscope for the rudder and one for the elevator. Direction was controlled by a magnetic compass and the entire system was powered by compressed air. The range was measured by a small propeller in the nose which ran a counter attached to a mechanism that simply closed and locked the shutters on the pulse jet engine as soon as the counter turned to the correct number of revolutions. Without an air supply, the engine simply shut off and the Fi 103 dove onto its target.

In addition to the problems posed by the high "g" take-off, and the requirement to fly a course accurately without a pilot, the Fi 103 presented a number of problems not found in other aircraft. For one, the aircraft was made completely of steel as opposed to manned aircraft, which were made of aluminum. Ferrous-metal steel adversely affected the aircraft's compass, sending the early test Fi 103s off course by several degrees. The problem was solved by the crude but effective method of taking the Fi 103 into a building that contained no iron and setting the course, taking into account the local magnetic deviation. After that the crew struck the shell of the airframe around the compass with a wooden mallet. This effectively zeroed in the compass on magnetic north and canceled out any effect the steel shell might have.

The major problem with the guidance system of the early experimental Fi 103s was the vibration of the engine, which threw the compass off as much as ten percent. To dampen the shock of take-off and the vibration, the compass was suspended with rubber springs in a wooden sphere. Wood offered two advantages. It meant that there was less metal to affect the magnetic compass and it was considerably cheaper that any other material in Nazi Germany. The sphere was mounted in the airframe on helical springs as an extra cushioning measure.[14] Vibration was also lessened by improvements in both the engine mounts and the airframe. A third problem that affected the course of the aircraft was that the engine was not perfectly parallel to the airframe due to flaws in manufacturing. This was an error for which the guidance system had to constantly correct in flight.

The motor mounts were changed to reduce vibration, and the way the engine was attached to the Fi 103 was modified. The engine was now attached to the bomb by a single mounting point atop the rear fin and a flexible fork near the air intake that allowed the fuel lines to pass from the fuel tanks into the body of the bomb and then to the engine itself.

These two modifications solved the vibration problem, but during the next launch the flying bomb flew into a strong crosswind, veered off course and crashed. The Fi 103 should have been able to fly into the crosswind without crashing. It was obvious that a new problem had surfaced and the scientists and designers set to work to uncover and solve it. Because the Fi 103 was tested as a whole, it was difficult to identify the source of the problem because the airframe, engine or guidance system and a long, detailed process followed in which each component was exposed to a crosswind to determine which had failed and how. After many trials and adjustments, the scientists discovered that the servos in the guidance system were upset by strong crosswinds and they were modified to accommodate for these. At the next test the Fi 103 performed as designed.

Convinced they had solved all the problems of the Fi 103, the designers decided to demonstrate the new weapon to the Nazi hierarchy. In January 1943, Hitler, Goering and Himmler were invited to watch a launch of the Fi 103 and they arrived at Peenemünde with expectations of watching the Fi 103 perform flawlessly. Unfortunately, the launch did not go as planned.[15] The Fi 103 sped up the launch ramp, the roar of the booster rocket followed by the unmistakable sound of the pulse jet engine as the pilotless aircraft left the sled. A few seconds later, however, it went out of control, skidded across the launch area and crashed nearby.

After promising so much and delivering only failure, the Fi 103 team were not only embarrassed, but they were afraid the entire project would be canceled. Fortunately for them, Hitler saw enough potential in the weapon to allow the development to continue. The engineers went back to the drawing board to find the source of the new problem, but after long hours of tests and experiments they were unable to pinpoint the trouble. Everything worked fine on the ground and there was absolutely no reason for the Fi 103 to crash. Frustrated, they decided that the only way to discover the problem was to use a test pilot, since the telemetry of that time was inadequate for the purpose. They built a special compartment in a Fi 103 with a pilot seat and a simple set of instruments and controls. In order to keep the aerodynamics of the Fi 103 as close to the production model as possible, the test pilot had a small periscope instead of a canopy for visually flying the Fi 103.

Finding a test pilot, however, was no easy matter. The Fi 103's propensity for crashing was well known around Peenemünde and there were no volunteers who wanted to fly a prototype flying bomb from an enclosed compartment when it was likely to crash. Luckily for the project, Flugkapitän Hanna Reitsch, one of Germany's top test pilots, agreed to do it. Crammed into the tight compartment, she made four hazardous trips in the flying bomb and only during the fourth flight was she able to isolate the problem. The wing mounts of the Fi 103 were not strong enough to absorb the shock of the pulse jet taking over from the rocket-powered sled. As long as Fi 103 was on the sled being propelled on a straight course it was fine, but when the pulse jet took over, the jolt broke the mounting bolts and the wings fluttered, causing the Fi 103 to spin out of control and crash. The mounting bolts were quickly strengthened and the test program continued.

The program experienced several other minor problems but these were quickly and easily corrected; a workable Fi 103 flying bomb appeared ready for production in May 1943. Fieseler invited Albert Speer, Grossadmiral Karl Dönitz and Feldmarschal Erhard Milch to the sham competition between A-4 and Fi 103 conducted on May 26. Once again in front of an audience of dignitaries, the launch failed, but the decision to produce Fi 103 had already been made. Two successful launches in June seemed to confirm the decision as correct.

The production version of the Fieseler Fi 103 was 27 feet long and 5 feet wide. It was made of sections of steel alloy that were bolted together. It had two short, stubby wings with a total span of almost 15 feet. The plane was powered by the new Argus 109-104 pulse jet engine, which gave it a maximum speed of 400 mph and a range of 180 miles. Its offensive punch was an explosive charge crammed into its nose. The bulkhead behind the compass assembly was 14-gauge steel and it separated the explosive from the controls of the Fi 103. The blast would come from 1,760 pounds of "high-blast" Amatol, an explosive more powerful than TNT. It was contained in a cylinder which conformed neatly to the shape of the fuselage. The warhead was triggered by fuses primed by switches in the nose and on the exterior of the belly.

The fuel tank was located in the compartment behind the explosives. The Fi 103 was powered by 1,333 pounds of "B-Stoff" fuel, which was a mixture of gasoline and additives to increase performance. The next compartment held two spheres that contained compressed air. The spheres had an internal pressure of 900 pounds per square inch and were wrapped with metal banding to keep them from exploding. The air was used to power the Fi 103's flight control systems simply and effectively. The flight controls were located behind the compartment containing the compressed-air spheres and were directed by the Askania guidance system. Any deviation sensed was translated into a pneumatic signal. The signals triggered a series of pistons that opened air inlets and moved an actuating cylinder. Air was directed to cylinders that corrected the appropriate control surfaces and returned the Fi 103 to a straight and level course. Actual direction to the target was controlled by the gyroscope, which compared the current flight path to the alignment that had been set in the magnetic compass of the Fi 103. Deviations between the two triggered a battery-powered electric motor that adjusted flight control surfaces, by means of a pneumatic servo motor, until the magnetic compass and gyroscope were back in alignment.

Controls to the flight systems were accomplished using thin actuator rods routed to the wings and tail through simple tubes. All flight control rods went through the Fi 103 flight log mechanism, which was located near the steering control. When the Fi 103 reached its target, the flight log severed the actuator rods to the rudder and elevators, locking the missile on course and, by electrical impulse, then set off two small explosive charges that activated a pair of spoilers under the tail plane. The spoilers dropped the nose by 4 or 5 degrees and threw the flying bomb into a shallow dive toward its target. Finally, the designers built a unique internal dog-leg metal brace that was located just behind the explosive. The top of the brace extended out the top of the Fi 103 and was used to lift the flying bomb onto its launch rail. The bottom of the brace extended down and out the bottom of the Fi 103 and served as the lug that kept the Fi 103 on the launch rail during launch. The large circular pipe and the steel rods that held the wings in place passed through the center of the brace.

Although the automatic pilot and guidance system were very sophisticated and could compensate for yaw and roll, they could not compensate for displacement in the same way the A-4 guidance system could, and a strong wind could easily throw the Fi 103 off course. Here, again, the Luftwaffe might have benefited from the Army's experience with the A-4 guidance system, but it did not. Another weak link in accuracy was the counter. A purely mechanical device, it was more prone to failure than an electric one, and malfunctioning counters often shortened or lengthened the range of the Fi 103 far outside the six-mile target radius claimed for it. The weapon was at best an "area weapon" barely accurate enough to hit large targets such as cities or ports. Its advantage was that it was cheap, easy to build and used no critical fuel. Even if only a few reached England, at least the Germans would be striking back at their enemy.

Milch and the Air Ministry hierarchy set December 15, 1943 as the opening date of the Fi 103 offensive against London. This was merely the first of many overly optimistic predictions for the Fi 103 made by the Luftwaffe leadership. From June 17 through 18, Goering, Milch and Generalleutnant Walther von Axthelm, the head of the Luftwaffe antiaircraft troops, met in Berlin to discuss production of the Fi 103. Since the Fieseler plant at Kassel lacked the capacity to produce the number of flying bombs planned for, they decided to start an additional assembly line for the Fi 103 at the Volkswagen plant at Fallersleben. They estimated that the program would require 2,990 workers whose production would start with 100 flying bombs in August 1943 and increase 500 per month until production reached 2000 per month in December.[16] In 1944, production would increase even more rapidly until a maximum of 5,000 per month was reached in May 1944 and maintained at that rate thereafter.

Goering, demonstrating his complete ignorance of the production capability of the Third Reich in general and the Fi 103 in particular, demanded an ultimate production goal of 50,000 units per month.[17] Had the entire German aircraft industry converted to Fi 103 production, it could not have produced that many units a month.

In order to have everything ready for the start of the Fi 103 offensive on December 15, the missile launch crews had to be assembled and trained and the equipment necessary to launch the Fi 103 had to be in place. Under the auspices of the Flak (antiaircraft) troops, von Axthelm appointed Oberst Max Wachtel to command a new instruction and test unit, christened "Lehr und Erprobungskommando Wachtel" (Training and Test Command Wachtel) after its new commander.

Wachtel was an excellent choice. An artillery officer in World War I, he had joined the Luftwaffe in 1936 and was an experienced, nononsense Flak commander. The new unit made its home at Zempin, a few miles south of Peenemünde, and was responsible for training the firing crews and maintaining liaison with the firms delivering the equipment necessary for their training and deployment. At the same time von Axthelm appointed Oberst Georg von Glydenfeldt Director of FZG 76, which meant he was responsible for both crew training and further development of the Fi 103.

By June 21, 1943, barracks and a new launch ramp were under construction at Zempin. In the meantime, operational planning and methods of deployment for the flying bomb were ironed out in a meeting on June 18, 1943 between Goering, Milch and von Axthelm. Milch agreed with Hitler's concept of large concrete bunkers to house the firing sites. The bunkers were to be as bomb-proof as the U-boat pens along the French coast and would allow the launch crews to fire under any conditions. Von Axthelm, who was more aware of combat conditions than either of his superiors, wanted small unobtrusive firing sites that were well camouflaged and difficult to find. Needless to say, von Axthelm did not get his way, but Goering offered to compromise on a combination of large and small sites.

Hitler agreed to the compromise and also to a number of large sites for both A-4 and Fi 103. On June 28 he ordered the construction of 252 concrete Fi 103 launching sites to be incorporated into the Atlantic Wall. The sites, extending from Dunkirk along the coast of France to the Cotentin Peninsula, were all identical. Each had a large square building made of concrete blocks and no metal for preparation of the Fi 103 before flight. A smaller building a short distance away stored the hydrogen peroxide and sodium permanganate used to generate the steam to drive the catapult. A long concrete launching ramp was usually aligned on London, but some were oriented on Channel ports. A launch site also had two or more long storage buildings with curved entrances to prevent Allied aircraft from shooting down the length of the building. From the air they looked like skis laid on edge so that Allied photo interpreters named them "ski sites."

At the end of July 1943, training began in earnest at Zempin. The 14th Company of the Luftwaffe Air Signals Experimental Regiment set up a series of radars along a 155-mile section of the Baltic coast to track the firings and record data.[18] A month and a half later, on August 15, "Lehr und Erprobungskommando Wachtel" began training "Flak Regiment 155(W)." The appellation "Flak" made it part of the Flak troops and provided additional cover for its dealings with FZG 76. The suffix "W" stood for "Werfer," which in German could mean anything from launcher to projector to mortar. In addition to their training at Zempin many of the troops were assigned to companies manufacturing major components of the Fi 103 to gain further experience with the system.

While the first launch crews were being trained, production of the new flying bomb was getting off to a rocky start. Of the 2,180 workers required for the production of the Fi 103, only 1,427, or roughly 65 percent, were actually available at the end of July.[19] After the bombing raids which devastated Hamburg from July 24 to August 2, Milch demanded that fighter production be given first priority in the Luftwaffe production program and the Fi 103 reclassified as a bomber replacement. If the confusion that reigned in the upper echelons of the Air Ministry was not enough, the Army's A-4 program was poaching on skilled labor reserved for the Fi 103. Milch complained loudly and Speer was forced to issue an order that the A-4 program was not to interfere with that of the Fi 103.

Nevertheless, there was friction between Milch and Speer. Professor Willi Messerschmitt waded in on Speer's side because he wanted to see the aircraft industry removed from Milch's control. He criticized the single-shift operation of the factories and recommended that only fighters and Fi 103s be produced. After the British air raid on Peenemünde on August 17, plans were made to move Fi 103 launch facilities to a navy base at Brüsterort, northwest of Königsberg. Once calm was restored, the launch facilities remained at Peenemünde West, but Brüsterort was used as an additional training facility. Like the production plans for the A-4, those for the Fi 103 began to unravel immediately. By the end of August not one Fi 103 had been delivered. Endless problems caused the Volkswagen and Fieseler factories to make numerous modifications, each of which delayed production a little longer. Of the pre-production units delivered for training and testing, many had to be repaired on site before they could be fired and some arrived with components missing. Of the firings that took place in August less than 60 percent were successful in leaving the launching ramp. The accuracy of those that made it off the ramps was extremely poor.

On September 1, 1943, the fourth anniversary of the start of the war, Flak Regiment 155(W) moved to the new training area at Brüsterort. The target date for completion of training was October 1, but this date passed with a large number of personnel yet to arrive.

The Fi 103 required high-quality personnel that front-line commanders were reluctant to lose, and even though their transfers could not be thwarted, they were delayed for as long as possible. The higher echelons of the Air Ministry were either unable or unwilling to force the issue because the regiment could not reach full strength until February of the following year. After three weeks of training, the catapult crews each launched two ballasted dummy missiles with the same weight as the actual Fi 103 into the dunes near Brüsterort.

The crews nicknamed the dummy Fi 103s "Bumskopf" (blockheads). After firing the dummies successfully, the crews were returned to Zempin and launched a live Fi 103 with a ballasted warhead. The crews then returned to Brüsterort, where they resumed training with dummies. Some soldiers who were in support and repair positions trained with industry to increase their specialist skills. The training of the launch crews was practical but it was hampered by the insistence on absolute secrecy. No training aids or illustrated materials were allowed and no notes could be taken by the trainees. Another difficulty, which became evident in September, was the lack of Fi 103s to launch. The pre-production Fi 103 in the "V" (Vorserienzellen—prototype pre-production) series, which were lighter than the production model, were nearly gone and there were no new models of the M series, a second pre-production type similar to the G series, the mass-production version coming out of the factories.

Hitler expected little from the Fi 103 due to its lack of accuracy, but Milch was still hopeful. "I will be satisfied if the Fi 103 works at all. . . . A weapon against which the public sees there is no real defense has such catastrophic morale effects that by itself—regardless of what the weapon is—it must have immense consequences."[20] Believing that Luftwaffe crews would be able to launch one Fi 103 every twelve minutes, he stated that the citizens of London would "never endure it. It will be the end of any real life in the city."[21] Colonel Viktor von Lossberg, a Luftwaffe bombing expert and later an authority on night fighters, recommended filling the Fi 103 warhead with incendiaries, because the Germans did so little damage to London with explosives whereas the English burned most of Hamburg to the ground.

By the middle of September, the Volkswagen Factory at Fallersleben began producing production Fi 103s at the absurdly slow rate of two missiles per day. This was not even enough to meet the training requirement of six per day. In addition, Askania and some of its sub-contractors had suffered bomb damage and could deliver only a small number of the guidance and control components necessary, and as late as October, Volkswagen was still short of skilled workers and machine tools.

The first section of Flak Regiment 155(W) was transferred to Zempin to complete its training and fired its first Fi 103 as a unit on October 26, 1943. At that time only 38 Fi 103s were available and only two launches could be made per day.[22] Nevertheless, technical problems continued. There were malfunctions in the counter, the engine and the guidance section. In some cases the telemetry failed to function. Tests continued and mass production was still a long way off when the RAF struck the Fieseler Factory on October 22, just before it was supposed to begin production of Fi 103. The air raid aroused suspicion that the British knew about the Fi 103, when they were actually attacking all of the aircraft factories in the area. The Nazis also suspected treason, so when the Fieseler Company relocated its factory in Rothwesen northeast of Kassel, only a few kilometers from the Bettenhausen site, it was not allowed to take the French and Dutch foreign workers that made up 45 percent of its skilled work force—a move which caused another serious delay in production.

The dislocation of the Fieseler factory was so great that they were unable to maintain the paltry production rate of two Fi 103s per month, but the British were unable to do to the Germans anywhere near the damage their faulty management did to themselves. The Volkswagen assembly line was plagued with modifications. Between August 1 and November 3, 1943 alone there were 150 changes. The few Fi 103s launched in November either turned over in flight due to improperly checked guidance/control systems or they fell apart in mid-air. The latter problem was caused by the fact that G model airframes were spot-welded instead of riveted like the V models had been.[23] The spot welding was badly done and "at the end of November 1943 the Volkswagen mass production series was halted for the time being, and the two thousand bombs already partially finished were scrapped as their structures were too weak."[24]

With this kind of wasted effort, who needed British bombs? Even if the airframes were inferior, it seems that some extra welding, no matter how crude, would have allowed the Luftwaffe to use some of them for training! The Air Ministry decided to have Volkswagen man-ufacture only one hundred new Fi 103s, with all of the modifications to date, after which a decision based on their performance would be made. Unfortunately, the one hundred missiles would not be delivered until February. At the end of November, Volkswagen and Fieseler were short 2,126 skilled workers and 540 specialists. Fritz Sauckel, the Plenipotentiary for Labor, was able to provide 8,417 workers, but these were all unskilled.[25] On November 13, von Axthelm had the temerity to suggest that the Fi 103 be used against potential invasion ports and other military targets. Unaware of how poorly the program was doing, he suggested 30,000 a month be fired to compensate for its inaccuracy. Hitler told him not to worry about the invasion but to concentrate on retaliation.

In December, Flak Regiment 155(W) began deploying to France, where it was to become subordinate to LXV Armeekorps, command-ed by army Generalleutnant Erich Heinemann. The corps activated on November 28 was a special-purpose unit set up solely for the long-range bombardment of England. In recognition of its unique organi-zation, Heinemann's chief of staff was Oberst Eugen Walther of the Luftwaffe. The marriage was not a happy one, as the coming months would show.

5

Allied Discoveries and Countermeasures

In London, the ultimate target for the new German weapons, decisions relating to the war rested in the War Cabinet, which consisted of Prime Minister Winston S. Churchill, who was also Minister of Defence, and the cabinet offices of the Foreign Secretary, Lord President of the Council, Lord Privy Seal, Secretary of State for War, Chancellor of the Exchequer, Minister of Food, Minister of Information, Minister for Civil Defence, Minister of Labor, the Air Ministry, and the First Lord of the Admiralty. Churchill was Prime Minister of a coalition government and many of his cabinet ministers came from other parties. He also relied on personal advisors who were not officially part of the cabinet. One of the most important of these was Professor Frederick Lindemann, a close friend, who became Lord Cherwell in 1943.

Below the War Cabinet was the Vice Chiefs of Staff Committee, whose members were the chiefs of staff of their respective services and formed the link between the War Cabinet and the armed forces. In addition, there was the Defence Committee, which was divided into Operational and Logistical subcommittees. The members of this committee were the Deputy Prime Minster and the three service ministers who were not part of the War Cabinet. There was no intelligence officer at cabinet level.

Prior to the war, Great Britain's intelligence-gathering effort was fragmented. The gathering of foreign intelligence by agent was the domain of the Special Intelligence Service (SIS), which worked through Foreign Office embassies. The identity of the head of SIS was kept secret and he was known only as "C." The gathering of signal intelligence (Sigint) was the responsibility of the Government Code and Cipher School. The War Office and the services also had their own intelligence agencies that gathered strictly military information on enemy order of battle and doctrine.

On February 7, 1939, the Committee for the Scientific Survey of Air Defence, chaired by Sir Henry Tizard, submitted a report pointing out the British government's ignorance of new German weapons technology. Acting on the report, the Air Staff attached a scientific and technical section to its Directorate of Intelligence. Tizard, asked to recommend someone for the post of scientific liaison officer, named Dr. Reginald V. Jones, a 27-year-old scientist working in the Admiralty Research Laboratory. Approached in May by A.E. Woodward-Nutt, Tizard's secretary, Jones accepted the post and agreed to start work on September 1, 1939, which, as it turned out, was the day on which World War II in Europe began.

Jones was a good choice. Educated at Oxford, he had studied under physicist Professor Frederick Lindemann, who was working on infrared detectors. Receiving his doctorate for research in infrared radiation at age 22, Jones went on to work with Tizard in the development of infrared for aircraft detection. His first task as Assistant Director of Intelligence (Science), or ADI(Sc), was to respond to a scare caused by a remark in a speech made by Hitler broadcast from Danzig on September 19, 1939, near the end of the Polish campaign. If England didn't make peace, Hitler threatened, he would attack the British with a weapon against which they had no defense. Jones researched the remark thoroughly. Between Hitler's execrable grammar and bad translations, it sounded as if the German dictator meant a secret weapon, but he really meant the Luftwaffe.

During his investigation, Jones discovered that none of Britain's intelligence services had much information on evolving German technology. Nevertheless, the inquiry was extremely beneficial because it put Jones in contact with many agencies and individuals in the intelligence community and these contacts would serve England well in the future. Another asset for British intelligence was the establishment of the Photographic Interpretation Unit (PIU) in 1940 at Medmenham under the auspices of the Air Ministry. In 1941 the PIU became the Central Interpretation Unit (CIU) and would be a major element in the discovery of the A-4 and the Fi 103.

The first break for British scientific intelligence came in the "Oslo Report," so-called because it was sent anonymously to the British Naval Attaché in Oslo, Norway in November 1939. The report, obviously written by a scientist or an engineer, contained information on the Ju-88 aircraft program, an aircraft carrier, remote-controlled gliders, autopilots, remote-controlled shells, the German aircraft research facility at Rechlin, methods of attack on bunkers, air raid warning equipment and countermeasures, an aircraft range finder, torpedoes and electric fuses for bombs and shells.[1]

The section on remote-controlled gliders mentioned an anti-shipping glider bomb propelled by rockets that was under development at Peenemünde, but it mentioned nothing about long-range rockets or flying bombs. The report also contained a part of one of the fuses it discussed. The "Oslo Report" was not precise and was not received well in many British ministries, but was extremely important in that it gave Jones an excellent idea of the directions German weapons research was taking. In several instances he was able to use the information in the Report to point him toward precise areas of inquiry.

For the next three years, Jones was deeply involved in the electronic war between the Royal Air Force and the Luftwaffe which concerned radar, radar detection and directional beams for aircraft, and he had little time to pay attention to the few rumors about rockets picked up by SIS agents. In December 1942, information concerning German rocket research became increasingly available but the picture it presented was anything but clear. On December 18, SIS received a report from a Danish chemical engineer who traveled extensively.

During a visit to Berlin, the engineer had had a conversation with a professor and an engineer who mentioned a rocket that carried five tons of explosive over a range of 200 km. He was pressed for more data and on January 1, 1943, SIS received a report "that the rocket's course and range were directed by a metal body, inserted into the projectile before firing and working automatically when the rocket reached its zenith, and that the rocket flew horizontally before turning over onto its target."[2] The credibility of the engineer was in question until he sent the British photographs of a Bf-110 fighter with the Lichtenstein radar. Also in January, the Military Intelligence Branch of the War Office (MI) informed CIU that the Germans were developing long-range rocket projectors that could hit England from the Channel coast and that they were to be alert for launching rails and other unusual construction in the area. This was followed by a third report from the chemical engineer on March 31, 1943, which claimed the rocket was manufactured by Opel and tested near Swinemuende.

A second source, this time a neutral, reported in January and February 1943 that a factory at Peenemünde was producing a new weapon that had been tested in Latin America—a statement received with justifiable skepticism. The source also reported a large airfield on Usedom island and a rocket that rose vertically, then disappeared suddenly in a horizontal direction. Another neutral source reported a rocket with a ten-ton warhead and a range of 100 km that was soon to be deployed on the French coast.

The Special Intelligence Service received a report that Krupp was mass-producing a rocket gun with a 120 km range. The common factor in all these reports was Peenemünde and Jones made the connection with the "Oslo Report." Peenemünde had been photographed once on May 15, 1942, as part of a general reconnaissance of the Baltic coast. Flight Lieutenant D.W. Stevenson, flying a Spitfire, photographed the airfield at Peenemünde West and parts of the rocket development center. Other than the airfield and a great deal of construction, the Central Interpretation Unit (CIU) at Medmenham reported very little. They could not explain the large circular embankments, which were the test stands, and the photographs were filed for future reference.

German prisoners of war were another valuable source of information. A prisoner in January said the rocket was as large as a car and that ranges of up to 100 km were hoped for. The most significant report from POWs occurred when, on March 22, 1943, MI recorded a conversation between German Generals Ritter von Thoma and Ludwig Crüwell, who had been captured in Africa. The two men, obviously aware they were being monitored, spoke in hushed tones and parts of their conversation went unheard even by the sensitive microphones in the room. Crüwell had been captured in May 1942 and Von Thoma in November. In bringing Crüwell up-to-date, von Thoma told of a large rocket he had seen tested, presumably at Kummersdorf, with Field Marshal von Brauchitsch. The weapon, according to von Thoma, went into the stratosphere and had unlimited range. The effects were to be frightful. He went on to say that he knew their prison was near London and since he heard no loud explosions there must have been a delay in the program because the major who did the briefing gave the impression the rocket would be ready in a year.

Another POW, described as a technical officer assigned to a panzer regiment, had already provided some reliable information in exchange for preferential treatment from his captors. Not wanting to kill the golden goose, he told his interrogators on March 29, 1943 a story of a rocket weighing 120 tons with a "a weight of explosive of 60 to 80 tons, a range of 1,500 to 1,800 km and a blast sufficient to 'wipe out' everything within a radius of 30 km."[3]

Photo-reconnaissance sorties of Peenemünde were ordered on January 9 and on March 1. The photographs revealed additional construction but could not confirm the existence of rockets or other secret weapons under development at the installation. On Saturday, March 27, Charles Frank, a fellow scientist who had the desk across from Jones, looked up and told Jones, "It looks as though we'll have to take those rockets seriously." Frank had been reading the transcript of the conversation between von Thoma and Crüwell. The transcript definitely got Jones's attention. He regarded von Thoma as "The intelligent pessimist and most technically informed of our galaxy of German generals."[4] and was suddenly in a quandary. What he had was enough to pique the interest of an astute intelligence officer and little more. The "Oslo Report" mentioned Peenemünde but not in the context of rockets, and the other sources had mentioned them only in passing.

Recording von Thoma's conversation had certainly been a coup, but none of these items either singly or together gave a very accurate picture of German rocket research. Since there was not enough information upon which to base a course of action, Jones was loath to cry "wolf" too soon and decided first to direct the sources at his disposal to find out more about the German rocket. He informed his former mentor, Prof. Lindemann, what he was doing and began his inquiries, not realizing that the Military Intelligence Section of the War Office had other plans.

Military Intelligence alerted the operation staffs to the von Thoma/Crüwell transcript and recent agent reports concerning the possibility that the Germans were developing long-range rockets.

After discussing the matter with the Scientific Advisor to the Army Council and the Controller of Projectile Development of the Ministry of Supply, the Vice Chiefs of the Imperial General Staff discussed the matter at a meeting on April 12, 1943. They then circulated a paper titled "German Long Range Rocket Development." It offered the technical opinion that the rocket would be multi-staged, thirty inches in diameter, ninety feet long and weigh about nine and a half tons. The warhead would weigh a ton and a quarter. The paper questioned the accuracy of such a weapon; indicated it would need to have a projector about 100 yards long; and offered three alternatives as to how the projector might be constructed.[5]

Three days later, General H.L. Ismay, Chief of Staff to the Minister of Defence, made the Prime Minister aware of the existence of German rockets. He reported: "The Chiefs of Staff feel that you should be made aware of reports of German experiments with long range rockets. The fact that five reports have been received since the end of 1942 indicates a foundation of fact even if details are inaccurate . . . The Chiefs of Staff are of the opinion that no time should be lost in establishing the facts . . . they therefore suggest you should appoint an individual who should be charged with the task forthwith. They suggest for your consideration the name of Mr. Duncan Sandys," who as a scientific investigator could "call on such Scientific and Intelligence Advisers as appropriate."[6] Churchill approved the recommendation the following day.

Sandys, the Prime Minister's son-in-law, appeared to be the perfect man for the job. At 35, he was a member of the House of Commons and the Joint Parliamentary Secretary to the Ministry of Supply. In the Norway Campaign, he served with an antiaircraft regiment and had later been the commanding officer of the first experimental rocket regiment, until an automobile accident ended his military career. After his recovery he returned to the House of Commons and became Financial Secretary to the War Office before transferring to the Ministry of Supply. In short, he was a politician with cabinet connections and military experience in the specialty that had fixed the interest of the Chiefs of Staff. The code name for Sandys' investigation was "Bodyline."

The appointment was not widely known and Jones did not learn about it until two weeks later. Lindemann, his former professor, called Jones in to ask him if he thought there was anything to the reports of

German rockets. When Jones reported that he did, the professor told him he didn't believe the Germans could develop a long-range rocket and informed Jones of Sandys' appointment. Jones was upset that someone had been selected to do the job he had been doing for the past three years, but there was nothing he could do about it. He was not a politician and the War Cabinet was not about to entrust the entire rocket investigation to one ministry, no matter how good its record. Nevertheless, Jones resolved to maintain the investigation of the German rocket he had started, and as ADI(Sc) he was fully justified in doing so. Agents were briefed and the Photographic Reconnaissance Unit (PRU) at Medmenham was asked to photograph Peenemünde again. Even though Sandys and Jones had never met, there was soon a turf battle between Churchill's advisor and the Air Ministry scientist.

Shortly after his meeting with Jones about the rocket, Lindemann advised Sandys to get in touch with the ADI(Sc) and take advantage of the latter's expertise rather than set up an entirely new organization. Following the meeting, instructions were issued to Group Captain Peter Stewart, Station Commander at Medmemham, who established a new cell to look specifically for secret weapons. "Flight Lieutenant André Kenny and three others were assigned to search for clues of experimental work and production, especially at Peenemünde. At the same time Norman Falcon and two of his army observers were to concentrate on . . . potential launching areas on the French coast."[7]

A special reconnaissance program, shared with the Americans, was set up to ensure that the coast from Cherbourg to the Belgian frontier was completely covered. As an additional instruction, photos of Peenemünde were to go to Sandys and no one else—a restriction that Jones easily circumvented. He was part of the RAF and was on excellent terms with the PRU, sometimes briefing the reconnaissance pilots himself. One of the squadron leaders personally assured Jones he would get copies of the photos he needed.

Another facet of Jones's attempt to discover something about the rocket was a stroke of genius. He was wondering how the Germans might track a rocket in flight and remembered the story of experiments with the Paris Gun related by Carl Bosch, a German friend, between the wars. Three shells fired from the gun at twenty-minute intervals "disappeared." A meteorologist reported the impact of three meteors twenty minutes apart, and the projectiles were later found much farther than anticipated from their expected point of impact. The shells had gone into the stratosphere, lengthening their range considerably. The gun was eventually fielded as the Paris Gun.

Jones reasoned that the problem of tracking a rocket by radar would be a lot easier. Since he had been working with radar for the past two years, he knew the German Army had little, if any, radar of its own. The Luftwaffe, on the other hand, had its expert radar operators in the 14th and 15th Companies of the Air Signals Experimental Regiment. Since these two units were monitored very closely by "Y," the British intercept service at Bletchley Park, Jones asked a friend, Prof. Frederick Norman, to see if either of the units had deployed to Peenemünde or someplace near it on the Baltic coast.

In June, Jones's inquiries began bearing large fruit, indeed. Two forced laborers from Luxembourg managed to smuggle out a sketch of Heeres Anstalt Peenemünde. One of them, who succeeded in getting letters to his father, a member of a Belgian underground network, told of a large rocket that made a noise like "a squadron at low altitude."[8] The sketch reached Jones on June 17, and five days later a report from a source inside the German High Command told of a winged rocket launched by catapult. Later, Jones learned that what he termed his "longshot" paid off. The 14th Company of the Luftwaffe Air Signals Experimental Regiment had set up a Würzburg radar at Peenemünde and had established an additional detachment on the Island of Rügen.

Additional PRU sorties were flown over Peenemünde in May and June. They revealed very little initially and this had partially to do with the uniqueness of the German weapons. One photo interpreter in the section at the Medmenham CIU set up to deal specifically with Peenemünde imagined that the Rhein-Metall ramps for launching the Fi 103 along the Baltic Coast were sludge pumps. Nothing else was found until Jones received copies of the photos from the squadron leader nearly a week after they were taken. When he studied photo N/853 under a stereoscope, Jones found what everyone else had missed. Although the photograph was not particularly clear, he could make out on a flat car, "a whitish cylinder about 35 feet long and 5 or so feet in diameter, with a bluntish nose and fins on the other end."[9]

Excited, Jones showed the photograph to Charles Frank, who concurred that it was a rocket. Instead of taking the news of the discovery up the chain of command, however, Jones took it directly to Lindemann, who recommended that Jones notify Sandys. It would give the two men a chance to meet face-to-face and put an end to the battle between them. Jones obligingly sent a note to Sandys, who didn't acknowledge it. Instead, Sandys' photo interpreter issued an addendum to his original report notifying everyone that a rocket had been found on N/853 without mentioning Jones. Lindemann was nearly as offended as Jones and arranged for Jones to attend a meeting with Churchill, who was already aware that Sandys and Jones were not getting along. While waiting for the meeting, Jones wrote a report about the rocket that included the dimensions of the object in the photograph, an estimated weight of twenty to forty tons and the fact that the German radar units were at Peenemünde. The report also included a recommendation to bomb Peenemünde as soon as possible.

Surprisingly, Sandys asked to see Jones as soon as he saw the report. The meeting was polite, and when the matter of the weight came up Sandys informed Jones that his experts estimated the weight at eighty to one hundred tons. When Jones looked surprised, they put a call through to Dr. William R. Cook, who explained about weight density ratios of solid-fuel rockets and noted that the shell of the rocket would have to be extremely heavy to withstand the pressure of the burning propellant. Jones was only partially convinced but changed the report to reflect Cook's expert opinion. Since the British only built solid-fuel rockets with cordite as the fuel, even their scientists were unable to imagine a liquid-fuel rocket, much less an inertially guided missile. On June 23, 1943, another sortie was flown over Peenemünde. This time a rocket could be seen clearly.

The meeting of June 29, to which Lindemann had invited Jones, was a full meeting of the War Cabinet Defence Committee (Operations). Sandys briefed on the rocket and, based on the latest photographic evidence, offered his estimate that the rocket was thirty-eight feet long, seven feet in diameter and weighed between sixty and eighty tons. The warhead was estimated at "two to eight tons."[10] He also speculated that tower-like structures in the photographs (the handling equipment at the test stands) were the projectors for the huge solid-fuel rockets. Sandys concluded with the estimate by the Ministry of Home Security that a single such rocket landing in a densely populated area would cause up to four thousand killed and wounded.[11] He recommended a heavy bombing raid on Peenemünde as soon as the RAF could arrange it.

When Sandys was finished, Churchill asked Lindemann for his opinion. The professor disagreed with nearly everything Sandys said and assumed the role of "devil's advocate." In addition to believing that the Germans were incapable of building a long-range rocket—because he believed they had to use solid fuel—Lindemann disliked Sandys for personal reasons and he warmed to his task. He stated his belief that the Germans had not built a long-range rocket and that the items seen on the Peenemünde photographs were either torpedoes or dummies designed to throw the British off the track of the real weapon, which was a pilotless flying bomb. Churchill then called on Jones, who refuted his old professor. The objects in question were too big to be torpedoes—and why put out dummies that would make the enemy even more curious? Before the meeting broke up, it was agreed to investigate the flying bomb, which Lindemann mentioned as a distinct possibility. In order to lessen risk to the bombers, the RAF had to delay the bombing of Peenemünde until the nights were long enough.

Information concerning the German rocket continued to pour in. Much of it concerned performance characteristics and was, in most cases, perplexing if not outright contradictory. Confusing the issue were indications that Lindemann's flying bomb might be a reality. However, there were concerns closer to home. In April 1943, SIS began receiving reports of the construction of concrete emplacements on an unprecedented scale in France close to the Channel coast. The seven "large sites," as they were later called, were begun at Watten, Wizernes, Sottevast, Martinvast or Equeurdreville, Mimoyecques, Siracourt and Lottinghem. They were planned during the meeting Hitler had had with Speer on November 22, 1942, and later confirmed on July 1, 1943. Hitler's reasoning was that the concrete U-boat pens protected U-boats against bombs and these emplacements would do the same for A-4 and Fi 103. The first site, begun at Watten, progressed rapidly.

To the photographic interpreters at Medmenham, its exact purpose was unclear, but most agreed it had something to do with German secret weapons. In fact, Watten and Wizernes were planned A-4 firing bunkers; Mimoyecques was for the high-pressure gun eventually labeled "V-3," which never worked very well; and the rest were firing and storage bunkers for Fi 103. These sites "were mainly underground [and] embraced related but sometimes separate structures thousands of feet long, often with steel and concrete walls 25 to 30 feet thick."[12]

The Watten site, inland from Calais, was supposed to take more than 156,000 cubic yards of concrete to complete. Major General Lewis H. Brereton, commander of the U.S. Ninth Air Force, who visited the site after it was captured by Allied ground troops, described it as "more extensive than any concrete constructions . . . in the United States, with the possible exception of Boulder Dam."[13]

In addition, several hardened field sites for A-4 were begun north of the Somme in the Pas de Calais area. This was the result of a training accident at Blizna in which soggy ground under an erected A-4 gave way, giving the commander the mistaken belief that A-4 needed a hard stand for launching. In fact, A-4 needed little more than a few timbers to brace the ground and in "some cases the Germans hardened a patch of hard soil just by spraying it with liquid oxygen to make the moisture in the soil freeze solid."[14] But that was in the future.

In early 1943 approaches were made to U.S. and Soviet intelligence agencies for any information on German secret weapons. If the Russians knew anything, they weren't saying. American intelligence officials had nothing, but agreed to question Fritz von Opel, who was interned in the United States. Opel had not dealt with rockets since 1937 and could offer little except to say he thought a long-range rocket impractical. If the Germans had invented one, he thought the best means of launching it would be by mortar. In the meantime, further sites were located at Wissant and Bruneval.

Sandys continued to coordinate the intelligence and began working on precautions for civil defense. On July 10, Sir Stafford Cripps, Minister of Aircraft Production, recommended that the large sites be bombed immediately and frequently, but on the basis that the purpose of the sites was unclear, the Chiefs of Staff were reluctant to divert bomber wings from their current schedule. They asked for a close-up photo reconnaissance of the sites and requested Vice Admiral Lord Lewis Mountbatten, Chief of Combined Operations, to study the possibility of making a seaborne or airborne attack on one of them to get more information. On July 29, Mountbatten replied that a seaborne attack on Wissant or Bruneval had little chance to succeed. He prepared a plan for an airborne operation on Wissant with the proviso that a successful withdrawal was highly unlikely. On August 2, the Chiefs of Staff decided that such a raid was not justifiable.

On August 6, Sandys also recommended bombing Watten because of the rapid progress the Germans were making. The Chiefs of Staff again demurred, but noted that a daylight attack by U.S. bombers on Watten and Wissant was under consideration even though the Air Staff doubted that Watten had anything to do with rockets, suggesting instead that "it might be a protected operations room."[15] Unwilling to attack the sites in France, the Air Staff at least agreed to attack Peenemünde on the night of August 17–18, 1943. and indicated that attacks on chemical plants at Leuna and Ludwigshafen would occur as soon as feasible. The Air Staff requested further information on the French sites and asked Sandys for more detailed information on the purpose of the sites and the dates firings might commence.

When the raid on Peenemünde was carried out, it was Sandys' idea to bomb the housing area to kill the scientists and technicians. A photographic reconnaissance was carried out the next day revealing the damage to the buildings in the housing areas to have been severe. However, much of the experimental and launch areas had been unscathed. Nevertheless, in what had to be one of the major blunders of the effort against the A-4 and the Fi 103, the "Air Staff asked the USAAF to defer its planned follow-up daylight attack on Peenemünde until there had been detailed assessment of the damage and Sandys had produced his next report."[16] The delay, combined with Dornberger's policy of letting Peenemünde appear as if it were heavily damaged, allowed work on the A-4 and Fi 103 to continue unimpeded for nearly a year. One unfortunate result of the bombing was that most of the bombs fell in the area holding the forced laborers and it was they who suffered the most. After the raid, the British received no further reports from this source.

Detailed photographic reconnaissance and agents' reports definitely ruled out any possibility that the Watten site was "a protected operations room." The structure was designed to handle huge objects and store large amounts of liquid that might be fuel. The reasonable assumption was that it was being built for a rocket offensive and that the structure would be complete some time in September 1943. This information was submitted in a report by Sandys dated August 21 and included the recommendation that the site be bombed before the concrete roof was completed. Sandys also conjectured that the German program might be delayed indefinitely if the site were destroyed. The Vice Chiefs of Staff accepted Sandys' recommendation and put into effect the plan to bomb Watten.

On August 27, the first American participation in the battle against the new German weapons took place in the raid on Watten, with 187 B-17 bombers of the 8th Air Force considerably damaging the site. A photo reconnaissance by PRU showed that the bombers scored a large number of direct hits, but the Germans had not abandoned the site and instead increased their Flak defenses. Further raids on Watten were made by medium and heavy bombers of the 8th Air Force on August 30 and September 7. The additional attacks did the trick. The PRU showed the site had been severely damaged and analysts suggested that the Germans would be better off starting over than attempting to repair the damage. The Germans agreed. While they looked at the possibility of using the Watten site to manufacture and store liquid oxygen, they no longer considered it useful for launching rockets and the Wizernes location was chosen as the main A-4 storage and launching site.

On August 31, 1943, a ministerial meeting was held to discuss Sandys' latest report. During the meeting, the Special Intelligence Service revealed a source who was getting information from a senior official in the Heereswaffenamt who revealed that there were two weapons under development. One was a rocket known as A-4 and the other was a pilotless aircraft known "officially" as PHI 7. The official's information concerning the A-4 was useful as it gave fairly accurate information on the range and size of the rocket, but the damage that could be done by the warhead was greatly exaggerated. The information also indicated that Hitler had set October 31, 1943 as the deployment date and that "100 A-4 projectiles had been fired and another 100 were on hand."[17] The official could not provide any information concerning the PHI 7 because the German Army was not in charge of the project. Sandys found that the distinction the Waffenamt source made between the two weapons made it easier to understand much of the earlier agents' reports of performance descriptions and he felt that this intelligence confirmed his previous conclusions; he now felt it "unlikely that the attacks with the weapons would take place on any appreciable scale before the end of 1943."[18]

Lindemann, who was now Lord Cherwell, disagreed and argued that the information was not scientifically accurate, even though "C," the head of SIS, considered the source reliable. Air Chief Marshal Sir Charles Portal, chief of the Air Staff, was particularly impressed by the report of the PHI 7 since one had crashed on the island of Danish Bornholm on August 22, 1943. The participants in the ministerial meeting agreed that everything must be done to discover more about the pilotless aircraft, and then turned to matters of civil defense, making plans for additional shelters as well as provisions for the evacuation of the British cities of London, Southampton, Portsmouth and Gosport. Plans for the evacuation of the government from London, which had been shelved after the Blitz, were dusted off.

During September, Lord Cherwell made a further attempt to discourage the notion of the rocket, as well as (in his view) some of the more fantastic aspects of it such as the ten-ton warhead and the estimate that each rocket might cause up to four thousand casualties. He recommended that a questionnaire concerning the available evidence be presented to a panel of scientists known as the Bodyline Committee to determine what was correct and what wasn't. In the meantime Sandys was to get a statement from "C" concerning the reliability of the existing intelligence.

The statement from "C" was actually written by Jones and rejected most of Cherwell's assertions that the rocket was a hoax to cover the true weapon, which was a pilotless aircraft. His conclusions were that the Germans had been experimenting with long-range rockets for some time and that they had encountered problems that were holding up production—otherwise Hitler would have used them. Jones also pointed out that technical and scientific objections to the rocket might not be valid if the Germans had developed a new technology. Jones's third conclusion was that there were most likely two weapons: one a long-range rocket and the other a pilotless aircraft. On the whole he'd made a fairly accurate assessment.

Evidence that the Germans had something other than a rocket had been accruing since April 1943. The sources included the Polish underground and a Luxembourger worker at Peenemünde who actually managed to smuggle a crude sketch of the launching of an Fi 103 out of the installation before he escaped. It described a cigar-shaped missile with a range of 150 km, with 250 km possible. This information made both Sandys and Jones believe there might be two weapons, but Cherwell continued to scoff at the rocket. Finally, on June 29, the Defence Committee asked Sandys to include a search for a pilotless aircraft in his investigations. By this time SIS knew that Peenemünde had both an Army and a Luftwaffe installation. The Luftwaffe installation was connected with the experimental station at Rechlin and was supposed to be involved in the testing of antiaircraft material and new aircraft armament.

The PRU photographs of June 23, 1943 showed four tailless aircraft on the Peenemünde airfield; they were christened "Peenemünde 30." However, the CIU agreed these were not pilotless aircraft but experimental ones. This was true enough, because the aircraft turned out to be early models of the Me 163 rocket fighter. Like reports concerning the rocket earlier in the year, reports of the pilotless aircraft began to multiply in June 1943. On August 1 a usually reliable source stated that a gyroscopically controlled self-propelled bomb designed by Argus was due for fielding that month. On August 7 another source stated that the rocket airplane exhibited serious deficiencies and that the intended production rate was not possible. Still later in the month, another foreign source described an aerial torpedo launched by catapult due for deployment in August or September.

An SIS report dated August 20, 1943 came from a new source in France, a network headed by Marie-Madeleine Fourcade. The source, who had spoken with a captain from the research center at Peenemünde, described the security pass system at the installation and indicated that research was "concentrated on:

(a) bombs and shells guided independently of the laws of ballistics.

(b) a stratospheric shell.

(c) the use of bacteria as a weapon."[19]

The report continued that Kampfgruppe (KG) 100 was working with guided bombs and went on to describe what was obviously the vertical launch of an A-4, but then began to describe Lehr und Erprobungskommando Wachtel, which was supposed to deploy 108 catapults able to launch a flying bomb every twenty minutes. The Army was supposed to deploy an additional four hundred catapults between

Brittany and Holland. Fifty to one hundred of the bombs were supposedly enough to destroy London, and deployment was scheduled for
November 1943. The source also connected Lehr und Erprobungskommando Wachtel with Flak Regiment 155(W). To Jones the
thought of 108 launchers was chilling.

On August 27 a most remarkable piece of information arrived in
the form of photographs of the Fi 103 that crashed on the Danish
island of Bornholm, along with a crude sketch of the apparatus. They
were taken by a Danish naval officer named Hasager Christiansen,
who sent them to Danish Naval Intelligence which, in turn, forwarded multiple copies to the British along with the sketch. The drawing
was extremely valuable despite the fact that it showed the pulse jet on
the underside of the airframe. A set of the photographs was intercepted by the Gestapo and Christiansen was arrested and tortured.
Fortunately he managed to survive and escape to Sweden. The initial
British reaction was that it was a larger version of the Hs 293 glider
bomb used against Allied shipping in the Mediterranean, because it
had been launched from an He-111 bomber.

What ultimately convinced Jones that the Germans were working
on two weapons was a pair of Enigma decrypts from September 7,
1943. One, from Luftflotte 3, urgently requested Flak protection for
Flakzielgerät 76 following the capture of a British agent who was on
the ground to establish the position of the FZG 76 organization, and
also in view of repeated bombing attacks on installations that the
decrypt referred to as "reception stations." The second decrypt stated
that Luftflotte 3 was solely responsible for flak protection of this organization in the area Belgium–North France.[20]

Using the "Oslo Report" which associated FZG development
numbers with gliders and pilotless aircraft, Jones concluded that FZG
76 was a code name for a pilotless aircraft intended for long-range
bombardment of England rather than the long-range rocket.
Meanwhile Sandys reviewed his position. He was responsible for the
investigation of long-range rockets, jet-propelled bombs, guided
bombs, jet planes, long-range guns and any novel projectile that might
appear. Having one man accountable for such a vast array of information was counterproductive and on September 6, 1943 Sandys recommended a redistribution of responsibility to the Chiefs of Staff. He
was to stay in charge of the investigation of the long-range rockets,

guns and unusual projectiles. The Air Ministry—Dr. Jones, to be precise—would continue the inquiry into jet aircraft, the glider bomb and pilotless aircraft, and provide Sandys with periodic updates for inclusion in his reports to the Defence Committee. The arrangement was workable and the Chiefs of Staff approved it four days later.

The flow of information continued. Air Intelligence passed on to Sandys an unconfirmed report that there were two types of pilotless aircraft. One was a light plane that carried incendiary bombs, most likely a reference to "Fernfeuer," and a rocket-propelled aircraft launched by catapult and controlled automatically rather than by radio control so it could not be jammed. Both devices were manufactured by the Fieseler Aircraft Company. Sandys included this information in his September 13 report.

On September 14 Jones submitted an "Air Scientific Intelligence Special Note on the Flakzielgerät 76." Paragraph 5, "Conclusion," read: "The Germans are installing, under the cover name of FZG 76 a large and important ground organization in Belgium–Northern France which is probably concerned with directing an attack on England by rocket driven pilotless aircraft. It is more than possible that the construction at Watten is associated with this project. It appears that aircraft are not to be launched from far back, but that supplies may be brought up to the forward areas."[21]

Cherwell disagreed with Jones and insisted "Flakzielgerät" meant "anti-aircraft predictor." Several new prisoner of war interrogations mentioned "liquid air," but usually in reference to the warhead. Diplomatic intelligence sources revealed even more information when German Foreign Minister Joachim von Ribbentrop notified all German missions that Allied bombing of the Reich was going to lessen when current measures were completed.

The Japanese ambassadors in Berlin and Rome also provided excellent Sigint when they reported to Tokyo that "new German methods of retaliation would be introduced before the winter in spite of the delays inflicted by the bombing of Peenemünde and Friedrichshafen—names which the ambassador in Berlin begged Tokyo to keep secret."[22] A decrypt of another message from the Japanese ambassador dated October 7, 1943 gave information concerning the accuracy of a form of artillery bombardment at a range of 400 km and that the weapon would be effective against London and other cities. This message was typical of the information available concerning the characteristics and performance of the weapons, in that there was no way to get a clear picture from the information available.

When the panel of Bodyline Committee scientists began deliberating the form of the rocket at the end of September 1943, they had at their disposal "159 reports from SIS, 35 from POWs and 37 from diplomatic posts,"[23] in addition to countless photographs from the PRU. The fuel panel of the committee was charged with discovering what kind of fuels were necessary to give the rocket the range necessary to reach its target, but, because the existing information was so confusing, got off the track and debated whether or not it was practical to engineer such a device. Dr. Alwyn Crow, Chief of Projectile Development, maintained that the high ratio of fuel to rocket needed for the ranges listed in the various intelligence reports could not be achieved using a single-stage solid-fuel rocket.

Recent information from the United States concerning experiments with liquid fuels made many of the members of the fuel panel realize that the necessary range might be achieved for a Peenemünde-size rocket with a one-ton warhead using liquid fuels. Unfortunately, they deemed it improbable that the Germans had developed such a weapon. Mr. Isaac Lubbock, chief engineer for the Asiatic Petroleum Company, who was developing a gasoline/liquid oxygen motor for the Chief of Projectile Development, had recently returned from the United States, and on October 10 was asked by Sandys to propose a design for a liquid-fuel rocket. Lubbock chose aniline and nitric acid for his fuels, based on American experience with the two chemicals, in the belief they were easier to handle than other combinations of fuels. The fuel was to be pumped by pressure or a turbine pump fueled by burning cordite or some of the rocket fuel. With six combustion chambers generating 150 tons of thrust, the theoretical single-stage rocket was capable of carrying a seven-ton warhead 140 miles.[24] Lubbock was aided in the design by Geoffrey Gollin, his assistant, and Colonel Kenneth Post, Sandys' military assistant.

On the following day, the Bodyline fuel panel met on the fourth floor of the Shell Mex House in London. Large photographs of Peenemünde with the rocket were on all the tables. Although he stated he would not be present, Lord Cherwell was there and sat opposite Lubbock and Post, who made the presentation about the liquid-fuel rocket. A number of attendees protested that this was new information they had had no opportunity to examine. Cherwell, no doubt seeing Post and Lubbock as Sandys' men, "stoutly declared that nobody could teach him anything about rockets; he could safely say that he and Dr. Crow knew more about rockets than any man in Great Britain."[25] At the end of the meeting, Sir Frank Smith, one of the scientists present, polled the rest of the attendees and asked if they felt the objects in the photograph were rockets. All replied affirmatively except Cherwell and Crow, who claimed they were nothing more than inflated barrage balloons. The statement brought a riposte from Colonel Post, who asked why the German Army transported balloons on heavy-duty railway cars. Were they heavier-than-air barrage balloons? Crow had no reply.

When Smith indicated he would record that the participants, after seeing Lubbock's sketch, were of the opinion that the object in the photograph might be a rocket, a furious Lord Cherwell rose from his chair and stalked out of the room. Colonel Post rose to open the door for him. He explained later to Lubbock that "no matter how infuriating the Professor was, one always had to be polite to him: he was an extremely powerful man."[26]

It was obvious that Sandys had purposely brought Lubbock's design to the meeting to put everyone off balance and was not sorry he angered Cherwell. What he had done was finally convince the British scientific community of the possibility that the Germans might be using liquid-fuel rockets. At the full Bodyline Scientific Committee meeting on October 22, most of the participants agreed and reported to the Defence Committee that "a rocket with a warhead of 10 to 20 tons and a range of 130 miles was scientifically possible, that ranges up to 300 miles would be possible with smaller warheads, and that a rocket possessing such performances could have the dimensions of the object seen at Peenemünde.[27] Two days later, Sandys offered the opinion that although the long-range bombardment of London that was planned by the Germans was unlikely to occur before early 1944, the long-range rocket was ready for operational use. He went on to suggest that massive numbers of rockets might be used against London in November or December 1943 unless the Allies took offensive action to prevent it.

In a further series of meetings, Lord Cherwell went on the offensive, pointing out all the engineering difficulties that existed in developing a rocket. On October 28, Sir Stafford Cripps pointed out that while Cherwell denied that the objects in the Peenemünde photographs were rockets, he had not offered any reason why the Germans had not been able to build one. Cripps was able to gain a consensus that scientifically there was nothing impossible about making one. While Cherwell raised some excellent points about the engineering difficulties involved with the rocket, the scientists finally reported to Churchill: "There is nothing impossible in designing a rocket of 60–70 tons to operate at a range of 130 miles."[28] Lord Cherwell did not agree, and he continued to insist that the Germans would find it far more practical to build a pilotless aircraft. He also had another concern, which went beyond his dislike of Sandys and a natural obstinacy: He was concerned that concentration on the German rocket, which he regarded as a marginal threat at best, would detract from the current bombing program.

Cherwell was correct about two things. The Germans were developing a pilotless aircraft and it would draw considerable resources from the campaign against Germany. He was also correct in his view that developing a long-range rocket posed enormous technical difficulties; he simply didn't realize that the enemy's scientific team, led by Wernher von Braun, was surmounting the problems one by one.

In October and November there were further intercepts from the 14th Company of the Luftwaffe Experimental Signals Regiment, which was obviously plotting an aircraft with an average speed between 200 and 300 miles per hour and with a possible top speed of over 400. Its rate of fall implied that it was a winged vehicle and that its range was about 120 miles. In December, Jones began plotting the accuracy of the Fi 103 using these intercepts. The CIU, possibly prompted by the intercepts, conducted a search for small aircraft.

Flight Officer Constance Babington-Smith, a photo interpreter at CIU, realized that something smaller than the Me 163 would only show up on good-quality photographs. She went to the print library and retrieved the photos taken on July 22 and September 30. When she re-examined them she found "a midget aircraft on those splendid photographs. The absurd little object was not on the airfield, but sitting in a corner of a small enclosure some way behind the hangars."[29] Designated "P20," the object had a wingspan of approximately twenty feet and was propelled by a rocket or jet. It was small enough to be an expendable pilotless aircraft and it was located near the airfield, not in the rocket development center.

While the CIU was backtracking to confirm the existence of the Fi 103, an ominous piece of the puzzle was discovered in France. In October, SIS learned from the French underground that the Germans had begun constructing six sites with either concrete platforms or lines of posts aligned on London. Missions to photograph the sites began on November 3, 1943, and by November 24 thirty-eight had been confirmed by PRU flights. Agents in contact with the SIS reported as many as sixty. The most advanced was one at Bois Carré. All sites were "set back up to 20 km from the coast in a corridor 200 miles long by 30 miles wide in the Seine-Inferieure and Pas de Calais."[30] By the end of November fifteen additional sites were located in the Pas de Calais region and seven in the Cherbourg peninsula. The sites were identical and had two or more buildings that looked like skis laid on edge, thus "ski sites." All those discovered were aligned on London.

None of the data could confirm that the ski sites had anything to do with either pilotless aircraft or rockets, because the British viewed the Fi 103 as a pilotless aircraft which could take off from an airstrip without need of a special apparatus—and the rocket needed a projector which was a large mortar or a tunnel in the ground. Regardless, something had to be done about them, and quickly. With the Germans still in control of the continent, bombing was the only solution, and the question arose of how to attack the targets. If the sites were built of reinforced concrete, then heavy bombs had to be used. If they were built of concrete blocks, then lighter bombs could be just as effective.

The SIS in Switzerland contacted the French underground. Michel Hollard, the French engineer who had alerted the British to the "ski sites," made a personal reconnaissance of the site at Bonnetot-le-Faubourg. Dressed as a workman, he picked up a wheelbarrow laying in a ditch and wheeled it in. Finding the location of the planned catapult, Hollard took out a compass and checked its alignment. Later that evening he confirmed it was aligned on London. Hollard then persuaded André Comps to apply to the Germans as a draftsman. When he got the job, he proceeded to copy all the plans for the ski site.[31] Hollard confirmed that the sites were made of concrete blocks and the information was in SIS hands by the end of November. But prior to this, on November 17, Sir Stafford Cripps issued a summary and assessment of the intelligence available to date, which offered nothing new and side-stepped the critical issues concerning the existence of the rocket or its fuel. It repeated a suggestion that there might be a smaller rocket than A-4, although there was no hard evidence to support the claim.

Cripps's report also dealt with German propaganda and production, which again added nothing new. The appendix on the pilotless bomb began, "There is no direct evidence of any preparations for the use of this weapon."[32] Lord Cherwell rightfully criticized the report because it failed to address the technological feasibility of the rocket. He then restated his position that the rocket was a hoax and that FZG 76 was a predictor for antiaircraft artillery. He further insisted that the pilotless aircraft was a newer version of the Hs 293 guided bomb and that it was not a great threat. Neither Cherwell nor Cripps made any account for the ski sites, since they were obviously not suited for a huge rocket. Nevertheless, the War Cabinet took the threat of German long-range bombardment weapons very seriously.

At the end of October 1943, Prime Minister Churchill informed President Roosevelt of the potential threat by telegram. Later, more comprehensive information was "passed verbally under the strictest security conditions, to the United States authorities at ETOUSA and COSSAC and in Washington."[33] ETOUSA (European Theater of Operations, United States Army) was the controlling headquarters for all U.S. troops in the European Theater. From May 1943 until December 1943 it was commanded by General Jacob L. Devers. COSSAC (Chief of Staff for the Supreme Allied Commander) was responsible for planning the Normandy invasion. It was a joint headquarters under Lieutenant General Sir Frederick Morgan.

In November the Joint Intelligence Committee established a subcommittee whose sole purpose was to deal with all intelligence regarding the new German weapons and the threat they posed. To avoid duplication of effort and compromising some of the "Most Secret" intelligence disseminated regarding the German weapons, the responsibilities of the Sandys Committee were taken over by the Air Ministry, assisted by the new committee. The code name "Crossbow" replaced "Bodyline" on November 15, 1943, and the Allied effort to counter the rocket and the flying bomb would remain known as Crossbow for the remainder of the war.

Also on November 15, the command structure of the Allied air forces changed to reflect the command structure for the invasion of the continent of Europe, preparations for which were then underway. The purpose was to centralize control of all air resources under Dwight D. Eisenhower, the Supreme Allied Commander. Directly subordinate to Eisenhower were the U.S. Eighth Air Force, commanded by Lt. General Carl A. Spaatz; Royal Air Force Bomber Command under Air Chief Marshal Sir Arthur Harris; and the Allied Expeditionary Air Force, headed by Air Chief Marshal Sir Trafford Leigh-Mallory. Eighth Air Force and Bomber Command were responsible for the strategic bombardment of Germany and German-occupied territory. The Allied Expeditionary Air Force was responsible for support of the invasion and contained the U.S. Ninth Air Force, the RAF Second Tactical Air Force and Air Defence Great Britain (ADGB), which, until the reorganization, had been RAF Fighter Command, an independent organization. Air Marshal Roderic Hill was appointed commander on November 15.

Air Defence Great Britain included three groups: Antiaircraft Command under General Sir Frederick Pile, Balloon Command under Air Vice Marshal W.C.C. Gell and the Royal Observer Corps. Hill's superior, Leigh-Mallory, was planning offensive air operations for the invasion of Europe and had no interest in Hill's mission, which was primarily defensive. This left Hill, who was a relatively junior air marshal, to his own devices unless he erred mightily. Hill commanded General Pile, who had been head of British antiaircraft since before the outbreak of the war. Pile was a baronet and was familiar enough with the Prime Minister to have lunch with Churchill at his home, Chequers. This presented another potentially awkward situation for Hill and more than once he was accused of being swayed by his influential subordinate. Fortunately for the Allies as a whole, and Great Britain in particular, the two men were thorough professionals who had a common goal.

One of their first tasks, delegated by Leigh-Mallory, was to prepare for the threat of the German pilotless aircraft—now perceived as a single threat with no connection to the rocket. The Air Staff estimated the speed of the pilotless aircraft as between 250 and 420 miles per hour and its altitude between 500 and 7,000 feet. The defenses were to be in place by February 1944. But these estimates were too broad for practical planning, so Hill asked for more specific information. The Air Staff replied that the average speed was 400 miles per hour and the probable altitude was 7,500 feet. They reduced the speed eventually to 330 miles per hour and the altitude to 6,000 feet. Hill concluded that in order to intercept and destroy pilotless aircraft over that range of speed and altitude he would have to coordinate the guns, balloons, searchlights and fighters as never before. Hill submitted his plan to Leigh-Mallory on December 16, 1943 and asked to be kept informed of proposals to divert the Fi 103 with radio jamming.

The first Crossbow report, issued on November 24, 1943, rejected Cherwell's assumption that the pilotless aircraft was a larger guided bomb and Cripps's suggestion that there was a rocket smaller than A-4. It emphasized that a pilotless aircraft was not yet in mass production and that the ski sites were designed for use by the Luftwaffe. It concluded: ". . . a number of reliable reports concerning the activity of Colonel Wachtel link the ski sites beyond reasonable doubt with some weapon, probably a large rocket, designed for long range attack against [England]."[34]

The Assistant Chief of the Air Staff for Intelligence disagreed, and on November 30 stated that the ski sites were intended for the pilotless aircraft. At the same time, photographs of Peenemünde West taken by the PRU on November 28 showed a pilotless aircraft poised for launch on one of the launching ramps. The CIU concluded that the ski sites were designed for the "projection of glider bombs of the Peenemünde type,"[35] and that the body of the bomb had to pass through the large rectangular building. The Crossbow committee accepted CIU's findings on December 4, 1943.

When the Chiefs of Staff received the report, they realized that jamming, balloons and antiaircraft fire might not be very effective and gave priority to bombing. By December 14, plans were drawn up for attacks on twenty-seven sites and bombing began on December 18. On December 24, the U.S. Eighth Air Force launched its first major strike against a Crossbow target. Escorted by fighters, 670 heavy bombers dropped 1,700 tons of bombs on twenty-three of the sites. For the first time the outside world learned of the German threat, and the *New York Times* announced that U.S. and British aircraft had hit the "Rocket Gun Coast."

On December 10, British Intelligence decrypted a Luftwaffe Enigma intercept of November 26. It instructed two of the observation groups of the 14th Company of the Experimental Signals Regiment to begin tracking the A-4 on its vertical ascent and track it as long as possible. Signal instructions were the same as for the FZG 76. Here, at last, was real evidence of two weapons! December 1943 was a watershed month in what was swiftly becoming another battle in an increasingly technological war. In a little over a year British Intelligence authorities went from near total ignorance to a realistic appraisal of the threat, and then to action by bombing not only Peenemünde, the seeming source of the German weapons, but also striking at production facilities and the huge concrete emplacements at Watten and Wizernes and ski sites elsewhere.

The grim responsibility of planning for civil defense was also begun on the premise that the German weapon had a huge warhead. Mr. Herbert Morrison, Minister for Home Security, estimated 100,000 new shelters would be needed, and two battleships—the *Lion* and the *Temeraire*—which had been laid down then suspended in 1941—were canceled and the steel used for those shelters.[36] Much of the credit for this belongs to Churchill, who would not let his own son-in-law cut Dr. Jones out of the picture and who refused to let Cherwell, his own scientific advisor, dominate the debate over the weapons. But there remained much to learn.

As the Germans hurriedly constructed launchers for the Fi 103 along the Channel coast, British intelligence still knew almost nothing about the nature of the flying bomb. Its method of propulsion, its guidance system and the size of its warhead remained a mystery. The A-4, which had been under development for far longer, was an even greater mystery. Cherwell and other members of the Cabinet were still unwilling to admit that the Germans had succeeded in developing a liquid-fuel, inertially guided missile. Skeptics, they concentrated on what they themselves had not been able to do rather than on what was possible, and they refused to see the Fi 103 as a serious threat.

6

The Germans Deploy the Flying Bomb

Despite the destruction of the Fieseler works in Kassel and the production problems on the assembly line at Fallersleben, the Luftwaffe still expected to bring the Fi 103 into action by the end of 1943. Superficially, the production problems did not appear serious and work on the launch sites was progressing satisfactorily. The original Fi 103 launch site system, later known as System I, was approved by Hitler on June 28, 1943. It consisted of 252 concrete launching sites that were incorporated into the construction program of the Atlantic Wall and extended from Dunkerque along the coast of France to the Cotentin Peninsula of western Normandy. Following Hitler's approval, German military construction teams began a search for suitable firing locations. Site selection was based on the organization of the firing unit, proximity to the Channel coast, fields of fire and safety.

Colonel Max Wachtel's Flak Regiment 155(W), the unit organized and trained to fire the Fi 103, consisted of four firing battalions, designated I through IV, which operated as independent units. A battalion consisted of a 60-man staff, four firing batteries and two supply batteries. The firing battery had a command post of 40 men and four 65-man firing squads. Each supply battery had 220 men each. The batteries were numbered one through 16 for the regiment, which was typical for German combat units at the time, and the eight supply batteries were numbered 17 through 24. The site planners sought four sites for each battery for a total of sixty-four battery sites in order to give the battery some protection from detection by Allied reconnaissance aircraft as well as alternate locations from which to fire, as the military situation dictated. A launch site included enough buildings to store the flying bombs, then assemble, fuel, align them on the target and launch them. The site also had to provide the sixty-five-man launch crew with food and shelter. A launch site had to be located near the Channel coast but at least twelve miles from the shore to minimize the unit's vulnerability to enemy landings and naval gunfire.[1] Obstacles that could possibly interfere with a flying bomb lifting off the launch ramp had to be removed from an arc three degrees left and right of the catapult, extending to approximately four miles from the ramp. In addition, the area behind the launching site had to be sloped to provide the launching crew with protection against an Fi 103 that malfunctioned and detonated prematurely.

These requirements made it impossible to find suitable areas with both natural camouflage and no obstructions in the prescribed area, and the engineers settled on orchards as a favorable compromise. The size and shape of most French orchards provided unhindered launch areas out to the prescribed distance, the trees offered some camouflage and most of them had natural slopes to allow for drainage. General Heinemann and the senior officers of Flak Regiment 155(W) expressed concern about the policy of locating the launch sites in orchards. Orchards certainly met the firing and safety criteria for the Fi 103, but they couldn't conceal the site from anything but the most casual observer and left it exposed to the wrath of Allied bombers.[2] However, no one was about to question an order from the Führer and construction proceeded.

The most easily identifiable buildings in the site were three curved "ski" buildings each of which stored, on wheeled dollies, ten Fi 103s with their wings removed. Firing procedure called for the bomb to be rolled from the storage building to the assembly building. There the wings were fitted and the bomb was fueled and filled with compressed air. From the assembly building, the Fi 103 went to the demagnetized building, where its compass was set and the fuses installed. The bomb was then moved to the launch ramp and fired. To support these activities there was a preparation store room; a workshop; a maintenance bunker; a water tank; a fuel tank; a launch control bunker; a fuse supply building; a divided building for storing sodium permanganate and hydrogen peroxide for generating steam for the catapult; and a personnel bunker that was the barracks for the firing crews. The heart of the site was the launch ramp, which was 138 feet long. With a 6-degree inclination, it was 15 feet high at its apex. The ramp was made of seven steel girder sections positioned between reinforced-concrete blast walls.

All of the buildings and the launch ramp were made of reinforced concrete except the demagnetized building, which was devoid of ferrous metals so that it would have no effect on the Fi 103's compass. The buildings were dispersed in order to minimize bomb damage, but, with the stereotypical German sense of order, all the sites were constructed in a standard layout, with every building in each site in exactly the same place. This failure to vary the layout and the curved storage buildings provided Allied aerial observers and photo interpreters with a distinctive signature that helped them identify the launch sites immediately.

Launch sites were grouped in three general areas along the French coast. The northernmost extended from Calais south to Abbeville and then southwest to Biennais just north of the Seine River. The launching ramps of this group were oriented on London. A smaller group of sites was clustered around Caen and another extended along the Cotentin Peninsula south of Cherbourg. The majority of the ramps in these two areas were oriented on the British ports of Southampton and Portsmouth.

Headquarters of Flak Regiment 155(W) was at Amiens, a fact quickly noted by Allied agents. The firing units were supplied by railroad lines that ran from Lille, through Arras and Amiens, and on to Rouen. The flying bombs, fuel and other supplies arrived in France by rail from Ghent through the marshaling yard at Mouscron, northeast of Lille. From there they were brought by rail to one of the forward unloading stations; these were located at Furnes, Bergues, Blendèques, Rènescure, Aire-sur-Lys, Berguette, St-Venant, Chocques, Wavrins, Bouque-Maison, Doullens, Canaples, Flixécourt, Longré-les-Corps-Saints, Liercourt and Airaines. The main depots were at Sautrecourt, Beauvoir, Domléger, Neuville-au-Bois, St-Martin-le-Hortier and Biennais. Each supply battery was responsible for one storage depot from which Fi 103s were forwarded to the launch sites. These were located at Lumbres, La Pourchinte, Raimbert, Auchy-les-Hesdins, Rollencourt, Agenville, Cramont, St-Ricquier, Pont-Rémy, Salouel, Bois-Etrejuste, Laval-Boiron, Beaumont, Authieux-Ratieville and

Monville. The supply sites were positioned in the rolling farmland just back from the coast and well camouflaged. At the time they became operational, each of the small launching sites was to have a stock of 20 flying bombs on hand. Since the launch site was only a short distance from its forward depot, the bombs were moved forward by truck, where they arrived mounted on a wheeled trolley. The wings were not installed; the guidance system was not set; and the fuel and compressed-air tanks were empty.

The Luftwaffe High Command delegated the responsibility for site selection and construction to Luftwaffe Headquarters Belgium and Northern France, located in Brussels, and Luftwaffe Headquarters Western France, located in Etampes. These two headquarters determined site location and allocated priorities for construction. Organisation Todt, the German labor organization, was assigned to build the sites and a Todt supervisor was assigned to each of the Luftwaffe headquarters to ensure that the work crews were complying with Luftwaffe specifications.

Originally, only German military engineers or German civilian laborers were supposed to work on the sites, but the construction of over two hundred launch sites, in addition to the intense work required to create the Atlantic Wall, were too much for the available German labor force. Work on the sites got underway in the first week of August 1943 and quickly fell behind schedule due to the lack of workers. Foreign laborers from Belgium and Holland were drafted to complete the project and soon over 40,000 non-German workers were involved in the construction of Fi 103 sites along the French coast.[3] The use of foreign workers increased security problems significantly, and information on the sites began to flow to the British, who very soon had detailed information about them.

At approximately the same time as construction of the small firing sites started, work began on the four large Fi 103 launch sites directed by Hitler's decision on June 28, 1943. Located at Seninghem, Tammerville, Couville and Siracourt, these were huge launch complexes 625 feet long built of steel reinforced concrete. The roofs were 15 feet thick—proof against all but the heaviest Allied bombs—and the walls were built to withstand direct hits from artillery shells. Each complex was designed as a self-sustaining facility that stored the bombs, fuel, compressed air and the chemicals for the launcher. In addition, it was to provide safe shelter for the crews so they could conduct an uninterrupted barrage of Great Britain, regardless of enemy bombing. Upon completion, the four facilities were expected to maintain a rate of fire of 90 bombs a day.

On September 23, 1943 the Luftwaffe and Organisation Todt met to discuss progress on the construction of the first 64 sites. They concluded that 58 of these would be ready by October 4 and Organisation Todt would have six weeks to finish the remaining ones.[4] In that same time period, Flak Regiment 155(W) would be able to man the completed sites.

The conclusion was unrealistic. The massive construction project was straining not only the ready supply of labor, but the supply of building materials and the transportation system tasked to carry them to the launch sites and the Atlantic Wall as well. To make matters worse, the Allies had begun a bombing campaign on the French supply, railroad and communication centers that was slowing the flow of rail traffic throughout Occupied France. The delays rapidly gained serious proportions and the confident mood of September gave way to a more realistic appraisal of the situation. The Allied bombing caused so much damage that in a meeting held on November 3, 1943, von Axthelm stated that he expected only one third of the sites to be operational when the time arrived to begin the offensive, which most assumed would be in December.

It was soon evident, however, that construction of the launch sites was the only thing concerning Fi 103 or A-4 that was anywhere near on track. A few days after the meeting, General Günther Korten, Chief of the Luftwaffe Operations Staff, arranged for von Axthelm to address the OKW staff. Only after the appointment was made was von Axthelm warned that Hitler would be in attendance. A tactician who was painfully unaware of Germany's industrial potential, von Axthelm wanted to fire 30,000 Fi 103s a month because he felt the numbers would make up for the flying bomb's inherent inaccuracy. He also felt that the Fi 103 should be used on targets like the Channel ports, which would be of greater military significance than London in view of the upcoming Allied invasion of the continent.

When the antiaircraft chief made his presentation, he mentioned that production was only a tenth of what was necessary to thwart Allied preparations for invasion. Hitler interrupted, stating, "Don't concern yourself with warding off an invasion. Keep to the subject of our retaliation offensive."[5] When von Axthelm insisted that there was no time to lose, Hitler snapped, "Get your bombs over there first. Then you will get the production you want!" Von Axthelm countered that valuable time would be lost as well as the element of surprise.[6] Without another word, Hitler left the room, ending the meeting.

On November 18, 1943 the last of Wachtel's firing batteries left for France, but the supply batteries were still short of qualified people. Bent on a policy of retaliation as soon as possible, Hitler received another unpleasant surprise when he attended a static display of Fi 103 at Insterburg Airfield with Reichsführer SS Heinrich Himmler on November 26. During a briefing by Luftwaffe Colonel Kröger, the leader of the Fi 103 experimental unit at Peenemünde, Hitler asked when the bomb would be ready. Kröger honestly indicated the end of March, meaning that development would be concluded at that time. He wasn't even addressing training considerations, but Hitler wasn't interested in hearing more. At 1330 hours, an hour and a half after arriving, he boarded a train and returned to his headquarters at Rastenburg.

The Germans needed a joint headquarters to coordinate and support the units firing the Fi 103 and the A-4, since both army and Luftwaffe units were involved. On December 1, Hitler approved the formation of LXV Armeekorps and it was activated under the command of Lieutenant General Erich Heinemann, a 67-year-old career artillery officer. In keeping with the joint mission of the corps, his chief of staff was a Luftwaffe officer, Colonel Eugen Walter. Heinemann and Walter quickly learned that the corps was looked upon by both services with hostility. On November 23, Goering had insisted that a Luftwaffe division control the Fi 103 rather than an army unit. When Heinemann, an army general, asked the Heereswaffenamt for information about the A-4, they refused to give him any. The LXV Armeekorps commander and his chief of staff gained whatever knowledge of the two weapons they could by visiting Peenemünde and Zempin and discovering, to their dismay, that neither weapon was close to deployment.

If that were not enough, Heinemann was appalled at the size of the large launch sites. He knew they could not be concealed from aerial observation, and the fact that they were swarming with foreign workers meant security was nearly impossible. On the day LXV Armee-korps was activated, Dornberger's hopes for a field command were crushed. Heinemann considered Dornberger a desk officer and he wanted someone with combat experience, so Generalleutnant Richard Metz, a seasoned veteran, was transferred from the Russian Front and appointed to the post of Höhere–Artillerie Kommandeur (Mot) 191 (Superior Artillery Commander, motorized, 191) or HARKO 191 that Dornberger had been filling since late 1943. Heereswaffenamt had supported Dornberger for the role, but from this time forward the project manager of the A-4 was considered a technical expert, not a field commander, and he and the A-4 developmental center at Peenemünde were moved even farther from the center of influence. Metz, as HARKO 191, was to prepare the units under his command for field combat and control their tactical deployment.

Meanwhile A-4 production lagged badly. A realistic report from Peenemünde dated December 5, 1943 indicated the A-4 could not be ready until April 1944. However, even this date proved entirely too optimistic. The SS controlled production at Mittelwerk, and training at Blizna was under SS "supervision," but in his haste to get control of the A-4, Himmler had created more bottlenecks to getting the weapon into the field. The rockets left the Mittelwerk in Nordhausen minus their electrical systems and warheads. From Nordhausen they made a rail journey of roughly 150 miles to the Demag-Fahrzeug-werke GmbH (Demag-Automotive Factory) at Falkensee, west of Berlin, for the installation of electrical equipment. From there they traveled either to Peenemünde for testing or to Blizna for training. By the end of January 1944, Mittelwerk had produced 56 A-4 missiles of such uniformly poor quality that "they could not even be used for sta-tic tests. They had hundreds of leakages, cracks, incorrect connections and other failures."[7]

Experts from Peenemünde were called to visit the Mittelwerk with suggestions on how to correct the problems. Not surprisingly, there was also a problem with sabotage since a great part of the workforce at Mittelwerk consisted of slave laborers. Under the constant threat of death, the inmates showed remarkable courage and continued to dam-age rockets that were leaving the assembly line. As a result of the untrained and unwilling labor force, the sabotage and a long train journey to which delicate machines like A-4 did not take kindly, approximately 19 percent of the A-4s arriving at their destinations had technical faults or broken or missing parts. At the end of December, the new-model Fi 103s were not yet available,[8] but a LXV Armee-korps meeting on December 30 established the firing rate for Fi 103 launch crews as three per hour—an unrealistically high firing rate that exemplifies the lack of objectivity on the part the German leadership.

On December 8, it was obvious that the attempt to erect huge bunkers at Watten and the other sites was being thwarted by Allied bombing, and Hitler asked Speer to look into the matter. By the middle of the month, it was evident that work on these sites had to be abandoned and Hitler ordered that only work that could be completed by the fall of 1944 would continue. Ironically, Hitler was rather sanguine about this turn of events and explained that he was not disappointed, because every bomb that fell on the large concrete sites in France meant one less bomb on Germany.

In a postwar interview von Braun claimed that Organisation Todt continued the construction just to prove it could do so in the face of heavy bombing.[9] The Allied victory over the large concrete installations forced Hitler and OKW planners to concede that the small mobile launcher was the only way to deploy A-4, a method that made it nearly impossible to detect. Hitler was obviously excited about the prospect of using both weapons against England, and during his daily war conference on December 20, 1943 he mentioned that the Allies were bombing the large sites because they were getting nervous. "They know exactly what we're up to," he said. "They are writing we've got rockets; they are saying that it's possible that we can fire one or two tons of explosives at them—and now they are believing it themselves."[10]

A discussion of Allied methods of attack followed and Hitler mentioned that attacking such small targets as the launching sites from 20,000 feet was not very effective. In response to Wehrmacht operations chief Alfred Jodl's report that some attacks were made from an altitude of 6,000 feet, Hitler ordered the antiaircraft defenses enhanced—a move that resulted in a significant increase in Allied aircraft losses. Misleading reports of Fi 103 production instilled confidence in OKW and on December 11, 1943 it ordered the flying bomb attack on London to begin by the middle of January. General Heinemann, Colonel Walter, his chief of staff, and Colonel Wachtel, commander of the firing units, were stunned. Heinemann pointed out that it was impossible because, if for no other reason, there were no Fi 103s then in production. The heavy bombing convinced Wachtel that the Allies were well aware of his unit's activities and would spare no effort to destroy the sites. Although the fixed launch sites with their permanent ramps and concrete buildings were preferred by Hitler, it was obvious that with their exposed position and clear signature they were easy targets. During the first three months of the attacks, repair crews tried to fix the damage but quickly found that attempts to mend the sites only brought the Allied planes back.

It was soon clear that the repair effort would best be served by concentrating on the most important sites. Wachtel designated 22 sites to be kept operational, and repair efforts were concentrated at these. It did not take the Allies long to detect the increased activity, however, and within a few weeks their bombers were concentrating their efforts on those 22. Clearly, Wachtel's men could not carry out a systematic bombardment of England if their launching sites were in constant need of repair. Something had to be done.

To clarify the situation, the first of two conferences was held in Paris on December 28, 1943. It was attended by representatives from the Army, the Luftwaffe and firms contracted to supply Fi 103 components. During the meeting, General Heinemann outlined the status of the A-4 and Fi 103 production programs and the state of the construction of launch sites along the French coast. Production of both weapons was far behind schedule. The OKW estimate that 1,400 Fi 103s would be ready for firing was, as usual, overly optimistic. In fact, the test program would not officially end until February.

Production problems were certain to follow the end of the test program as modifications and alterations were made. In light of the problems, General Heinemann felt the OKW estimate that 55,040 Fi 103s would be built in 1944 was extremely unrealistic. At the conclusion of the second meeting on January 2, 1944, the general drafted an unvarnished report to OKW that the flying bomb campaign could not start for another four or five months. Heinemann recommended that the Fi 103 be given first priority since it was closest to completion, and that some of the materials used for A-4 should be used to produce more Fi 103s. Next, he recommended that construction on the 42 fixed launch sites that had not been destroyed or damaged continue, as a ruse to lure Allied bombers away from the new launch sites, which had a different and much smaller signature than the existing ones. All work on the new sites was to be done exclusively by German laborers and plans were made to station a counter-espionage unit in the area to protect them from Allied agents.

Heinemann's report was taken very seriously by Generaloberst Hans von Salmuth, commander of the 15th Army, which controlled LXV Corps, and he adopted all of Heinemann's proposals without change. The launch date was moved back to February 15, 1944 and on January 4 Generaloberst Jodl met with von Axthelm and Bree to determine whether that date could be met. Neither man was willing to give Jodl bad news. Von Axthelm declined to answer the question on the grounds that he was responsible only for development and production, and Bree stated that as an engineer he was unable to comment on issues regarding deployment. Jodl naturally read between the lines, but he was unwilling to give Hitler the bad news and break the spell under which the Nazi leadership seemed to exist regarding the new weapons.

Joseph Goebbels, Hitler's Minister of Propaganda, meanwhile waxed ecstatic to Wilfred von Oven, his press secretary: "For three and a half years they [the people of London] have had no sirens. Imagine the terrific awakening that's coming! Our weapons are absolutely unprecedented. There is no defense, no warning at all. Wham. It hurtles down into the city, all unawares. I cannot picture a more devastating attack on their morale . . ."[11]

The euphoria came to a rapid end a few days later. On January 10, 1944, there was a 15th Army conference at Tourcoing, outside Lille, attended by Feldmarschall Wilhelm Keitel, chief of OKW. During the conference, Heinemann repeated his recommendations to expedite the long-range engagement program to Keitel. The Fi 103 was to be given priority over A-4 because it was more refined; new launching sites that were simpler to build and easier to camouflage were to be built to compensate for the ones destroyed; construction of the new sites was to be done by German labor only; and counter-espionage efforts were to be increased.[12]

A few days later Heinemann presented an extremely realistic assessment of his new command, stating that the Fi 103 would not be ready for deployment for four or five months. He asked Jodl to pass this information to Hitler, but Jodl again demurred. This down-to-earth appraisal did not endear Heinemann to the Luftwaffe. When the commander of LXV Armeekorps asked the Luftwaffe for additional information concerning the Fi 103, Feldmarschall Gerhard Milch, head of the Air Ministry and de facto chief of the Luftwaffe, was furious. During a meeting at the Air Ministry on January 18, 1944, Milch exploded when informed of Heinemann's request, shouting that it was none of LXV Armeekorps' business. He forbade his subordinates from giving Heinemann any information concerning the Fi 103, on the basis of secrecy. Concerned that Heinemann would only use the information to make himself look good at Milch's expense, the latter further instructed that, according to the Führer, "only those who absolutely need this information may be given it, and the Generalkommando [Heinemann] does not in the least belong to those."[13]

Denying the only unit organized to fire the Fi 103 information about the weapon didn't help the situation. Production of the Fi 103 was on hold and the war wouldn't wait. The following day, Milch downgraded the Fi 103 program, diverting materials to the production of fighters, which were accorded top priority in order to defend Germany against Allied bombing raids.

As 1944 dawned, the Third Reich faced increasingly grim news across its battle fronts. In the east the Soviet Army had arrived at the Dnieper, the river the Germans reached in September 1941. Italy, Germany's only ally in the West, was gone and the Allies were slowly making their way up the Italian boot. Here the Germans had a distinct advantage since they were fighting a deliberate defensive war to tie down as many British and American divisions as possible; but attrition is a two-way street and the Italian Front continued to consume first-class troops that could have been used elsewhere. In the west, everyone knew it was only a matter of time before the British and Americans invaded the continent—the most probable time spring or early summer. The situation at sea was equally grim. The German surface fleet was merely a fleet-in-being, bottled up in harbors and fjords. The once powerful U-boat arm was suffering terribly from long-range aircraft that patrolled the sea lanes, up-to-date Allied escort vessels with modern detection equipment accompanying nearly every convoy. In the air the Allies continued to gain ascendancy, although the Germans were exacting a heavy toll of Allied bombers over the Reich.

Since November 1943, German intelligence had become increasingly aware of the British effort to find out as much as possible about the Fi 103 and its deployment in France. Because the British also knew that Wachtel was the commander of Flak Regiment 155(W), German counterintelligence decided to throw the British off the trail by creating the impression that Wachtel had returned to Zempin by giving Flak Regiment 155(W) the cover designation "Flakgruppe Creil." The headquarters was moved from Doullens to the Château Creil, north of Paris, and they reported that the Flakgruppe was commanded by "Oberst Martin Wolf"—who was none other than Wachtel. At varying times the commander of Flak Regiment 155(W) dyed his hair, grew a beard and traveled in civilian clothes. In addition, an independent 130-man Luftwaffe motorized signal company was deployed to the area around the launch sites to convince the Allies that the flying bombs were radio controlled and cause them to waste precious time and resources trying to jam Fi 103s as they crossed the English coast.

These measures appear to have had some degree of success as they provided Allied intelligence with a baffling series of dead ends. In the short run, Allied intelligence interest in Wachtel deflected it from a thorough investigation of LXV Armeekorps until the summer of 1944.[14] Increased surveillance of the workers at construction sites by the Gestapo was also paying off. On February 5, Michel Hollard, the French engineer who had alerted the British to the "ski sites," and made a personal reconnaissance of the site at Bonnetot-le-Faubourg, was arrested by the Gestapo. Although the Germans tortured him, he refused to talk. He was sent to a concentration camp, where he was fortunate enough to survive the war.

On February 12, 1944, LXV Armeekorps submitted a progress report on Fi 103 launch site construction that listed three different "systems" of sites. Each system included both launch sites and support sites. System I included the sixty-four original "ski sites" and the eight supply sites. System II consisted of the replacements for the sites in System I since they were being systematically destroyed by Allied bombers. System III called for sixty-four additional sites, some of which were oriented on the Channel ports of Bristol, Southampton, Portsmouth and Plymouth. In addition to the launch sites, System III also included nineteen storage sites.

The new sites in Systems II and III were considerably different from the old style sites planned in June 1943. The fixed installations, with their characteristic ski-shaped storage buildings and numerous reinforced concrete buildings, had an unmistakable signature, and once damaged were difficult to repair. The new launch site, which both Heinemann and Wachtel preferred, was much smaller and difficult to detect from the air. In woods or some other well-camouflaged position, engineers leveled a 250-foot strip of ground oriented on the target and poured seven pairs of concrete pads. Sections of 6-inch steel rail were laid on either side of the pads and a gantry was built on the rails. The assembly crew then used the gantry to hoist the seven support legs, each taller than the one preceding it, into position. Once in position they were fixed to the concrete pads and the launch rail sections were hoisted onto the support legs and bolted in place. The site needed only a workshop, fuel storage area, compass setting platform and firing point. Only the fuel storage buildings were concrete. To diversify the signature, the remaining structures were built to resemble farm buildings indigenous to the area. Power to the site was provided by a mobile generator, to eliminate its dependence on the civilian power grid.

In an environment in which the Allies held air superiority, the new sites were far more viable. Smaller and more easily camouflaged, they could be easily rebuilt if damaged or destroyed. The steel parts of the launch ramp were prefabricated, and sections of the ramp damaged by bombing or a malfunctioning Fi 103 could be removed and replaced in a matter of hours. New generators could be brought forward if the one at the site was destroyed. In some cases, barracks and workshop buildings were prefabricated to speed construction and repair. To underline the need for the new type of site, LXV Armeekorps issued a report on February 18 predicting that the old sites would soon be destroyed and that continuing repairs would be useless.[15] It emphasized that the new simplified sites would be ready in sufficient numbers by the time the attack on London started. Heinemann's recommendation to maintain repair work on the old sites as a deception measure proceeded, and Allied planes continued to bomb them.

The A-4 program meanwhile continued to attract the attention of the Nazi elite. In February 1944, seemingly out of the blue, Wernher von Braun was summoned to the headquarters of Reichsführer SS

Heinrich Himmler at Hochwald in East Prussia. It was not far from Hitler's Wolf's Lair and von Braun obeyed with some trepidation. Even though he held the rank of honorary major in the SS, he was extremely suspicious of SS motives, particularly those of General Hans Kammler, who he felt was plotting to gain control of the A-4 program. Himmler was, as usual, extremely polite, if not charming. "I hope you realize that your A-4 rocket has ceased to be a toy and that the whole German people eagerly await the mystery weapon . . . I can imagine that you've been immensely handicapped by Army red tape. Why not join my staff? Surely you know that no one has such ready access to the Führer, and I can promise you vastly more effective support than those hidebound generals."[16]

Von Braun replied that he couldn't ask for a better boss than General Dornberger and added that delays were due to technical troubles rather than red tape. He also added that the A-4 was "rather like a little flower" that needed a gentle gardener along with the proper amount of sunshine and fertilizer to grow. Von Braun feared that Himmler was planning to give it "a big jet of liquid manure . . . that might kill our little flower."[17] According to von Braun, Himmler smiled a bit sardonically at the simile. One has to be skeptical concerning the last part of von Braun's account. If he was indeed trying to be careful, why would he make a remark that was bound to irritate a man as ruthless and powerful as Himmler? What is certain is that Himmler offered von Braun a position in the SS and the engineer declined. As usual, however, Himmler would find an alternate means of getting his way.

On March 1, 1944, LXV Armeekorps held a typical German Kriegspiel for deployment of the Fi 103. (Literally translated, "Kriegspiel" means "wargame," but it is really a staff map exercise similar to U.S. command post exercises.) The scenario was a retaliation firing in response to a British bombing raid on a German city. An analysis of the exercise showed that the crews could have launched from 768 to 960 bombs on the nights of March 1 and 2. This was a sustained rate by each crew of approximately five bombs every three hours. While this rate of fire was much more reasonable than that of three per hour established in the meeting of December 30, 1943, it would also prove to be extremely unrealistic.

The tightening of German security continued to pay dividends.

Two British intelligence groups landed in France in early March and both were captured soon after they arrived. Between March 1 and 5, German counterintelligence rounded up eleven British agents. One of these had sketches showing the detailed layout of four ski sites. In the Beauvais region, an area that contained Fi 103 supply facilities and headquarters, counterintelligence confiscated over a thousand containers of arms, ammunition and explosives that had been parachuted into Occupied France. A short time later the Germans found sixty-one more containers with the radios and papers—of British agents, an incredibly valuable find. In the middle of March, Headquarters LXV Armeekorps issued two circulars warning that the "Gaullist Intelligence Service" was observing the setting up of secret weapons units, the construction of the large sites and any "long range guns that might exist."[18]

In January, Reichsminister Albert Speer had fallen seriously ill with a knee infection and a month later had to be hospitalized. He was unable to return to work until April and, as he was not available for Hitler's conferences, many attempted to increase their influence at his expense. Some even went so far as to tell Hitler that Speer would not recover. In March, the Fi 103 was finally in full production and Milch used Speer's absence to impress Hitler with the speed of Fi 103 production in comparison to A-4. He also convinced Hitler that the Fi 103 needed some of the A-4's labor and resources, and on March 5 Hitler ordered the Mittelwerk to begin Fi 103 production.

The decision was not as politically motivated as it seems. The A-4 program was experiencing a considerable amount of trouble. By mid-March there had been fifty-seven launches of A-4s at Heidelager. Only twenty-six actually left the launch pad, and of those only two reached their target. From the time A-4 was first tested with live warheads, the rocket exhibited a regrettable tendency to break up at 6,500 feet or more above the target.[19] In some cases the warhead fell to earth and exploded, but in most instances the warhead exploded when the rocket broke up, making the A-4 totally ineffective. In addition, there was a tendency for many rocket engines to explode a few feet above the launch pad or simply stop. Either way, the results were hazardous for the crews and damaged hard-to-replace ground support equipment.

At first the airburst problem was dismissed as the result of rough handling during transport, and every rocket arriving at Blizna was given a thorough inspection. Despite these precautions, the malfunctions persisted nevertheless, and the experts at Peenemünde set to work to solve the riddle. The problem of the engine cutting off or exploding was fairly straightforward; it was due to faulty tubing and connectors in the fuel-feed mechanism. In some instances the tubing and connectors were loose or cracked; in others the fuel lines to the motor were not bent correctly and were improperly stressed when they were connected to the engine. The shock of ignition and the vibration of lift-off cracked the lines and the fittings. These defects caused two very different failures. Sometimes fuel and oxidizer did not reach the combustion chamber and the engine cut off. At other times, the same defects allowed fuel and oxidizer to accumulate in parts of the rocket other than the combustion chamber, where the mixture was set off by electrical sparks that caused an explosion which destroyed the rocket. To prevent recurrences of the trouble, the pipe-bending machinery was adjusted to insure a tension-free fit and the connectors were fitted with locking devices to insure they could not vibrate loose.

During the tests at Heidelager, the first integrating accelerometers for automatic fuel cut-off arrived. These devices were designed to make the rocket independent of the Campania radio control cut-off system, which Dornberger and other German military men felt left the A-4 vulnerable to enemy jamming. They also meant that a lot of expensive ground equipment and vacuum tubes in the guidance section could be done away with. Mounted in the rocket, the accelerometer was sensitive to acceleration. It indicated the rocket's speed, then was pre-set to switch off the fuel flow to the rocket motor as soon as the proper velocity was reached. As with the other components of the A-4, there were problems with the accelerometers. The ones made by Kreiselgeräte GmbH increased the problem of lateral dispersion, while those designed by Professors Buchhold and Wagner of Darmstadt gave the rocket roughly the same performance as Campania.

During this period Generalleutnant Metz conducted a comprehensive inspection of his firing units and was extremely disappointed by what he found. Abteilung 836, the best unit he had, needed considerable field training, and Abteilung 485 was far below strength and only starting its training. A third unit, Abteilung 962, was in the process of being broken up to fill the other two units. Metz was also dissatisfied with the Abteilungs' leadership. The HARKO 191 was accustomed to a much higher level of discipline on the Russian Front. Since neither the personnel, the A-4, nor the ground-support equipment was ready, he asked to be reassigned. Heinemann denied Metz's request for transfer and he continued to prepare the A-4 firing units for combat.

By the middle of March, Himmler was ready to take the next step in his plan to seize the A-4 project for his own. At 2:00 A.M. on March 15, three Gestapo agents arrested Dr. Wernher von Braun at his apartment and incarcerated him in Stettin. A short time later they arrested Klaus Riedel and Helmut Gröttrup, two of von Braun's close friends and associates. The charges brought against the engineers were based on conversations overheard by agents and informers of the Sicherheitsdienst (the security service of the SS) since October 1943, shortly after the RAF attack on Peenemünde. However, this wasn't the first attempt to gain control of the A-4 program by discrediting those who built it. Himmler first used the approach in March 1943 when he tried to disgrace Colonel Leo Zanssen, the Commander of Peenemünde.

Because von Braun and his associates often spoke of building spaceships instead of weapons, they were charged with giving peacetime projects precedence over wartime work, a violation of one of Speer's regulations. They were also accused of making treasonable statements by claiming the war was going badly and that the A-4 was an "instrument of murder."[20] A final accusation was that they formed a Communist cell. This latter charge may have been close to the truth; Gröttrup was the only Peenemünde engineer who opted to go to the Soviet Union after the war.

Arresting three top engineers of a weapons development project just as the weapon was going into mass production would generally be considered a self-defeating move, but in Hitler's Third Reich power mattered more than logic. It is not difficult to assess Himmler's reasoning for making his attempt at such a critical time. Since Speer was ill and could not defend his turf, it was an opportune moment to strike. From Himmler's limited viewpoint, the A-4 had been completed and was now in production, so he could get rid of its creators and take it for his own. Either he could not grasp the idea that the A-4 needed further refinement or he felt that it would be an easy matter to force someone else to do it.

Dornberger, headquartered in Schwedt, received a phone call at

2:00 A.M. from General Buhle, chief of the army staff serving with OKW at Berchtesgaden, requesting him to come to a conference with Feldmarschall Keitel immediately. Reservations had already been made for Dornberger at a local hotel. He left Schwedt at 8:00 A.M. and arrived in Berchtesgaden late in the afternoon. As soon as he was settled in his room, Dornberger called Buhle, who came to see him in his room and tell him that von Braun and the others had been arrested. Dornberger was astounded at the news. "I could not believe my ears," he wrote. "That couldn't possibly be true! Von Braun, my best man, with whom I had worked in the closest collaboration for over ten years and whom I believed I knew better than anyone, whose whole soul and energy, whose indefatigable toil by day and night, were devoted to the A-4, arrested for sabotage! It was incredible."[21]

After what he described as a nearly sleepless night, Dornberger met with Keitel the following morning and the Field Marshal wasted no time telling him the charges were very serious. Dornberger informed Keitel that he vouched for the three, even though he didn't know exactly what the charges were. Amazed that Dornberger reacted so quickly, Keitel cautioned him and asked, "You would vouch for these men with your own life?"[22] Dornberger replied, "It surely goes without saying, sir, that I would stand by my closest colleagues without hesitation or reservation."[23]

Keitel then went on to detail the "evidence" against the three rocket engineers, relating what the SD had overheard. Dornberger repeated his willingness to vouch for the three men, went on to state that they had indeed shown the way to outer space, and that if his men had been arrested for sabotage for expressing such thoughts, then he should be arrested also. Keitel emphasized that the "sabotage" consisted of their not giving their all to the A-4 weapon because they were thinking in terms of outer space. Dornberger wanted to know who the informer was and advised the chief of OKW that the entire project would be ruined if the men were not released. Keitel, unwilling to put himself at risk, told Dornberger that Himmler had taken over and there was nothing he, Keitel, could do. Dornberger reminded Keitel that all the men involved were legally under the Army's jurisdiction and should, therefore be transferred to an army confinement facility. Keitel balked. Even after Dornberger detailed the seriousness of the loss of the three engineers to the project, Keitel refused to intervene.

Dornberger then replied, "It is my duty to demand immediate release of these men in the interests of the program."[24]

Keitel was appalled at being placed in a situation in which he had to make such a difficult decision. He replied pathetically that he could not appear to be less zealous than the Gestapo: "I am watched, all my actions are noted. People are only waiting for me to make a mistake. If I ever have to go, the Officers' Corps will have lost the last intermediary between itself and the Führer."[25] Dornberger ignored Keitel's excuse and asked to see Himmler in order to try to get the engineers released. Keitel phoned Himmler, but the Reichsführer SS refused to see Dornberger. Instead, Dornberger was instructed to "apply to the SS Security Office in Berlin and ask for General Kaltenbrunner."[26] Keitel timidly asked Dornberger to keep what had transpired between them in the strictest confidence, then dismissed him. By his own account, Dornberger returned to Schwedt "in a white hot rage"[27] and drove to the bomb-damaged SS Security headquarters in the Prinz Albrechtstrasse in Berlin accompanied by Lt. Colonel Georg Thom, his chief of staff. It was advisable to have a reliable witness.

Kaltenbrunner was not available and Dornberger met with Gestapo Chief Heinrich Müller, one of the most ruthless and merciless men in the Third Reich. Dornberger remembered him as physically nondescript, with piercing blue eyes. When Dornberger asked for the release of the men arrested by who he thought were agents of the SD, Müller insisted they were being held in protective custody and then proceeded to lecture Dornberger on the difference between the SD and the Gestapo. Undeterred, Dornberger told him that protective custody and arrest were the same to him. He informed the Gestapo chief that the A-4 project was in jeopardy if the three remained in prison and explained the situation with regard to space travel and the rocket.

Possibly unsure of how next to proceed because of the consequences to a major project, Müller agreed to brief Kaltenbrunner in order to expedite the matter. He then attempted to intimidate Dornberger with the threat that the Gestapo had a large file on him, but Dornberger refused to be cowed, especially after Müller admitted that Dornberger was considered Germany's greatest rocket expert. Dornberger left for Stettin as soon as he left Müller's office, and by working with a Major Klammroth of the Abwehr (Army intelligence) managed to get von Braun transferred to Schwedt.

During this time Hitler visited Speer while he was convalescing in Klessheim. Hitler was so solicitous that Speer used the opportunity to intercede for the three men. The combination worked. In a few days, von Braun was released on the basis that he was vital to the war effort and would remain free for three months, after which the case would be reviewed. The other two men were released a short time later. After the beginning of the A-4 campaign against London, the case against von Braun lapsed. Riedel was killed in an auto accident in August 1944 and Gröttrup remained free until the end of the war.

While the A-4 program experienced problems with defective rockets and attempts by Himmler to appropriate the weapon for his own, work on the Fi 103 proceeded at a steady pace. On March 14, 1944, wingless flying bombs with the motors attached but not operating were dropped from bombers flying at an altitude of around 6,500 feet in order to test various fuses and the effect of the warhead on a target. After successful completion of the tests, Flak Regiment 155(W) personnel moved to the SS testing ground at Blizna to begin live firings in April.

The end of March brought another bizarre event in the development of the German long-range weapons, this time involving the Fi 103. Over seven hundred Fi 103s had been manufactured by the end of the month and Milch, along with General Karl Koller, chief of the Luftwaffe operational staff, decided to give Hitler a surprise present for his birthday on April 20. The plan, published March 29, called for a "Great Reveille" of three Fi 103 to be fired at London a few hours before dawn on the Führer's birthday. The Great Reveille was to be followed by a similar "Salute" of one hundred around noon and then a mass firing of the final two hundred in a "Tattoo" that night. In full agreement with Hitler's concept, Wachtel insisted that the Fi 103 could only be effective as a weapon of terror and this was a good way to employ it. He explained his position to von Axthelm, who obviously didn't agree with him. The controversy over whether the Fi 103 should be used strictly as a terror weapon or against military targets had not been solved by Hitler's pronouncement the previous November. In January, Milch had indicated that the Allied ports of embarkation were under consideration as targets.[28] Nonetheless, the proposal was forwarded to General Korten, the Luftwaffe chief of staff. Heinemann was against the project from the first. Launching the flying bomb early and in small numbers would prematurely reveal the operational sites and give the Allies a chance to retaliate. Hitler agreed with Heinemann. He wanted the Fi 103 used in mass and he wanted it to be a surprise. He was also concerned that the enemy might find an intact Fi 103, duplicate it and use it against Germany. He, therefore, issued an order that the flying bomb was not to be used until mid-May.[29]

On April 11, a second secret Kriegspiel was held at LXV AK headquarters in Paris. During the exercise the flow of Fi 103s from the factories to the storage areas to the firing sites was realistically considered in the face of Allied bombing. Not only was the firing rate lowered again, but it was obvious to Colonel Walter, the corps chief of staff, that the eight concrete storage sites in the launching zone were totally vulnerable to air attack. As a result of the exercise, the existing reinforced-concrete storage sites were abandoned, and in May the bombs were stored in well-protected and easily camouflaged caves and railroad tunnels. Caves were selected at Nucourt southwest of Beauvais and at St-Leu-d'Esserent in the Oise Valley. The former was codenamed "Nordpol" (North Pole) and the latter "Leopold." Later, a third storage area for air-launched bombs was established in a tunnel at Rilly-la-Montagne. Each of the storage sites held between a thousand and fifteen hundred bombs. This proved to be an excellent decision since none of the new storage sites were attacked by Allied aircraft until after the beginning of the campaign against London.

From April 14 to 17, 1944 the firing crews of Flak Regiment 155(W) fired a total of thirty Fi 103 with live warheads at a target area between Lublin and Cholm, a distance of roughly 105 miles. Eighteen, or 62 percent, hit the target. The remaining twelve either failed to leave the launching ramp or traveled only part of the distance. At least one of the "short rounds" landed in the village of Adampol, killing several people and some animals and reducing a number of buildings to ruins.[30] Additional firings in May indicated that the Fi 103 and its firing crews were slowly improving.

Gosslau and the engineers involved in the design and development of the Fi 103 were also learning a number of things about their creation. For tactical reasons it was best to deploy the Fi 103 at the lowest altitude possible in order to obtain the highest speed, the maximum range and the shortest flight time possible. This was because the air was denser at lower altitudes and there was better combustion in the engine. While the firings at Blizna showed an average of 62 percent successful firings, some crews had 82 percent success. However, only 25 percent of the hits landed in a circle 9.32 miles in diameter. Gosslau concluded: "Dispersion in longitude mainly is caused by a wrong estimate of the wind. Dispersion in latitude is also influenced by that factor, but tolerances of airframe and failures of the compass decisively add to this."[31]

The steady improvement in Fi 103 was not matched by the A-4. In one incident von Braun traveled to Blizna to observe A-4 launchings and was nearly killed by a rocket that fell back to earth after its engine cut out. He was saved by a second malfunction, which caused the rocket to explode in mid-air. In that particular case the incident was attributed to a bad electrical connection, but the airbursts continued. Von Braun and the engineers blamed the failures on the firing crews, who they claimed were not technically proficient enough to work with the rocket. They went further to maintain that the rocket could only be fired from large bunker complexes because of the laboratory-like conditions needed to handle the weapon properly. Dornberger strongly disagreed and later wrote, "Many of the soldiers . . . were keen, and interested in the technical aspects. . . . As a result of shooting in all kinds of weather and the most varied field conditions the skill of the crews rose to a degree of perfection that had not been reached even . . . at Peenemünde."[32] To him it seemed the fault lay at the feet of the production staff at Nordhausen.

The industrial experts at Mittelwerk in turn blamed the designers at Peenemünde. They specifically blamed von Braun for claiming the rocket was fully developed in October 1943. In the spring of 1944, major modifications were required in the engine and the turbo pump assembly to make them suitable for mass production, and they blamed the entire design team at Peenemünde for not designing the rocket for ease of mass production. Both complaints were justified, but the condition stemmed from the fact that Peenemünde was a research and development project tasked with building a rocket that worked. Mass production was only of secondary importance as long as they were denied the resources to build a production facility. The A-4 having been taken away from the engineers at Peenemünde before all the flaws could be dealt with contributed greatly to the problem.

After a short investigation, Dornberger believed the flaw in the A-4 was in the fuel and oxidizer tanks. Strict quality control was imposed over the manufacture of the fuel tanks, but the air bursts continued. The next theory was that the spot weld securing the fuel tank in its suspension in the rocket was breaking. The fuel tanks in two experimental rockets were riveted before they were fired and both were destroyed by air bursts. Neither did modified fuel tank suspensions solve the problem.

Major General Josef Rossman, department head of the Heereswaffenamt suggested stationing observers in the impact area of the A-4 to find the reason for the airbursts and Dornberger took his advice. There was no telemetry at Blizna and the incoming rockets had to be tracked visually. In May, Dornberger and von Braun set up camp in the impact area. Both were extremely lucky they were not seriously injured. On one occasion, an A-4 landed within 300 feet of Dornberger, hurling him into the air.[33] Fortunately for the A-4 program, he was unscathed. He did manage to observe through his binoculars one rocket that broke apart and "saw one part of the rocket flying on and recognized the warhead and instrument compartment."[34] The warhead then struck the ground. Had this been the only problem there would have been no difficulty in deploying the A-4. In most cases the warhead was either disintegrating or exploding thousands of feet in the air and the problem was obviously a longstanding one.

The warheads of the A-4s launched over the Baltic were filled with green dye and on numerous occasions the dye had been spread over a large area of the ocean in a pattern inconsistent with the impact of an intact warhead. Only in the spring of 1944 did Dornberger and his subordinates realize the significance of the dispersion of the dye. Nevertheless, the problem of the airbursts remained a mystery and in June the staff at Peenemünde began vertical launches from Greifswalder Oie in order to visually track the rockets as they plunged toward the earth. Some of these rockets were adjusted to burn all the available fuel and they, too, experienced the airburst phenomenon. The Greifswalder Oie observations were inconclusive and General Rossman, who felt that the heat of reentry might be causing a structural failure in the rocket, suggested the installation of fiberglass insulation inside the hull. The suggestion worked to a great extent and the airburst problem thereafter affected only 30 percent of the rockets fired at Blizna.[35]

Another solution was to use a very insensitive fuse that lessened the effect of the blast because the warhead would not go off until it had penetrated the surface of the earth. Of course, if it penetrated a building before it went off the effect would be catastrophic—as the campaign on London later showed. These two modifications, plus a number of other minor changes, reduced the failure rate of the A-4 to 20 percent. Much later, the engineers at Peenemünde discovered that the problem lay with a structural weakness in the front end of the hull. Dornberger and his staff "found the final solution by reinforcing the front end of the hull with a sheet steel collar that we riveted in place. In the end we achieved 100 percent impacts."[36]

From May 18 to May 20, a three-day exercise was conducted at Heidelager to determine the readiness of the A-4 rocket, its launch crews and support equipment for deployment to France. It was then decided to continue training for another two to three months before deployment was practical. However, preparations for deployment to France continued. Prior to the Allied invasion of Normandy, A-4 rockets were to be stored in field supply dumps in northern France. There was a large dump at Hautmesnil which had underground galleries serviced by a rail spur. Smaller sites were located at La Méauff, Bois-de-Bouge and Sottevaste. Together there was enough space to store roughly 150 rockets. An aboveground site at Monchy-Cayeux in the Pas de Calais had barracks, a huge gantry and wooden shelters for the storage of 28 rockets. In addition to the storage sites, a number of "launch sites," which were little more than patches of concrete, were constructed throughout the deployment area. This was because Heinemann, who had witnessed an A-4 nearly tip over during a practice firing, was convinced the A-4 needed hardstand as a launch pad. All of these positions had to be abandoned before they were put to use.

At the end of May 1944, Albert Speer put in motion the machinery to privatize Army Installation Peenemünde. This time he had the assistance of Dornberger, who had vehemently opposed such a move in a meeting with Prof. Karl Hettlage and Heinz Kunze at the Ministry of Munitions in Berlin on February 3, 1943. In a little over a year a great deal had happened, however, including the increased influence of the SS in the rocket program. Himmler had been attempting to get his hands on the project since he tried to discredit Leo Zanssen in 1942. His recent attempt to circumvent Speer while he was ill and his willingness to imprison von Braun and the other engineers showed he was ready to make overt moves to seize the project.

At the time, Speer and Dornberger were at odds because the former hadn't mentioned Dornberger in a reorganization of the A-4 program. Whether this was from an oversight or was a genuine attempt to lessen the general's influence is not known, but Dornberger, who was still "Beauftragter zur besonderen Verwendung Heer" (Commissioner for Special Duties–Army) took it as a threat to his position and went directly to General Fromm, commander of the Reserve Army and Chief of Armaments, with a demand that he (Dornberger) be made head of the entire A-4 project from development to deployment. He threatened to go over Fromm's head to Hitler if nothing was done, and Fromm threatened him with a charges of dereliction of duty and cowardice. Neither general carried out his threat, however, and the incident blew over.

Dornberger continued to lose influence and it became evident to both himself and Speer that something had to be done to protect Peenemünde from Himmler and Kammler. The groundwork was laid for Paul Storch, a top manager for Siemens, to take over Electromechanische Werke GmbH as general manager in a very short time. One reason privatization was now more palatable to Dornberger was that Degenkolb, the ruthless former head of Speer's Special A-4 Committee, was out of the picture, having delegated his responsibilities to Kunze. By the end of June 1944, documents were already referring to Peenemünde as Electromechanische Werke.

While the "modified" sites, as the Allies called them, were under construction, General Heinemann also streamlined the supply system. A few supply sites were in Belgium; several were in northwestern France in the area of Département du Nord; a final group was located south of the Somme River in the Pas de Calais. Trains arriving from Germany delivered Fi 103s and supplies to unloading stations near one of the eight supply depots located near the launch sites in Belgium and the Département du Nord. The field munitions depots at Nucourt and St-Leu-d'Esserent became the two main storage facilities for rocket sites south of the Somme. These two sites provided Fi 103 flying bombs and fuels to the launch sites. Other supplies and equipment were stockpiled at a dump located in Paramain-L'Isle-Adam, near Pontoise. The supply net was served by the railroad which provided priority service to Fi 103 sites. The Fi 103 flying bombs and the supplies needed to assemble fuel and launch them crossed the Belgian/German border near Aachen, then moved through Belgium via Ghent or Brussels and arrived in the marshaling yard at Mouscron. There the trains were divided into those going to the sites in Belgium, northwestern France or the Pas de Calais.

Special Rail Battalions were organized and stationed along the rail line to repair track and bridges damaged by Allied air attacks, and the number of railroad police along the line was increased to guard against sabotage. In addition, each train carried a special security detachment to protect it from attack while en route. The new sites and supply system were in operation in time to receive the flying bombs that were coming off the assembly lines in ever-increasing numbers. German industry turned out 1,700 Fi 103s in April and 2,500 in May. The flying bombs and supplies were moved to the storage areas by truck each night. From there they were loaded on specially designed trucks and trailers and moved to forward dumps from which they were sent to the firing sites as needed. To limit the sites' signature and vulnerability, only enough supplies and bombs were kept at them for the next set of launches.

As preparations for the flying bomb offensive proceeded, relations between Headquarters LXV Armeekorps and Flak Regiment 155(W) grew increasingly strained. A certain amount of friction from inter-service rivalry was to be expected, especially in this case, when the only operational unit in an army corps was a Luftwaffe regiment. Wachtel later joked that Flak Regiment 155(W) was the only Luftwaffe regiment "with its own Army Corps."[37] There was definitely friction due to the fact that what the corps and the regiment were doing was entirely new and they had to learn as they went along. The main source of discontent came from the relationship between the three principal figures in the corps: General Heinemann, the commander; Walter, his chief-of-staff; and Wachtel, commander of the firing units.

Wachtel, rightly, considered himself the expert when it came to the operational aspects of the Fi 103. He had formed the unit and taken it through the birth pangs of any new weapon system and its supporting organization. Heinemann was an astute commander and a realist and appears to have been content to let Wachtel have his own way. Walter, the chief of staff and a strong personality, had his own ideas on how things should be run and he was often at odds with Wachtel. Neither man was willing to compromise. One of their basic differences was the selection of targets for the Fi 103. Walter wanted the flying bomb to be used against military targets such as the port of Southampton and was willing to order Fi 103s diverted to that target on his own initiative. Wachtel, on the other hand, felt that the Fi 103 was only useful as a terror weapon, and insisted it be confined to that purpose. Wachtel was so frustrated that he wrote to von Axthelm in June to protest Walter's attitude. This is surprising considering von Axthelm's lukewarm response to Wachtel's concept in April. As a commander, Heinemann failed to control the growing animosity between the two and seemed unable to impose his will on either. Because of this the chief of staff Walter became the de facto commander of the corps and even Heinemann deferred to him.

On May 14, 1944, Headquarters LXV Armeekorps moved from St. Germain in Paris to Maisons-Lafitte southwest of the city, and two days later received an order from Hitler to begin preparations for the offensive against London. The launches were to begin in the middle of June, at the discretion of the German Commander-in-Chief–West. The codeword to signal that the start of the campaign was imminent was "Rumpelkammer" (Junk Room). Immediately upon receipt of the code word, the launching ramps in the modified sites were to be assembled and supplies and flying bombs were to be brought forward to the launch sites. The Fi 103s were to be prepared for launch as soon as they arrived. Heinemann and Wachtel estimated that this part of the operation would take ten days to complete. Once completed, the code word "Eisbär" (Polar Bear) would start the operation.

In the original plan, the attack was to be supported by long-range coastal batteries hitting selected targets along the English coast and an attack by bomber units of Luftflotte 3. Several Fi 103s were also scheduled to be launched from aircraft to test their effectiveness. As soon as Hitler's order was received, the technicians who were repairing the old-type sites rejoined their units. The supply network began to move and stockpile flying bombs and supplies in preparation for operations. Ninety-five of the sites were now fully operational and another 31 could be made ready in a week.

On the morning of June 6, 1944, the Allies invaded France at Normandy. It was the largest seaborne invasion in history and one of the greatest strategic surprises. Hitler was convinced the landings were a feint and that the actual invasion would come through the Pas de Calais. For that reason he refused to commit his reserves to the battle in the crucial early hours when the beachheads were in jeopardy. One of the reasons he thought the attack would occur farther north was because of the Fi 103 launchers and the large concrete sites along the Pas de Calais. In a Top Secret directive dated November 3, 1943 he explained that the Pas de Calais was "the region from which we shall be opening our long-range bombardment of England. For it is there that the enemy must and will invade; and it is there—if I am not deceived—that our decisive invasion battles will be fought and won."[38]

Hitler was in fact deceived and at 1745 hours on June 6 the code "Rumpelkammer," was received at Headquarters LXV Armeekorps. The offensive was scheduled to begin at 0545 on Monday, June 12, only six days after notification, not the ten days originally planned. The order prompted a flurry of activity at the launch and supply sites as the men of Flak Regiment 155(W) brought up flying bombs and drew the necessary supplies to begin operations. There were numerous delays in getting the right equipment to the sites on time. Allied interdiction of the transportation system in France naturally played a role, but the Germans' insistence on absolute secrecy added to the confusion. The depots in Germany didn't know what they were storing, and when the order came to ship equipment to France they often failed to send complete sets of launch ramps or failed to send all the correct sections. In some cases the prefabricated supports for the ramps did not match the poured concrete supports and troops had to adapt the misfitting parts without power tools. In others there was not enough fuel for the Fi 103s or enough chemical to power the catapults.

Thousands of minor technical problems were fixed and supply glitches worked out; communication problems were solved and myriad other details checked and rechecked. The firing, supply and maintenance crews of Flak Regiment 155(W) worked around the clock. Few of them got any sleep, but there was not enough time to do it all and Wachtel protested the shortened preparation period to no avail. On June 11 he received specific orders to launch the first two salvos of rockets so they would hit London at 2340 and 0040 hours on the night of June 12–13, and then maintain "independent fire" until 0445 hours. The Fi 103 took approximately 22 minutes to cover the distance to London, so coordinated launches would need to begin about 2318 hours. There were only 873 Fi 103s in France available for launching, and if everything went according to plan this was no more than a two- or three-day supply of flying bombs. Regardless, there could be no more delays. This was Germany's last chance to defeat the enemy before he became too strong to eject from the continent.

In the early morning hours of June 12, Wachtel assembled his battery commanders in the headquarters command bunker and reminded them of the grave situation. To his men he exhorted, "Soldiers! Führer and Fatherland look to us, they expect our crusade to be an overwhelming success. As our attack begins, our thoughts linger fondly and faithfully upon our native German soil. Long live our Germany! Long live our Fatherland! Long live our Führer!"[39]

Despite this entreaty, Wachtel's sites could not complete their firing preparations and he was forced to call LXV Armeekorps headquarters at 2300 on June 12 to ask for a one-hour delay in the start of the offensive. According to Walter, the corps chief of staff, Wachtel claimed that only an hour was necessary.[40] It was granted, but when the time was up the firing units were still not ready. On his own initiative Wachtel delayed the firing until 0330 hours. Shortly after midnight only the huge coastal guns opened fire for the offensive, firing thirty-three shells at Maidstone and Folkestone. No flying bombs or manned bombers joined them. Most of the bombers had been destroyed on the ground when Allied planes attacked their airfield at Beauvais-Tille that afternoon.

When the Fi 103 launches finally began, there was no massive barrage. Each battery was ordered to fire when it was ready. Only ten Fi 103s had been fired from the 54 designated to be launched during the night. Five crashed near the sites, one crashed into the Channel and four reached England. Only the dreadful supply situation prevented Wachtel from being court-martialed for the abysmal first effort of the Fi 103. Operations were temporarily suspended until June 15. Meanwhile, the crews slaved to get their flying bombs and launchers ready for a new start. It would be significantly different.

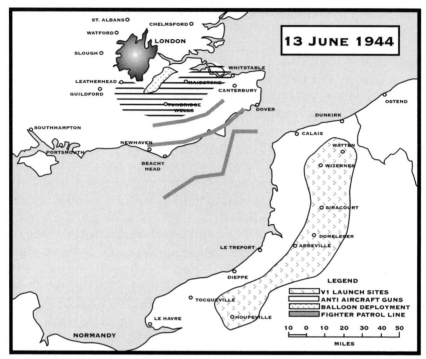

13 JUNE 1944

LEGEND
V1 LAUNCH SITES
ANTI AIRCRAFT GUNS
BALLOON DEPLOYMENT
FIGHTER PATROL LINE

10 0 10 20 30 40 50
MILES

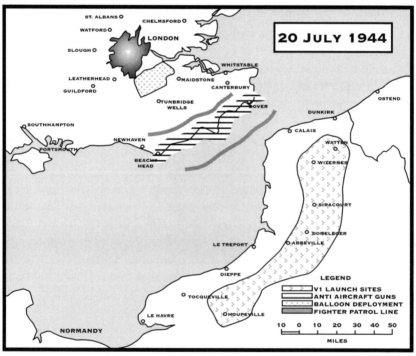

20 JULY 1944

LEGEND
V1 LAUNCH SITES
ANTI AIRCRAFT GUNS
BALLOON DEPLOYMENT
FIGHTER PATROL LINE

10 0 10 20 30 40 50
MILES

7

The Allies Strike Back

In the closing months of 1943 everyone except Lord Cherwell and a few other obstinate British officials agreed that the Germans were developing two long-range weapons, but beyond that the experts in British intelligence knew precious little. There were no hard facts concerning production other than information about the Fieseler works in Kassel, and no one really knew how the Fi 103 was powered. The plans of the ski site provided by the audacious Michael Hollard showed a divided building labeled "Stofflager," which Dr. R.V. Jones interpreted to mean a fuel-storage building. Since there was no connecting door in the wall dividing the two compartments, Jones correctly deduced that the two halves of the building were separated by a blast wall. He knew that the HS 293 and Fritz-X glider bombs were powered by hydrogen peroxide and sodium permanganate, which were known respectively as "T-Stoff" and "Z-Stoff" to the Germans, and he also knew that some of the personnel who had used the two chemicals in KG 100, the air group that had launched the HS 293, had been transferred to Flak Regiment 155(W).

Jones then calculated that the building could hold enough fuel "for twenty flying bombs and give them the necessary 200 kilometers' range for London."[1] Always careful, Jones searched for another building that might hold another type of fuel and found none. He therefore assumed the flying bomb "would be driven by a larger version of the hydrogen peroxide rocket that had previously been seen in the HS 293 glider bomb,"[2] and went on to recommend that the Allied air forces attack hydrogen peroxide production facilities. While Jones's logical deduction turned out to be wrong, his recommendation, if carried out, would have had considerable consequences for the Fi 103, the A-4 and the German Navy. Unfortunately for the Allies, air assets were limited and planners for the air offensive against Germany could not make hydrogen peroxide a priority target.

Of the A-4, the British knew even less. Other than a number of intercepted Enigma signals warning German radar stations that the rocket was about to be fired, there was no hard intelligence about its size or performance. There was also no hard evidence on the function of the large sites or their connection with the rocket, although all of them were within 150 miles of London. A part of the problem arose from "the failure of agents to distinguish in their reports between the rocket and the pilotless aircraft and 'the lack of definite corroboration . . . by photography or other means.'"[3]

With the Germans in control of the Continent, the only way the Allies could prevent the enemy from launching the new weapons was to attack his installations with air power. The man responsible for the Crossbow campaign was Air Marshal Sir Norman Bottomley, who had succeeded Duncan Sandys as the chief investigator for Crossbow on November 18, 1943. As Deputy Chief of the Air Staff, he was responsible for coordinating the initial air effort against the new German weapons.

His staff identified three types of targets that were vulnerable to Allied air attack. The firing sites that included both the ski sites and the large sites were the most obvious. The transportation net that moved the Fi 103 flying bombs and their supplies from Germany to the launch sites in France was also a visible target that was exposed to attack. The production facilities that made the flying bombs were listed as the third target, but the Allies knew very little about these. The supply sites were added to the list as a fourth target when they were discovered later.

Although the destruction of any of the targets listed by Bottomley's staff would severely hinder the effort to launch the Fi 103, the only way to guarantee that none would be fired against Allied targets was to destroy the launchers. Therefore, Bottomley's staff recommended a campaign to bomb the launch sites already identified in the coastal areas of France and to continue to monitor the area and destroy new sites as construction began. None of the air planners believed this would be particularly difficult since the majority of the sites were in the open and could be easily attacked from the air. The large number of sites required a great number of raids, and the plan called for attacks by heavy bombers, medium bombers and fighter bombers to accomplish the mission.

Bottomley's plan to use strategic bombers to destroy the sites brought grave protests from both Marshal Arthur Harris, commander of RAF Bomber Command, and General Carl Spaatz, commander of the U.S. Eighth Air Force. Both men argued that attacking Crossbow targets with heavy bombers was a waste of valuable strategic bomber assets, at the expense of continuing to attack industrial targets inside the Third Reich. Any diversion of assets from that mission were deemed unacceptable. The two commanders were also not particularly worried about the Crossbow targets. Harris and Spaatz were convinced that their aircraft would either destroy the rocket manufacturing facilities as part of the general bombing campaign against German industry or, once the factories were located, they could allocate a few well-timed raids that would obliterate them.

Another point of contention against using heavy bombers for Crossbow was that Operation Pointblank—the effort to destroy the Luftwaffe by attacking its production and ground facilities—was underway. As a compromise, both RAF Bomber Command and the American Eighth Air Force recommended that their part in the campaign be restricted to hitting the factories and transportation network that supplied the sites. In this way, they could continue their strategic bombing campaign and still contribute to the destruction of Crossbow targets. This was a curious recommendation since the Allies knew nothing of the production of Fi 103 except for the Fieseler plant in Kassel which had been bombed in October 1943.

Both strategic bomber forces did agree to allocate bombers to attacks on launching sites if no other targets were available or if weather kept them from the Continent. On paper the air campaign against the launching sites in France consisted of RAF Bomber Command, U.S. Eighth Air Force, RAF 2nd Tactical Air Force, U.S. Ninth Air Force and the fighters of Air Defense Great Britain earmarked to provide tactical air support for the Allied expeditionary forces set to invade France in the spring of 1944. In reality, the majority of the responsibility for attacking the launch sites fell initially to the latter three organizations, which bore the brunt of the losses in the early stages of the campaign.

Allied planners first consolidated all the intelligence available on the sites and prioritized the targets. First priority was the launch sites, with the transportation system second. French railroads that led from the coast to the interior of France and then into Germany were carefully scrutinized for "choke points" such as bridges, tunnels and railyards. The railroads and supply facilities in France were also not a matter of great concern to the Crossbow planners because both the strategic and tactical air forces were attacking the transportation net in France as a prelude to the invasion. The air planners were certain that their efforts would not only rob the German Wehrmacht of the ability to move and receive supplies by rail, but also destroy the ability of the rocket troops to bring supplies and missiles to the launch sites. The main matter of concern, then, was the destruction of both the large sites and the "ski sites."

By late 1943 the Royal Air Force had amassed a lot of useful information on both types of sites. The launch sites and the surrounding areas were photographed and the photographs analyzed in detail. The proximity of the sites to antiaircraft installations, Luftwaffe airbases and radar sites were plotted and the potential of German reaction to attacks on particular sites calculated in order to determine the optimum method and strength of attack. Allied air staffs then assembled mission profiles that gave commanders all the available information necessary to successfully attack a site. There were four previous attacks on Crossbow targets: the bombing of Peenemeunde and the attack on the large rocket-launch complex at Watten in August 1943 by Bomber Command; the attack on the Fiesler factory in October 1943; and the attacks on several construction sites associated with flying bombs by the U.S. Ninth Air Force in November. Although these were attacks on Crossbow targets, at the time they were not part of an overall plan to systematically destroy the support and firing structure of a particular weapons system.

The discovery of the ski sites in late November 1943 injected a note of urgency into the equation and on December 2 the air campaign against Fi 103 launch sites began in earnest. The Office of the Combined Chiefs of Staff gave the campaign a new priority and directed RAF 2nd Tactical Air Force and U.S. Ninth Air Force to begin a bombing campaign against those sites considered most threatening. The aerial battle to prevent the Fi 103 from becoming operational was underway.

On the morning of December 5, fifty-four Martin B-26 Marauders of the Ninth Air Force struck twenty-one ski sites, while rocket-carrying Hurricanes from RAF 2nd Tactical Air Force attacked eight other launch sites. A further eight additional sites were hit by Bomber Command to determine if area bombing was effective against a target as small as a ski site. An additional two hundred bombers were forced to turn back due to heavy overcast. Three groups of 18 Martin B-26 Marauders from the 323rd Bombardment Group, Ninth Air Force, arrived over the sites at Liegescourt, St-Josse-au-Boise and Boise-de-St-Saulve, but were unable to drop their ordnance because all three targets were covered by clouds. Some of the other bombers got through and damaged a number of sites.

Post-strike analysis revealed that the lower the altitude of the attack, the better the results. Area bombing by Bomber Command proved particularly ineffective. Bombing at night, using Bomber Command's standard method of attack—designed for large cities—was inappropriate for attacking a small target. In the attacks on the ski sites bombs fell over a large area, often killing and wounding French civilians while missing the ski sites entirely. The big bombers would have been more effective had they attacked in daylight, but that would have required a fighter escort and the fighters would have been better employed attacking the ski sites themselves. To reduce enemy air activity around the launch sites and to reduce the Luftwaffe's ability to interfere with air operations over Allied bases, 200 medium bombers of the Ninth Air Force bombed Schiphol airfield in the Netherlands on December 13.

The attacks on the launching sites brought an immediate response from the Luftwaffe, which launched a 20-aircraft strike against the Ninth Air Force bases at Earls Colne, Gosfeld, Andrews Field and Gread Dunmow. The attack killed 8, wounded 20 and damaged some of the airfield facilities.[4] Also in response to the attacks, Luftwaffe headquarters and Flak Regiment 155(W) established new directives for camouflage and defense of the sites. All the sites were camouflaged so that, from the air, buildings appeared to have been dismantled and all shadows of facilities remaining at the sites erased. Labor gangs were assembled to repair the sites or build new ones if necessary. Most important, the sites were given antiaircraft protection. The number of light and heavy guns around the sites grew quickly. Since the weather over Germany was bad in the month of December, on the 15th of that month, Chief of the Air Staff Sir Charles Portal urged an all-out attack by the 8th Air Force against the ski sites, with the dual objective of destroying the sites and luring the German day fighter force into the open in an area where Allied bombers had fighter cover. In this General Ira Eaker concurred and the Chiefs of Staff committee requested that Eighth Air Force give "overriding priority to Crossbow bombing."[5]

One area on which there was a good deal of objective information was the site of German tests of the Fi 103 along the Baltic coast. The intercepts of transmissions of the 14th Company of the Luftwaffe Experimental Signals Regiment gave an excellent picture of the aircraft's performance, and it was obvious that all was not well with the flying bomb. After reviewing the plots, R.V. Jones estimated that "In December the accuracy and reliability of the missiles were still so poor that if they had been launched from the ski sites, only one in six would have hit London."[6]

In January 1944 the Germans moved additional bombers to France. This was the beginning of Operation "Steinbock," an attempt to bomb British population centers in retaliation for the Allied bombings of German cities. The Germans managed to mass over 500 bombers of various types, but many of the aircrew were new and poorly trained, as were many of the mechanics. Even the veteran mechanics were working on entirely new aircraft like the He 177. Despite intensive additional training, many of the crews had difficulty with night navigation and failed to find their target, even if it was the city of London. In several cases, raids of over a hundred bombers were unable to drop more than thirty to forty tons of bombs on the British capital.

British defenses were tough and losses rose. Although the raids continued into April, from the German point of view they were failures. Jones saw these raids as a substitute for the flying bomb campaign and further indication the flying bomb would not be ready soon. Jones went on to estimate that the Fi 103 would not be ready for deployment until March 1944—an estimate very different from that of the Joint Intelligence Committee Crossbow subcommittee report of December 18, 1943, which stated that the Germans would be able to launch an offensive capable of delivering "300 tons of bombs in an eight hour period by mid-January 1944."[7]

Cherwell did not concur with the committee's conclusion. Using Jones's data, he wrote, on December 18, to Churchill of his concerns that vital resources were being diverted from D-Day preparations and strategic bombing. With uncanny accuracy Cherwell predicted that each flying bomb "would carry a payload under 1 ton; less than a third of those launched would travel the full 130 miles; [and] with the weapon's average error of ten miles possibly one would arrive per hour in London." He also stated that the offensive—which he did not believe would start before March or April—would claim an average of two to four casualties per aircraft."[8] Later, Cherwell predicted that the flying bomb would be powered by a pulse jet rather than a turbine and as a result the warhead would be lighter than the ton and a half the experts were predicting; he lowered his estimate of those killed to one per flying bomb.

Cherwell's prediction was remarkably accurate, yet it missed the point in that he did not address the destruction, injuries and psychological problems that 24 tons of explosive hitting a major city every day might cause. Nevertheless, Lt. General Frederick E. Morgan, Chief of Staff to the Supreme Allied Commander, or COSSAC, did not concur with his estimate of the situation because on December 20 COSSAC was advised that the threat was so serious that he needed to consider locating Overlord bases beyond the range of the Fi 103. The following day the Chiefs of Staff issued a statement skeptical of Jones's report that the Fi 103 was inaccurate. Cherwell disagreed with the Chiefs of Staff and openly stated that he considered the threat exaggerated.[9]

In late December 1943, Jones received a report from the French agent Amniarix that the "Wachtel" antiaircraft regiment had moved to Creil under conditions of great secrecy. The report went on to describe the proposed symbol or patch of the unit as the letter "W" over an "8" expressed as a fraction, a pun on Wachtel's name since one-eighth in German is "achtel." The patch was never used because the pun was so obvious.[10]

Another massive raid against the Fi 103 was conducted on

December 20 when 185 medium bombers of the Ninth Air Force attacked various sites along the French coast. However, many of the targets were obscured by clouds and ground fog. Only 35 B-26s actually found and bombed their targets. Eight-four mediums of the Ninth Air Force went in against the ski sites the next day and 210 B-26s took off for a maximum effort the following day but were recalled because of inclement weather.

Bad weather continued to hamper operations. Of ninety bombers that took off to bomb sites in the Pas de Calais area on December 24, only 60 managed to bomb their assigned targets. The weather then closed in and kept the bombers on the ground until December 30, when 200 B-26s took to the air. One hundred bombers managed to find their targets but the rest were forced to return to base without dropping any bombs. On the last day of the year, the Ninth Air Force staged one more maximum effort. Two hundred B-26s hit rocket sites and support facilities along the French coast. These strikes were aided by 500 heavy bombers from the 8th Air Force, which also bombed targets along the coast. The December raids delivered 3,000 tons of bombs on the launching sites. Seven sites were totally destroyed and 14 severely damaged. Then, poor weather prevented any further attacks until January 4.

The raids were also instrumental in developing tactics for aerial attacks to destroy the sites. Each air force developed its own method. The British heavy bombers, which had been allocated five sites to destroy, used a combination of high-altitude area bombing and extremely heavy bombs to destroy their targets. Eighth Air Force heavy bombers flew in boxes of six at altitudes ranging from 13,000 to 20,000 feet and used their extremely accurate Norden bomb sights to hit the targets, but the bombardier had to pick up his target at least six miles; therefore, in the early part of the campaign visibility was the key. The American medium bombers, usually B-26s of the Ninth Air Force and British B-25s from various organizations in AEAF, bombed in boxes of 12 to 18 aircraft at altitudes between 10,000 and 12,000 feet, although they sometimes went as low as 5,000 feet to see their targets and assess bomb damage as they left the target area.

The British pilots of the 2nd TAC used extreme low-level attacks to hit the sites. Flying just above the waves in complete radio silence, they crossed the coast of France below the effective altitude of German

A meeting of Germany's early rocket pioneers, including Rudolph Nebel at left, Hermann Oberth, to the right of the rocket, Klaus Riedel, holding the small rocket, and behind him the dapper young Wernher von Braun.

After the rise of Hitler, von Braun found himself with a new circle of acquaintances, as well as a new research facility at Peenemünde.

Throughout 1942 the Germans attempted to perfect the A-4 rocket, later to be known as the V-2. The majority of tests during this early period met with disappointing results, as below.

Although it started later, the Luftwaffe was able to deploy the Fiesler 103, later to be known as the V-1, before the Army could field the V-2. A simpler machine, the Fi 103 was launched from catapults aligned on its target.

As the A-4 neared completion, the SS maneuvered to take control of the weapon from the German Army. Below, an obviously impressed Heinrich Himmler, standing next to Walter Dornberger, makes his first visit to Peenemünde in April 1943.

A vast factory complex called the Mittelwerk was constructed in the Harz Mountains to conceal and protect rocket production from Allied bombers. Below, a view of one of the underground galleries.

Oberst Max Wachtel, the commander of Flak Regiment 155(W), which fired the V-1s. Below, Wachtel inspects a flying bomb that is ready to be launched.

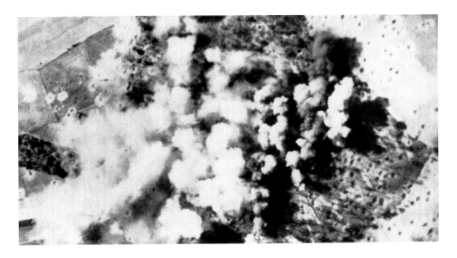

Allied intelligence was able to identify the "ski sites" originally designed to launch the V-1. While Operation Crossbow unleashed thousands of bombers against the sites, the Germans meanwhile switched to more flexible, and inconspicuous, launch methods.

The gigantic V-2 storage bunker at Wizernes, France after absorbing 14 Allied air attacks. Today the bunker is a museum run by the French government called La Coupole. It contains originals of the V-1 and V-2 and also celebrates space travel.

Once the SS had muscled its way into the rocket program, Obergruppenführer Hans Kammler was placed in charge of the combined V-1/V-2 offensive.

A V-2 supply train.

Carefully considered German camouflage schemes were designed to conceal the weapons among trees.

The Meilerwagen provided a mobile launch platform for the V-2.

Some V-1s were air-launched by He-111 bombers in order to flank fixed Allied defenses.

A V-1 descends on London.

Devastation caused by V-weapons in Antwerp.

In Antwerp, a British vehicle is caught in a blast.

Below, the result of a V-2 explosion.

American Engineer casualties after a V-weapon attack on Antwerp.

General Carl Gray greets two soldiers from his hometown of St. Paul, Minnesota after dedication of a locomotive to Private H.J. O'Brien, killed in Antwerp by a V-weapon.

Damage caused by V-weapons to the main railroad station in Liège.

A V-1 makes a
direct hit on
the Antwerp
docks.

A U.S. officer injured by a V-weapon blast in Antwerp.

Another scene from "The City of Sudden Death."

Walter Dornberger, Wernher von Braun (in cast) and other scientists after surrendering to the U.S. Seventh Army in May 1945.

Below, in May 1946, the Americans fire off a captured V-2 at the White Sands proving ground in New Mexico.

radar. Avoiding known flak concentrations they hit the sites at high speed with great accuracy and were gone before the Germans could react. This method of attack required great skill; any mistake flying at treetop level at high speed meant a fatal crash.

At the beginning of 1944, the British and Americans looked across the English Channel with reserved optimism. They had driven the enemy from North Africa and knocked Italy out of the war, but Germany still held most of Europe and was far from beaten. The invasion of France that planners were finalizing would not be easy. On January 1, 1944 the JIC Crossbow subcommittee revised its pessimistic assessment of the potential of the Fi 103 and indicated that the Germans would not be able to launch it in January. They were unsure which type of engine powered the Fi 103, but they remained highly skeptical of reports that it was rocket propelled. Therefore the committee could not make a precise assessment of the warhead, which could be as heavy as 1.8 tons if the Fi 103 was powered by a turbojet. The latest estimate stated that the Germans could launch from 75 sites by late February or from 150 by late March.[11]

Allied superiority in the air was growing, yet the United Kingdom was bracing for an assault by weapons that had never been fired, because the leaders of Great Britain were not about to allow civilians to suffer through another bombing attack like the Blitz of 1940. The threatened German invasion of 1940 had been thwarted by the British victory in the Battle of Britain, but the Luftwaffe had continued to carry out raids against targets in England. Thus, the threat for the British was real and immediate. They continued to press for attacks on the launch sites, going so far as to recommend that 10 percent of the tactical aircraft assigned to the invasion be devoted to hitting launch sites until D-Day.[12] On the other hand, Americans viewed the German secret weapons as a potential threat to Overlord, the planned invasion of the Continent.

The overall assessment by the Allies was that the raids in December were a success, and they were scheduled to continue. Analyzing Photo Reconnaissance Unit (PRU) photographs in early December, the Central Interpretation Unit (CIU) identified 64 sites, of which 27 were close to completion. These sites were scheduled for the first attacks in January. The Ninth Air Force alone had flown six raids with 531 bombers and struck 21 of the sites on the target list, but the threat remained. By Christmas, CIU identified 75 sites, of which 54 were near completion. The number continued to rise and by January 8 there were 88 sites, 79 of which were near enough to completion to pose an immediate threat.[13] The first attack of the new year occurred on January 1, 1944 when 253 Ninth Air Force B-26 Marauders took off to bomb ski sites along the French coast. Once again weather proved to be a major obstacle and the results of the raid were disappointing.

During the month of January, ski sites became the sole mission of the Ninth Air Force, and of the 1,146 sorties that took off from their airfields, 802 actually reached the target. Unable to bomb targets in Germany due to bad weather, the Eighth Air Force added its weight to the attacks near the French coast. In January it launched large raids on four days for a total of 1,444 sorties, 1,034 of which found their targets. In some cases the heavy bombers tried bombing sites obscured by clouds with the new Gee-H blind-bombing device, although with indifferent results.

The RAF 2nd Tactical Air Force continued its low-level attacks and achieved better results per raid than either the medium or heavy bombers, but with increasingly higher losses. The Germans not only increased the number of guns around each site but changed their position so that aircraft using aerial reconnaissance photographs to circumvent German Flak positions often ran straight into the defenses they were trying to avoid. Despite reports of heavy damage, the number of sites continued to grow. On January 30, 1944, CIU reported 97 sites under construction, with 95 so close to becoming operational that they were designated primary targets.

The problem posed to the British by the Fi 103 and the A-4 was further complicated by the fact they clearly needed American help in dealing with the threat. Not only did they need American aircraft to assist in bombing the large sites and the ski sites, but they also needed new radar equipment and proximity fuses for their antiaircraft artillery units. American antiaircraft radar sets were much better than the available British ones, and while the proximity fuse was a British invention, only the Americans had succeeded in mass-producing it. However, many British officials were reluctant to give their ally the full story. This resulted partly from a desire to protect sensitive intelligence as well as from some natural xenophobia. The lack of shared information generated a great deal of American skepticism about the new German weapons. Thanks to the friendship between Roosevelt and Churchill, the Americans were eventually informed of the new weapons' potential.

On December 20, 1943, the U.S. Joint Chiefs of Staff began a survey titled Implications of Recent Intelligence Regarding Alleged German Secret Weapons. The title reflects the skepticism with which some American officers viewed the entire subject. Lt. General Carl R. Spaatz, who commanded the United States Strategic Air Forces in Europe (USSTAF), thought the ski sites were nothing more than an "inspired German feint."[14] Two days later, General George C. Marshall, the U.S. Army Chief of Staff, directed Lt. General Jacob L. Devers, commanding general of European Theater of Operations, United States Army (ETOUSA), to report on existing British countermeasures.

The response was immediate and Devers briefed Marshall on the information available and sent a courier with copies of plans of the ski sites to Washington that very night. At Marshall's behest, Secretary of War Henry L. Stimson established what amounted to an American Crossbow committee under the direction of Major General Stephen G. Henry, director of the War Department's New Developments Division. Henry was instructed to coordinate with all American services and the British to find a timely solution to the new weapons. The British were still reluctant to share all the available information with their Allies and it took a strongly worded note from Marshall to Field Marshal John Dill, chief of the British Joint Staff Mission to the United States and senior British member of the Combined Chiefs of Staff, before the American were satisfied.[15]

Concerned that the Germans would deploy the new weapons just in time to thwart Overlord, the Americans openly considered changes to the plan to minimize the damage the German weapons might cause. Lt. General Morgan, COSSAC, gave an appreciation of the threat in mid-December 1943 in which he considered any appreciable change in the Overlord plan impractical, but warned that the German weapons could prejudice an assault mounted from the southern coast of England. The American reaction to the threat was to use the "worst case" scenario, which was particularly depressing in its consideration that the Germans might use gas, biological weapons or even explosives of a new and "unusually violent character," which was probably a euphemism for an atomic bomb.

The Joint Chiefs of Staff directed the Supreme Commander, General Dwight D. Eisenhower, to prepare for the possibility of gas or biological attack, but suggestions for either a gas attack or ground attack against the ski sites were dismissed. There was no choice but to continue Crossbow air operations against the sites in France and the Americans felt that this could be done a great deal more scientifically.

General Henry "Hap" Arnold, Commanding General Army Air Forces, felt that there had been too much guesswork in the previous attacks on the sites in France and was positive that low-altitude attacks could achieve better results. To see if he was right, he decided to conduct a practical test. On January 12, 1944, Marshall approved the suggestion of the War Department committee investigating the German weapons that the Army Air Forces be given as a task of the highest priority a "technical and tactical inquiry into the means, methods and effectiveness of air attacks against Crossbow targets in France."[16] The original intention was to conduct the tests close to the actual theater of operations, but the decision was made to conduct the tests at the Army Air Forces Proving Ground at Eglin Field in Florida.

On the morning of January 25, Arnold telephoned Brigadier General Grandison Gardner, the commander, to direct him to conduct the tests. At first, Arnold's language was circumspect, but then the urgency of the situation became evident. "I want some buildings reproduced. I want to make simulated attacks with a new weapon. I want the job done in days not weeks. It will take a hell of a lot of concrete . . . give it first priority and complete it in days—weeks are too long."[17]

Despite shortages in labor and building materials, Gardner mobilized the full resources of the proving ground, doing nothing less than reproducing a ski site in the pine barrens of the Florida panhandle in the minutest detail. Purchasing agents roved the countryside for hundreds of miles hiring contractors and buying materials, thus by-passing the red tape normally required for such an enterprise. While construction materials poured in by truck, train and airplane, army and civilian engineers and laborers worked twelve-hour shifts to construct the critical buildings of the ski site in less time than the Germans had been able to build one. Before the concrete was dry, Army Ground

Forces sent in an antiaircraft battalion and a camouflage unit to prepare the site.

In mid-February the test attacks began, with Gardner reporting to Arnold daily. On February 19, 1944, Arnold brought Air Marshal Sir Norman Bottomley, who was Deputy Chief of the Air Staff, and Air Vice-Marshal Frank Inglis, Assistant Chief of the Air Staff (Intelligence), to personally observe the tests in progress. The grueling and rigorous tests were carried out with live ammunition in as near to combat conditions as possible. High-, low- and medium-altitude attacks were carried out with every type of ordnance then available. What the pilots at Eglin did not have to face were the expert Flak gunners of the Luftwaffe—something with which the British had already had considerable experience. At the end of February Gardner was convinced he had tested every possible option and submitted a final report on March 1. The exhaustive tests confirmed beyond any doubt that "minimum-altitude attacks by fighters, if properly delivered, were the most effective and economical aerial countermeasures against ski sites."[18] The findings reflected the unanimous opinion of Arnold, the U.S. War Department Crossbow committee and the American Air Commanders currently in England.

The test results brought a sense of relief to the Americans. Medium- and high-altitude bombing was the least effective form of attack and meant that these air assets would not have to be diverted from the ongoing Operation Pointblank, the Allied air operation designed to sweep the Luftwaffe from the air by April 1, 1944. Armed with the results of the Eglin tests, a group of officers headed by Brigadier General Gardner traveled to England to present his findings to Eisenhower, ETOUSA and American and British air commanders. While American generals Carl R. Spaatz, Hoyt Vandenberg and Lewis Brereton strongly supported the low-altitude attack proposal, the British, predictably, were against it.

Air Marshal Sir Trafford Leigh-Mallory was particularly opposed to the idea. During the early days of the Crossbow air campaign, the Royal Air Force had tried fighter attacks and had found them too costly for the results obtained. On March 4 he wrote to Spaatz, "I think it is clear now that the best weapon for the rocket sites is the high altitude bomber."[19] Leigh-Mallory also drew on a Combined Chiefs of Staff Directive to support his position. Dated February 13, 1944, the directive listed Crossbow targets as the second priority for heavy bombers, and Leigh-Mallory wrote to Arnold late in March, "I feel certain we must continue to rely on the Heavies."[20] The British also voiced skepticism concerning the way the tests were conducted at Eglin, stating that the American version of the ski site was much better constructed than the actual version; in addition, they disputed the American contention that 1,000- and 2,000-pound bombs delivered at low altitude with delay fuses were better than the 250- and 500-pound general purpose bombs then in use against the ski sites.

To the Americans the British logic was curious and they were unable to understand their ally's position. It was in fact a simple matter of combat experience versus a well-conducted test, the only unrealistic aspect of which was the lack of live German gunners firing back. The Americans, who had already flown combat missions but did not have the long-term combat experience of their allies, were not able to understand that one of the primary British concerns was their critical shortage of manpower; therefore they were unwilling to face the high losses that experience showed might occur in low-level attacks. Eisenhower was inclined to side with his countrymen, but he was a coalition commander dealing with an ally who had been in the war far longer, so he conceded the point to Leigh-Mallory and approved the continuation of the policy of using heavy bombers to attack the ski sites. Nevertheless, Americans air commanders refused to take no for an answer. They were still concerned about the diversion of high-level bombers from Pointblank and did not give up on using fighters to bomb the ski sites.

While the U.S. Army Air Force and the Royal Air Force argued over the best way to attack the ski sites, Air Marshal Roderic Hill, commander of Air Defence Great Britain (ADGB), and his chief subordinate, Lt. Gen. Sir Frederick Pile, commander of Britain's antiaircraft troops, were determined to use their own means to prevent the flying bomb from reaching London or any other target in England. Based on the Air Staff estimates that the flying bomb had a speed of 330 miles per hour and an altitude of 6,000 feet, Hill, in coordination with Pile, formulated his first plan in December 1943 and presented it on January 2, 1944. It called for a defense-in-depth that relied on early warning by radar and observers of an imminent attack.

On first alert, one group of fighters was to be launched to patrol twenty miles from the English south coast between South Foreland and Beachy Head at an altitude of 12,000 feet. When the flying bombs were spotted, a second group of fighters was to be launched to patrol the same area at 6,000 feet and shoot them down. For the flying bombs that got through the fighters, "Hill and Pile proposed to deploy 400 heavy and 346 light antiaircraft guns and 216 searchlights immediately south of London; a further 96 heavy guns and 216 light guns and 132 searchlights near Bristol, which was threatened by the sites near Cherbourg; and 32 heavy and 242 light guns, with a smaller number of searchlights, round the Solent, where there were several likely targets. As a further line of defense for London, 480 barrage balloons would fly at all hours of the day and night above the belt of high ground between Cobham, Kent and Limpsfield, Surry."[21] Hill also asked the Air Ministry to keep him informed of any progress made in the efforts to jam the flying bomb's signal should it be found to be remote controlled or to create a magnetic field to upset the flying bomb's magnetic compass and make it veer off-course.

Pile first learned about the flying bomb at the end of October 1943 while he was having lunch with Churchill, Beaverbrook, Cherwell and Sandys. The antiaircraft commander thought they would not be much of a problem "because with the Air Force that we had we ought to be able to bomb it out of existence in a very short time."[22] Without being alarmist, Churchill informed Pile in no uncertain terms that dealing with the flying bomb wouldn't be that easy and Pile took the admonition to heart.

On the surface, to the air defense chief, the flying bomb did not appear to be a great challenge. The Fi 103 flew at a constant altitude at a constant speed on a straight and level course: the ideal situation for antiaircraft gunners. Had the Fi 103 been a manned aircraft, the situation would have been little different from the Battle of Britain and the Blitz, but in the end the fact that they were not dealing with a manned aircraft changed the way the target had to be engaged and forced the defense to adopt much more sophisticated methods of target detection and tracking.

The Fi 103 was a very small target. It had a wingspan one-fourth that of the He 111 bomber and nearly half that of the Fw 190 fighter, and it was only marginally slower than the latest Allied piston-engine

fighters. Mechanically, it had a much simpler engine and fewer working parts than manned aircraft and was, therefore, less susceptible to
damage. The Fi 103 also gave the defenders much less time to react. It
left the launcher and flew straight to the target without having to
climb to altitude and check its formation, so the defenses had little
more than twenty minutes from launch to impact. As an unmanned
aircraft the Fi 103 was not restricted by the lack of daylight. While
high winds might blow it off course, it was not restricted by rain and
other bad weather that constrained the operations of manned aircraft.
In fact, bad weather was an excellent cover for the Fi 103. Perhaps the
most disagreeable aspect of the unmanned flying bomb was that after
it was hit it remained a bomb. Once it was damaged, there was no one
on board to keep the aircraft level while the crew bailed out or who
might try to return to base with an aircraft that could be repaired. As
soon as it was no longer airworthy, the flying bomb fell to earth to
explode wherever it crashed. Because "shooting down" or "damaging" no longer sufficed, Pile's gunners needed equipment that allowed
them to detect, engage and destroy an approaching aircraft in less time
than any antiaircraft gunners in history.

Since the Fi 103 had to be engaged within seconds, the gunners
had to have a gun with power traverse and elevation that was directed by radar—something the British antiaircraft forces didn't have. The
primary British antiaircraft weapon for medium- to high-altitude targets was the 3.7 inch (94mm) gun, which came in permanent and
mobile configurations. All of the guns on permanent mounts had
power traverse and elevation, while very few of the mobile guns did.
As field weapons the majority were still hand-operated. None of the
British guns had radar direction. However, it was not just the Fi 103
that was causing Pile's gunners trouble. The Germans had resumed
carrying out air raids on England during January 1944 and they were
successfully using "Window"—strips of aluminum foil dropped before
an air raid to confuse enemy radar. This was particularly galling to the
British, who had invented it.

The answer to Pile's problems of directing the guns was the
American S.C.R. 584 radar, the one used on the American 90mm antiaircraft gun, which had power elevation and traverse and an automatic fuse setter. The S.C.R. 584 was a gun-laying radar and "the
most successful single application of the micro-wave ten-centimeter

technique to ground fighting in World War II. It could automatically track an unseen target at night or in cloud or fog, supplying range, azimuth and elevation data to a gun director."[23] The S.C.R. 684 had a range of 90,000 yards for early warning, and as a target got within 32,000 yards the set acted as a gun layer. It had no blind spots and could detect low-flying targets like the Fi 103. Unlike the British radar sets, it was also immune to Window. However, it was a complex piece of electronic equipment and required a number of scarce materials like tantalum, molybdenum and tungsten, as well as 140 vacuum tubes which were then in short supply in the United States. The fielded version weighed several tons and cost $100,000.

Pile initially requested 134 of them, which he called "amazing instruments," and eventually hoped to get 430 of them. The first contract for the S.C.R. 584 called for the production of 2,750 sets, which meant that Pile was requesting over 15 percent of the initial output. As might be expected, Cherwell was opposed to additional expenditure for antiaircraft equipment because he considered bombers essential. After listening to Pile's reasoning behind the request, Churchill ordered the war office to do everything it could to obtain the S.C.R. 584. Pile considered Churchill's decision of great importance and later wrote, "Without this equipment it would have been impossible to defeat the flying bomb."[24]

Guns were not the only British equipment that needed radar. From early in the war, searchlights had been radar directed. Unlike modern radar sets, which are better than lights at night, the radar of the 1940s had severe limitations. Electronically it was frustratingly low and not very precise, so at night the best way to mark an enemy aircraft was by triangulation with lights. By 1944, as the "Elsie" radar used early in the war was becoming increasingly ineffective due to the German use of Window, Pile also needed a new radar to enable his gunners to coordinate with night fighters. The British had the S.L.C. 9X, which was good for both applications but not in adequate numbers. The need to destroy the target rather than damage it also meant that the British needed proximity fuses for their shells. The proximity fuse had a small transceiver that detonated the shell whenever it came within a set distance from the target. Prior to the invention of the proximity fuse, antiaircraft shells had time fuses. The time on the fuses was set in accordance with the time of flight of the projectile needed to reach the range and altitude of the enemy formation. Thus, improperly timed projectiles would explode before reaching the formation or pass through it without exploding. The proximity fuse was a British invention but they were unable to mass-produce it. The Americans did so, and used proximity fuses for both antiaircraft and field artillery, eventually supplying them to their allies.

On February 2, 1944, the Chiefs of Staff for the Defence Committee used new estimates to determine the timing and scale of the missile threat. Their estimates indicated that the warhead weighed approximately one ton and that an initial attack could begin as early as mid-March, with the Germans capable of delivering 400 tons of explosive in a ten-hour period—a rate that approximated the level of the German bombing raids of April–May 1941. The estimates were discussed before the Defence Committee the following day, but no judgment could be reached because the weight of the warhead remained unknown. Early in February, CIU at Medmenham discovered the Germans' eight supply sites for the Fi 103, each of which was heavily defended by antiaircraft guns. These were not immediately chosen as targets, while the Allies stepped up the intensity of their raids on other sites.

During the month, the Ninth Air Force made twelve attacks with a total of 2,311 aircraft, 2,177 of which reached and bombed their assigned targets and also carried out smaller diversionary raids on German airfields. These raids represented the entire bombing effort of the Ninth Air Force during the month. The Eighth Air Force was also hard at work. During the month, 1,341 heavy bombers, out of 1,741 dispatched, located and bombed launch sites along the French coast. At this time the attacks on the ski sites seemed to be going well and the threat from the flying bomb appeared to be much less than originally anticipated. Accordingly, Air Vice-Marshal Roderic Hill was asked to revise his plan for the defense of Great Britain in order to release as many antiaircraft guns and searchlights as possible to the invasion forces. The revised plan called for the eventual reduction of the guns south of London to 192 heavy and 246 light,[25] a reduction of 52 percent and 29 percent, respectively. In Bristol, heavy guns remained untouched, but the light guns were to be reduced from 216 to 36. The number of guns around the Solent was not changed. If needed, there was a considerable number of antiaircraft units assembling in the area for the invasion.

Hill submitted the revised plan for the reductions in guns to Leigh-Mallory at the end of February. He included in it a proviso that allowed the number of guns for defense to be increased if necessary, and he also warned that the gunners would face a difficult challenge if the Fi 103 flew at an altitude of 2,000 to 3,000 feet rather than the 6,000 feet predicted by the Air Staff because they would be too low for efficient engagement by the heavy guns and too high for the lights.[26]

During the month of February 1944, the Special Intelligence Service received an increasing number of reports from its agents in France concerning peculiar construction going on at places other than the ski sites. Some of the reports indicated that these were new sites, very different from the ski sites but still designed to launch the flying bomb. The overall evidence was that 120 of the new sites would by ready at the end of May. The fact that the new sites were far less substantial than the ski sites was taken as an indication that the bombing campaign was working.

By the first week in March, photo reconnaissance was showing that the bombing was producing positive results. The CIU was still unsure of the exact number of sites and thought there might be as many as 120. Of the 96 sites identified, 54 had suffered major damage but only nine were under repair. Thirty-one of the damaged sites showed no signs of repair work at all. [27] By March 16, no further sites had been located and the total was estimated to be 100. At this time the Air Ministry gave the Chiefs of Staff a revised estimate that the number of sites intact on April 1 would be about 8. At worst, 10 sites would be ready by April 15, so that the Germans would be unable to deliver more than 160 tons of explosive in a 12-hour period—and this only at 48-hour intervals. The one unpleasant piece of news during this period was that the plots of the Fi 103 fired along the Baltic coast were becoming more accurate and the Germans had gone from firing five flying bombs every two days in January to firing nine by the end of March. By that time it was estimated that 60 percent of the flying bombs would hit London as opposed to the 33 percent that would have hit in December.

Allied raids continued into March. The Ninth Air Force sent out missions totaling 2,040 bombers, 1,653 of which reached their targets.

During the month, all but four of the raids carried out by the Ninth Air Force were directed against Fi 103 installations. The Eighth Air Force flew Crossbow missions on seven days for a total of 1,136 B-17 Flying Fortresses and B-24 Liberator sorties, which dropped bombs on designated sites along the coast of France. As of March 17, the Allies had dropped 2,500 tons of bombs on the larger sites in thirty raids. Photo reconnaissance estimates indicated that Martinvast would take three months to repair and Lottingheim would take between a month and a half and three months to repair. The damage to Siracourt and Sottevaste would take two to six weeks. Watten, Wizernes and Mimoyecques escaped serious damage, and at this time it became evident that Mimoyecques was being developed along different lines than the other sites. It had two tunnels and a SIS agent reported that "a concrete chamber was to be built near one of the tunnels for the installation of a tube, 40 to 50 metres long which he referred to as a 'rocket launching cannon.'"[28] The report was basically correct because the Mimoyecques site was under construction for the "Hochdruckpumpe" or high-pressure pump gun known sometimes as V-3.

The weather closed in on March 27 and the medium bombers were not able to fly another mission until April. Since other agents had also reported rocket-firing guns, and British scientists continued to assume that the A-4 had to be launched from a projector, the results of this information strengthened the association of the sites with the rocket in British eyes. As a consequence the Air Chief of Staff for Intelligence forwarded the photo reconnaissance information for Mimoyecques with a note that "the nature of the works supports the statement put forward in a recent intelligence report that they may be intended for the launching of a large rocket."[29]

On March 21, 1944 the Chiefs of Staff discussed the lack of information on the sites and Duncan Sandys pressed for a greater effort. R.V. Jones told them that they were already high-priority intelligence targets, but that there was little information available because the Germans were not using foreign labor, a main source of data. Sandys had already suggested a special operation to capture a German technician from one of the sites, and on February 8 the Chiefs of Staff approved the idea. Air Intelligence Branch of the Air Ministry briefed the Special Operations Executive and gave them the names of five Germans who were suitable targets. An SOE agent began a search on

March 19, locating one of the men in April, but was unable to capture him.[30]

Since October 1943, the Polish underground in the Blizna area had been a valuable source of information concerning the A-4 and the Fi 103. In December the Poles reported the Germans evacuating villages and building a railroad to Lemberg (Lwow) and sent a photograph of an A-4 in flight. In February two additional Polish reports indicated rocket dimensions that were very close to the dimension noted on photographs taken of rockets at Peenemünde. These reports also indicated weights that were much lighter than previous agents' reports. The rocket was 12 to 14 meters tall, a meter and a half in diameter. It weighed 11 to 12 tons with a one- to two-ton warhead.[31] The Poles observed a number of firings between November 29, 1943 and January 17, 1944, but it is not clear which of these were A-4 firings and which were Fi 103. They observed some firings from as close as a kilometer and a half from the "projector," which they described as rails mounted on a lattice construction set at angle of 45 degrees. This probably meant the launching of an Fi 103.

The Poles heard some firings from ten kilometers away and described a missile that was launched with a loud roar and trailed a stream of fire and smoke. The missile stayed vertical until it reached 1,000 meters in altitude, then changed trajectory. The Polish reports also mentioned tank cars full of liquid air. Two Enigma decrypts of SS messages sent in March 1944 lent further weight to the Polish reports. The messages exchanged between Heidelager and Peenemünde, with copies furnished to SS officer Hans Kammler in Berlin, discussed the construction at Heidelager being delayed because of the German Army's "secret command project."[32] While the information was confusing, one thing was certain: the A-4 was not ready for deployment.

With news that the ski sites were badly damaged and the invasion imminent, Allied target priorities shifted. The bombardment of enemy tactical targets in the area of the planned invasion required a maximum effort during April and May if the invasion were to succeed. Accordingly, on March 4, 1944 the medium bombers of Ninth Air Force were assigned Overlord targets as their first priority. However, photo reconnaissance of Crossbow targets did not lessen. The Allied planners determined that 61 of the 97 identified sites had been destroyed or suffered major damage. Supreme Headquarters Allied

Expeditionary Forces noted in March that the pilotless aircraft threat was one of the smaller hazards of the war to which Overlord was vulnerable.[33] As the frequency of air attacks against all the sites lessened, the Germans appeared to increase their repair efforts and Air Intelligence estimated that they might have as many as 41 sites operational at the end of the month, with several more coming on line.

This estimate was lowered to 25 by the middle of April, but it was still unacceptable. On April 17 the War Cabinet "pressed for an intensification of the attack, and the next day the Chiefs of Staff agreed that it had become a matter of urgency to neutralize the threat at once so as to avoid the need to divert forces during Operation Overlord, when the situation might be more critical."[34] Eisenhower acceded to the wishes of the War Cabinet, and on April 19 Air Marshal Tedder informed Spaatz that for the time being Crossbow missions had priority over all others. This decision was met with grave concern at Army Air Force Headquarters. They complained that Crossbow had grown out of all proportion to the seriousness of the threat and complained that it was "so uneconomical 'as to be wasteful, and should be curtailed.'"[35]

The headquarters also was of the opinion that the resources absorbed by Crossbow missions could make the difference between success and failure in Overlord. While the Ninth Air Force directed the majority of its efforts at attacking airfields, bridges and marshaling yards, it still found time to launch six strikes totaling 1,852 aircraft at ski sites during April. The Eighth Air Force contributed heavily in April, directing 1,649 heavy bombers in seven different raids against the launch sites. At the end of April, photo reconnaissance showed that construction was continuing on the large sites at Sottevaste, Siracourt and Mimoyecques, but that it had ceased at Martinvast and Lottingheim. At Watten, bomb-damaged buildings were not being repaired but a new building was nearing completion, as was a large domelike structure which was supposed to be a bomb-proof cover. At the working sites the antiaircraft defenses had increased. Once again heavy raids were directed against the large sites.

The first eyewitness account of the flying bomb in flight was obtained by the Naval Intelligence Division of the Royal Navy from the naval attaché in Stockholm on April 16, 1944. On March 15, the captain of a freighter had witnessed two Fi 103s that had been fired from a shore installation some ten miles from his ship. The captain reported that they were the size of a small fighter, had short camouflaged wings and were "propelled at very high speed by a rocket tube which gave approximately 300 detonations a minute. . . . Each detonation appeared to give two flashes in the form of a ring." Needless to say, the report caused a number of questions concerning the time between launches; the exact location of the "rocket motor" (was it above or below the fuselage?); whether or not there were actually a series of explosions or a rumbling sound; and how were the explosions counted. The questions were answered by the attaché on April 24 and, from hindsight, it is obvious the captain of the vessel observed the flight of two Fi 103s and accurately counted the explosions using the master's watch. However, little use could be made of this information at the time it was obtained, because so little was known about the design of the flying bomb.[36]

On April 27, 1944, Robert Rowell of the CIU was examining the latest reconnaissance photos of the Cherbourg peninsula when he suddenly gasped. Near the village of Belhamelin he found a long concrete pad with pairs of studs embedded in it, constructed between two farm buildings. A short distance away was a well-camouflaged square building. These were the two essential constructions required for a launching site, but there were no large concrete buildings and no ski-shaped storage buildings. It was obviously a new type of launching site, designed to be as unobtrusive as possible. In the words of one member of the CIU: "the Germans had evidently learned their lesson over the ski sites, and had made new plans with Allied interpreters as well as Allied bombing in mind. The new sites were horribly difficult to spot, but within a few days twelve had been identified."[37]

By the middle of May the list of new "modified sites" was growing rapidly and to Allied intelligence officers it was an ominous development. The headquarters of the Allied Expeditionary Air Force (AEAF) took little notice of them, however. In fairness to Leigh-Mallory and the officers of AEAF, they were planning for Overlord and had time for little else. There was also the attitude that the modified sites were less efficient that the concrete ski sites and were less of a threat. Air Marshal Harris was probably typical when he wrote, "By forcing the enemy to abandon his first method of launching [the ski sites] . . . the enemy was compelled to use a much less efficient form of temporary site."[38] Harris' deputy, Air Marshal Sir Robert Saunby, expressed a similar opinion: "Instead of the hundreds a day which the ski sites were designed to operate, the modified sites, with an energetic and well trained crew, could expect to launch one flying bomb every half hour."[39] The statement is even more fantastic considering that even the lowest rate of fire Saunby suggested was far beyond anything Wachtel's troops could manage.

A third excuse for not attacking the modified sites was that they were difficult targets to find and damage. This one was offered after the fact and really makes little sense, considering the defenses of the ski sites in some areas. The discovery of the modified sites also brought up the discussion that the ski sites were, in reality, dummies designed to mislead the Allied air effort. In the long run they did turn out to be dummies, but this was never the original intention, and Cherwell's suggestion on January 18, 1944 that the ski sites were dummies was wrong. On January 22 and on February 5, photo reconnaissance demonstrated that they were genuine.[40]

As soon as the first of the modified sites was discovered, another huge Allied photo reconnaissance mission was set into motion. Aircraft from "No. 106 Squadron of the RAF at Benson, the Tactical Reconnaissance Squadron of the RAF 2nd Tactical Air Force, the Strategical Squadrons of the American 7th Photo Group and the Tactical Reconnaissance squadrons of Ninth Air Force once again set about covering the whole of northern France within range of London and the area of the Cherbourg peninsula within range of Bristol."[41] By May 2, CIU had identified only five of the new sites and three of these were on the Cherbourg peninsula. However, between May 2 and June 7, CIU interpreters identified 38 north of the Somme River, 20 in the Cherbourg peninsula and three in Calvados: a total of 61 sites. Agents of the SIS also reported 100 such sites and 31 of these were later confirmed by photo reconnaissance.[42] Due to the fact that none of the new sites were complete, it was impossible for CIU to determine their ultimate configuration. It was obvious, then, that the sites were more than a mere expedient.

It appeared that the Allies had been duped into bombing the fixed sites while the Germans built modified ones. In addition, the first attack against one of the new sites, by low-flying Hawker Typhoon fighter bombers, proved difficult and unsuccessful. The attack had to be delivered against the launch rail itself. This involved hitting a target that was 250 feet long and 12 feet wide, was usually situated in a grove of trees and which had its approaches covered by multiple flak guns. It was a daunting task at best, and the new sites proved very resistant to attack. Even as the Allies discovered and attacked more of the modified sites, the launch teams were preparing for action.

In May, the Americans tried one more time to get the British to agree that a low-altitude attack with fighter bombers was the most efficient way to attack the ski sites. On May 6, Spaatz informed Arnold of a low-altitude attack carried out by the 365th Fighter Group. "After intensive briefing by Eglin Field officers, four fighter pilots attacked four ski sites with P-47s carrying two 1,000-pound delayed-fuse SAP [semi-armor piercing] bombs. Though very heavy machine-gun fire was encountered at each site, three of the four attacking P-47s achieved Category A damage (sufficient to neutralize a site for several months), with no loss of aircraft."[43]

These were excellent results despite the fact that the Eglin tests showed the P-38 and not the P-47 was the best aircraft for this type of mission. Thus the fighters achieved Category A damage at the cost of one ton of bombs per site as opposed to the expenditure of 1,947 tons per site expended by heavy bombers. General Doolittle thought the British Mosquito the best aircraft and wrote to Arnold that they "achieved the highest degree of damage with less tonnage, fewer attacking sorties, and fewer losses than any other type of aircraft."[44] Though the British conceded that the Eglin method worked and used the system themselves on occasion, they continued to insist on the use of heavy and medium bombers to attack the ski sites.

With Overlord drawing near, Allied bombers continued to attack Crossbow targets in May 1944. On May 9, 40 B-26s of Ninth Air Force carried out an attack against the sites at Beauvoir. They experienced intense antiaircraft fire in spite of the fact they used "Window" to confuse enemy radar. The pilots reported that the Flak was so severe and erupted so suddenly that there were several near-collisions among aircraft taking evasive action. Nineteen of the forty aircraft participating in the raid were damaged, four so severely they had to land at forward bases in England instead of their home fields. Eighth Air Force contributed 800 sorties, which dropped a total of 2,600 tons of bombs chiefly on the large sites; AEAF flew 3,800 sorties, dropping

2,000 tons. RAF Bomber Command was conspicuously absent in May due to the need to stand down after suffering particularly heavy losses during Pointblank raids over Germany. From January to April 1944, RAF Bomber Command suffered at least 2,729 aircraft shot down or damaged, with a loss of thousands of aircrew.[45]

At the end of May, the Allies got their first look at the Fi 103 when British experts were allowed to examine the wreckage of two flying bombs that had crashed in Swedish territory. One had been recovered from the Baltic by the Swedish Navy and the other had crashed in Sweden on May 13. The experts found that it was a midwing monoplane with a wingspan of 16 feet, made mostly of steel. Powered by a pulse jet that used low-grade aviation fuel, it was controlled in flight by a rudder and two elevators. This finally put to rest the theory that it was powered by a hydrogen peroxide rocket. Little could be learned about the guidance system other than it had three gyroscopes and was directed by a compass rather than by radio control. Nothing could be learned about the actual warhead since both were fitted with dummies. The flying bomb was definitely designed for mass production. This information was reported to the Air Ministry on June 8 and to the Chiefs of Staff the following day. What amounted to an intelligence coup, however, was overcome by events a few days later when the flying bomb offensive against England began.

From June 4 to 10, Crossbow photo reconnaissance flights were canceled due to Overlord requirements and the weather. When they resumed on the 11th, activity was reported at modified sites in the Pas de Calais area. At several of the sites the square building had been erected and some showed that rails had been installed on the launchers. A reliable SIS agent in Belgium reported a train of 33 cars, each loaded with three "rockets," that passed through Ghent on its way to France and that more trains were expected. Air Intelligence reported to the Chiefs of Staff on June 12 that as many as 42 sites in the Pas de Calais might be ready to launch flying bombs. The report concluded that "the indications are the Germans are making energetic preparations to bring the pilotless aircraft sites into operation at an early date."[46]

As late as June 2, 1944, just four days before D-Day, 633 B-17s and 293 B-24s of the Eighth Air Force attacked ski sites in the Pas de Calais. By this time Allied air forces had caused Category A damage to 107 ski sites. An analysis by the USAAF showed that the Eighth Air Force accounted for 35 sites, the Ninth Air Force for 39 and British units of AEAF for 33. The average bomb load per damaged site varied by aircraft. For heavy bombers the B-17s expended 195.1 tons per aircraft per target destroyed and for B-24s it was 401.4 tons. For the medium bombers it was 223.5 tons per aircraft per target, while the B-25s expended 244 and the A-20s 313. Attacks by fighters and fighter bombers verified the Eglin tests. The Mosquitos led with 39.8 tons per aircraft per target, and the Spitfires 50.3.

Between December 1943 and June 1944 the Allied air forces had expended 36,200 tons of bombs in 25,150 bombing sorties, a greater effort than that expended on any single enemy target up to that time in the war. RAF Bomber Command contributed little to the effort due to its commitment to Pointblank. The cost to the Americans was 49 heavy bombers, 30 medium bombers and 771 airmen.[47] British losses were 75 aircraft and 161 men. Between May 1, 1943 and March 31, 1944, the Allies flew 10,310 photo reconnaissance missions over occupied Europe. Over 4,000 of these mission, nearly 40 percent, were in search of Crossbow targets and included both A-4 and Fi 103 sites and support activities.

On the evening of June 12, 1944, Allied airmen considered they had done an excellent job in destroying the large sites, the ski sites and the supporting supply sites. Ironically, early in the campaign they had made the Germans realize that permanent concrete launching sites were not the answer, and despite Hitler's wishes the Germans were forced to adopt simpler measures. For the Fi 103, the solution was the modified site with its simpler launcher that was easily camouflaged and easy to repair. For the A-4, the Meiler truck-drawn launcher replaced the huge sites at Watten and Wizernes.

The ski sites became, in effect, one of the most expensive and extensive deceptions in history. Both American and British air officers claimed the bombing delayed the launch of the Fi 103 by as much as four to six months; however, this cannot be supported. It is doubtful that the bombing delayed the German effort more than a few days. The primary reason for the delay in deploying the Fi 103 was the difficulty the Germans experienced in fine-tuning, and then manufacturing, the weapon. As soon as sufficient flying bombs were ready, the Germans began to launch them. The fitful start of the campaign on the

night of June 12–13, 1944 initially made the Allies think they had succeeded in erasing the enemy threat. Lord Cherwell laughed heartily at
the few flying bombs that reached England and said, "the mountain
hath groaned and given forth a mouse!"[48] These were words that
Londoners would soon regret.

8

Diver, Diver, Diver

The protective measures in place to counter the flying bombs attacking Great Britain in the early morning hours of June 13, 1944 were a combination of defenses developed before the war, during the Battle of Britain and the Blitz, and plans made by Air Marshal Roderic Hill as commander of Air Defence Great Britain (ADGB) in January 1944. The number of guns required by the plan was later reduced when the bombing of the ski sites seemed to be going extremely well. Even before the opening of hostilities in World War II, British military officials had been aware that aerial attacks from the continent would be directed against London and other key targets in southern and southeastern England.

To defend the approaches to these areas, the British built two chains of radar stations, known as Chain High and Low, along the southeastern coast in the late 1930s. These radar stations allowed the British to detect enemy raids forming over France and alert the Royal Air Force of the impending attack. Once the RAF was alerted, the information was fed to a plotting room that monitored the Germans as they flew across the Channel and assigned fighter squadrons to attack enemy formations as appropriate. After being vectored to the enemy, once the RAF fighter pilots made visual contact they were free to attack the Germans as they saw fit.

If the enemy managed to get through the radar and over British soil, they came under watchful eyes of the Royal Observation Corps (ROC). The ROC consisted of teams of observers, stationed on rooftops, hills and other key locations, who spotted enemy aircraft

187

visually or with sound detectors. After making the sighting, the ROC team recorded the passage of the enemy and reported the information back to the RAF plotting room. The ROC teams inland continued to observe and report the enemy's course, altitude and position. As the enemy neared London, he entered an antiaircraft belt consisting of guns and searchlights which extended from the Thames to Southampton in a wide arc. The mission of the guns was to shoot down any enemy aircraft that had survived the fighters. Behind the AA gun belt was a final defensive belt of antiaircraft, or "barrage," balloons. These huge, gas-filled bags were tethered to the ground by stout steel cables and were designed to disrupt enemy formations by making aircraft fly over them. Any aircraft foolish enough to enter the balloon barrage was likely to have its wings and propeller ripped off by the cables.

In addition to the combat defenses consisting of fighters, guns and balloons, the British also had a huge civil defense organization. Civil Defence was the responsibility of Mr. Herbert S. Morrison, the Home Secretary. Prior to an attack, the organization alerted cities and towns along the likely courses of attacking aircraft. For protection during an attack, it provided shelters from the bombing. These ranged from large elaborate shelters that included underground (subway) stations in the major cities to small shelters for individual or family use. Civil Defence also coordinated fire fighting and damage control measures in the target area. After a raid, the organization provided medical attention and evacuation for the wounded, cleared the damage and rubble and provided food and shelter for those who had lost their homes and possessions in the raid. The civil defense organization stretched across the entire length and breadth of England and was refined during the Battle of Britain in 1940 and the Blitz. It proved remarkably efficient in coping with the chaos caused by widespread bomb damage.

When the first news of the potential rocket bombardment reached the British authorities, they took a serious look at their defenses. Certainly, the main thrust of the operations against the flying bombs would be to obliterate them before they were launched. However, there was little doubt that a certain percentage would reach the English coast, and the defenses were realigned based on that possibility. To coordinate the effort, Air Marshal Hill, commander of ADGB, had under his direct command airborne forces groups 9, 10, 11, 12,

13, and 38; 60th signals group; and 70th training group. By June 1944, ADGB had at its disposal 24 squadrons of Spitfires, two squadrons of Typhoons, nine squadrons of Mosquitos, two squadrons of Beaufighters, a squadron of Hurricanes, five mixed squadrons and two specialized flights. The pilots and support personnel were all veterans who had little doubt that if the flying bombs could be intercepted and shot down, they could do it. The fighter pilots were ably backed by the RAF's 30th, 32nd and 33rd Barrage Balloon Groups, which were in place around London in June 1944. Also subject to Hill's authority was Anti-Aircraft Command, an army organization.

Commanded by veteran Lt. General Sir Frederick Pile, Anti-Aircraft Command had been an integral part of the defense of Great Britain throughout the war. It began life as the First Anti-Aircraft Division on December 13, 1935, when it consisted of a few 3-inch guns and a paper strength of 5,200 men. The command grew rapidly as war threatened and it provided the United Kingdom's ground defense for the Battle of Britain and the subsequent Blitz. It gained further experience during the so called Baedeker Raids of 1942 and 1943, and by early 1944 had grown to two divisions and two independent groups. The command had a strength of over 250,000 personnel and a total of 2,800 heavy guns plus several thousand light guns, rocket launchers and hundreds of searchlights. The Royal Navy also contributed to the defenses by building several antiaircraft platforms in the Thames estuary and off England's southeastern coast. These were integrated into the overall antiaircraft program and their mission was to engage low-flying enemy bombers trying to attack Allied shipping.

The plan to defend England against the flying bomb followed the pattern used to defend her against the Luftwaffe during the Battle of Britain. When radar operators detected an incoming flying bomb, they alerted the plotting room, which vectored the fighters to the target. The fighters were responsible for the area from the English Channel to the area just south of Whitstable on the coast, running in a convex arc to approximately East Grinstead. Antiaircraft guns took up the battle from that point and continued on a line extending from Chatham on the coast to Limpsfield, which was covered by barrage balloons. To keep the antiaircraft gunners from shooting down friendly fighters, the rules of engagement gave pilots and the gun crews separate zones of action and the pilots were not allowed to fly over the gun belt.

On February 10, 1944 the Ministry of Home Security dispatched a "Most Secret" Letter to the Regional Commissioners of the civil defense regions most likely to be affected by the flying bomb and the rocket. The subject was absolutely secret and information regarding any possible attack could not pass below the level of Civil Defence controller or chief constable. In reporting a flying bomb or rocket attack, they were to use the code name "Diver" for the flying bomb and "Big Ben" for the rocket. The British established the central headquarters for defense against a new enemy attack at the RAF base at Biggin Hill. However, the precise performance characteristics of the flying bomb, the exact time it would be employed and the volume of the attack were all unknowns. Since enormous resources were dedicated to defense against this weapon, these unknowns were critical and a matter of great concern. Once "Diver" was activated, all the resources of ADGB, aircraft and antiaircraft would be dedicated to destroying flying bombs.

Allied planners were leery about committing ADGB resources too early or to a minor threat. Allied resources were not infinite and if the actual campaign did not live up to expectations, only a small portion of command resources would be needed and the rest could be used by the invasion forces. In fact, as the flying bomb campaign began, the Chiefs of Staff subcommittee met to discuss the demise of Anti-Aircraft Command and how best they could use the 50,000 men and 27,000 women made available by its diminished role. Needless to say, Air Marshal Hill and General Pile resisted the temptation to strip the defenses any more than had already been done earlier in the year. Until the Germans acted, nothing further could be determined.

Shortly after 4:00 A.M. on June 13, 1944, Edwin Woods, a farmer on duty as a member of the Royal Observer Corps at Observer Post Mike Three at Lyming on the Kent Downs, received a message from the Maidstone ROC Center that something was going on at Boulogne. Through his binoculars, Wood thought he saw a "fighter on fire," but it was outside his sector. He gave the position to the center at Maidstone, which passed it on to the observers in Observer Post Mike Two, which was fittingly enough a Martello Tower at Dymchurch, built to give early warning against a French invasion during the time of Napoleon. Observers E.E. Woodland and A.M. Wraight, manning the post, spotted a flying object spurting flames from its tail and making a noise like a Model T auto. Aimed at the Tower Bridge in London, the first V-1 "flying bomb" fired at England passed within five miles of the post and Woodland picked up the phone and rang Maidstone: "Mike 2, Diver, Diver, Diver—on four, northwest one-o-one."[1]

The plotter at the operations center called out the code, sirens sounded, the report was relayed to No. 11 Fighter Group at Uxbridge and as rapidly as possible up the chain of command to both London and Washington. Other reports followed this first Fi 103 fired in anger until its engine stopped some five minutes later and it dove to earth to explode in an open field.

The second Fi 103 to cross the coast landed in a potato field. The third reached Bethnal Green. In addition to destroying a railroad bridge and two houses, it killed six people, among whom was 19-year-old Ellen Woodcraft and her eight-month-old son, Tom. Another thirty people were injured. The few flying bombs in the first attack did not cause a great deal of concern in the meetings called the following day. Air Marshal Hill was disappointed that the heavy bombing of the ski sites had not completely prevented the Germans from employing the flying bomb, but most British authorities were relieved by the pathetic few that reached England. One American intelligence officer characterized it as a hit by a "powder puff."[2] Lord Cherwell was contemptuous of the German effort and many others felt it was prudent to wait to see if any further attacks occurred before committing all available resources to "Diver."[3]

Dr. R.V. Jones, who had asked Cherwell not to laugh the flying bomb campaign off, and Duncan Sandys warned against being so complacent about the German effort, but they were a distinct minority. The weakness of the attack convinced the British War Cabinet, meeting that afternoon, that the flying bomb was not much of a threat after all, and they passed their new evaluation to Air Marshal Sir Trafford Leigh-Mallory, commander of the Allied Expeditionary Air Forces. Mallory immediately cut a planned attack on the flying bomb launch sites from 3,000 to 1,000 sorties.[4]

Meanwhile, despite numerous launch failures, the commander of Flak Regiment 155(W) was not upset. At least some of his missiles had gotten through. Colonel Wachtel knew that he was working with an untried weapon subject to an accelerated deployment schedule and that "teething" problems were to be expected. The Flak Regiment spent June 14 correcting the errors of the previous day in preparation for a major launch as soon as possible.

The most significant problems during the Germans' first attempt were mistakes in launch procedures and mechanical malfunctions on the launchers. By June 15 every launcher had been test-fired, the missiles readied and the crews prepared. After they were readied, they were checked and rechecked again.[5] Reports of the crews' preparedness were passed to Colonel Wachtel, who reported to LXV Armeekorps headquarters that fifty-five launchers were operational. At 1900 hours, General Erich Heinemann, certain that all was ready, ordered Wachtel to open fire on "Target 42," which was London. Wachtel radioed to his four firing detachments, "Open fire on Target Forty-two with an all catapult salvo, synchronized at 11.18 P.M. (impact at 11.40 P.M.). Uniform range 130 miles. Then sustained fire until 4.50 A.M."[6]

Shortly before the designated time, German launch crews hauled the two-ton pilotless aircraft to the launchers and emplaced them, then readied follow-on missiles. General Heinemann traveled to Wachtel's command bunker and received good news. Two minutes before the designated time, the second battalion launched the first flying bomb of the new offensive. It was followed by launches from the 54 other operational sites. The first flying bomb crashed into London at 2340 hours. Shortly after midnight the weather worsened and it began to rain—perfect weather for the flying bomb. By noon of July 16, the Flak Regiment had launched 244 Fi 103s. Of these, 45 crashed, in the process wrecking nine launch sites. One crashed in a village shortly after take-off, killing 10 Frenchmen.[7] One hundred forty-four Fi 103s crossed the English coast. Seventy-one fell in southeastern England and seventy-three reached London. Thirty-three flying bombs were shot down by fighters or AA fire.

Air-raid sirens came to life as the Chain Low Radar Stations picked up the first of the flying bombs catapulted from their launchers on the northwestern coast of France, gained altitude and headed out over the English Channel. Twenty minutes later, the Fi 103s of the second wave of flying bombs arrived over London and antiaircraft guns and searchlights around the capital swung into action. Shooting down a flying bomb traveling at speeds in excess of 350 mph proved harder than expected and most of the antiaircraft shells exploded harmlessly behind them. Only 11 of the 33 Fi 103s destroyed were brought down by antiaircraft fire, but the misses added to the damage. Showers of shell fragments fell onto the buildings of Greater London, shattering skylights and breaking roof tiles.[8] Professor Jones was "horrified to see our anti-aircraft gunners firing enthusiastically at the bombs as they crossed London, which was the worst possible thing they could do. For if a bomb were hit, this made sure it would fall on London rather than pass over and explode harmlessly beyond. Cherwell needed only the slightest persuasion to intervene and the practice was stopped in a few days."[9]

The alert continued through the night as Flak Regiment 155(W) kept up a steady stream of bombs. After five hours of steady firing there was a 50-minute break to allow the crews some rest, after which they returned to their launchers to begin "disruptive fire": flying bombs launched at random intervals to keep the British in a constant state of alert, and to preclude them from cleaning up damage or putting out fires. Firing continued for another seven hours and the bombardment finally ended some 12 hours after it began.

The first pilot credited with shooting down an Fi 103 was Flight Lieutenant J.C. Musgrave in a Mosquito of No. 605 squadron with Flight Sergeant F.W. Somwell. In the early hours of June 16, they spotted a flying bomb over the Channel and went in pursuit. After a short chase, Musgrave opened fire and the bomb exploded with a "tremendous flash," crashing into the sea. Most interceptions were far more difficult. Wing Commander Roly Beaumont, commander of No. 150 Wing, expended all his ammunition before his Fi 103 started to go down and it was left to his wingman to finish. Beaumont thought he and his wingman were the first to bring down an Fi 103, but Musgrave had beaten them to the punch an hour before. One pilot of No. 91 squadron only shot his target down after a twenty-mile chase.

Early on the morning of June 16, a spotter plane from the Luftwaffe Ninth Air Corps flew a discreet distance behind the wave of bombs leaving their launchers. The pilot radioed a report to General Heinemann that he saw "a glow of fires in the target area" brighter than any he had seen after conventional attacks on England. Jubilant, Wachtel was convinced that the tide of war was about to turn, and he dispatched a number of telegrams to his superior. These messages concluded: "May our triumph justify all the expectations which Front and Fatherland have bestowed upon our weapon."[10] The German High Command, intimately familiar with the Reich's dangerous military situation, was less enthusiastic. They merely announced, "Southern England and the London area were bombarded with very heavy high explosive missiles of novel design during the last night and this morning."[11] Joseph Goebbels, the Nazi Minister of Propaganda, made sure that no mention of "revenge" was made in any of the broadcasts or reports, because no one knew precisely what damage had been done to the British capital.

Initially, the British public did not quite know what to make of the flying bomb. Residents of London thought the antiaircraft gunners were doing a magnificent job, shooting the Fi 103s down like flies. Because of the glow of the Fi 103's exhaust at night, one man thought the Germans were purposely sending over planes that were on fire. When the newspapers initially reported that the Germans were using pilotless planes, many thought they were radio-controlled aircraft which dropped their bombs and returned to base. Very quickly everyone learned to recognize the odd rattle of the Fi 103 engine, which sounded like a hum in the distance and grew into a deafening rattle or stutter as it flew overhead. Those who could hear it held their breath for the deadly moment when the engine stopped. While this feature undoubtedly saved a number of lives, many Londoners felt this was the most disagreeable aspect of the flying bomb. Nicknames for the infernal things proliferated and the names ranged from the prosaic "P-planes," for pilotless planes, to the colorful "Farting-furies," but the names that stuck were "Doodlebugs" and "Buzz Bombs."

British officialdom was stunned by the magnitude of the renewed bombardment. Members of the Royal Observer Corps tried to keep up with the sightings and impacts, and by dawn on June 16 they were exhausted after a long night's work. The civil defense organization that had been built up during the Battle of Britain and the Blitz had been, to a great extent, dismantled since 1941 due to the need for labor in other parts of the British economy. Harried Civil Defence workers found it difficult to cope. Unlike a conventional bombing attack—which occurred in a short space of time in a relatively small area—the flying bombs came down in widely dispersed intervals in different locales. There was no way to dig out the dead and wounded quickly or even find out how many there were. In some civil defense districts, only "many killed" or "many hurt" were written in the local logs. As bombs continued to fall throughout the morning of June 16, Herbert Morrison, the Home Secretary, went before the House of Commons to report that Britain had indeed come under attack from German missiles and announce that countermeasures were being implemented. Detailed reports of strikes and casualties would not be reported to the press in order to prevent giving the enemy any information on the effectiveness and accuracy of the strikes. The area of southeast England crossed by the flying bombs on their way to London, an area in which they often came down, became known as "Bomb Alley."

Shortly before noon on June 17, there was a full meeting of the cabinet, and then Churchill called for a staff conference at five that evening. Usually attended by the chiefs of staff or their representatives, this conference was considered so vital that the Chiefs of the Air and Naval Staffs felt obliged to cut short a visit to the Normandy beachhead and attend personally. The Secretary of State for Air as well as the Deputy Supreme Commanders, Hill and Pile, also attended. The main issue on the agenda was countermeasures to the flying bomb. The first course of action taken by Leigh-Mallory was to increase air attacks against Crossbow installations. The targets selected were the eleven ski sites the Allies thought were still operational and another dozen modified sites. The Allies also selected the concrete installations built for the System I launch sites.

Apparently Leigh-Mallory was under the impression that no modified sites had been discovered in the area from which many of the flying bombs came and that the supply sites were in use. Where he got his information is unclear because the Germans had totally abandoned the ski sites, and both aerial reconnaissance and agents on the ground reported no activity at the those sites while there was plenty of evidence of activity at the modified sites. British intelligence had never found any activity at the supply sites. The one positive result of the meeting was that Churchill gave Hill, with Pile's assistance, authority "to redistribute the gun, searchlight and balloon defences, as necessary, to counter the attacks."[12] The prime minister also asked General Eisenhower to make every effort, short of interfering with the battles in Normandy, to neutralize the launch sites.[13]

The Germans also held meetings on June 17. In one of his rare appearances near the front, Hitler secretly flew to France, where he spent the day at Margival discussing with his generals the battle raging in Normandy. On hand were General Heinemann and Walther, his chief of staff. Though the Führer was "pale and bleary-eyed," he expressed his gratitude for the success of the flying bomb and indicated that he expected a great deal from the offensive. Heinemann and Walter both emphasized the seriousness of the supply situation, especially the shortage of bombs, and stressed that no significant success could be achieved in the attacks on London unless Hitler increased the output of the Fi 103 above the current level of 3,000 per month. Before the meeting ended, the Führer told Heinemann and Walther he was proud that Germany was fighting with new and modern weapons. He also stressed that London was the only target to be engaged.

Hitler took Heinemann's request for increased production to heart, and when he returned to Berchtesgaden, he declared that A-4 production was to be lowered to 150 a month and the materials saved were to be used for the Fi 103. Armaments Minister Speer was disappointed but obeyed. The promise was made that as soon as the A-4 was ready for deployment the production targets of 600 to 900 units a month would be resumed.

On the Allied side, by June 17 all the resources called for in the "Diver" Plan were committed to the defense, and any intentions to dismantle Anti-Aircraft Command were, for the moment, suspended. The staff of the antiaircraft units estimated that it would take 18 days to move the guns into new positions, build the necessary facilities, reestablish communications and be ready to fight the battle. Even though they were caught off guard by the unexpected barrage of flying bombs, Anti-Aircraft Command accelerated their redeployment time table and did it in less than four days. In addition to the gun and balloon defenses around Greater London, the defenders included 12 squadrons of fighters, which were assigned to one of three lines of defense. The first line was a standing patrol at 12,000 feet over the English Channel between Beachy Head and Dover; the second line was above the coast between Newhaven and Dover; and the third was further inland between Haywards Heath and Ashford. Once flying bomb launches were detected, the patrol area would be lowered to 6,000 feet.

The fighter defense lines did not close down at the end of the day. During the hours of darkness, the day fighters were replaced with night fighters. The night fighters were augmented by searchlight batteries spaced one and a half miles apart along the coast from Seaford to South Foreland. Once the bombs were past the fighter screen, they entered into the gun boxes. There were four rows of eight-gun batteries. Each of the batteries was spaced 6,000 yards apart, each row 3,000 yards behind the other. Combined, these guns covered the southeastern approaches to London. Behind the guns were the 480 barrage balloons.[14]

The flying bomb posed unique problems for the defenders and it was obvious they were having little success at stopping them. One of the problems was that the "diver" defenses were based on the speed of conventional bombers. Another was the way the flying bomb approached. During the German aerial attacks of 1940 and later, British radar was able to detect raids as they formed over the Continent. Masses of German bombers required a relatively long time to assemble into a formation. First individual aircraft and squadrons lifted off from their airfields; then they climbed to altitude over France, awaiting other bomber groups and fighters. All of this activity was clearly visible to the English radar. Thus, the English usually had 20 to 30 minutes' advance notice before a Luftwaffe bomber formation crossed the Channel. The flying bomb needed no formation, nor did it climb to any great altitude. By the time it was illuminated by British radar, it was were already out over the Channel traveling at six miles a minute. The average distance from the launch sites to London was 130 miles and in theory the defenders had 22 minutes to identify and destroy the flying bomb. This was not a simple process, however.

During June 1944, the English Channel and coast of France were covered with swarms of Allied fighters, bombers and cargo aircraft. The sudden appearance of a blip on the radar screen could be a flying bomb or it could be an Allied airplane, so the radar operator was obliged to watch the blip for a few seconds in order to make a positive identification. If it was flying a straight-and-level course, as only the Fi 103 did, it was a flying bomb. After positively identifying the flying bomb, the radar operator had to notify the British defenders and then vector an aircraft onto an intercepting course. All of this took precious time, and the flying bomb was often over England before the fighters could close with it.[15]

Furthermore, fighter pilots had little experience fighting such a weapon. Although the bomb flew straight and level and so, in that sense, made an ideal aerial target, it was still a difficult target to bring down. The Fi 103 was fast enough to tax all but the abilities of the swiftest fighters. It crossed the coast traveling at 340 mph and gradually increased speed, as the weight of its fuel was burned away, to 400 mph before it reached London. The earlier versions of the Spitfire, Hurricanes and Typhoons could not overtake it and were obliged to position themselves in front of the flying bombs and launch a head-on attack. Such an attack could be particularly dangerous for the closure speed between the fighter and bomb was more than 600 mph. At such speeds the pilot had only an instant to line up his target, fire and get out of the way, because a hit on the Fi 103's nose might well detonate the warhead, which could destroy both the flying bomb and fighter.

The Tempest V and Spitfire XIV could catch the Fi 103 from behind and these were positioned closest to "Bomb Alley," as the sixty-mile-wide swath of southeastern England became known. However, even attacking from behind posed significant problems. If a fighter pilot was fortunate enough to catch up with a V-1 there was the problem of range. Most of the pilots were taught that to insure an air-to-air kill they had to fire at ranges of 500 yards. At such short ranges the flying bomb was sure to be shot down, but if the warhead detonated it might also destroy the fighter. Initially, the pilots opted for long-range fire on the bombs. In order to catch the Fi 103s the fastest aircraft, the Tempest Wing from Newchurch and the Mustang IIIs of 129 Squadron and 315 (Polish) Squadron, became the first line of defense.[16]

On June 18, 1944, Flak Regiment 155(W) launched its 500th flying bomb. Already the Fi 103 offensive had claimed 500 lives, seriously injured over 2,000 more and wounded countless others. To that date the largest single number of deaths was 24, when a flying bomb hit the street outside a pub in Battersea.

June 18 was a Sunday and the Royal Military Chapel at Wellington Barracks, approximately a quarter of a mile from Buckingham Palace and less than half a mile from the government offices between Whitehall and St. James Park, was packed with worshipers. A flying bomb, perhaps the 500th, was seen crossing Queen Anne's gate at 11:20 A.M. A short distance away, Dr. Jones and his assistants were at work and heard the "unmistakable noise of a flying bomb." They quickly got under their desks. The congregation at the chapel heard the buzz become a loud roar. The flying bomb struck the roof, which had been reinforced to withstand the Blitz, and penetrated before exploding.

The side walls and supporting pillars were blown down as smoke and dust billowed into the sky. Rescue workers arriving at the scene discovered debris ten feet deep on the floor of the chapel. The death toll from this single bomb was appalling. Fifty-eight civilians and 63 military personnel had been killed and 114 injured. Only the Bishop of Maidstone, who was conducting the service beneath the dome above the altar, was unhurt.

A disaster of this magnitude would have affected any city, but this Fi 103 had hit at the heart of English power and society. Among the dead were Lt. Colonel John Cobbold, commanding officer of the Grenadier Guards, Lt. Colonel Lord Edward Hay of the Grenadier Guards, and the entire Coldstream Guards Band. Among these latter was the band director, Major James Causley-Windram, known to many in London for the entertaining way in which he directed the band's concerts in St. James Park. This flying bomb incident brought home the seriousness of the situation as had none other. People of every walk of life knew something had to be done to improve the military defenses and civil defense.

The tragedy of the Royal Military Chapel overshadowed the fact that flying bombs also hit eleven factories in London that same day. The following day Churchill ordered Parliament to move from the House of Commons to Church House, just as it had done during the Blitz. Church House was a modern steel structure far more substantial than the older building. Shortly after the move, one member of Parliament asked the prime minister why they had to return to Church House. Before he could reply, another member suggested to the MP that he walk a few hundred yards to Birdcage Walk and look at the damage to the Royal Military Chapel if he wanted to know the reason.

On June 19, Air Marshal Hill changed the rules of engagement for the guns and fighters. The latter complained that they often had to break off engagement over the gun belt just as they caught up with their prey. Under the new rules, the fighters had free reign, in the area from the Channel to the balloon barrage, during periods of good weather, since the planes had the best chance of shooting down the flying bombs. When fighters were chasing the bombs, the antiaircraft gunners were forbidden to fire. In periods of marginal weather, the antiaircraft gunners were allowed to fire freely at targets below 8,000 feet while the fighters patrolled above that altitude. When the weather turned bad and the fighters could not fly, the gunners could engage any target they spotted.[17]

Two days later, without Goebbels' consent, the *Berliner Ausgabe* ran an article stating that the Germans were having their revenge on the British. Goebbels was furious. His initial optimism about the flying bomb had turned to doubt and he didn't want to raise the hopes of the German public that the new weapons would win the war. He was so angry that he threatened to have the reporter shot, but the damage had been done. In a few days the Germans were referring to the Fi 103 as a weapon of revenge. Having no choice, Goebbels turned the misstatement to his advantage. On June 24, he made an official announcement in which he coined the term "Vergeltungswaffe Eins," or "Vengeance Weapon Number One"—thus conveying the impression that more weapons would follow. The new name was abbreviated and the Fi 103 designation was seldom used again; instead, the weapon would henceforth be known as the V-1.

The new name did not improve the weapon and there were still bugs to work out. The steam generator that propelled the V-1 up the ramp did not always work correctly. In many instances the flying bomb fired but the steam generator failed to move it up the ramp. The bomb was now "live" and the counter at the nose of the bomb was spinning, meaning that the bomb would explode in 20 to 25 minutes. Most of the crews evacuated the site and let the bomb explode and destroy the launch ramp. Some crews, who can only be described as daring, disassembled the warhead on the launcher and removed the fuses.[18] Problems notwithstanding, the Flak Regiment launched its 1,000th V-1 against London on June 21.

Very soon after the issue of the new rules of engagement, Hill must have realized that British defenses were still seriously flawed. Certainly his pilots and antiaircraft gunners were doing their best, but they were not bringing down anywhere near the number of flying bombs initially assumed. The expectation that the V-1 would be easy to shoot down was quickly proved false. There were few vulnerable areas in the flying bomb and there was no pilot to wound or kill in an aircraft that was much smaller than a conventional fighter. There was also a grave danger from the exploding warhead. Some pilots received burns from the explosion of a V-1, and over the course of the campaign five pilots were killed. In one case the explosion blew the wing off the pursuing pilot's Spitfire. A sixth pilot was killed when he accidentally flew into the balloon barrage.

A method of avoiding the danger of having the V-1 warhead explode was to tip the wing of the flying bomb and throw it off course. The first pilot to accomplish this amazing feat was Flying Officer Ken Collier, an Australian serving in No. 91 Squadron. At 9:50 P.M. on June 23, 1944, he was scrambled with other pilots to intercept "divers." Collier sighted one flying at 2,500 feet and swooped down to intercept. He hit the pilotless aircraft again and again but failed to bring it down before running out of ammunition. Frustrated, he flew alongside the V-1 and tried to flip it over on its back. Failing the first attempt he tried again, and succeeded, watching it crash in an empty field. Reporting his unorthodox success at his squadron, he was met with considerable skepticism until the mechanics reported fresh black paint on the wing of his Spitfire. Except for a party at the squadron mess, Collier never received the recognition he deserved. He was killed in December 1944 and the squadron's records were lost after the war, only to be rediscovered decades later.[19]

The antiaircraft gunners were having even worse luck, bringing down, at most, only 13 percent of the targets engaged.[20] The problems facing the gunners were legion. Equipment headed the list. The mobile 3.7-inch guns were not capable of engaging a fast, low-flying aircraft. The British had not yet received the American S.C.R. 584 radar set or the proximity fuses. The radar sets they did have were placed in defilade to avoid jamming by German radar, and this limited their effectiveness. Further, the rules of engagement favored the pilots and severely hampered the gunners' freedom of action. Not all guns were under the command of Anti-Aircraft Command and many of the light guns were not concentrated in the "Diver Belt." Another problem Lt. General Pile had was working as part of a joint command. When he decided to concentrate his light guns in the North Downs right behind the belt of main guns, he found the RAF had already decided to emplace more balloons in the same area; Pile's command therefore had to find a new area in which to emplace the light guns. Then, more changes were made to the rules of engagement and the fighters were given even greater latitude. The gunners' score fell to only nine percent of the targets engaged. Even with this further restriction of the gunners the RAF was not increasing its percentage of flying bombs shot down. By June 26, largely because of fluctuations in the German rate of fire, the number of flying bombs reaching London each day had fallen from 70 to 25, but Hill realized that something more needed to be done.

As if to punctuate the necessity for action, another disastrous V-1 explosion occurred on Friday, June 30. By then, approximately 50 flying bombs a day were reaching London. The alerts came so often that many people had gotten in the habit of ignoring them, waiting instead to listen for the sound of a V-1 engine as it passed over and stopped. Bush House was a large office complex on a crescent-shaped street called the Aldwych, right off the Strand. Across the street was the Air Ministry Building. There was a Royal Observer Corps station on the roof of Bush House where some of the office girls were sunning themselves. Below, scores of people were out on the street, and buses lined the curb. Shortly before 2:00 P.M., a flying bomb passed over Wellington Station, and when its engine cut out went into a sharp dive, hitting the street just in front of the Air Ministry. Few people heard it over the din of the traffic. The buses were demolished and people were cut to pieces by flying glass. WAAFs in the Air Ministry Building who had looked outside to see the flying bomb were sucked from the windows and hurled to their deaths. More than a hundred were killed instantly. Hundreds more were hurt, and later nearly another hundred died of their injuries. The incident was known as the Aldwych Massacre.

Pile was understandably frustrated. The results attained by his gunners were far below expectations and he voiced his discontent at every opportunity. At a periodic "night air defence" meeting Churchill offered Pile carte blanche for the gunners for a week, but the general wisely declined: "I was not anxious to assume the major role in the defence until I had got more American equipment, and even then I wanted a combined show, in which the best results from the RAF as well as from the guns were obtained."[21] In this he was reflecting the views of his commander. Hill's new rules of engagement had improved the situation and the number of flying bombs being shot down rose from roughly 20 to 40 percent. Nevertheless, Hill had achieved this success at the expense of paralyzing the antiaircraft portion of his command. Not willing to rest on his laurels, he was determined to get maximum results from both the guns and the fighters.

On July 10, Hill decided to make another change in the defenses to improve them. In some ways it was a return to the original arrangement. The fighters and guns were each to have their own operational zone. There was, however, a major change in the deployment of the guns. On Pile's recommendation, all the guns except for those needed for marking rounds on the coast were to be moved into a single dense belt on the North Downs. This would concentrate the guns in a last line before London and clear the way for the fighters everywhere except over the gun belt. Hill, positive he had found the solution, ordered the redeployment of the guns. It was no small task. The redeployment meant not only the movement of the guns and their crews but also their support personnel and signal equipment. Four hundred forty-one static guns had to be moved to replace mobile guns from all over England.

A major hurdle was the fact that these guns had to be mounted on permanent platforms that were built of concrete. Even if the time and material were available for this major construction project, the labor was not. The solution was developed by Brigadier J.A.E. Burls, Pile's engineering officer, who designed a "moveable lattice-work of steel rails and sleepers which, when filled with ballast, was as static as anybody could desire."[22] The "portable" platforms involved 8,000 tons of material that also had to be moved. Three hundred sixty-five guns went by road and the remainder by rail. Tractor trailers and heavy cranes were borrowed from the Americans. New gun sites had to be found with sufficient water and drainage. Thirteen thousand Anderson shelters and three million sand bags were needed to protect the gun crews.

Hill gave the assignment of explaining the move, and new rules of engagement to the pilots of ADGB, to Air Commodore G.H. Ambler, his Deputy Senior Staff Officer. Ambler was not a professional military man. He was a successful Yorkshire textile merchant who looked forward to returning to the family business after the war. As a staff officer, he was a valuable asset to Hill because he could deal with problems objectively and did not have the ingrained service prejudices inherent in many professional military officers. Since his postwar career was not in jeopardy, he was willing to give his commander unwelcome news if necessary. He accepted his assignment to explain the move and agreed with his superior that the guns had to be concentrated in a single belt and the fighters had be excluded from it. However, he was uncomfortable with the decision that guns on the coast had to be moved to the North Downs.

To clarify his own uneasiness, Ambler decided to set his thoughts down on paper in accordance with the format prescribed in the War Manual. He reasoned that Hill's objective was not to redress a grievance but to put the guns in the best position to shoot down incoming flying bombs. That position had to be the coast, where they would have a clear field of fire over the widest possible area. Any malfunctioning shell would fall harmlessly into the sea. This was an important point since American proximity fuses had not yet arrived. The coast was also the best place for the radar sets since they, too, had a clear field of observation. Ambler also recognized that conditions for the radar had changed. Advancing Allied troops had cleared the coastal areas of France and there was no longer any danger of jamming.

It took two days for Ambler to finish his paper, and during that time he sought advice from his friend Sir Robert Watson Watt, the inventor of radar, who agreed with him and confirmed that the coast was the best place for the radar sets. For the pilots, Ambler saw one major disadvantage. Their area of operation would be split by the gun belt into two zones, one over the water and one over land. On July 13, the day he saw Ambler's paper, Hill received a visit from Watson Watt, who told him that he was also of the opinion that the south coast was the best place for the guns.

Hill belatedly recognized that interception over water and over land should be treated as two separate problems, and after Watt's support of Ambler's recommendation gave himself a day to think it over and look for any technical flaws or omissions. When he was sure the idea was sound he called for a meeting to be attended by Pile, Air Vice Marshal Saunders, who was the commander of No. 11 Group, and a representative from Headquarters, Allied Expeditionary Air Force

(Hill's higher headquarters). He also asked Watson Watt to attend. Pile naturally supported the idea. A plan to place all the guns on the coast had been recommended in his headquarters, but had been shelved because it was felt the pilots would not agree to such a radical change.

In its final version the plan called for a dense, 5,000-yard-deep gun belt stretching from Beachy Head to Dover that could fire 10,000 yards out to sea. This gave the fighters plenty of room for interception over the Channel and plenty of room behind the guns. The barrage balloons remained a final defense. The fighters would not be allowed to fly at any altitude less than 8,000 feet over the gun belt, which gave the gunners absolute freedom up to 6,000 feet. One attractive feature of the plan was that it allowed a maximum number of defenders to engage the flying bombs while they were over the Channel, thus sparing many civilians the misfortune of being under a flying bomb shot down on its way to London or being hit by badly fused antiaircraft shells.

Rather than objecting to two zones for the fighters, Saunders surprisingly supported the idea, saying it was the best proposed to date. This meant the gun belt had to be moved to the coast; Pile's batteries were already on the way to the North Downs and some were emplacing as they spoke. Any delay in moving further would be amplified if the gun units were allowed to settle into their North Downs locations.

Convinced that this was the right course of action, Hill took a bold step. Rather than submit a strong recommendation up the chain of command, he decided to redistribute the defenses as he saw fit, acting on the authority given him by Churchill on June 16. He ordered Pile to move his guns. Perhaps no other incident demonstrates the close working relationship between Hill and Pile. As soon as he left the meeting, Pile returned to his headquarters and ordered the move. Stopping a move in progress and ordering the batteries to redeploy was no simple process, however. There were already plans to move 376 mobile heavy guns and 526 light guns. Thirty-two static guns were already in place on the North Downs and the platforms for seventy more had just arrived. Forty more static guns on the move had to be diverted. The signals network that supported the Gun and Searchlight Operation Room had to be set up prior to arrival of the guns, and this meant thousands of miles of wire, including 3,000 miles for inter-battery communications alone.

As the move got underway the defenses were increased by another twelve mixed heavy batteries and 312 static guns. In all, 30,000 tons of stores, 30,000 tons of ammunition, and 23,000 men and women who crewed the guns were moved by 8,000 trucks manned by 9,000 drivers who covered 2,750,000 miles in one week. Pile gave his subordinates full rein and admitted, "All the normal rules went by the board. Routing and movement control were forgotten. For this move one brigade issued no movement orders at all: no one seemed any the worse. The movement was a flood, but a well-managed and orderly flood."[23] It was indeed. By July 17, 1944 all the heavy guns were in position and by July 19 the light guns had closed. In six days Hill and Pile had created a belt containing nearly 1,600 guns of all calibers and 200 rocket projectors.

Just after he set the new deployment in motion, Hill told Air Marshal Sir Trafford Leigh-Mallory what he had done. Leigh-Mallory's only question was whether or not a trial deployment on a short stretch of coast would not have been better. Hill replied that it was all or nothing, and the head of the Allied Expeditionary Air Force let the matter stand at that. The Air Ministry, however, was furious. Convinced Hill had yielded to Pile, who, after all, knew Churchill and perhaps Duncan Sandys, who was chairman of the cabinet Crossbow Committee and a former antiaircraft officer, the ministry chose to look at the entire matter from a parochial point of view. They believed that Hill had sacrificed the fighter force for the guns and took him to task for not inviting them to the July 13 conference as well as for moving the guns without authority. This was stretching the point. Hill had kept his higher headquarters informed; Saunders had represented Leigh-Mallory at the conference; and Hill had spoken with his superior after the decision was made. Hill also had Churchill's authority to exercise his initiative. Hill was informed that he could expect dire consequences if his plan failed, but he knew that already. He had exercised his initiative and the Air Ministry couldn't call the move back.

In the first six days of the new arrangement the defenses brought down 269, or 56 percent, of the 473 flying bombs that reached the coast.[24] Although the number of flying bombs brought down by the fighters declined, the number shot down by the guns rose and this had been Hill's objective. In the first week the gunners brought down 17 percent of the targets engaged and in the second week 24 percent.

Aside from the redeployment, one of the reasons for the gunners' success was that new equipment had arrived. Anti-Aircraft Command received 135 of the long-awaited S.C.R. 584 radar sets and Pile was able to "borrow" an additional 165. Adapting these to the static British 3.7-inch gun required 200 modifications to the gun. Along with the radar sets came proximity fuses and 20 American batteries armed with the radar-controlled 90mm gun.[25] Hill ordered barrage balloons from all over England, with the exception of those at the Scapa Flow naval base. Redeployed to Kent and Surrey, the number of balloons covering London rose to 750 and then 1,000, and finally on July 8 reached a peak of 1,750. In its final form the balloon barrage covered an area twenty-six miles wide and eleven deep. At this point AA Command was asked to contribute another 25,000 men to the invasion forces in France. They were able to do so only because Cherbourg had been captured and the Bristol defenses were no longer needed. The remainder were made up from searchlight companies.

The U.S. Army Air Force meanwhile looked for new ways to attack the large sites and on June 20, 1944 General Carl A. Spaatz, Commander of the United States Strategic Air Forces in Europe, asked General "Hap" Arnold, Commanding General Army Air Forces, to direct General Gardner of the AAF Proving Ground in Florida "to begin experiments with radar-controlled "war-weary" heavy bombers which, with excess loads of explosives, could be expended as single 'missiles' against otherwise impregnable targets."[26] Spaatz also initiated efforts in the European Theater to find methods to control a bomber by "radar" so that it could be used as a "guided missile." The experiments, code-named Aphrodite, were quickly conducted and because American methods of radio control could not control a bomber on take-off, the method of attack looked strikingly like Sperry's experiments with the Curtiss N-9 in World War I. The bomber, loaded with explosives, and equipped with radio control, had to have a live crew to get it off the ground. It was followed by a control aircraft and when it got close to the target, the crew bailed out. The control aircraft then guided the "missile" to the target.

The process was not without hazard. On August 4, 1944, Lieutenant Joseph Kennedy, Jr. and his radio operator lifted off in a B-24 Liberator stripped of its armament, loaded with 22,000 pounds of explosives and with only enough fuel for a one-way flight. Shortly after take-off the B-24 was followed by the control plane. As they neared the channel, the Liberator blew up in a blinding flash, killing both men in the bomber. Tragic accidents notwithstanding, Spaatz had initiated the world's first two-way guided-missile war.

Another welcome addition to Britain's defense was the arrival of five Meteor I jet fighters assigned to No. 616 Squadron on July 23. The Meteor was not that much faster than a propeller-driven aircraft at the operational altitude of the flying bomb, but at greater altitudes it was considerably faster. The Meteors were initially supposed to go to the Continent to provide a counter for the new German jet fighters; however, they were held in England to counter the V-1. The first Meteor kill of a flying bomb occurred on August 4. The Meteor's guns jammed and the pilot tipped the bomb over with his wing.

After a decline in the number of bombs shot down in the first week following the move to the coast, the score improved rapidly, but not everyone was satisfied. The pilots thought they had been sold out and used their declining scores to prove their point. Hill was not a desk-bound general. He was also a pilot who pursued flying bombs when he had the chance and he spoke the same language as his fliers. Exercising personal leadership, Hill flew from airbase to airbase in his Spitfire. He went to great lengths to explain directly to the men who risked their lives chasing the deadly V-1 what the new rules of engagement meant and how the defense was doing. When he was shown fragments of antiaircraft shells that had wound up in British fighters or had fallen on British airfields to demonstrate the incompetence of the antiaircraft gunners, he told the station commanders to discuss the situation directly with their counterparts in Anti-Aircraft Command. He was taken at his word and the results of these personal visits were extraordinary. Antiaircraft gunners were not as quick on the trigger, and many a pilot who thought he had free rein suddenly found himself standing before his commanding officer receiving a good "dressing down" for violating the rules of engagement.

The proportion of flying bombs observed shot down steadily rose until it reached 74 percent in the third week in August. The following week it fell to 62 percent, then climbed to a new high of 83 percent. Here was proof positive that Hill's decision to move the guns to the coast was the right one; and though it was a remarkable achievement, it wasn't the whole story. Despite the best efforts of Hill and Pile and the men and women who made up ADGB, flying bombs were still getting through. Each one carried nearly a ton of amatol and in some cases, trialen, a far more powerful explosive. Coming down at a shallow angle, the blast could take down rows of houses, and while killing fewer than in conventional bomb attacks, the number of injured was very high. Each flying bomb had the potential for great tragedy.

At Lewisham in southeast London, the morning of Friday, July 28 began routinely. The post office was full of pensioners and the stores of Woolworth's, Marks and Spencer's and Sainsbury's were crowded with shoppers. Outside the stores was a row of stalls that attracted more shoppers and the traffic was normal. As two buses drove down Lewisham High Street, no one heard a V-1 as its engine cut out. At 9:41 A.M. the flying bomb struck the top of an air raid shelter on the corner. The buses, the stalls and the shoppers took the full force of the blast. Most of the casualties came from the blast and from flying glass which made the scene particularly appalling. Less than ten minutes after the blast, Civil Defence workers began to arrive. Just as Britain's defense had been modified, the Civil Defence organization had adapted to the new situation. The damage caused by the flying bomb was not localized the way damage from a conventional bombing raid was and Civil Defence was short of resources and personnel. However, the area hit by a flying bomb could be determined in a matter of minutes so that personnel and resources could be concentrated in a relatively small area.

Civil Defence teams were organized as flying squads directed by observation posts to reach the damaged area with the necessary equipment in a short time. One aspect of the flying bomb was fortunate from Civil Defence's point of view. It usually landed at a shallow angle and rarely destroyed gas or water mains or underground electrical cables, thus minimizing the chance of fire. On the other hand, it had a tendency to hit crowded streets. This meant fewer casualties trapped in collapsed buildings than would have occurred in the Blitz, but it multiplied the number of casualties in the open. As in Lewisham, the injuries caused by flying glass and exploding cars and buses were frightful. Night rescue work was made easier by the fact that there were no German pilots or observers to guide on sources of light so rescuers working at night could use floodlights to work faster. Due to its

superior explosive and the angle at which it fell, the flying bomb did
more damage to buildings than a conventional attack would have,
however, and during the first two weeks of the campaign damaged
200,000 houses in addition to killing 1,600, seriously injuring 4,500
and slightly injuring 5,000 more.

Instead of large regional centers to take care of the newly homeless, it was more effective to have mobile units available to help those
dispossessed by a V-1. "It was often found better to bring in mobile
canteens, bath and laundry units rather than make the people concerned go to the facilities."[27] The large number of houses damaged
called for swift action, and repair units were sent to the damaged area
as quickly as possible. When houses were demolished, arrangements
were made for the removal and storage of furniture.

Shelters were an important responsibility of Civil Defence and,
like rescue operations, the flying bomb created shelter problems very
different from those of the Blitz. While a great many people slept in
the subway, or "tube," stations, there was not a "deep shelter mental-
ity" as there had been during the Blitz and the deep shelters were used
for troops on leave. The same types of sanitation problems caused by
people staying in the subways without bathing and lavatory facilities
also existed, and inconvenienced people using them, but it was a relatively minor problem. Large shelters could not be placed in convenient
centralized locations since the threat was widespread and random, and
the demand for two types of smaller shelters rose dramatically.

The "Anderson" shelter was similar to a culvert and was designed
to be dug into a family's yard (garden to the English). The other was
the "Morrison," which was a crush-proof table located inside a house.
A family could get under the Morrison, and if the roof collapsed they
would not be crushed while they waited to be dug out. The major
advantage of the Anderson and Morrison shelters was that they
enabled people to find shelter at a moment's notice because the V-1
gave little or no warning. In the beginning of the campaign, Civil
Defence used the warning system already in place for conventional
bombers, but so many alerts were sounded that citizens became con-
fused. Finally they decided to sound the early warning when large
numbers of flying bombs crossed the coast in a wave. As with the shelters, the warning system became decentralized and many large buildings and factories stationed observers on the roofs to report the

approach of a flying bomb.

Morale in London during the V-1 campaign became fragile and the British government could not allow its citizens to continue under such a sustained bombardment. The nature of the flying bomb and the seemingly quixotic way it killed frayed the nerves. The flying bomb affected everyone from the humblest shopkeeper to the Supreme Commander Allied Expeditionary Forces. On July 21, General Dwight D. Eisenhower wrote his wife that he was unable to write two long papers because he and his stenographers had been forced to go to the shelter nineteen times.[28] Registration of school children for evacuation began on July 3, and by July 17 some 170,000 had been evacuated. By the middle of August approximately 1,450,000 people had left London to escape the flying bombs—a much greater number than those who left to escape the Blitz. Of these only 275,000 were official evacuees.[29] Productivity in the British capital fell 25 percent and by September there was not a pane of glass left in the buses in the city. Morale at the front in Normandy was also affected by the bombardment. British soldiers were understandably concerned about their loved ones, but Americans who had been stationed a long time in southern England were also concerned about the people who had shown them many kindnesses during their stay.

Even as Air Marshal Hill worked to refine his defenses, top British and American military men were meeting in London to discuss the problem. The British Chiefs of Staff considered an idea proposed by Sir Charles Portal in January 1944 to hold certain German cities "hostage" and not bomb them if certain conditions were met—in this case suspension of the V-1 campaign. They also proposed reprisal raids against German cities if the flying bomb offensive was not halted. However, General Sir Alan Brooke, Chief of the Imperial General Staff, vetoed the plan because he did not feel that the Germans would abandon a relatively inexpensive campaign that was currently diverting about 50 percent of the Allied bombing effort from targets in the Reich.[30] A recommendation to use gas on the launching sites was also rejected because the danger to French civilians in surrounding areas was too great. Throughout the war, the Allies were prepared to use poison gas if the Germans used it, but there was no danger of that happening. Hitler, who had been gassed as a soldier in World War I, had a loathing for chemical weapons and refused to consider gas an option. In the final analysis, the use of massive Allied air resources against non-military targets was a waste of precious aircraft, and when the idea of retaliation was broached to Eisenhower, his reply was straightforward: "As I have before indicated, I am opposed to retaliation as a method of stopping this business."

One offensive measure the Allies could take was to attack the flying bomb launching sites and their sources of supply. By the end of June, Allied air forces had stopped their wasteful attacks on the ski sites and concentrated on the modified sites, because the volume of flying bombs launched against England depended on the number of operational launchers in Flak Regiment 155(W) rather than the number of flying bombs being produced. Although the modified sites proved to be very difficult targets, the number of sites identified by photo reconnaissance and radar continued to rise. Not counting the 20 sites in the Cherbourg Peninsula, which had been overrun by June 30, there were 63 identified sites. The number rose to 72 by July 2 and 94 by the end of the month.[31] It was impossible to effectively maintain photographic surveillance of roughly 5,000 square miles and the Germans had become masters at camouflage, making it difficult to find them from the air and nearly as difficult to identify them on photographs. An examination of the sites captured on the Cherbourg Peninsula showed that the sites were simple in construction and that the Germans could repair the heaviest damage in roughly ten days.[32] Forty percent of the Allied air effort was now directed against the launching sites, but it didn't affect the numbers of bombs launched. The Allies had better luck attacking the supply sites.

The new German supply sites were discovered by radio intercepts. In May, Enigma intercepts showed that LXV Armeekorps was interested in a cavern at Nucourt, near Pontoise. On June 10, the intercepts mentioned three supply dumps that were storing components for Maikäfer (May bug or dorbeetle), the old codeword for the Hs 293 guided bomb. On June 17 and June 19, further intercepts confirmed the existence of dumps at Nucourt, St-Leu-d'Esserent and Rilly-la-Montagne in the Oise Valley. Other intelligence also indicated that the Germans had assembly depots in these areas. Early in July, another Enigma decrypt gave the number of flying bombs received and issued by the site at St-Leu.

In the last week of June the Eighth Air Force made heavy attacks on Nucourt and St-Leu. Heavy damage was done to Nucourt, where 241 flying bombs were buried and 57 seriously damaged. St-Leu was not seriously damaged because of its thick roof. On the nights of July 4 and 7, using blueprints and other detailed information from French agents and advice from Dr. R.V. Jones, Bomber Command's famous No. 617 Squadron, "The Dam Busters," mounted raids with 6-ton "Tallboy" bombs. On the first raid, the giant cave was hit seventeen times by the huge bombs carrying delay fuses, and part of the roof collapsed. On July 7, the entrance caved in, entombing the missiles stored there. Thereafter the number of flying bombs dropped from a hundred a day to roughly seventy a day for nearly ten days.

On July 10 and July 15, Nucourt was attacked again and this time more of the roof caved in. On July 17, Allied aircraft attacked Rilly-la-Montagne, which the Germans began to repair as soon as the raid was over. There was only one other decrypt concerning supply sites after the raid on St-Leu, but agents reported the Germans rapidly decentralizing their supply arrangements at Bois-de-Cassan, Forêt-de-l'Isle d'Adam and Mey-sur-Oise. There were reports of over fifty different locations from which bombs were being transferred to the launch sites at a rate of ninety per night.[33] After July 27 the rate of fire rose once again and Allied bombing did not affect it thereafter.

The Japanese ambassadors in Berlin and Vichy continued to be additional useful sources of information. During June and July 1944, the Japanese Ambassador in Berlin reported that the Germans were disappointed in the flying bomb and no longer felt it would alter the situation in Normandy. On June 19, the Naval Attaché in Berlin reported that the Germans were hoping to use the flying bomb against England's south coast ports. He reported that unless the flying bomb was used against the Allied divisions then waiting to embark, it would have little chance of turning the situation in Normandy to Germany's favor. On July 5, the Japanese Ambassador in Vichy reported that Otto Abetz, the military governor in France, admitted that the flying bomb would not have an effect on the military situation in Normandy.

A little over two weeks later, on July 22, Japan's Naval Attaché in Berlin reported to his government that Luftwaffe authorities had told him it wasn't possible to use the flying bomb against the Allied landings. As with most intercepts, this one could not be accepted without confirmation, but indications were that the flying bomb would not be used against the invasion ports or any military or logistical targets.

Given the Allies' fear that the flying bomb might disrupt the invasion, this must have come as good news, but another telegram, on July 25, from the Japanese Ambassador in Berlin contained a more disturbing item. Foreign Minister Ribbentrop had told him that although the flying bomb was inaccurate and would produce no dramatic change in the military situation, the Germans had great expectations for their forthcoming rocket, the V-2, which was much more accurate.

The British War Cabinet moved quickly to deny the Germans any useful intelligence about the flying bomb. On July 16, a Military Intelligence official, whom Dr. R.V. Jones referred to only as "George," informed him that the Germans had instructed their agents in London to report where the flying bombs were falling in the city and this put the intelligence agency M.I.5. in a quandary. Most of the "German" agents in Great Britain were, in fact, controlled by the British and were maintained to feed false or misleading information to the enemy. If they fed back deliberately false reports, the Germans could very well learn their spy network was compromised. Jones reasoned that agents' reports of location were usually accurate, but their sense of timing might be off. Jones knew from his experience with the photographs from Peenemünde and Blizna that the flying bombs had a tendency to fall short. He also noticed that the bombs now hitting London were falling in the southeast, a less densely populated area of the city. Jones saw a solution to M.I.5.'s dilemma: "In a flash I saw that we might be able to keep the bombs falling short, which would mean fewer casualties in London as a whole, and at the same time avoid arousing any suspicions regarding the genuineness of the agents."[34]

Jones suggested to "George" that the agents should report the correct points of impact for bombs which had fallen beyond London, with the times of bombs which had fallen short. "Thus, if the Germans attempted any correlation, they might be led to think that even the bombs which they had reason to believe might have fallen short were instead tending to fall in northwest London. Therefore, if they made any correction at all, it would be to reduce the average range."[35] If the Germans did manage to obtain aerial photographs of the damage, there was no way they could match a particular bomb with a reported incident.

The Germans never noticed the deception. In the first week of the attack, a "very reliable agent" sent accurate details of bomb damage all over London. By June 22, the agents never reported a flying bomb south of the Thames when, in fact, 75 percent of the bombs were falling south of the river.[36] What should have been a simple matter of agent control for M.I.5, however, somehow reached the War Cabinet, where it was hotly debated on August 15, 1944. Lord Cherwell and Duncan Sandys, who had been appointed Chairman of the War Cabinet Crossbow Committee on June 19, supported the policy. On the other hand, Herbert Morrison, who chaired the cabinet while Churchill was away, complained that they did not have the right to say who lived and who died. Morrison was a socialist and felt to some extent that the British leadership was willing to have bombs fall on working-class London rather than in the areas in which government officials lived. He insisted that the plan be abandoned immediately and the cabinet agreed, but that didn't end the matter. Group Captain Alfred Earl, Air Secretary to the War Cabinet and an acquaintance of Jones's, was present at the discussion and had the minutes concerning agent reports of flying bombs struck from the record by reason of the fact they concerned agent control and were extremely sensitive. He then told Jones what he had done. Since there was no longer a record, Jones felt free to tell "George" to continue the policy, and that was done.

As steps were taken to control the agents' reports, the British newspapers were publishing the obituaries of those killed by the bombs and listed the boroughs or districts in which the deceased had lived. Cherwell thought the information would give German agents in neutral countries a belated but accurate plot of the fall of the bombs, so one of his statisticians plotted roughly seventy cases from *The Times* and eighty from the *Daily Telegraph,* to come up with two different centers of impact. Both were close enough to the actual center of mass to give Cherwell cause for concern. He called Sir Finlander Stewart, Chairman of the Home Executive, and British newspapers were no longer allowed to list addresses or districts of victims in obituaries.

While the Allies struggled to sharpen their defenses, General Heinemann and Colonel Wachtel worked diligently to make Flak Regiment 155(W) more efficient. Photo reconnaissance was out of the question, so Heinemann had to rely on agents' reports to determine where the flying bombs were hitting in London. There was a delay in getting information out of England and he and Wachtel needed something more timely and objective. They decided to track the flying bombs themselves by installing a small FuG 23 transmitter in the bomb. Once the bomb was launched, a 153-foot-long antenna was released to trail behind the bomb. To limit the chance of interception of the signal, the FuG 23 did not begin transmitting until it was roughly thirty five miles from the target. The coded signal was picked up and triangulated by three receivers at Le Tilleul, Cambrai and Poix, and the stations followed the signal until it stopped transmitting, which amounted to five or six minutes depending on the actual speed of the particular V-1. The cessation of the transmission was taken to mean point of impact. The tracking beams were not precise but presented a small triangular area into which the bomb fell. The center of the triangle was accepted as the coordinates of the impact and this location was reported to LXV Armeekorps headquarters, where it was plotted on a large map of London. From June 15 to August 1, 440 of the 6,046 V-1s launched at London were equipped with the FuG transmitter.[37] Neither the reports from the agents nor the information from the transmitters gave Heinemann or Wachtel any reason to change the range.

The Germans were also aware that the balloon barrage just south of London was a major obstacle to the V-1 because the pilotless aircraft could not fly over it. Over the course of the campaign, the stout cables that tethered the balloons accounted for 278 flying bombs. To overcome this obstacle, the Germans adopted an improvement suggested by Wachtel. These were sharp-edged cable cutters inside the leading edge of the V-1 wing that the Germans called *Kuto-nasen* (Kuto noses). The cutters enabled the fast-flying missile to cut through any cables it encountered without bringing down the missile. The modification was not complicated and by the end of June, V-1s with the cable-cutting wings were reaching the launch sites. Somewhat more than 20 percent of the V-1s were equipped with the *Kuto-nasen* and by the end of the campaign they accounted for the loss of 630 British balloons.[38]

By the middle of July, Flak Regiment 155(W) was a veteran unit, skilled in the preparation and launch of their unique weapon.

Combined production of the V-1s at Nordhausen and Fallersleben rose quickly to nearly 3,000 a month and the availability of missiles and the number of modified sites enabled the crews to launch an average of 100 missiles a day at London. Supply arrangements were difficult but workable. The missiles from Germany were delivered by rail and then taken to the storage sites at night, usually in small groups of three trucks or less. Storage was the weakest link in the V-1 chain, as Allied bombing of Nucourt and St-Leu-d'Esserent had demonstrated. Fortunately for the Germans, the ability of the launch crews to fire so many missiles a day kept the number of missiles at the storage sites at a minimum. The loss of three hundred V-1s was bad enough, but had the depots been filled to capacity there might have been nearly three thousand lost and the V-1 campaign would have come to a halt for several weeks. From the storage sites the missiles went to the firing sites, also at night and in small groups.

Conditions for the launch crews were far from perfect. In addition to Allied bombing raids, they faced the danger of failures on the launching ramp, V-1s that crashed and exploded shortly after take-off and bombs with defective guidance systems that circled for twenty minutes before they crashed and exploded nearby. As of July 24, 245 missile failures due to technical reasons had been reported. Seventy (28.6 percent) were due to airframe failures; 62 (25.3 percent) due to catapult failures; 40 (16.3 percent) due to engine failures; 34 (13.9 percent) due to control equipment failures; 5 (2.0 percent) due to crew errors; and 34 (13.9 percent) for unknown reasons.[39] Nevertheless, the number of launches per day increased.

On July 20, the day a group of German officers attempted to assassinate Hitler, the Flak regiment received new instructions to carry out a saturation attack on London. That night, the launch crews fired 193 missiles at London and the next night they launched 200. Heavy launch schedules, however, could not be maintained over a long period. Supply shortages, Allied air attacks as well as fatigue quickly took their toll. Some days Flak Regiment 155(W) launched only a handful of flying bombs, but on the whole the numbers were impressive. On August 2 the crews succeeded in launching a total of 316 bombs in a twenty-four-hour period. As a result of the damage to Nucourt and St-Leu, Wachtel established five new underground storage facilities to serve a new line of 64 proposed launch sites extending from St-Omer to the port of Le Havre. These new sites came with a proposal to bring the launching establishment to brigade strength. A second regiment, Flak Regiment 255(W), was approved on July 17, 1944, as were the new launch sites. A third regiment, a brigade headquarters and more sites were also in the planning stage.

Throughout July and the early part of August, British defenses continued to improve, and the guns and fighters began bringing down an ever greater number of the flying bombs approaching England's coast. Hill's decision to move the guns to the coast was obviously the correct one, but the defense had one glaring weakness in that it faced only to the southeast. This didn't seem to matter until the Germans added a new dimension to their assault.

On July 9, the first air-launched V-1 out-flanked the defenses and fell on London. The concept of launching the V-1 by air was an obvious result of the air-launch tests of the missile at Peenemünde during the winter of 1943–44. A series of tests to determine the practical application of the concept began at the "Erprobungsstelle der Luftwaffe" at Peenemünde on April 6, 1944. Tests were conducted to find a suitable aircraft for the purpose and the Dornier 215, Dornier 217 and Focke-wulf 200 were considered, but the Heinkel 111H was chosen. With a bomb capacity in excess of 6,000 pounds it could easily carry the weight of the missile, and a modification program was set up at Oschatz, about 40 miles east of Leipzig.

The aircraft was adapted to carry one V-1 beneath either the port or starboard wing between the fuselage and the engine. To save weight, the internal bomb racks were removed. In order to launch the flying bomb the aircraft had to be adapted to release its missile at the proper place and at the proper altitude. To this end, the same air log as that installed in the V-1 was installed in the He 111H along with an altitude-control device that was connected to the log. Other modifications allowed the crew to start the pulse jet engine and release the bomb at the proper time.

Not everyone was enthusiastic about aerial delivery of the flying bomb. Feldmarschal Erhard Milch was skeptical that air-launching could ever be a routine method of V-1 delivery but he did see its value as a feint to outflank, and thus disperse, the defenses. The third group of Kampfgeschwader 3 was equipped with modified aircraft and trained at Peenemünde in May.

Its training ended with the launch of fifty-four V-1s in the first nine days of June. The air launch was a simple affair. The aircraft maintained an altitude of 2,000 feet and its speed was sufficient to keep the pulse jet engine running after it was ignited. When the air log indicated the correct distance, the bomber dropped the V-1, which fell a few hundred feet before its pulse jet engine reached full power. Once that happened, the flying bomb flew on toward its target.

According to existing policy, the group should have come under control of LXV Armeekorps, but on June 16, 1944 the Luftwaffe stated that air delivery of the V-1 was the same as any other bombing mission and so maintained control of its effort.[40] With the tests complete and the question of who was to control the air launches settled, the Luftwaffe ordered III/KG 3, stationed at Dutch airfields at Venlo and Gilze-Rijn, and Beauvais in France, to carry out a series of operational tests.

Major Martin Vetter, the commander of the unit, was an acknowledged bomber ace and took to the project with great relish. After several experiments he came up with the ideal delivery method. The He-111H was an obsolete bomber with an official maximum speed of 217 mph under full load. In fact, the speed of the aircraft carrying the two and one half tons of flying bomb was less than 200 mph and sometimes as low as 170, which made it an easy mark for Allied fighters. To make matters worse, English radar coverage in June 1944 extended far out into the Channel and the North Sea. A slow-moving He-111H heading toward England was bound to be picked up by radar, intercepted and shot down.

In order to give his bomber crews a fighting chance, Vetter knew they had to avoid observation, so he ordered them to attack only at night. When the bomber took off, it headed for a radio or light beacon on the Dutch coast at an altitude of 1,600 feet. Over the North Sea it dropped to a very low altitude, in many cases less than 200 feet, to fly below the British radar envelope. Just prior to the launch point, the bomber climbed to about 1,700 feet and started the pulse jet engine. At that point the aircraft was visible to British radar at Foreness, North Foreland and St. Margaret's Bay. After a ten- to thirty-second warm-up, the bomber dropped the flying bomb and, as it headed for its target, the crew executed a sharp turn, dove again to minimum altitude and headed for home.[41]

The group began operations on July 18, 1944, with an authorized strength of thirty aircraft, but there were seldom more than eight operational at a given time. In the first three days the group launched about fifty V-1s at London. Before its last five launches, on September 5, the group managed to send three hundred bombs against London, ninety against Southampton and twenty against Gloucester.[42]

During the month of July, Crossbow authorities were faced with a mystery in that they couldn't identify the origin of flying bombs coming in from the east. The conclusion was that they had come from Belgium or Holland, but by July 27 photo reconnaissance revealed no flying bomb launching sites in either of the suspected areas. A re-examination of the evidence by Air Intelligence concluded that the flying bombs that were arriving from the east had to be air-launched. From July 11, a series of daily Enigma transmissions concerning III/KG3 had been intercepted. In the first, Fliegerkorps IX ordered a reconnaissance of London with the added instruction that if it had to be postponed because of V-1 operations, then III/KG3 had to be informed. There were further communications between Fliegerkorps IX and LXV Armeekorps concerning III/KG3 and some of them suggested a reconnaissance of the Portsmouth–Southampton area.

Suggestions were put forward that III/KG3 might be a new designation for Flak Regiment 155(W), but when the PRU and CIU failed to find any launch sites that might be the origin of the radar tracks, a further re-examination was called for and Signal Intelligence revealed that transmissions intercepted from the air launch training program at Peenemünde had been overlooked. Baltic plots clearly showed the air-launched flying bombs and the fact that training had intensified in May and June. The British were slow in reacting to the new threat and were unable to change the ground defenses before III/KG3's airfields were captured by advancing Allied troops. British defenders managed to shoot down several of the air-launched flying bombs and night fighters caught a few of the bombers over the North Sea, but shortage of fuel limited the operations of the Heinkels far more than enemy action. Before its airfields were captured, III/KG3 was pulled back to Germany to await events.

Defenses against the main V-1 effort from the Pas de Calais improved rapidly. Even as they improved, however, the tragedies continued to mount. On Wednesday, August 2, a bomb landed near a pub in

Beckenham at lunch hour and killed forty-four. August 28, 1944 was one of the defense's best days. Out of 97 bombs that approached the coast, 65 were brought down by guns, 23 by fighters and 2 by balloons. That meant 92.7 percent of the incoming flying bombs had been brought down. The score is impressive but it also means that seven tons of explosive got through. Two of the bombs landed in Kent and the other five went on to London. On the average, in the last seven weeks of the offensive, the guns and pilots brought down more than 60 percent of the flying bombs, but there was no way to stop them all until the launching sites were overrun.

On July 18, the Americans captured St-Lô and a week later the breakthrough the Allies had been hoping for occurred when Operation Cobra, a massive air bombardment, opened a huge hole in the German lines. On August 1, Patton's Third Army was activated and it raced through the Avranches gap. A German counterattack failed and the Allied armies encircled the tattered German forces in the Falaise Pocket, which they closed on August 19.

On August 12, LXV Armeekorps Headquarters withdrew from France to Waterloo in Belgium. Six days later, they ordered Flak Regiment 155(W) to make a phased withdrawal from its positions in the Pas de Calais to Belgium in the area of Antwerp. The third and fourth battalions of the regiment had already been forced to withdraw north to avoid the advancing Allies. The first and second battalions began an orderly withdrawal as soon as notified, and Wachtel, some of his staff and the third and fourth battalions of the regiment remained at Saleux until August 23, when they withdrew to Roubaix. The sites were dismantled, and equipment and supplies collected and moved back toward Holland to new sites surveyed along the Dutch coast. What could not be taken was destroyed. All movement was done at night, but even during the hours of darkness Allied bombers disrupted the retreat, destroying the trains and bombing the roads over which the Flak Regiment was withdrawing. The first and second battalions set up in the Amiens–Abbeville area, but before they could get any orders to dismantle and evacuate their equipment they were threatened by advancing Allied tanks.

On August 31, with Armeekorps Headquarters leaving Waterloo, most decisions were left to the section commanders. They fired the last nine V-1s from France at 0400 on September 2 and fled after destroying their equipment. They gathered at Maria ter Heide in Holland, where Wachtel and most of his men were preparing new sites. As the German front disintegrated, the retreat took a heavy toll on the German missile crews and their equipment. Driving and towing their equipment across roads choked with military vehicles while under constant Allied air and artillery attack accounted for the loss of much equipment and supplies. By the time the Flak Regiment made it out of harm's way, much of the launching equipment and most of the vehicles of the second and fourth battalions had been destroyed or abandoned to the onrushing Allied armies. Only the first and third battalions managed to save any substantial amount of equipment.

Oberkommando der Wehrmacht had little idea of what was happening to the men of LXV Armeekorps or Flak Regiment 155(W). After the fall of Paris on August 25, Hitler ordered the Flak Regiment and the long-range artillery to open fire on the city, but there was no place or time to build catapults. On August 29, OKW ordered General Heinemann to provide sufficient launching sites to engage both Paris and London. Sites selected by Heinemann in the first phase of the corps' withdrawal had already been overrun by advancing Allied troops and the order could not be obeyed. The first phase of the German V-1 campaign was over.

Flak Regiment 155(W) and Headquarters LXV Armeekorps had accomplished much during the eight months from January through August 1944. Their mere presence had diverted thousands of Allied sorties and tens of thousands of tons of bombs from the cities of the Reich. Under conditions of extreme difficulty they fired roughly 8,000 flying bombs, of which 2,300 made it to London. They killed a total of 2,419 people, roughly one per missile as Cherwell had so smugly predicted. The V-1 injured thousands more, destroyed 170,000 houses in Greater London and damaged 800,000 additional. Militarily, they tied down more than a quarter of a million men, 2,000 guns and 900 aircraft that could have been employed on the Continent. All this at a cost of less than 500 men killed and wounded.

With the withdrawal of Flak Regiment 155(W) from effective range, the massive bombardment of London ceased and only a few air-launched V-1s remained. Great Britain and the United States, convinced they had erased the V-1 threat, congratulated themselves on their victory. After August 30, the U.S. Army Air Force flew no more

Crossbow sorties and in early September the British Vice Chiefs of Staff announced that all the launching areas in France had been captured. On September 5, Sir Charles Portal, Chief of the Air Staff, noted that the attacks on storage depots and transportation facilities could cease, and the following day the Vice Chiefs of Staff announced that the flying bomb attacks presented no further danger as all the launching sites were overrun.

On September 7, Herbert Morrison, the Minister of Home Security, officially ended the evacuation of London and the British population rejoiced as thousands streamed back into the capital. On the same day, Duncan Sandys gave a press conference in which he praised the people in London and in "bomb alley" for their courage, and thanked the Americans for their assistance. During the conference he said, "Except possibly for a few last shots, the battle of London is over."[43] It was an unfortunate choice of words.

9

Vergeltungswaffe Zwei

When the flying bomb offensive was finally underway, Erhard Milch was delighted. The Luftwaffe had succeeded in launching a long-range weapon at London before the Army. Wernher von Braun and his supposedly brilliant team of engineers at Peenemünde had labored eight years and spent billions of Reichsmarks and had yet to produce a viable weapon, while the Luftwaffe had done it in little more than two years. Walter Dornberger was naturally chagrined. To make matters worse, A-4 rocket #4089, used as a test bed for Wasserfall, an air defense missile, went astray after a normal launch on June 13, 1944 and had crashed near Malmö, Sweden. Dornberger explained that, "while the rocket was still traveling slowly the control engineer had changed its direction by eye and lost contact with it when it unexpectedly moved sideways into a low flying cloud."[1]

Dr. R.V. Jones's information on the event was that "the control officer had been selected for this particular trial on the basis of his expertise as a controller of guided bombs, and had never seen a rocket take-off before. He was said to have been so awestruck by the sight that he unwittingly left his hand on the controls so the rocket swerved to the left too [far] and by the time he pulled himself together it was too late to gain control."[2]

When Dornberger reported the incident, he was asked if the rocket would give away any secrets if it fell into enemy hands. Dornberger assured headquarters that the Wasserfall control equipment would give them some difficulty. After his explanation, he was ordered to report to Rastenburg for a reprimand from Hitler, even though he was not responsible for the Wasserfall project. By the time he arrived, Hitler's temper had cooled and he avoided experiencing one of the Führer's legendary tantrums.

The local inhabitants in Sweden were startled by the rocket's impact. Eyewitnesses reported one explosion several thousand feet in the air and then a second when the rocket smashed into a cornfield. No one was hurt, even though one man and his horse were thrown to the ground by the blast. Scattered everywhere were pieces of wreckage that included Swedish ball bearings. The natural assumption was that an aircraft had crashed and the site was quickly surrounded and cordoned off by the Swedish home guard. The crew of the crashed aircraft could not be found but men, who were most likely German agents, attempted to enter the restricted area. One group with a hearse claimed they were there to retrieve a corpse. They were turned away and Swedish authorities called for local citizens to turn in anything they had found, going so far as to search the homes of souvenir hunters, who were reluctant to give up their prizes.

The following day, the British Air Attaché in Stockholm notified the Chief of the Air Staff of the crash. Swedish air officials took the two tons of wreckage they collected to Stockholm for examination. By June 22 they discovered the wreckage had a turbo pump and was not another flying bomb. Negotiations continued with Swedish authorities, and two RAF officers who were experts on air crashes were allowed to examine the wreckage. This was the beginning of "Operation Big Ben," the Allied effort to piece together a German rocket. The experts' first concern was that the whole thing might be a German ruse, but they quickly realized the wreckage was genuine.

On July 7 they reported that it was larger than a flying bomb, rocket propelled and controlled by fins and jet vanes in flight. They also concluded that it had radio guidance similar to that found in the German guided bomb Hs 293. It was approximately six feet in diameter and they "guessed that the weight of the warhead could not be less than 10,000 pounds and might be considerably more."[3] The conclusion that A-4 was radio guided was understandable in view of the Wasserfall instrumentation installed in the rocket. There was little evidence to indicate what the rocket's fuel was, other than blue and violet stains on the main burner unit and reddish brown stains on fragments from the fuel tank. These strongly indicated that the fuel was hydrogen peroxide, but it was quickly learned that the stains were from the dyes the Germans used to recover their rockets at sea. Neither of the dyes could be used as a fuel, and as there was no trace of hydrogen peroxide in either the motor unit or the fuel tanks, that chemical was finally ruled out as a fuel. An Air Ministry finding dated July 23, 1944 stated that an alcohol–liquid oxygen fuel combination could not be ruled out. The estimate of the weight of the warhead was the result of continued British overestimation of the size of the A-4's payload.

The Malmö rocket was a major intelligence coup even though the errors concerning guidance and warhead once again threw British investigators off track. The Air Chief of Staff for Intelligence included this information in his report of July 9 along with a Polish report that the A-4 was powered by hydrogen peroxide, had a range of 200 miles and was radio controlled. Information from the Baltic plotting stations indicated that seven rockets had been fired from June 7 to 30. By this time the large site at Sottevast had been captured by advancing Allied troops, and air intelligence could find no firm evidence that it was a "rocket projector" site, but conjectured it might have been designed for the bulk storage of rockets. The report concluded that the Germans were capable of firing a few rockets at England at any time, provided the firing bases in France were completed. After a Chiefs of Staff meeting on June 27, Field Marshal Sir Alan Brooke, Chief of the Imperial General Staff, expressed concern about the rocket, which appeared to most knowledgeable British leaders as an indistinct but darkening shadow behind the flying bomb.

After the Malmö incident Dornberger was increasingly seen as the bearer of continual bad tidings, instead of as the project manager of a revolutionary new weapon. It was a situation the SS was quick to exploit, and on July 8 Hans Kammler denounced Dornberger as a public danger in the presence of General Walter Buhle, chief of the OKW Army Staff and two other generals. The SS officer went on to state that Dornberger should have been court-martialed for undermining the war effort of the Reich by virtue of his supposedly hopeless project. While Kammler denounced the A-4 project as hopeless, Reichsführer Heinrich Himmler meanwhile demanded that Field Marshal Keitel subordinate the rocket project to one strong personality—no doubt meaning himself—with Kammler as his deputy. Keitel diplomatically declined, while Dornberger continued his attempt to gain control of every aspect of the A-4 from development to production to firing. A few days later, Dornberger's and the Army's hopes were dashed. After surviving the attempt to assassinate him in the "Officers' Plot" of July 20, 1944, Hitler lost whatever trust he may have had in the Army. On July 21, he dismissed General Friedrich Fromm as head of the Reserve Army and head of armaments and replaced him with Himmler, who now became the second most powerful man in Nazi Germany. Albert Speer, who had been able to maintain some control over the A-4 project, lost influence because his name had been found on a list of proposed ministers made up by the conspirators who tried to kill Hitler.

In an information report to the Crossbow Committee dated July 10, Duncan Sandys stated that Allied attacks on the large sites would continue. To delay the development of the rocket and improved flying bombs, another heavy raid on Peenemünde was planned. On July 11, the Chiefs of Staff advised Churchill to get the remains of the rocket that had crashed in Sweden and obtain permission from Stalin for British experts to inspect the site at Blizna as soon as it was overrun by the Russians. Churchill, who had been keeping the Soviet leader informed of the flying bomb since the beginning of the attacks, made the request on July 13. Lord Cherwell now admitted the rocket existed, but expressed his doubts that the large sites had anything to do with it. Rather he thought they were for the flying bomb. Sandys disagreed and Churchill felt compelled to have another meeting that same day to discuss the "conflicting intelligence" about the rocket.

At the meeting the Chief of the Air Staff left no doubt that the long-range rocket did exist. The next day, censorship and deception plans based on experience with the flying bomb—to deny the enemy information about impact areas and damage—were drawn up and submitted to the Chiefs of Staff. Concern about the rocket increased when the British intercepted a diplomatic message from the Japanese ambassador in Berlin to Tokyo, in which he once again reported that Germany would be employing a weapon, or weapons, more devastating than the flying bomb.[4]

Concern about the rocket continued to deepen, and Air Vice Marshal Frank Inglis, Assistant Chief of the Air Staff (Intelligence), asked Jones to report immediately on what he had on the subject.

Jones was not happy about issuing what he considered an incomplete report, and he complied "under the strongest possible protest." On July 16, he issued an assessment of intelligence about the rocket. For it he used the information from the rocket that crashed at Malmö; reports of Polish observations of the rocket; photo reconnaissance; radio intercepts from the Baltic tracking stations; and information from prisoners of war. The conclusions were that the rocket had a range of approximately 200 miles, based on Polish observations of nineteen launchings between April 30 and May 7, 1944, and the fact that the Malmo rocket crashed 200 miles from Peenemünde. From the radio intercepts, it was clear that the Germans had fired between thirty and forty rockets from Blizna and Peenemünde in the month of June and that the accuracy of the rocket had improved to the point where 50 percent of them were falling into a circle 20 miles in diameter.

Photos of craters in the Blizna area indicated a warhead weight of three to seven tons—still a gross overestimation—and since the Malmö rocket investigation was not yet complete, Jones still believed the rocket was fueled by hydrogen peroxide. There was no worthwhile information on rocket production. One source stated that production had been curtailed in March in favor of fighter aircraft, but no one knew if the rocket was in mass production, how many were being made or where it was manufactured. Jones's conclusion was basically the same as that of the Chief of the Air Staff: that the Germans could launch a few rockets at any time, providing launch sites were available in France. Jones also cautioned that, considering the military situation in Normandy, the Germans might commit the rocket before all the mechanical problems were solved. Two days later, on July 18, Cherwell conceded that the rocket could not be disregarded but that the results of such an attack were not likely to be very serious, adding that the engineering problems involved in devising this weapon must be formidable.

That evening, Churchill made one of his rare appearances as chairman of the Crossbow Committee. In what turned out to be a "stormy" session, the Prime Minister exclaimed that they had been caught napping. The outburst was the result of two particularly upsetting pieces of information, both presented by Dr. Jones. The first was Jones's conclusions that the Germans had already fired upwards of 150 experimental rockets and that, in all probability, they had manufactured around a thousand. A few days before the meeting, Jones had seen decrypts from the Baltic that reported serial numbers of "Geräte" (devices) traveling from Blizna to Peenemünde. The numbers ran from 17053 to 18036.[5] Jones correctly deduced that these were the serial numbers of rockets that had been fired at Blizna and the wreckage was being returned to Peenemünde for analysis. There was no direct proof that these were rocket serial numbers, but the flying bomb catapults at Blizna had been dismantled, so all he needed was proof that the rocket was at Blizna. Working very late, Jones re-examined the photographs of Blizna taken on May 5. In the early hours of the morning he discovered a white blur on a flat car of the narrow-gauge railway that served the camp. It was a rocket.

Churchill was aghast at the thought of a thousand tons of explosive falling on London. Jones's bland assertion that a thousand tons was less than that delivered on a single night by Bomber Command or Eighth Air Force did little to mollify the prime minister.

The second piece of information that Churchill found so upsetting was the fact that the Germans didn't need a large bunker from which to fire the rocket. It could be launched from a mobile launcher set on a small piece of concrete or other hardstand. Jones had identified small concrete pads on a Blizna photograph the day before, and the information was a surprise to Churchill, but evidence of the ability to fire the rocket from a small piece of hardstand had been available from POW interrogations for some time. Near the end of June the Allied troops captured POWs from "Sonderstab [Special Staff] Berger," a unit under the control of a Lieutenant Colonel Berger, responsible for selecting, surveying and constructing rocket installations. The POWs reported fourteen areas in which there were twenty-four firing sites. "Each site consisted of three rectangular platforms of different depths of reinforced concrete, so built that they would be scarcely distinguishable from the nearby road; the rocket was to be fired on the platforms from a metal tripod."[6]

The POWs went on to state that a site at Bernesy had been completed in January and one at Bray was close to completion. They also listed four supply dumps in which the rockets were to be stored in tunnels before they were taken to an assembly shed prior to firing. One dump was in a quarry, while another at La Meauffe was being dug as a series of tunnels serviced by a narrow-gauge railroad. This information had been reported to the Chiefs of Staff by the Assistant Chief of the Air Staff for Intelligence in a regular report on July 9, but was not discussed at later meetings of the Chiefs of Staff or the Crossbow Committee. In the discussions between Cherwell and Sandys, the subject had not come up. Nevertheless, Jones was put in a bad light and accused by Sandys of withholding information. During the next scheduled meeting of the Chiefs of Staff, Sandys repeated his accusations and was supported by Herbert Morrison, who had not been present at the July 18 meeting. Sandys complained that he could not do his job properly if he had to depend on periodic digests of intelligence material instead of raw data and that Air Intelligence should not wait until it was certain of the facts before circulating them. His recommendation that he receive raw data could not be approved because of the danger of compromising intelligence sources, but the recommendation that Jones no longer be the one to decide what was to be disseminated was accepted. Cherwell attempted to defend Jones in a memorandum, but Churchill and the committee were very frustrated and Jones had become the target of their ire.

On July 30, 1944 the Assistant Chief of the Air Staff (Intelligence) appointed RAF Group Captain Jack Easton Director of Intelligence (Research), responsible for coordinating the work of all Air Intelligence sections responsible for Crossbow work and for providing other agencies with the intelligence they required. Jones was understandably angry and drafted a letter of resignation, but then thought better of it. He was afraid that scientific intelligence concerning the rocket would not be properly controlled, or perhaps used for political purposes, and decided to remain.

In the midst of the controversy about rocket intelligence it was obvious the two British experts in Stockholm could learn just so much in Sweden from mere observation. Jones strongly recommended to Sir Charles Portal "that the acquisition of all available components is a matter of vital interest to the defence of this country and that we should not hesitate to pay any reasonable price which would satisfy the Swedes."[7] Negotiations were made through military staffs, and a deal for "two squadrons of tanks" was presumably struck. Shipments of the rocket wreckage by air began immediately and the heaviest parts by sea later. On July 31, experts at Farnborough began their difficult task. Using wood and wire to fill in the empty spaces, they painstakingly assembled the fragments and parts recovered from the Swedish crash in an attempt to reproduce an A-4.

The Polish underground, known as the Home Army, had waged a long and difficult war against the occupying Nazis. They had a well-organized intelligence network that observed and recorded German experiments and training with long-range weapons at Blizna. They kept in contact with the Polish government in exile in London and provided R.V. Jones and other British agencies a great deal of information on the Germans' progress. After observing launches of both the Fi 103 and the A-4, the Poles realized the potential of the weapons and went to extraordinary lengths to obtain information about them. At one point they even considered attacking the German installation at Blizna and holding it long enough to seize important documents obviously stored there. The plan was wisely given up because the SS garrison at Blizna was strong and reprisals against the local population were bound to be excessive. A less ambitious but still dangerous plan involved stealing an A-4 from a train, taking it to a little-used siding and transferring the load to a truck.[8] Fortunately, this plan didn't have to be used either.

The Polish underground not only observed launches of the Fi 103 and the A-4 but, in the case of the latter, it established teams to collect wreckage from crashed rockets. They were the first to discover the revolutionary hydrogen peroxide turbo pump that pumped fuel to the engine of the A-4. Often the Poles reached the impact point of the rocket before the SS units that were searching for it.

On May 20, 1944 an A-4 fell on the swampy left bank of the Bug River near the village of Klimczyee without exploding. The local Home Army unit found the rocket, and before the SS recovery team arrived managed to hide it by rolling it into a pond and moving a small herd of cows around it. When the SS team arrived, it was unable to locate the rocket and after a few days the Germans gave up their search. The Research Committee of the Home Army was then given responsibility for the find. Jerzy Chmielewski, the head of the committee, and Antoni Kocjan, a committee member who was an engineer, arranged to have the rocket partially dismantled and carted away. Under Kocjan's supervision, the rocket was disassembled and its internal arrangements photographed. In mid-July 1944 the British and

Poles arranged to have a large amount of the stolen rocket picked up by cargo aircraft in Poland and flown to England. While they were not made frequently, flights to Poland from Italy had been carried out twice before, in May and June, 1944.

In Poland this airborne operation had the code name "Most," which in Polish means bridge. In England it was known as "Wildhorn." Each of the flights brought in equipment needed by the Polish Home Army as well as agents. The return flights brought out agents and intelligence the Poles had gathered. Kocjan, the engineer and the man most qualified to describe what he had seen, was ordered to take with him to England as much material as he could and make an oral report to the Polish authorities in London. Unfortunately, he was arrested by the Gestapo shortly before the operation was to take place and Jerzy Chmielewski was selected to go in his place.

Chmielewski cycled nearly 200 miles to arrive at an airfield that was supposed to be held by the Polish underground, only to find it occupied by a Luftwaffe detachment with two German Storch aircraft and their crews. After a tense few hours, the aircraft flew away and the field was occupied by an underground unit ready to fight off any Germans who might want to reoccupy it. The RAF Dakota arrived on schedule and Chmielewski and several other passengers got on. When the aircraft tried to take off, however, the wheels sank into the marshy ground. The aircraft was unloaded and straw placed before its wheels. The engines roared but it again refused to budge. After a serious discussion about whether to burn the aircraft, Home Army soldiers placed boards in front of the tires and the pilots severed the brake lines because they thought the brakes were jammed. This time the aircraft managed to take off—to the cheers of the Home Army men guarding the field. The aircraft had spent an hour and twenty minutes on the ground, but was unmolested by the Germans. After take-off, it flew south and landed safely in Italy. The Polish emissary arrived in London on July 28, but refused to speak to anyone but a man known to him. After some tense hours, this man arrived and the information was turned over to the British. Unfortunately, the pieces Chmielewski and the Poles had gathered at such great risk were of little use; they were only duplicates of those recovered from the Swedish A-4.

With considerable experience with the flying bomb and definite technical intelligence about the rocket in hand, on August 24 Anti-

Aircraft Command proposed a method of destroying the rocket before it might arrive. With radar able to predict the path of the rocket, the gunners planned to put up a barrage near London to explode the rocket's warhead in the air. The estimated ammunition expenditure for each barrage was about 320,000 rounds. A drawback was that even with the proximity fuse, about 2 percent of the shells fired would fall to earth in the local area and explode. At 28 pounds per projectile, this came to 89.6 tons per barrage. It was obvious that the one-ton warhead of the rocket would do far less damage and, furthermore, that the defenses would quickly run short of ammunition. The idea was sensibly shelved, but the fact it was even considered demonstrates the seriousness with which the British viewed the destructive potential of the rocket.

On Tuesday, July 18, 1944—a bright summer morning—the workers at Peenemünde were alerted that enemy planes were approaching. Air raids along the Baltic coast became a common occurrence in 1944 and Peenemünde was alerted for raids on Stettin and other nearby cities. The warnings were not only for bombers but also for reconnaissance planes, and sometimes workers at the installation had to wait hours for the "all clear" signal before returning to work. About two hours after the initial warning, the antiaircraft guns opened up and the drone of approaching bombers could be heard in the distance. Thirty-five B-17s of the Eighth Air Force dropped thousand-pound bombs on the installation. The American bombardiers toggled a little too late, however, and many of the bombs fell in the woods near Test Stand VII, but the damage was bad enough. Test Stand XI, the one used for calibrating engines, was a complete loss. The hangar in Test Stand VII was hit, as was the concrete-reinforced control room. Beams buckled, but no one in the building was hurt and it could still be used. One of the cranes, the cooling water pump house and the battery room at the test stand were also destroyed, but this was damage that could be repaired, and before the end of the month rocket V-205 was launched from the stand. Altogether, fifty people had been killed, but the dispersion ordered by Dornberger the year before had resulted in minimal casualties.

On August 1, Heeresversuchsstelle (Army Research Installation) Peenemünde officially became Electromechanische Werke GmbH (Electromechanical Industries, Inc.). The monthly expenditures were to be approximately 13 million marks. Eighty-nine percent of it was to be spent on A-4 research and 11 percent spent on Wasserfall, the antiaircraft missile. Even with Electromechanische Werke in control of the A-4 and Wasserfall projects, the site still belonged to the Army and it was administered by the installation commandant of what was now the Karlshagen Test Range. Motor pools, housing and aircraft had to be shared, which led to some friction. Fortunately, both the Army and Electromechanische Werke had its own launch equipment. Many of the "employees" were also soldiers and airmen. There was a total of 3,580 German civilians, most of whom became employees of Electromechanische Werke and received substantial pay raises, not that it did them any good with strict rationing and the Reichsmark declining in value. There were 1,283 German soldiers and airmen and 379 forced laborers and prisoners, who were also under direct control of the military.[9] It was not the best arrangement, but it worked. Von Braun, the talented engineer, gifted, too, with considerable charm and tact, could work in any environment and so remained de facto leader of the effort at Peenemünde.

A day later, another American raid caused further damage to the facility and put an end to static firings at Test Stand VII because of further destruction of the water-cooling system. Hangars in the southern part of the installation were also badly damaged. Since most of the workers were in their shelters, only about ten people were killed and these were for the most part antiaircraft gunners.

On August 4, 1944, Hans Kammler was promoted to SS-Gruppenführer (major general), and two days later Himmler placed him in charge of the A-4 program, making him responsible only to the Reichsführer and SS-Obergruppenführer Hans Jüttner, who was Himmler's chief of staff for the Reserve Army. Thus, at the stroke of a pen, Kammler suddenly had all the power that Dornberger, as head of the A-4 program, had worked for years to obtain. Disheartened, the latter considered resigning as "Beauftragter zur besonderen Verwendung Heer" (Commissioner for Special Duties–Army, or B.z.b.V. Heer) and requesting another assignment. He wrote: "I felt like a man who has devoted years of toil and affection to making a superb violin, a masterpiece which only needs tuning and who then has to look on helplessly while the instrument is grabbed by a tough, unmusical woodman and scraped with a jagged lump of wood. I was in a state of appalling weariness and despair."[10]

Dornberger was talked out of resigning by von Braun and Dr. Ernst Steinhoff, who both felt that, for the good of the project, Dornberger should remain and even help Kammler. The engineers thought they could negotiate with Kammler, but Dornberger had his doubts. Nevertheless, he agreed to remain if for no other reason than to see his creation in action. Meanwhile, the U.S. Eighth Air Force carried out a third air raid on Peenemünde on August 25, 1944. Again the damage was serious and it was six weeks before test firings could resume from Test Stand VII.

Even though the reconstruction of the Malmö rocket was still in progress, Dr. R.V. Jones was able to report on August 10 that the rocket was not the sixty-ton monster with a five-ton warhead often mentioned in intelligence reports. Instead he was finally able to report something close to the true weight and dimensions of the A-4 and its payload. On August 27, he submitted another report that was widely circulated. The head of British Fighter Command, Air Marshal Roderic Hill, and his staff were relieved that the warhead was much smaller than anticipated, but they also learned that the rocket was not as easy to intercept as the flying bomb and that the launch and storage areas for the rocket were much more difficult to locate and damage than even the modified flying bomb sites and their storage areas in caves and tunnels. The only visible vulnerability appeared to be during preparation for launch, when the rocket was being fueled. Any plans to deal with the rocket in France had to be changed quickly when German resistance collapsed and Allied troops overran all the potential launch sites.

During the last weeks of August, the Chiefs of Staff urged Hill to use his fighters for armed reconnaissance over France and Flanders, in search of new launch sites for both the V-1 and the rocket; then, suddenly, the Chiefs of Staff were treating the entire long-range weapon threat as if it were over. Indeed, for a few days it appeared that Sandys' remark about the Battle of London having ended except for a few last shots might be true.

On August 29, Hitler ordered the A-4 offensive to begin under the code name "Operation Penguin." At this point, the matter of who was actually in charge of German long-range weapons came to a head. The

Heereswaffenamt was still pressing for Dornberger to take over the A-4 offensive. Only on August 31 did Colonel Walter, Chief of Staff of LXV Armeekorps, learn that Himmler had been appointed Special Commissioner for rocket weapons with Kammler as his deputy. He also learned that the SS General was calling a meeting in Brussels at which the rocket offensive was part of the agenda. Walter demanded clarification and the Army High Command called him back with the decision that LXV Armeekorps was sole director of rocket operations and Kammler had nothing to do with the offensive. Walter hurried to the Brussels meeting, where he found Dornberger, Metz and Kammler, who was issuing instructions on the deployment of units for the offensive and the sites they were to occupy. When he finally gave Walter a chance to speak, the LXV Armeekorps Chief of Staff read the High Command's decision on the matter to the generals in attendance and "stressed the purely local duties of Dornberger; emphasized the complete irrelevance of Kammler; and warned Metz of his responsibility to the Corps."[11]

Kammler, for once unsure of himself, replied that he would get confirmation from Himmler, the only superior he recognized, and suggested menacingly that Walter also get confirmation from the Army High Command. Walter did request confirmation and two days later discovered that Kammler was, indeed, in command and that the Corps was required to brief him on the course of the offensive although the corps still had responsibility for conducting it. The SS was firmly in control. General Heinemann then requested that LXV Armeekorps be disbanded since it had no real function, but the Wehrmachtführungsstab refused the request and reaffirmed the LXV Armeekorps' control of Flak Regiment 155(W) as a need for its continued existence. Three weeks later, on September 20, Richard Metz resigned his position as HARKO 191, in which he had directed field training and tactical deployments. With the SS in charge, there was nothing for him to do.

The collapse of the German forces in France and the subsequent rapid advance of the Allied armies took Kammler and his new organization by surprise. The firing points north of the Somme selected by Heinemann could not be used. The attempt to establish a headquarters near Antwerp in August was quickly abandoned as was the suggestion that it be located in the city of Metz. At the end of the month Kammler established his headquarters at Cleve. Then, as the Allied advance slowly came to a halt, he moved it forward to Berg en Del in Holland, near the city of Nijmegen. On September 3, A-4 launch sections, organized into Gruppe Nord (Group North) and Gruppe Süd (Group South), began moving forward into western Germany and Holland. These included a total of 5,306 personnel and 1,592 vehicles,[12] more than in most German combat divisions at the time. Gruppe Nord, with two batteries of Artillerie Abteilung 485 was under the command of Colonel Hohmann. It assembled near Cleve and on September 5, Kammler ordered it to The Hague to begin the offensive against London. Gruppe Süd, with batteries two and three of Artillerie Abteilung 836 and Lehr und Versuchs (Training and Experimental) Batterie 444 under the command of Major Weber advanced from the Rhineland to Venlo, Holland but later returned to Euskirchen to attack targets in France and Belgium. The SS battery had not yet completed training.

Lehr und Versuchs Batterie 444 had the special mission of attacking Paris. Ordered to open fire as soon as possible, the unit had traveled first to Euskirchen, arriving there on the night of September 2–3. From there it went to its operational area at La Roche-en-Ardenne in Belgium, roughly 30 miles south of Liège. The launching area was not more than two miles away in the area of La Roche.[13] The moves went unnoticed by Allied reconnaissance and agents. In July, R.V. Jones had argued that the Allies would certainly know when the Germans moved their rocket-launching troops and equipment into France, but Holland was not France. The Germans had much tighter control of that country and, of course, very little information regarding tactical moves got out of Germany.

Kammler's new command was styled "Division zur Vergeltung" (Vengeance Division). On September 6, 1944, he issued his first command directive. In it Kammler assumed command, reaffirmed the formation of the two Gruppen and established command relationships. The directive concluded with the location of the Gruppen command posts. As fielded, the V-2 firing battery consisted of a headquarters and and three other platoons. The headquarters platoon took care of unit administration and communication with higher headquarters. The launching platoon had three firing sections, each with its own launch pad; this platoon was expected to launch two to three rockets per day. The technical platoon unloaded the rockets, minus warheads, from the trains that carried them to the front, tested them and pre-pared them for the launching platoon. The fuel and rocket platoon had three distinct sections. The first section transported the liquid oxygen, the second section the alcohol, and the third transported the warhead to the assembly area and was responsible for handling the sodium permanganate for the turbo pump. Besides the equipment peculiar to the rocket, the platoons carried the usual weapons and communications equipment typical of a combat unit.

The V-2 rockets arrived in twenty-rocket lots by train. A V-2 took up an entire flat car and for every two missiles there was a third flat car which carried the warheads and jet vanes for the two rockets. Normally, the warhead car was positioned between the cars carrying the rockets. After verification of the cargo, the technical platoon removed the rocket from the flat car with a Strabo crane, a mobile electrically powered horizontal crane of 16 tons capacity. Towed into position, it was wide enough to span the railroad tracks and an adjoining platform and was high enough for a rocket on a flat car to pass underneath. The technical platoon transferred the rocket from the rail car to a Vidalwagen, a light trailer roughly 46 feet long designed to transport the V-2 by road to a camouflaged position where the platoon checked the rocket's "propulsion unit, steering mechanism, alcohol tank pressurization system, wiring, and the switch-over from ground to internal power."[14]

It took roughly three hours to make the tests, and minor faults such as defective valves could be corrected with replacement valves by a Repair and Tail Removal Platoon; otherwise, the rocket was turned over to a field maintenance workshop or returned to Nordhausen. Once the rocket passed the initial tests, it was taken to the warhead mounting section, where the warhead was removed from the shipping container and attached to the missile. Shortly thereafter the technical platoon used the Strabo crane to transfer the rocket from the Vidalwagen to the Meilerwagen erector-launcher. The Meilerwagen was the trailer that towed the horizontal V-2, fins first, into the firing position and lifted the 8,800-pound rocket into the vertical position so it could be placed on the launch pad. It consisted of an elevating boom mounted on a wheeled chassis, which held the hydraulic mechanism and high-pressure pump for erecting the elevating boom.

The V-2 rested on the boom, which had numerous functions. In transit, the boom provided a secure cradle for the rocket, which was held in place with a ring clamp at the nose and one near the fins. It also transported the jet vanes in their containers, the connections for fueling, and tools and other items necessary for launching the missile. For traveling, the Meilerwagen also had a camouflage cover on a tubular frame that completely covered the rocket. At the firing position, the boom erected the rocket to the vertical position so that it could be placed on the launch pad and had built-in pipes for fueling the rocket. For fueling and last-minute checks, the boom had a ladder and two folding platforms for crew members who were doing the work or making any final checks.

The Feuerleitpanzer (armored fire control vehicle), towing the portable launch pad, preceded the Meilerwagen into the firing position, along with another vehicle towing a portable generator. The fire control vehicle was a SdKfz 7 eight-ton halftrack in use throughout the German Army for towing the 88mm gun and other artillery. On the back of the halftrack was an enclosed armored shelter that housed a switchboard for communicating with members of the launching platoon; panels for monitoring the tests of the rocket; and the firing controls. It had seats for the crew, and the vision slits in the armored shelter were covered with two-inch-thick glass. The launch pad consisted of the launch table on which the V-2 actually rested, supported by tubular legs above a slightly concave pyramidal steel blast deflector, known in German as the Bodenplatte. The plates of the launch table could be raised or lowered to ensure that the V-2 remained vertical throughout the preparation to fire.

Integral to the launch pad were the cable mast that provided power to the rocket until lift-off and a box that contained the valves that regulated the supply of compressed air to the rocket and its electrical connections. The igniters for the rocket's motor were in a small container on the side of the valve box. In most cases, the ground upon which the launch pad rested was reinforced with logs prior to occupation of the position. As soon as the launch platoon arrived in the position, the crew set up the portable launch pad and laid out the electrical cables. The fire control vehicle was positioned 100 meters from the V-2 along the azimuth of fire and dug in up to the tracks if possible. Slit trenches were dug for the crew between 150 and 200 meters from the launch pad. Camouflage was the order of the day, and as soon as the battery arrived in position the process began.

The Meilerwagen was positioned approximately 50 feet from the launch pad. The prime mover was detached and the crew removed the camouflage cover and the rudder protection cases. The tools and other items needed by the crew were placed in a box attached to the top end of the boom. The Meilerwagen was then moved to the launch pad by means of hand-operated winches. Brackets on the launch pad engaged lugs on the Meilerwagen chassis when the two were properly aligned, then the Meilerwagen was leveled using the outriggers on the chassis and the rocket was raised to a vertical position. When the V-2 was completely vertical it remained suspended until the launch crew made any necessary, last-minute adjustments to the position of the launch pad by hand. The crew raised the launch table and, when the plates of the table touched the fins, the ring clamps of the Meilerwagen boom were released. The Meilerwagen, boom still erect, was pulled three feet away from the vertical V-2 and the platforms lowered while the V-2 was rotated 90 degrees so the crewmen on the platform could fuel the rocket.

During fueling and preparation for firing, the missile was checked to ensure that it remained vertical by the use of two collimators 90 degrees apart. Corrections were made using the manual jacks of the launch table as the rocket was prepared for a final series of pre-flight tests. Three of the graphite jet vanes were installed and the motor and injection nozzles were inspected for dirt or any other obstructions. Once the motor passed inspection, the last jet vane was installed. During engine inspection, other members of the launch crew installed batteries in the control compartment, charged the cylinders with compressed air and connected electrical power to the valve box.

Following the initiation of tests of the steering mechanisms, the rocket motor, the internal sequencing and the switches that controlled the changeover from ground to internal power, the pressure cylinders of the fuel system were charged and the fuel vehicles were brought into position by the fuel and rocket platoon. The alcohol for one launch was carried in two 765-gallon tanks, each carried on a three-ton truck. The fuel was pumped into the rocket by a towed rotary pump capable of pumping the fuel from both trucks simultaneously. After the alcohol tanks were full, the liquid oxygen was pumped into the rocket from a trailer holding a 7.425-ton insulated tank. Five minutes after the start of liquid oxygen fueling, the 33.3-gallon measuring tank on the Meilerwagen was filled with "T-Stoff" (hydrogen peroxide) from a waiting truck. The sodium permanganate, or "Z-Stoff," was transferred to the rocket and then the fueling process was complete. If there were no other problems, the fuses were installed in the warhead and all access hatches were sealed. The rocket was then rotated again so the number 3 fin was aligned on the firing azimuth. The igniter was installed in the motor, the final steering tests were made and the gyroscopes were turned on. Finally, all vehicles and personnel were evacuated from the firing site, and once the battery commander was satisfied that all his personnel were clear and there were no enemy aircraft nearby, he gave the order to fire. If the rocket was equipped with radio-control fuel cut-off, the control equipment was placed six to twelve kilometers behind the rocket, aligned on the firing azimuth.

The first attempt to begin the rocket campaign against the Allies fizzled when Lehr und Versuchs Batterie 444 made two unsuccessful attempts to launch rockets at Paris on September 7. Early on the appointed morning, the firing sections fueled rockets 18,589 and 18,593 and prepared them for launch. The first lifted slowly off its launch pad; then the engine cut out and it dropped back on the pad. It swayed, but managed to stay upright, its jet vanes still hot from the exhaust. Captain Kleiber of the technical battery ordered it defueled. Rocket 18,953 did exactly the same thing. An analysis of the two rockets showed that both had faulty accelerometers that cut off the fuel prematurely. There were, however, two bright spots to the affair. Neither rocket crashed or exploded to damage valuable ground support equipment or injure the trained crews; and the element of surprise had not been lost. Two days later they succeeded, but Himmler ordered his units to stop firing at French targets and the unit soon moved to Walcheren Island, in the Scheldt estuary near the coast of Belgium, to assist in the bombardment of London.

Shortly after 6:35 P.M. on Friday, September 8, 1944, the Germans launched their first V-2 against London. At 6:43 P.M. it landed at Chiswick, where the evening was dull and rainy. Because of the weather, nearly everyone was indoors except for Frank Stubbs, caretaker of the Stavely Road School, who was walking across the school's playing field, and British Army Private Frank Browning, who was on leave and on the way to see his girlfriend. Without warning, Stubbs was hurled twenty feet and thrown to the ground while Browning was killed instantly. When Stubbs got to his feet, he discovered that houses on both sides of the street had been demolished. In all, two people had been killed and twenty others injured, most of them trapped in the ruins of their homes. Witnesses from other neighborhoods described the explosion as a sharp sound and one of them said it was "like a gas main going off."

The rescue squad arrived quickly to get the injured out of the rubble and tend to their wounds. On the heels of the rescue squad came two RAF officers to examine the crater, which was 30 feet wide and 10 feet deep in the middle of a concrete road. They probed the crater, picking up pieces of wreckage, which they put in their briefcases. Shortly afterward, they were joined by two American officers and some Civil Defence officials. A reporter who asked one of the CD men if the explosion had been caused by some kind of new robot bomb was given the reply, "We can't tell you what it was. It might have been a gas main explosion."[15] The reporter didn't believe this and it's doubtful that the official expected him to. Another rocket fell a short time later at Epping, but caused no casualties or damage. After moving to Walcheren Island, Lehr und Versuchs Batterie 444, now transferred to Gruppe Nord, opened fire on London on September 11, one day later than Artillerie Abteilung 485 had opened fire from The Hague. The Germans were surprisingly quiet about their achievement and Goebbels' Propaganda Ministry made no mention that the latest "V" weapon was in action.

The mobility long sought by Dornberger and Heinemann was exploited to the fullest by the firing units in Holland. Several of the firing areas were in large parks such as the Haagse Bos northwest of the center of The Hague, and the parks at Beukenhorst, Bloemendaal, Wassenaar, Loosduinen and Rijswijk. The parks provided almost perfect terrain for the launchers. While there were lots of trees, there was little underbrush, good roads and a lot of hardstand. In some cases the parks had a wall to provide extra security. It made the entire process of fueling the missile and preparing it for launch much simpler, and after the missile was fired it made possible a high-speed withdrawal to minimize Allied counterstrikes from the air.

On September 15, Gruppe Süd was authorized to open fire against Lille, Mons, Roubaix, Brussels, Tourcoing, Charleroi, Amiens, Arras,

Tournai, Liège and Cambrai. The air burst problem with the rocket continued. Most of the time the warhead and the rocket came down separately, causing two distinct craters. In other cases, the disintegration of the rocket caused the warhead to detonate and small fragments would be scattered across the landscape. These caused very little damage except for large pieces like the engine coming down in populated areas.

In the first ten days of the campaign only 25 rockets were fired at London, most of them from The Hague. Of the 25, 16 actually hit the city while the others landed in surrounding areas. Luckily, many of the rockets landed in lightly populated areas and only 50 people were killed and property damage was kept to a minimum. The low rate of fire was the result of defective rockets rejected prior to launch. Nevertheless, the rockets caused quite a stir. British officials refused to acknowledge that London and the surrounding areas were once again under bombardment. The excuse of exploding gas mains quickly wore thin, but the press was strictly forbidden from even speculating about what the sharp explosions around London might be. Nevertheless, the restrictions didn't help. The British public knew what was happening and along with speculation regarding the exact nature of the attack came the sarcastic reference to "flying gas mains," the only nickname ever used for the V-2.

One factor made the V-2 bombardment different from the Battle of Britain, the Blitz or even the V-1 offensive just two months before. Because of the Allies' breakout from Normandy and the rapid advance to the German border, the public assumed that Germany was on her last legs and the war was nearly won. Whereas the other attacks had been greeted with a certain amount of resignation, no one wanted to be killed or injured just before the war was won. The buzz bomb refugees, as the people who evacuated London were called, were returning. School children, mothers with infants and others poured back into the city at a rate of 10,000 a week. The authorities wanted them to stay away, but could not bring themselves to release accurate information about the new attack.

Some British officials, notably Lord Cherwell, remained genuinely nonchalant. He rightly guessed that the Germans could not produce the rocket in anything like the quantities in which they produced the V-1. It was a large, complicated machine with a warhead of "only" a ton of explosive. For the Allies that same one-ton payload could be delivered more easily and cheaply by a manned bomber and it seemed to Cherwell a waste of resources. But, he forgot that the Germans had no bomber fleet and this was the only way they could strike at the British homeland. He also forgot the aspects of V-2 that made it unique among the weapons of World War II. There was very little risk to the launch crews and it could not be intercepted.

The first two rockets that fell on London had an effect on the course of the war totally out of proportion to the casualties or damage they caused in the British capital. The Allied advance on the Continent was slowing down due to the inability to get supplies from the beaches and the ports to the troops in the combat divisions advancing along a broad front. However, there were enough supplies for a major push by one wing of the Allied army. Field Marshal Montgomery conceived a plan to seize a bridge across the Rhine with paratroopers, followed by an armored thrust to the bridge. Once the bridge was captured the North German Plain and the Ruhr—the industrial heart of the Reich—would lay open to an Allied thrust. Montgomery's original plan called for the advance to be made across the Rhine at Wesel, on the northern flank of the Allied armies. Shortly after the two rockets hit London, however, the Vice Chief of the Imperial General Staff sent a message to Montgomery's headquarters: "2 rockets, so called V-2, landed in England yesterday. Will you please report most urgently by what approximate date you consider you can rope off the coastal area contained by Antwerp–Utrecht–Rotterdam. When this area is in our hands the threat from this weapon will probably have dispersed."[16]

Upon receipt of this message, Montgomery changed his plan to accomplish two objectives at once. He recalled in his memoirs, "On the 9th September I received information from London that on the previous day the first V-2 rockets had landed in England; it was suspected that they came from areas near Rotterdam and Amsterdam and I was asked when I could rope off those general areas. So far as I was concerned that settled the direction of the thrust of my operations to secure crossings over the Meuse and the Rhine; it must be towards Arnhem."[17]

The concept of the operation was to drop three airborne divisions to capture the bridges across the Wilhelmina Canal at Eindhoven, the

Maas (Meuse) at Grave, the Waal at Nijmegen and the Lek (Lower Rhine) at Arnhem so that British XXX Corps could clear a 60-mile corridor that opened out into the North German Plain. The operation began with a massive paratrooper drop on September 17, 1944 to seize the bridges along the way to Arnhem as well as the Rhine bridge itself. Initially all seemed to go well and the second objective was gained as Kammler immediately ordered the withdrawal of all A-4 launch units from The Hague. He relocated his headquarters near Münster inside Germany and the firing units near Zwolle, still in Holland but near the German border. From there they fired a few rockets at Ipswich and Norwich. As for London, it meant that ten days after the start of the campaign the rockets stopped.

Unfortunately, for the Allies, Operation "Market Garden" began falling apart as soon as it began. Bad weather, inadequate planning, faulty equipment and lack of aircraft all played their part, but stiff German resistance was the main reason for its failure. Four days after Kammler's units evacuated The Hague and the surrounding area, one battery of Abteiling 485 returned to The Hague; by October 22, the other battery of Abteilung 485 and Batterie 444 were also back at their original positions to resume firing at London.

The end of September saw the end of the one and only attempt the British made to cooperate with the Soviet Union concerning the German secret weapons. By the middle of July 1944, the Soviet Army was rapidly approaching Blizna and Professor R.V. Jones thought the British might be able to gain invaluable information about the rocket if a team of British experts could visit the place after the Soviets captured it. He approached Air Chief Marshal Sir Charles Portal, Chief of the Air Staff, who thought it was a good idea and brought the subject up with Churchill. In a meeting on July 25, the prime minister indicated he had received a "very civil reply from Mr. Stalin."

Jones was disappointed that he was not allowed to choose the team. Instead, the team was selected on the basis of the turf battles going on in the Crossbow Committee. Lieutenant Colonel T.C.B. Sanders of the RAF was chosen as chief of the team, which included Squadron Commander Wilkinson, a Sandys nominee who had investigated the Swedish rocket, and Eric Ackerman, an expert in radio control who was Jones's nominee. The rest of the team were not as knowledgeable.

They arrived in Teheran on August 3, but the Russians refused to let them into their country because they had no visas. In a few days the team was down with dysentery—two of them with cases bad enough to require hospitalization. Ackerman felt the mission was hopeless because of the incompetence of the team members and the Russians' obvious reluctance to let them see Blizna. He sent Jones a private cable asking to return to England, and Jones honored the request. The Soviets, in the meantime, had captured Blizna and held the rest of the party up until they had a chance to strip it of everything deemed useful. The team finally left for Moscow in the last week of August, and after a short stay left Moscow for Blizna on September 1. They arrived the next day. Despite Russian resistance they spoke with a number of local inhabitants and managed to gather approximately a ton and a half of wreckage and some documents.

By September 27, the team was back in Teheran; however, Sanders had to cable that the Soviets had "lost" their material. Eventually, two large crates arrived in England, and when opened were found to be full of wrecked aircraft parts instead of the wreckage the team had collected—an indication of the Soviet-Allied missile competition yet to come. The team learned nothing at Blizna that they hadn't learned from the Swedish rocket and the parts from the Polish Home Army. In the long run, the team did more harm than good as the Russians took down the names of those Poles who had spoken so willingly with the team as "pro-British."

The British used sound-ranging equipment and flash spotting on the Continent as well as radar and crater analysis to determine that the rockets were originating in Holland, possibly near The Hague. The Special Operations Executive (SOE) asked the Dutch underground to find out what it could, but this was precious little. Intensive photo reconnaissance of the area surrounding The Hague revealed nothing. Since the British still believed the rocket was radio controlled, measures were taken for both ground and airborne jamming of the rocket's guidance system. From September 15, an intercept unit operating in the Brussels–Eindhoven–Liège area, close to the rocket launching sites, attempted to intercept and interpret radio signals controlling the rocket but was unable to find any evidence of radio control. By September 17, sixteen rockets had landed in England and three had fallen into the sea.[18]

The beginning of Operation Market Garden curtailed the firings, and Dutch underground reports indicated that German launch units were leaving the area. This news led to the assessment that the attack was "not likely to reach serious proportions,"[19] a view reinforced when rocket launchings ceased the following day. Five days later, the Deputy Chief of the Air Staff warned that new launchings could not be ruled out until the Allies overran the entirety of Holland west of Eindhoven. Considering the available information, and no doubt hoping the rockets would not return, the War Cabinet accepted the advice of the Chiefs of Staff and decided to make no public announcement about the rocket for at least another week.

Two major challenges faced the V-2 crews as they labored to launch the huge 12-ton monsters at their assigned targets. The first was the shortage of liquid oxygen. Dornberger drew everyone's attention to the problem on September 22, when he noted that all of the planned liquid oxygen facilities in France had been captured by the advancing Allies, and the existing aboveground facilities had all been bombed at least once. The current output was 260 cubic yards. Counting losses from evaporation during transport, storage and fueling, this meant there was barely enough for 25 tactical firings a day. Nothing was left over for training or experimental firings. Equally serious was the matter of A-4s rejected by the crews before firing, failing to take off or malfunctioning while in flight. Approximately six percent of the rockets delivered to the firing units crashed shortly after take-off.

Typical of the reports submitted by the firing crews was: "Unit No. 18383, September 21, 1944, 6:57 P.M. Unit did not achieve the prescribed thrust after normal take off and crashed at a distance of 4.35 miles. Cause not ascertainable."[20] Or "Unit 18374, September 22, 1944, 4:45 A.M. Thrust fell off shortly after take-off for unclear reasons."[21] Approximately fifty-seven percent of the V-2s failed pre-flight checks and had to be returned to supply depots as unserviceable. Other hazards to the rockets also existed. Because of the need to operate in total blackout conditions, more than a few rockets were damaged when fins hit low-hanging tree limbs or other obstructions.

Even with the problems of lack of fuel, malfunctioning missiles and accidents, the A-4 was not used to best effect. Kammler, typical of someone with no military experience, tried to accomplish too much with his limited resources. By October 3, Kammler's units had fired a total of 156 rockets, but these were divided among 14 different targets. London, the most frequently hit, received only 22 missiles during the period, little more than 14 percent of the total. St-Quentin, France was hit by only one rocket. Kammler was neither relieved nor reprimanded for the waste of firepower. What mattered to Himmler was that the SS was in control and that rockets were being fired. However, the waste could not continue.

An order from Hitler concerning the engagement of targets for the A-4 was sent to Field Marshal Gerd von Rundstedt, Oberbefehlshaber [Commander-in-Chief] West, on October 12, 1944: "The Führer has ordered that from now on the firing of the V-2, with all batteries ready for operation, is to exclusively be concentrated on London and Antwerp. The fighting against all other targets must be given up."[22]

One of the major problems with the first rockets that Kammler's launch crews attempted to fire was corrosion. Many rockets on their way to France when the Western Front collapsed were held in storage until the situation was stabilized. The storage areas were not suitable to storing sensitive pieces of equipment for long periods of time, and some parts rusted while others deteriorated. After a large number of rockets arrived in unusable condition, Kammler developed a system of only firing rockets fresh from the Mittelwerk, code-named "Warme Semmel" (Hot Cakes). This method of rapid resupply aided the Germans in that there was a much higher proportion of functional rockets. It also presented Allied aircraft with no large storage area to attack, although it restricted the rate of fire, not to the crews' proficiency but to the number of rockets on hand. Once the "Warme Semmel" program was in place, approximately 500 unserviceable rockets were scrapped. Storage in the open caused the bearing bushings in the servo mechanisms to swell, and replacements were not forthcoming.[23] This represented a month's production of rockets and it seems incredible that they could not be reconditioned by a team from Mittelwerk or Peenemünde, had the Germans only made the effort. But it was similar to the decision to scrap the 2,000 defective Fi 103 airframes in November 1943 rather than make them available for training.

At the end of September, Kammler took two steps to improve the performance of his units. He assigned Oberst Hohmann, the commander of Abteilung 485, as his operational chief of staff to capitalize on his practical experience as a V-2 commander; and on September 30, appointed Dornberger as his deputy and inspector of all the rocket troops, basically the same job Dornberger did as B.z.b.V. Heer. There was considerable friction between the two men and Himmler's chief of staff now entered the picture. As Dornberger wrote, "In the middle of September, Jüttner, now Commander-in-Chief of the Home Front, took a hand. he demanded a clear definition of duties. After long discussion I came to an agreement with Kammler. The order setting out once and for all the limits of authority on each side was issued on September 30, 1944, and bore, as a military novelty, three signatures. Jüttner, who knew Kammler, would not sign it until we two had attested by signing ourselves that we regarded the order as binding upon us."[24]

Even with the agreement Dornberger was not happy: "The first two months after Kammler's appointment were hard and bitter ones. I had to endure a whole series of humiliations. I had to submit to a chaotic flood of ignorant, contradictory, irreconcilable orders from this man who was neither soldier nor technician. They took the form of as many as a hundred teletypes a day . . . At first I could only look on helplessly while the influence of my staff was weakened by gross interference and efficiency dropped. I also had to stand by calmly as, among my own men, the chaff separated itself from the wheat, and driftwood I had trusted floated over to the opposite bank."[25] On October 10, SS Werferbatterie 500 arrived, to fire against Antwerp. Later in the month, the remaining firing units joined their parent units. The third launcher of Batterie 444 began operating from a site near Stavern, Holland on October 21 and the third battery of Abteilung 485 opened fire on Antwerp from Bergsteinfurt the same day. At the end of the month, Abteilung 836 closed on the Hermeskeil area southeast of Trier, Germany and commenced operations.

While the men of the V-2 firing batteries struggled to launch the new missiles at London, General Heinemann, the commander of LXV Armeekorps, and Oberst Max Wachtel, the commander of Flak Regiment 155(W), were doing their best to reconstitute the V-1 regiment. The headquarters of the Armeekorps was positioned at Alfter, near Bonn, and the operational command post of the Flak Regiment was set up at Wipperfürth, about 20 miles northeast of Köln. On

September 7, LXV Armeekorps proposed to begin operations against Brussels, Antwerp and Lille. This was part of a plan conceived by Generalleutnant von Axthelm to recommence operations as quickly as possible by targeting Belgian and French industrial areas; it required the approval of the Wehrmachtführungsstab. The army council, however, envisioned a reduced role for the Flak Regiment.

The loss of captured territories in the east and west was imposing a severe strain on German resources and both production and personnel were cut back. On September 23, Speer noted that Hitler ordered the resumption of peak A-4 production at 900 units per month as an urgent priority. Only the quantities of sheet steel and high explosive surplus to the production of 1,500,000 hand grenades and 50,000 210mm artillery shells could be used to make V-1s.[26] However, the Führer ordered the production facilities for 9,000 V-1s to remain in place if needed. The first and third battalions of the regiment, who managed to save a considerable portion of their equipment during the retreat, were ordered to resume firing. The personnel of the second and fourth battalions were sent to railroad Flak units, an utter waste of specially trained personnel.

The selection of firing sites was the next obstacle to overcome. In order to support von Axthelm's plan to fire on Brussels, Antwerp and Lille, the LXV Armeekorps issued an order to begin the construction of 32 "modified" sites in the Eifel, a heavily wooded area west of the Rhine and ideally suited for camouflaging V-1 launch sites. Eight sites were begun immediately. However, on September 17, von Rundstedt ordered the construction of two zones of launch sites on either side of the Rhine. On September 19, Oberst Walter, Chief of Staff LXV Armeekorps, asked that the deployment of Flak Regiment 155(W) be confined to the west of the Rhine in order to simplify security and supply arrangements. After the campaign in France, he knew how vulnerable transportation choke points like the Rhine bridges were to Allied fighter bombers. Von Rundstedt declined to consider Walter's recommendations and LXV Armeekorps issued an order on September 21 that delineated the firing area as "Wipperfürth-Olpe-Hörgrezhausen-Siegburg-Burscheid . . . In the area of Münster–Eifel–Mayen–Cochem–Minderlingen–Daun, the mobile employment of one battery is intended for those eight sites which are under construction."[27]

The allusion to "mobile employment" referred to the use of a new catapult that was even more easily constructed than the one in the modified sites. Designed by the von Saurma brothers, it needed no concrete bases, merely hardstand or railway ties. It was braced by tying stout cables to stakes in the ground or to surrounding trees. To implement the Armeekorps order, Headquarters, Flak Regiment 155(W) proposed the target areas of Mons–Charleroi; Maastricht–Liège; Brussels; targets of opportunity such as massed troops, and the ports of Antwerp and Rotterdam, should they fall into Allied hands.

This order indicated a shift in philosophy for V-1 targets. Hitherto, the regiment was restricted to the city of London by order of Adolf Hitler. Since the V-1 could no longer reach London, it was freed from the Führer's order and could be employed as the military situation dictated. The targets were selected on the basis of their military value and the fact they had to be large enough in area for the V-1 to hit. Between the deployment of the two battalions and the regiment opening fire, LXV Armeekorps headquarters belatedly recognized the danger of firing the V-1 in areas densely populated by German citizens. A note dated October 6 addressed the safety problems so familiar to the veterans of the firing sites in France; it deployed III/155(W) in the Eifel; while I/155(W) was to remain east of the Rhine, it was moved south so that it could fire into the gap between Köln and Bonn, a sparsely populated area.

The rejuvenation of the V-1 battalions did not go unnoticed by Allied intelligence. On October 2, Air Marshal Tedder received a report that correctly identified the sites in the Ardennes and estimated that the Germans could begin launching flying bombs in the middle of October at a sustained rate of 100 per day, with intense salvos of 30 to 40 an hour possible. The report identified Brussels, Antwerp and Rotterdam as possible targets.[28]

On October 1, the Allied attack to capture Antwerp began and Hitler stepped in to once again dictate the targets for the V-1 and V-2. The first V-2 fell in Antwerp on October 7 and the first V-1 four days later. The next day, October 12, Hitler made it official and ordered non-stop fire against Antwerp and Brussels. The Führer demanded an immediate expansion of the sites east of the Rhine. The expansion was slow due to the transfer of trained V-1 crewmen to conventional Flak regiments the previous month. In order to effectively attack targets in

Belgium, a third launching area was set up in Holland. Sixteen launch and eight reserve sites were begun in a triangular area the points of which were Zwolle–Almelo–Apeldoorn. On the same day, Kammler requested that Flak Regiment 155(W) be placed under his command. The Führer declined on the basis that the Flak Regiment's performance under the current commanders was "thoroughly unobjectionable,"[29] and operational control over the weapons remained divided.

Hitler's refusal to place all of the V-weapons under one headquarters makes sense only if it is viewed from his philosophy of "divide and rule." The LXV Armeekorps had been organized to control all of the V-weapons, but at the last minute he had allowed the SS to take control of the V-2. It would have been logical, then, for the SS to take over the V-1 as well and combine both weapons under a single headquarters as originally intended. After giving Himmler power over the Reserve Army and armaments production, however, the Führer probably felt the SS had enough power for the time being.

The first four sites in the Eifel were ready on October 20. Wachtel knew that as soon as he started firing, the Allied air campaign would resume against his sites; he therefore made provisions both to camouflage the sites and provide alternate firing areas. Based on his experience with the modified launch sites in France, the new sites were made even simpler and were harder to detect. The majority of the sites were situated in evergreen forests which maintained their foliage even in winter. When trees around the launch site were cut, the tops of the felled trees were lashed back onto the stumps to make it appear as new growth. Vehicle traffic into the sites was severely restricted to avoid leaving obvious track marks. As for the sites themselves, a small concrete pad was poured to allow the heavy trucks to offload the flying bombs. The launch site consisted of little more than a launcher on concrete piers, a firing pit, a wash-down point and a compass alignment platform that was an open area covered with a tarpaulin. There were no provisions for storage of fuel or parts, as the sites' proximity to Germany allowed immediate access to the supply network.[30]

Despite an assurance by von Rundstedt on October 15 that the V-1 sites were set up so they wouldn't be firing across any large German population centers, OKW took the precaution of alerting the Kreisleiters (the local Nazi district leaders) of the impending attacks and ordered them to report any incidents of V-1s crashing in their area under the code name "Donnerschlag" (Thunderbolt),[31] a prophetic name as it turned out.

Shortly before the scheduled start of the operation against Antwerp, engineers checked the supply of flying bombs and found that 200 of the 320 available were defective. Both Heinemann and Wachtel wanted to delay the start of the offensive until an adequate supply of reliable weapons was available, but von Rundstedt would not countenance delay and ordered the offensive to begin on time.

Early on the morning of October 21, the 23rd battery of the regiment began firing from Büchel, about 12 miles south of Mayen. By that afternoon, thirteen had been launched, but four of them had crashed. With the resumption of firing, Headquarters, LXV Armeekorps moved to Meschede, a small city on the Ruhr about 35 miles east of Dortmund, with excellent communications to both Holland and the Eifel. For security purposes the corps was redesignated XXX Armeekorps, with the code name "Ingeborg."[32] The 22nd battery opened fire on October 24 from Laufeld. With the first battalion of the regiment east of the Rhine and the third battalion in the Eifel, the question was who was to open fire from the sites in the Netherlands. Had the personnel of the second and fourth battalions been retained, the answer would have been simple. As it was, both battalions had to give up a battery to form a new second battalion with its headquarters near Deventer.

By the end of the month, Flak Regiment 155(W) managed to launch 337 flying bombs, of which 47 (13.9 percent) crashed shortly after take-off. Little had been done with the Fi 103 after the retreat from France. No developmental work had proceeded and it was obvious that both quality control for production and measures to preserve the flying bombs during storage had been ignored. On November 3, the regiment held a meeting to discuss improving the reliability of the V-1 and increase its range. A few days later, on November 7, the urgency of their task was highlighted when the regiment received a complaint from General Siegfried Westphal, Chief of Staff to von Rundstedt, that 65 V-1s had crashed in the LXVI Armeekorps area, causing substantial damage.

Behind the scenes, the fate of LXV Armeekorps was finally decided. With Kammler firmly in charge of the V-2 firing units, there was no way it could become a joint headquarters for the V-weapons. The

Luftwaffe saw this as a way to regain complete control of the V-1, and pressured for an independent command. Seeing the handwriting on the wall, Generalleutnant Heinemann resigned as commander on October 26. He was replaced by General von Treskow, who stayed but a few days until he was replaced by General Kieffel in early November. On November 14, headquarters, LXV Armeekorps was ordered to form the Luftwaffe firing units into the 5th Flak Division with an operational staff. With that order, the LXV Armeekorps, alias XXX Armeekorps, ceased to have a direct influence on events without ever fulfilling its role as a joint headquarters controlling all of the V-weapons. The following day, 5th Flak Division was activated under the temporary command of Oberst Eugen Walter, the former chief of staff of the LXV Armeekorps.

As soldiers of most nations are apt to do, the firing crews of Flak Regiment 155(W) disregarded the shift in the chain of command and continued to launch flying bombs. On November 18, 1944 they fired the 10,000th V-1 since the opening of operations on June 12. The change in headquarters had no effect on the performance of the flying bomb, which continued to have a high percentage of premature crashes and the "circle runners" that had been the bane of the launch crews in France. Whereas the Wehrmacht had not been overly concerned about V-1s prematurely crashing into French villages, it could hardly ignore those crashing into German ones. The incidents of circle runners and premature crashes were so frequent that the inhabitants of villages near the launchers nicknamed the V-1 the "Eifelschreck" (Terror of the Eifel). 5th Flak Division could no longer justify the risk to German life and property posed by the V-1 and transferred the 1st Battalion of Flak Regiment 155(W) to Holland, where the fate of the civilian population was of less concern to the occupying Nazis.

There had been plans in the 5th Flak Division to use the V-1 to form a front on the Rhine when the Allied armies approached, but the plan had to be set aside for the political considerations of the safety of the local population. The problem of defective flying bombs continued to plague the offensive. One irate German villager from Traben-Trarbach, which was 27 miles south of the line of fire, sent a letter to Kammler complaining that the local inhabitants lived in constant fear of the V-1s. By December 6, 1944, 2,738 flying bombs had been launched against continental targets and 818, a phenomenal 29.9 percent, had crashed or gone awry. On that date all launches were suspended until the cause of the malfunctions could be determined. A check of the Fi 103s in the system revealed that many of them had defective elevators, which had to be repaired. Flak Regiment 155(W) did not resume launches until December 11, just shortly before the German attack in the Ardennes.

In England, on September 25, the six-day lull in V-2 launches ended when a rocket fell in the Norwich area. In the next five days the British detected nine more launches. The rockets, fired from Friesland, some 250 miles from London, fell in the Norwich, or East Anglia, areas. Between September 25 and October 8, 21 more launches were detected, but three landed in the Greater London area. Ground reports indicated that at least two of these last came from Apeldoorn, and agents in The Hague reported that the launch crews and their equipment were returning. On October 12, the Germans ceased firing at Norwich and concentrated on London. Beginning in mid-October and continuing for the next five weeks, Bomber Command and fighters based in the United Kingdom flew 600 sorties against suspected rocket sites south of The Hague, and Mosquitoes of 2nd Tactical Air Force, based in France, attacked the railway stations at Leiden that were suspected of being a transportation node for the shipment of rockets.

By October 25, it was obvious that London was once again the main target, but only six of 63 rockets fired between October 3 and October 25 actually fell within the London Civil Defence Region. Nevertheless, casualties continued to mount. On October 30, the Becton Gasworks was heavily damaged, as were the Victoria Docks in West Ham. On November 1 seven people were killed in Woolwich, and later in the day a V-2 landed behind a row of houses killing 24 and severely injuring 17. That evening, a rocket plowed into Shardeloes Road, Deptford, as people were coming home from work. The explosion killed 31, severely injured 62 and slightly injured 90 more. The blast also wrecked houses a hundred yards from the point of impact.[33]

Despite these blows, the government refused to admit that the United Kingdom was once again under attack. The first week in November was the worst yet. Twelve rockets landed inside London while another fifteen landed outside the city limits. Two of the rockets landed within two miles of the Ministry of Home Security, leading to the speculation (correct, as calculations later showed) that the aiming point of the V-2s was Tower Bridge. On Sunday, November 5, at 10:45 A.M. one of the V-2s scored a direct hit on an iron bridge on Southwark Park Road in Bermondsey and tore up 250 feet of railroad track. That evening, another struck in Islington, killing 31 and severely injuring 84. At the end of the day thousands were homeless.[34]

On November 6, a V-2 damaged the Commer-Karrier Factory in Luton, killing 19 and injuring 196. The increasing number of incidents now led to widespread apprehension, but Churchill adamantly refused to admit that the United Kingdom was once more under bombardment. This was a strange reaction from a man who claimed that Londoners could handle anything as long as they were told the truth.

By Wednesday, November 8, 150 rockets had landed in England, killing 235. This was a death rate of approximately 1.6 per rocket, slightly more than Cherwell predicted. As usual, Cherwell's clinical predictions failed to take into account the injured, the psychological casualties and the property damage. In the same period, 711 had been injured seriously enough to require hospitalization, hundreds more had been slightly injured and thousands of homes had been destroyed or damaged.

On that same Wednesday, Goebbels could no longer remain silent about Germany's latest achievement and the daily communiqué of the German Home Service reported: "The German High Command announces: The V-1 bombardment of the Greater London Area, which has been carried out with varying degrees of intensity and only brief interruption since 15 June, has been supplemented for the last few weeks by another and far more effective explosive missile, the V-2."[35] The initial announcement was followed by a more rousing one later that evening. The British press reported the German broadcasts but made no editorial comment, much to the chagrin of Dr. Goebbels. The Germans used the British reluctance to admit that London was under bombardment and reported: "Nothing speaks more eloquently of its [the V-2's] devastating effect than the silence on the other side of the Channel."[36]

Churchill was left little choice in the matter. On November 10, he made a speech in the House of Commons in which he said that the Germans had been using a long-range rocket to hit the nation and that official silence was imposed to deny the enemy any information. He indicated that the rocket gave no warning and could not be intercepted, but indicated there was "no need to exaggerate the danger. The scale and effect of the attacks have not hitherto been significant." He concluded with an appeal to his countrymen to maintain secrecy. "Doubtless the enemy has hoped by his announcement to induce us to give him information he has failed to get otherwise. I am sure this House, the press and the public will refuse to oblige him in this respect."[37]

Goebbels could not resist taking a potshot at Churchill, and later that day a German radio commentator remarked, "In accordance with his tactics, the liar on the Thames has thus withheld from the world the fact of the German V-2 bombardment until today."[38]

Throughout November the number of "Big Ben" incidents involving multiple deaths rose dramatically. On November 19, a V-2 landed outside a crowded pub, killing 23 and injuring 63 more. The pub and surrounding buildings were demolished. Three days later, 25 people were killed and 44 injured in Bethnal Green. On Saturday, November 25, Kammler's batteries fired their 250th V-2. As it happened, it was an airburst which destroyed both the rocket and the warhead and caused little damage. Two subsequent rockets did far more: at 11:15, one came down on a block of apartments and offices in High Holborn, killing only six but injuring 292. In the East London District of Deptford, the Woolworth's and the Co-op next door were crowded with shoppers, mostly women and small children. Woolworth's had just received a shipment of aluminum saucepans—a rare item in wartime London—and the news of its arrival had spread rapidly. Outside the store, traffic was heavy but moving normally. At 12:25 P.M., a V-2 hit just to the rear of the store. When it exploded with a tremendous roar, the walls of the Woolworth store bulged outward, then the building collapsed. Next door, the Co-op disintegrated.

The shoppers never had a chance. Rescue workers toiled around the clock to extricate the injured and dead from the twisted mountain of rubble that was once a store. Eventually, it took four cranes, 16 heavy and 8 light rescue parties and 100 members of the National Fire Service. Searchlights were provided by a British Anti-Aircraft unit. U.S. Engineers provided a generator. Casualties could not be tallied until the following week. At the end, the official toll stood at 160 killed, 77 seriously injured and 122 slightly injured. Eleven could not be accounted for. The actual toll of wounded was much higher because passers-by helped the injured to hospitals and aid stations before they could be tallied. It was the worst single V-2 incident of the entire campaign against London. What made the incident even worse was that everyone in the district seemed to know someone who had been killed or hurt. But it was only one of many.

Londoners once again began to sleep in shelters. Because of the wide dispersion and low number of V-2s hitting London, the civil defense authorities dealt with them primarily as they had the flying bomb. Because V-2s came straight in and penetrated the ground before they went off, they were more likely to damage electrical wires, gas and water mains, but the aboveground area they damaged was less than the V-1.

In coordination with the V-2 attacks, the Germans launched Operation "Martha," a massed aerial-launched V-1 attack against the midland city of Manchester, on Christmas Eve 1944. The raid used up the remaining supply of fuel allotted to KG53, but the German planners felt the raid was worth the effort. Manchester hadn't received a severe bombing since 1940 and was not included in any of the existing defenses against the V-1. The planners hoped that the attack, coming on the northern flank of British defenses, would force Air Defence Great Britain to redeploy aircraft and antiaircraft guns to protect Manchester and other important cities in the area. If the political repercussions were severe enough, the diver boxes along the coast might have to be extended to cover the majority of England's east coast. If nothing else, the pummeling of a virtually untouched English city would raise the morale of German citizens, who were now enduring round-the-clock bombing at the hands of RAF Bomber Command and Eighth Air Force.

In the early evening of Christmas Eve, fifty He-111s of KG 53, each carrying a V-1, taxied onto the runways at various airfields in Germany. The date selected was designed to cause the maximum psychological effect on the British population. The bombers ran their engines up to full power and sped down the runway. Once in the air, they rose to only three hundred feet and headed out over the North Sea. Shortly after midnight, the fifty German bombers reached the launch point over the sea. Each bomber climbed to 1,700 feet and started the pulse engine of its V-1 rocket. After ten seconds the rockets were launched at Manchester. The bombers all turned for home. Thirty-five V-1s crossed the English coast and headed toward their target. The fate of the other fifteen is not known. However, the British air defenses were active. In fact, one night fighter shot down a bomber shortly after it had launched its flying bomb.

On Christmas Day 1944, V-1s began impacting all over the north of England. Only one flying bomb hit Manchester. Eleven landed within a fifteen-mile radius of the city and the remainder blasted farms, villages and pasture land along the route of the attack. A total of thirty-seven people were killed and sixty-seven were wounded that night. The raid caused little panic among civilians, and emergency services, which had been drastically cut after the Blitz, were able to handle the casualties and damage. The physical results of the raid were less than impressive, but it compelled the Allies to redeploy a number of night fighter squadrons.

1944 drew to a close with the war-weary population of London not knowing what to expect. The Allies had stopped Hitler's last great offensive in the Ardennes, but the V-weapons continued to fall. At 10:30 P.M. on New Year's Eve, a large crowd was celebrating at the "Prince of Wales" Pub in Islington when a V-2 hit in Mackenzie Road, a few yards outside the pub. The floor collapsed, sending the crowd into the cellar; then the roof and the masonry walls collapsed in upon them. Fires started and the local firefighters had to break up ice to get the water flowing. It took all night and the next day to get the dead and injured out of the debris. The final death toll was 68. There was no end in sight.

10

The City of
Sudden Death

L ong before the Allies landed on the beaches of Normandy on June 6, 1944, World War II had become more a war of resources than a contest of maneuver and combat. The Allies had enormous resources on both fronts while German assets were shrinking as they lost conquered lands in the east to the advancing Soviet Army. On the days following the assault on Normandy, the Allies secured a bridgehead on the Continent, but then German resistance stiffened and the Battle of Normandy settled into a nearly static front with gains measured in yards rather than miles. The supply situation for the Allies was relatively simple since there was no great forward movement. Supplies could be delivered from the beach to the combat troops with very little motor transport. While the Germans could not dislodge the Allied hold on that strip of the French coast, they limited the supplies and ammunition that could come ashore by keeping the front narrow and denying the Allies the use of any of the French ports. Hitler, realizing the ports were critical, ordered them held to the last. Garrisons of some ports, like St-Nazaire and Lorient, held out until the war was over.

The Allies captured Cherbourg on the tip of the Cotetin Peninsula on June 27, but the Germans had done such an efficient job of demolition that the port did not open until July 19. A few days later, the Americans ruptured the German line with Operation Cobra, a carpet-bomb attack, and the German position in Normandy collapsed. Allied armies raced to the Seine and the Germans, under Hitler's orders, mounted an ill-conceived counterattack at Mortain on August 6. The

German attack created a salient, however, and the Allies used the opportunity to surround the enemy forces in the "Falaise Pocket," destroying thousands of vehicles and killing or capturing tens of thousands of German troops. The battle for the pocket was over on August 25 and Paris was liberated the same day. All organized German resistance west of the Seine River collapsed and the Allies pursued, crossing that river before the Germans could mount any meaningful opposition. Nevertheless, the rapid pursuit took Allied units farther and farther from their main source of supply, which was the port of Cherbourg and the beaches of Normandy. For many units this meant a distance of more than 500 miles. The long supply lines led to shortages, particularly fuel and ammunition, and resources had to be rationed—a process that led to a certain amount of bitterness between the Allies. One U.S. First Army staff officer complained that the race across France had been impaired because the gasoline had been given to "the British to enable them to take the channel ports, to capture the V-1 bomb sites and to bring them faster into Antwerp."[1]

In 1944, U.S. Army Transportation doctrine called for the greatest possible use of railroads to move supplies because this was the most efficient means of hauling large amounts of cargo. Using railroads wasn't possible in France in late summer 1944, however, because Allied bombers had destroyed much of the French rail system, and while Allied railroad crews worked day and night to repair the damage, supplies piled up on docks and beaches. In addition to repairing the railroads the Allies embarked on two other courses of action to improve the logistical situation in this theater of war. The first was a short-term measure using trucks to operate one-way circular routes to supply U.S. troops. The "Red Ball Express," perhaps the most famous, was only one of several such truck operations. The plan called for 141 truck companies, which the Allies did not have because they had declined to bring additional support troops into the narrow beachhead. There were also not enough drivers, so personnel and trucks had to be stripped from existing units.

To make matters worse, the majority of the trucks were $2^1/_2$-ton light trucks instead of 10-ton tractor trailers designed for line haul operations. The round trip was 1,276 miles and the operation, begun on August 25 and supposed to end in September, was extended until November. It took a terrific toll on the trucks and personnel but it moved 412,000 tons of cargo in its 81 days of operations.[2]

The British had their own problems with transportation. They discovered that 1,400 of their three-ton trucks were defective and the vehicle shortage reduced the supplies to Montgomery's troops by 800 tons a day.[3] A long-term measure was to capture ports closer to the front. In rapid succession, the Allies captured Rouen on August 30; Antwerp on September 4; Le Havre on September 12; and Brest on September 18. Because the Germans had systematically wrecked most of the ports, it took some time before they were serviceable. Le Havre was opened on October 9 and Rouen on October 16. Brest was so far from the front that after it was captured no effort was made to repair and use it.

The large port of Antwerp was seen as the solution to the Allies' logistical difficulties. The importance of the port to the Allies can be summed up in a message Eisenhower wrote to General Marshall on October 23, 1944 stating that "the logistical problem has become so acute that all plans had made Antwerp a sine qua non to the waging of the final all-out battle."[4]

Antwerp, one of the world's great natural harbors, lies on the Scheldt River, which flows into the North Sea. The river is divided by South Beveland before it reaches the sea, dividing it into the Eastern and Western Estuaries. It is the latter that is used for sea access to the port of Antwerp. At the extreme western end of South Beveland is Walcheren Island, occupation of which controls access to the port. The Germans were well aware of the potential the port held for the Allies. In early September, Hitler ordered General von Zangen's Fifteenth Army, which occupied South Beveland and Walcheren Island, to block the Scheldt estuary and render the port useless to the Allies even if they captured the city. According to an Associated Press release issued after the battle, Canadian troops captured enemy documents "indicating that the defense of the Scheldt approach to Antwerp was the decisive factor in the further conduct of the war. According to the same source, an order was issued on October 7 by von Zanger showing that the German High Command feared that with the port of Antwerp in Allied possession, a death blow might be dealt to northern Germany and Berlin before winter. German troops were urged to defend the Scheldt blockade position at all costs.[5] Before they left, the Germans warned the inhabitants of Antwerp that they would send over 3,000 planes to bomb the city on the day the first Allied ship entered the port.

The port itself was occupied relatively easily and quickly. On September 4, the British 11th Armored Division raced into the city and captured the port intact. However, they failed to seize the bridges over the Albert Canal, and when the British decided to cross two days later the Germans blew these up. The Germans occupied South Beveland and Walcheren Island, but the seriousness of the Allied failure to capture the two was not immediately evident. "Market Garden" was in the works and that operation promised to end the war quickly. With the failure of the paratrooper-led offensive, the Allied need for a port close behind the advance to the German border suddenly became acute.

In retrospect, the failure of the British to completely occupy Antwerp in September has to be considered one of the major Allied blunders of the war in Europe. In October the areas blockading access to the port finally had to be cleared. The Canadian 2nd Division attacked South Beveland along the narrow isthmus that connects it to the mainland. On the night of October 25–26, the British 52nd Division conducted an amphibious assault on the south shore of the island and the two forces mounted a two-pronged attack that cleared the area by October 30. An amphibious assault against Walcheren Island was conducted the next day, and by November 9 the island was in Allied hands. The cost of the entire operation was 27,633 Allied casualties.[6]

With the land occupied, the Allies expected to open the port on November 15, but the Royal Navy needed an additional two weeks to clear the mines the Germans had sown in the estuary. They finished the job on November 26. The port officially opened two days later, when the *James B. Weaver*, a liberty ship with the personnel and equipment necessary to set up a port headquarters, the 268th Port Company (and a critical cargo of war correspondents) berthed in Antwerp. Unloading began immediately, albeit nearly three months after the city and docks had first been occupied.

Still, the Allies had every reason to feel pleased with themselves. Unlike Brest and Cherbourg, which had been totally wrecked by the retreating Germans, Antwerp, with its modern berthing facilities, 592 cranes, dry docks and storage capacity for 120 million gallons of fuel, was mostly untouched. Only a few sunken craft had to be raised and some dredging done. Antwerp was considered a British advanced base and the Americans were only to operate their part of the port to discharge cargo from arriving ships. American supplies were to be put on rail cars, barges or trucks at quayside and moved without delay to their forward depots at Liège and Luxembourg City. Command of the port fell to a British Naval Officer who had as subordinates a British and a U.S. port commander, which meant that Antwerp was run as two separate ports. This particularly suited U.S. Army transportation officers, who had not liked the way the British ran their ports in England and preferred to run things their own way.

The U.S.–British Agreement called for a discharge rate of 17,500 tons per day for British and 22,500 tons per day for the U.S. The discharge rates were exclusive of bulk petroleum, oil and lubricants (POL). The planned Allied rate of discharge was much lower than the port was capable of. Antwerp had a peacetime discharge capability of 80,000 to 100,000 tons of cargo per day. The lower rate was planned because port storage was limited and the Allies wanted a manageable rate that allowed for immediate clearance.

On an average day over 9,000 Belgian civilians worked in the port, and during one peak period over 13,000 were employed there. As a further assurance that things would run smoothly, Colonel Hugh A. Murrill, who was Chief of the Control and Planning Division for Major General Frank S. Ross, Chief of Transportation ETO, became Ross' personal representative at the port. Colonel Doswell Gullatt, an officer who had commanded the 5th Special Engineer Brigade on Omaha Beach, was the American port commander. General Ross allocated large numbers of supporting stevedore, truck, rail and military police units. The Americans were determined to make Antwerp work.

The Germans were unable to send the 3,000 planes they threatened, but random Luftwaffe bomber attacks and flying bombs and rockets were employed against Antwerp even before the Allies opened the port. With so much importance attached to it, the Allies took prudent steps to defend the port against both aircraft and the flying bomb. Major General A.M. Cameron, an experienced British antiaircraft officer, was appointed to conduct the air defense of the Allied-held cities in Belgium. Since he had little experience with flying bombs, Cameron immediately asked for assistance from Air Defence Great

ANTWERP X

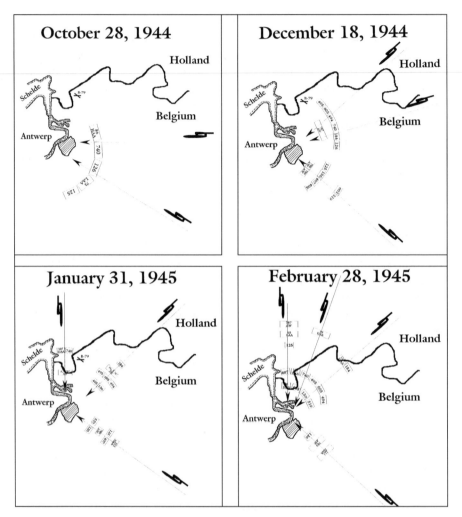

In some ways, the defense of Antwerp against the V-1 was more difficult than the defense of London because the weapons were closer and the Germans had more flexibility in launch sites. The above diagrams show two parallel developments: The Germans continued to spread out their attacks (their sites in Rotterdam and The Hague were north of Antwerp); and the Allies learned to array their defenses in depth against known sites.

By the time the last V-1 fell on the city on March 30, 1945, the gunners of Antwerp X had achieved an excellent rate of success. Against an airborne V-2, however, there was no means of defense.

Britain and an advisory team was assigned to his headquarters. Cameron's was a joint command and the responsibility for the defense of Brussels was assigned to the British, while the defense of Antwerp was assigned to the Americans under the command of Brigadier General Clare H. Armstrong. Armstrong had been commissioned a lieutenant in the infantry when he graduated from West Point in 1917, but in 1930 he transferred to the Coast Artillery, the branch responsible for antiaircraft artillery in the U.S. Army. He took command of the 86th Coast Artillery Regiment in May 1942, then commanded the 50th Antiaircraft Brigade in February 1944. He took the unit to Europe and commanded it until the end of the war.

Based on experience with the recent flying bomb offensive against England, Cameron's staff estimated that 105 V-1s and 40 V-2s could be launched against the city daily. However, they felt the actual number of hits on the port would be very low and calculated that the daily damage to the 12 square miles of the actual port and its facilities would be .025 percent per day. Indeed, the Allies estimated it would take the Germans several months to seriously affect the functioning of the port. They believed the war would be over by the end of 1944—a dangerous arrogance they shared with the tactical planners—and the situation would not leave the Germans enough time to seriously damage Antwerp's facilities.

The planners also noted that both German V-weapons were exceedingly inaccurate and had the potential of destroying 885 homes somewhere in the 339 square miles of Greater Antwerp on a daily basis. They anticipated total casualties of dead, seriously wounded and slightly hurt to be somewhat less than 1,000.[7] Allied logisticians, therefore, looked upon the flying bomb and the rocket as more of a nuisance than a serious threat to port operations. Part of their attitude stemmed from the fact that the V-1 campaign against London had just ended except for a few air-launched flying bombs, and that the V-2 was not yet a major headache.

General Armstrong's command initially consisted of 11,500 men assigned to three antiaircraft brigades. The 56th Antiaircraft Brigade was commanded by American General George M. Bader and the 80th Antiaircraft Brigade was led by English General H.W. Deacon. The 50th Brigade remained under General Armstrong's personal command. Several Polish antiaircraft batteries were also attached to the command, which was designated the "Anti-Flying Bomb Commando Antwerp X." Over the course of the campaign the number of men nearly doubled to 22,000, and at its height the defenses had 208 U.S. 90mm guns, 128 British 3.7-inch guns, 188 37mm and 40mm guns, and 72 searchlights.

The port of Antwerp was the center of a "critical zone" fourteen miles in diameter and it was the mission of the guns to keep the flying bombs out of this area. Tactical doctrine called for the guns to be deployed ten miles from the zone so that crippled flying bombs could not glide into the zone after they were hit. Observers stationed on the approaches to the city reported targets to the two antiaircraft operations rooms, which then alerted the gun sites located along the flight path of the target. The three antiaircraft brigades were designated solely for defense against V-1s, and in order to keep their positions as secret as possible all commanders and gun crews, to avoid revealing their locations, were strictly forbidden from firing at German aircraft.

The defenders and their advisory team had little time to prepare and work went forward at a rapid pace. The initial deployment of the defenses was established on October 28, 1944. The guns were placed in an arc facing roughly southeast from 90 to 124 degrees. From left to right were the British Heavy Anti-Aircraft Regiment (3.7-inch guns); the U.S. 740th Antiaircraft Artillery (AAA) Gun Battalion (90mm guns); the U.S. 126th AAA Gun Battalion; the 73rd British Light AA Regiment (37mm guns); and the U.S. 126th AAA Gun Battalion. Like the experience with London, the defense was initially hampered by restrictions designed to protect friendly aircraft taking off from and landing on any one of the numerous airfields surrounding Antwerp. Until November 5, the gunners of Antwerp X were restricted to firing at targets that could be visually identified as V-1s.

Due to the restrictions and inclement weather, the defense brought down very few flying bombs. After the rather poor initial showing, Headquarters Antwerp X established an "inner artillery zone" that included the lanes of approach of the flying bombs as well as the defensive area itself. Aircraft were instructed to stay out of this area, but friendly craft frequently violated the ban. In the two-week period from November 26 to December 11, a total of 357 friendly aircraft entered the zone.

On November 10, 1945, all British units except the 42nd Searchlight Regiment were withdrawn from the Antwerp defense and the line was thickened by additional U.S. gun battalions with their center facing 125 degrees. From left to right were the 740th, 184th, 126th, 125th, 407th, 405th, and 494th AAA Gun Battalions. Forward of the main line were the 789th and 788th Automatic Weapons (AW) Battalions, armed with the 40mm antiaircraft gun. Throughout the campaign the 40mm was used but was only marginally effective. The flying bomb's steel fuselage and limited number of vulnerable spots meant that the 40mm gunners had to score a direct hit in order to bring it down. On December 6, an eighth gun battalion was added to the main defensive belt and four addititonal gun battalions were deployed forward of the main belt. The AW battalions were pulled behind the main belt and reinforced with another battalion.

This was the beginning of a trend much different from the defenses of London. The V-1s were coming in along narrow corridors with little deviation, so the defenses were gradually arranged in depth along the corridors. Flying bombs that were obviously not going to hit Antwerp were called "flankers" and were not fired upon. On December 15, in conjunction with the Ardennes Offensive, the Germans began firing V-1s from Holland. The flying bombs began arriving from a direction roughly 60 degrees from the city, effectively outflanking the defenses. Due to the emergency caused by the Ardennes offensive there were no gun battalions to spare, so the existing ones were spread in an arc between 50 and 75 degrees. The main belt consisted of six battalions backed up by one AW battalion covering about three times its normal area. The original V-1 route was covered by a forward belt of two gun battalions and a main belt of four gun battalions, backed up by two AW battalions.

As if the battle against the flying bombs was not enough, the gun crews were also organized as infantry battalions and had to pull extra duty at roadblocks in case there was a German breakthrough in the Battle of the Bulge. As the enemy offensive reached its peak, five gun battalions and all the AW batalions were withdrawn from Antwerp X, leaving four gun battalions covering the northern route. The southeastern approaches were reinforced by the British 98th Heavy AA Regiment and the 296th Light AA regiment. The units were deployed so that there were two units in the forward belt and three in the main belt, the Light AA regiment backing up the main belt.

By January 11, 1945, the German offensive had been blunted and the guns were recalled. The V-1 attack from Holland reached serious proportions, however, since the volume of fire was heavy and the bombs deviated less from their course because the range was so short—in some cases less than 60 miles. The southeastern defenses were thinned and the northeastern became very narrow with four belts of heavy guns, consisting of eight U.S. gun battalions, one partial British 3.7-inch battalion and one AW battalion.

In the last week of January, Wachtel's troops began launching nearly due south from the area of Rotterdam. A major complication for the defense was Airfield B79, one of the largest on the Continent, located due north of Antwerp and directly under the path of the newly directed incoming V-1s. With the flying bombs coming in at low altitude and antiaircraft shells exploding near the runways and approaches, the airfield could no longer be used safely, so it was closed and moved. By January 31, the new approach was covered by one U.S. gun battalion and one British heavy AA regiment, backed up by two AW batteries. The northeastern approach had been thinned to four belts consisting of six gun battalions and two AW batteries. The southeastern defenses consisted of five heavy gun units, one of which was British, and one AW battalion. A month later, V-1 attacks increased to the point that the defenses had to be reinforced once again.

On February 28, the guns were deployed in a double belt stretching from due north to due east. There were five U.S. gun battalions and a British Heavy AA regiment in the forward belt and three U.S. gun battalions and a British Heavy AA regiment in the second. Along the northern route were two AW battalions and a gun battalion, arranged one behind the other. A gun battalion was deployed forward of the main belts at 20 degrees and a U.S. gun battalion and a British Heavy AA regiment were placed side by side at 54 degrees. The southeastern belt had been thinned to a British Heavy AA regiment, one AW battalion and a U.S. gun battalion, arranged in that order. The defenses remained in that configuration until the flying bombs stopped falling after March 30.

The equipment of the units in Antwerp X was some of the finest in the world. Even so, there were serious obstacles to overcome. The conditions in Belgium and Holland were less than ideal for the S.C.R. 584 radar, and presented radar officers Major Victor Rabbe of the

50th AAA Brigade and Major Claude Parish of the 56th AAA Brigade with considerable difficulty. The V-1 presented a smaller "pip," as radar sightings were called in World War II, than did fighter aircraft. To the experienced radar operator a V-1 could be further distinguished by its straight and level flight path. Occasionally, Typhoons and Spitfires were mistaken for V-1s because they used a straight and level approach to land at the numerous airfields surrounding Antwerp.

Another problem was the terrain. The ground was flat and wet and was dotted with numerous villages with tall steeples and chimneys. The combination caused a lot of ground clutter and the radar officers, when they could, stationed their sets behind one of the local pine woods that dotted the landscape to mask the villages and reduce the clutter. The radar sets along the northern route had a particularly difficult time because of water and windmills. Since there were few woods, the radar crews set up wire fences 50 yards in front of the sets, and this also served to mask the clutter.

When controlled by the S.C.R. 584 radar set, the U.S. 90mm M1 Antiaircraft Gun was the finest antiaircraft gun of World War II. During the campaign they were operated 22 hours a day with two hours a day for maintenance. Like every other mechanical device, the gun wore out after prolonged use. The gun tube's life expectancy was 1,500 to 2,000 rounds, and many batteries wore out three or four sets of tubes over the course of the campaign. After the third wore out, the gun slide had to be replaced as well. Due to shortages of replacement barrels, some tubes were retained until they had fired as many as 2,500 rounds. But this was a dangerous practice: when the tube became that worn, muzzle velocity grew erratic and, in some cases, the lands in the tube began to peel. For much of the four months December 1944 to March 1945, nearly every 90mm antiaircraft gun barrel produced was sent to Antwerp. The antiaircraft units in the Pacific and the Mediterranean had to wait. In February, ammunition ran low despite emergency deliveries by air. The M-13 fuze setter and the hydraulic rammer were considered problems. In the case of the latter, many gun crews resorted to ramming by hand, a practice many a section chief maintained was better than hydraulic ramming anyway.

Because of the short flight times and low altitude of the approaching V-1s, aircraft could not be used to intercept them the same way they did in England. Nevertheless, aircraft played a major role in

countering the V-1. The flying bomb attacks were supported by a specially equipped He-111 spotter aircraft that flew over Antwerp on a
nightly basis. The Allies believed the aircraft was equipped with a
powerful guidance beacon that directed the V-1s to their target in the
city and then used a "cut-off" beam to activate the flying bombs' diving mechanisms at the right moment.[8] The Allies also suspected that
guidance beacons from the transmitter at Bonn-Hangelar and a new
site built just east of the Rhine were guiding flying bombs onto their
targets. Neither of these suppositions proved to be true. The increased
accuracy of the flying bomb was a simply a consequence of the short
range from the launch sites in Holland to Antwerp.

In late October, General Cameron asked that aircraft be assigned
to help destroy the flying bomb threat. The request was approved by
SHAEF Headquarters in early November and the British 2nd Tactical
Air Force was instructed to form a wing of fighters to deal with the V-
1. Since there was so little time to detect them and shoot them down,
the only way aircraft could interdict the flying bombs was to destroy
them before they were launched. The original wing was augmented by
twelve squadrons of No. 12 Group's Spitfires, assigned to Air Defence
Great Britain. These squadrons were based at Matson in England and
on good flying days they would leave Matson in the early morning and
fly to the 2nd TAF airfield at Ursel in Belgium. These fighters hunted
for V-1 sites during the day and returned to England at night.[9]

The system gave the Allies a tremendous increase in the number of
aircraft searching for V-1 launch sites. As in France, the first attacks
were against the launch sites, but these were mostly unsuccessful. The
new launch sites had a smaller signature than the modified sites in
France and were far more difficult to find and hit. Also, even when the
sites were hit, there was little in them to damage or destroy, and minor
damage could be repaired very quickly. The Allied command then
decided to stop the launches by attacking the rail net that was supplying the sites. Consequently, the aircraft of No.12 Group began fighter
bomber raids against the railroad lines and sidings that might be supplying the sites. These aircraft, carrying 250- and 500-pound bombs,
proved quite effective at cutting the rail lines.[10]

The Germans countered the rail line attacks by forming railway
repair gangs in the various towns and villages along the lines. Each
gang was assigned a section of track to repair in the event it was dam-

aged. This system of repair proved particularly effective, and although rail traffic was disrupted during the day, the tracks were quickly repaired during hours of darkness.

There was no respite for either side at night. Many V-1 launches were made then for the double purpose of avoiding detection of the sites by Allied aircraft and making it more difficult for Allied aircraft and gunners to shoot them down. What the Germans could not have known was that for many of the Allied gunners the V-1 was a much easier target to track at night. The Allies took advantage of their excellent night fighters and assigned the destruction of V-1s as a secondary mission to the 422nd and 425th Night Fighter Squadrons. These two squadrons flew the Northrop P-61 Black Widow night fighter. As with the fighters of Air Defence Great Britain, however, the Black Widow found the V-1 a difficult target because it flew at roughly the same speed as the night fighter, which made closing on a flying bomb ahead of the aircraft nearly impossible. The short flying time of the V-1s to their target and their low flying altitude also made interception difficult, so the night fighters turned to interdiction missions, with rail as the primary target.

Flying over the area at night, Black Widows of the 422nd and 425th Night Fighter Squadron attacked the rail lines east of Bastogne during December. During the period of December 16–27, the 425th destroyed three locomotives and 16 rail cars during night ground interdiction missions.[11] Despite the Allied efforts to interdict the German transportation system, however, V-1 launches continued.

During the nearly six months of the campaign to defend Antwerp, the personnel of Antwerp X were called upon to to perform under exacting conditions, not to mention the danger of being hit by a V-1 or V-2. Army Tables of Organization didn't provide for crews that allowed 24-hour-a-day operations, so the existing crews had to operate short-handed around the clock. In the 175 days of the campaign they suffered 32 soldiers killed and 289 wounded. What they accomplished was the downing of 2,183 V-1s. In one week near the end of the campaign, they succeeded in shooting down 94 percent of the incoming V-1s. To accomplish this, they expended 532,000 rounds of 90mm ammunition and used 3,255,000 sandbags, 1,000,000 gallons of gasoline and over 4,250 tons of coal. Like Pile's gunners defending

London, they could not keep them all out, and every flying bomb that got through was a potential disaster. For the entire campaign the Allies logged 4,248 V-1s falling in the vicinity of greater Antwerp. This meant that flying bombs were hitting the city every day, excluding the six days in December when 5th Flak Division suspended firing for faulty elevators, and March 17, 1945, when no V-1s fell on Antwerp. Two hundred and eleven got through to the critical zone. Of those, 150 actually hit the dock area.

The first V-2 hit the city on October 7 and the first V-1 was recorded on October 11, ten days before the campaign ordered by Hitler began. The first serious incident in the city occurred when a V-2 slammed into Schilderstraat at 9:40 A.M. on October 13, more than a month before the Allies cleared the port. Thirty people were killed and forty-five injured. The intelligence report for the British 7th Armored Division on the following day stated tersely: ". . . something beastly fell in Antwerp yesterday."[12] There were three more serious incidents before the end of October. A V-2 that fell in Kroonstraat on October 19 killed 44 and injured 98. A week later, a V-1 fell in Tuinbouwstraat, killing 30. Two days later, a V-2 hit Bontemantelstraat, killing 71 and wounding 80. Just these four incidents accounted for a total of 177 dead and 226 seriously injured.

The new antiaircraft defenses were barely in place when the heavy V-1 bombardment began on October 21. Other cities such as Ghent and Brussels were also targeted. Ghent escaped serious damage, but fifty-five flying bombs landed in Brussels in a four-day period, causing considerable damage and frightening the inhabitants. Antwerp, however, was destined to take the brunt of the bombardment. By October 25 a total of 79 flying bombs had been launched. By the end of the month the number had risen to 337. These attacks proved very effective both in terms of damage done and by ranging the various cities for more concentrated attacks by the various launch sites. While the launch crews proved they could hit any of a number of cities, Colonel Walter knew the most important target was Antwerp, and after the initial ranging attacks began a sustained bombardment of that city's crucial port.

Throughout November an increased number of V-weapons hit their mark. There were at least six incidents in which 30 or more people were killed. On November 11 a V-2 fell in Broydelstraat, killing 51 and severely injuring 62. Among these were some of the first military casualties: fifteen soldiers were dead and six wounded. On November 13, even before the port opened, ComZ Headquarters issued Passive Air Defense (PAD) instructions for both soldiers and civilians working in the port area. They included directions for staying away from windows, taking cover and not looking out windows to see the V-1s as they passed over. Less than a month later, the defenses were increased. Perhaps the most tragic incident of the period occurred when a V-1 slammed into the Boy's Orphanage on Durletstraat at 1115 hours on November 16. Thirty-six were killed and 125 injured, many of them children. The 350th Dispensary was one of the U.S. units that assisted in the disaster and was destined to play a major role in many of the flying bomb and rocket incidents. It helped evacuate many of the injured despite the fact that the ruins of the orphanage were in danger of collapsing. Several Belgian Agencies, including the Belgian Red Cross, praised the dispensary's efforts.

The following month, the report of the Chief of Transportation of the ETO said, "The heroic rescue and first aid work done by the officers and enlisted men of the 350th Dispensary during December was outstanding. Working with the Belgian Red Cross, at their request, they (sic) answered calls for help any hour of the day and night. They treated civilians and military personnel at the scene of V-bomb hits and moved victims to the dispensary. Many times they were called from one such distress to another. They also carried out their mission of providing medical aid for approximately 4,500 troops of the U.S. Army, Navy and civilian employees of the U.S. Government."[13] Of the twenty officers and enlisted men in the 350th Dispensary, two officers and eleven enlisted men were wounded in the course of the campaign. Two of these were wounded when their billets were flattened by a V-1 on December 29.

The day before port operations began, a V-2 hit at Kerserlei & Meir, killing 128, of which 26 were military; another 113 soldiers were injured. On December 7, the PAD instructions became more comprehensive when headquarters instituted siren warnings in the port. A single 30-second wail indicated a flying bomb attack and two 30-second wails separated by five seconds was a conventional air raid. For conventional raids, workers were to lower their loads and find cover. For V-1 attacks they were instructed to find cover immediately.

The incidents in November were not allowed to interfere with discharge operations. In the first week, the Americans were well on their way to achieving their goal: unloading 10,000 tons of cargo per day. The 13th Major Port was reinforced by the 5th Major Port at the end of November and the discharge rate climbed to roughly 19,000 tons a day in the first week of December. From that point there was a steady decline in productivity. Sometime after the port opened, logistical planners revised their estimates of the port's capabilities downward. They expected the U.S. side of the port to discharge 15,000 tons per day in December, 21,500 tons per day in January and 22,500 tons per day in March. The target tonnage was lowered again in December to 16,000 tons per day in January, 18,000 tons per day in February, and 17,775 per day in March.[14]

In the third week of December, the actual daily discharge rate fell to 13,700 tons per day. This was slightly more than 60 percent of the target goal and only 91 percent of the new goal. In Volume II of "Logistical Support of the Armies," Roland G. Ruppenthal attributed the slowdown in discharge rate to the lack of port clearance capability, particularly the lack of rail cars.[15] The shortage was caused by the amount of cargo loaded on some 35,000 cars in Liège and Luxembourg City, ready for evacuation in the face of the advancing Germans during their December counteroffensive. Another reason Ruppenthal gives for port congestion was the embargo on shipments to forward depots during the Battle of the Bulge. Cargo was not shipped to Liège and Luxembourg City because of concern it might be captured by the advancing Germans.[16] For the short time cargo was unloaded during November and early December, the port clearance rate was 50 percent, which meant that the port authorities were storing one ton of cargo for every two tons discharged. The rate of clearance subsequently improved, so that by the end of the month "there was an excess of forwardings over tonnages discharged."[17] The increase was so marked that the average discharge for the month of December was 73 percent. In January the average rose to 92 percent.

One reason for the increase in port clearance was the "ABC Haul" created by U.S. transportation authorities specifically to clear cargo from the port. Named ABC for Antwerp–Brussels–Charleroi, it involved an average of 16 truck companies, most of them equipped with five-ton tractors pulling ten-ton semi-trailers. The ABC began on

November 30, 1944 and ran until March 26, 1945, during which time it hauled 245,000 tons of cargo from Antwerp.[18] Two of the truck companies were used specifically for pier clearance within the port. In February port clearance rose to 113.6 percent as the backlog was being cleared. Even then the ship discharge rate did not reach 22,500 tons a day. Since the planned discharge rate was less than 25 percent of Antwerp's actual discharge capacity (in order to ensure that the port was not congested by backlogs), it is evident from these statistics that port clearance was not the main reason for the drop in the discharge rate. What was holding up the productivity of the port was the German bombardment with the V-1 and V-2.

In addition to the port discharge rates, the German bombardment also affected rail and barge traffic. Rail traffic problems were caused to a great degree by hits on rail lines, bridges and rolling stock by flying bombs and rockets, as the following excerpt from a report from the 2nd Military Railway Service for the period November 15 to 30 shows:

> The German robots are doing considerable damage to rail facilities in Belgium, particularly in the Antwerp and Liege areas, which is being further aggravated by the fact that Belgian workers are refusing to work in these areas. A considerable number of trains have been held up waiting for repair of track in order to get through the Liege area. The Military Railway Service is coping with this situation as expeditiously as possible; however, the additional help of Belgian labor is urgently needed to speed up the flow of traffic.[19]

The situation was no better in December, as described in this report dated January 3, 1945:

> The month of December represented for the 2nd MRS a period of continued change, reaching a peak in tonnage handled, followed by a sharp downward trend brought about by the tactical situation, bombing and strafing of installations and trains on the move, losses in equipment and personnel due to the offensive of the enemy in Belgium, and increased activities in attacks by V-1 and V-2 flying bombs.[20]

The north yards in Antwerp were manned by American rail units that were normally considered "rear area" personnel, yet many units suffered a considerble number of casualties. The 729th Railway Operating Battalion listed twenty-eight Purple Hearts awarded for wounds, and the 743rd Railway Operating Battalion listed sixty-eight personnel wounded, three of them twice. Barge traffic was initially a problem because the Albert Canal remained blocked by the remains of the Yserburg Bridge until December 23. This was mitigated to a certain extent by trucks hauling cargo from the piers to a spot beyond the blockage, and loading the barge from there. Even after the canal was cleared, barge traffic from Antwerp never reached its potential and the logistical chain of command was unhappy about it. The reasons were summed up in this report from March 1945.

Mid-February saw Antwerp visited by the Commanding General, Com Z who was not pleased with the barge situation. In assisting to prepare an answer to his report, Movements gave the revised program for Inland Waterways and an explanation of how floods and civilians unwilling to work under buzz-bomb fire had hampered the previous one.[21]

From October 1944 to March 1945, the Germans maintained a bombardment of the city and port of Antwerp that lasted 175 days. During that time the only day in which no V-weapon fell on the port was March 17, 1945. By the end of December the number of V-1 launches against Antwerp rose to 924.[22] Just less than half that number slammed into the city and port area, many landing within a few hundred yards of their targeted point. The damage and casualties grew rapidly. By the end of the year, more than 1,000 homes had been destroyed, and more than 13,000 were heavily damaged. An estimated 1,500 civilian residents of Antwerp and its suburbs were dead as a direct result of the V-1s and thousands of others had been wounded.

The Allies recorded a total of 4,248 V-1s and 1,712 V-2s falling in the Greater Antwerp area and the west side of the Scheldt River. Of these, 150 V-1s and 152 V-2s actually fell within the dock area. Another 47 V-1s and 31 V-2s fell north of the dock area between the docks and the city limits. Those falling in the dock area killed 53 military and 131 civilians and severely injured 174 military and 380 civilians.[23] Damage within the dock area consisted of two warehouses destroyed; twenty berths damaged; a canal lock damaged; a 150-ton floating crane sunk by a direct hit from a V-2; and 150 ships either sunk or damaged by V-weapons. One of the warehouses took a direct hit that caused 148 casualties.

Personnel were constantly diverted from discharge duties by an endless stream of warnings to take cover and by rescue and repair details. The damage did not have to be extensive to use up valuable labor, and repairs to buildings and facilities was an ongoing process. One report from the 13th and 5th Major Ports near the end of the war stated: "The rehabilitation of sheds and structures was carried out, and badly damaged buildings were repaired where possible. Because of the damage done by German V-1 and V-2 bombs, as well as by jet planes, it was necessary to keep crews at work repairing structures, roofs, doors, windows, and walls. About 90 percent of all glass in port installations was shattered and had to be replaced with plywood blinds of a temporary nature."[24]

Close calls were frequent. One ABC driver stated, "We can really put out the stuff and the only difficulty we have is with the buzz bombs. They hardly ever enterfere (sic) with our operations but they area a constant nervous strain. The closest bomb I ever came to was when driving from the [Antwerp] marshaling yard to the port area. A buzz bomb hit an old factory along the route about a hundred yards in front of me. It caved in the whole roof and walls of the factory and littered the streets with debris. Some civilians were killed and other (sic) were injured but none of our drivers were injured and we had to reroute temporarily until the street was cleared off with a bulldozer."[25]

The constant "nervous strain" is a common theme among first-person accounts of life in Antwerp and Liège during the period. Many G.I.s simply referred to Antwerp as the "city of sudden death."[26] Units outside Antwerp found themselves the targets of V-1s that overshot the city. On November 11, the headquarters of the 709th Railway Grand Division arrived in Malines to discover its quarters had been destroyed by a V-1. It took them two days to find another place, which itself had been damaged by V-1s exploding nearby. The first ship hit by fragments from a V-2 was the *Timothy Bloodworth*, operated by the Lykes Brothers Steamship Company. On December 24, a V-2 disintegrated in an airburst overhead, causing no damage. A second V-weapon, probably a V-1, then hit nearby and caused slight splinter damage on the hull near the number-one hold.[27]

The bombardment made conditions in the port so dangerous that concerns about bringing ammunition into it were raised by Supreme Headquarters as early as November. SHAEF requested that the headquarters involved present its views regarding the subject. The Communications Zone (COMZ or ComZ) "recommended that ammunition be excluded entirely, and proposed that all Class V [ammunition and explosives] continue to be handled at Cherbourg and Le Havre."[28] The Allied naval command and the British 21st Army Group felt that ammunition ships could be brought into the port if their numbers were strictly limited and the ships were adequately dispersed. The policy laid down by the chief administrative officer of the port a few days later did not forbid ammunition ships in the port but restricted the quantity to operational requirements "at the discretion of Communications Zone and 21st Army Group, and specified that [they] be handled in a separate and remote section of the port, that no dumps be permitted even for sorting, and that special fire fighting preparations be made."[29]

However, shortly after the port opened, its Executive Committee asked that all ammunition ships be temporarily excluded from Antwerp, a request approved by SHAEF Headquarters with the provision that no ammunition would be brought into the port for the next fourteen days. An exception was soon granted to admit a few British ammunition vessels, but this did not become standard practice. Ammunition did come into Antwerp on a regular basis, but it was primarily antiaircraft ammunition for the guns defending the city. According to the Office of the Chief of Transportation, ETO: "Because the danger from constant bombardment by V-bombs forbade it, not many shiploads of ammunition came through the port. However, on several occasions a total of 3,000 tons of amunition cargo consigned to the other depots were diverted to the AAA batteries defending the Antwerp area. Trucks were rushed to the ships, loaded with the needed ammunition and driven to the gun emplacements directly for distribution."[30] Most of the ammunition for the theater had to be transported the 500 miles from Cherbourg or 275 miles from Le Havre by rail and by truck, using up additional fuel and resources.

On January 1, 1945, at twelve minutes past midnight, a V-2 fell in Burgerhout killing 46, one of them military, and wounding 33 civilians. A week later, on January 8, a V-2 hit pier 123 about fifty yards from the freighter *Blenheim*, operated by the Waterman Steamship Company. Reports had it that "The concussion cracked all the bulkheads in the cabins and the forecastle, blew off or damaged all the doors, broke water pipes, and ripped radiators and bunks from the bulkheads."[31] The blast injured twenty of those on board and the ship needed nearly a month to make temporary repairs. She finally left for England in a convoy on February 2. Less than a week after the *Blenheim* was damaged, a V-2 hit berth 218 near the starboard quarter of the *Michael De Kovats,* damaging the superstructure and causing blast damage below. The explosion injured three aboard the ship and reportedly killed a soldier on the pier.[32]

The citizens of Antwerp suffered the same agony as the citizens of London but they lacked one advantage of their English allies: there were no subways or deep shelters because Antwerp rests only a few feet above sea level. One of the unique problems facing the Belgian authorities as well as the Allies was getting Belgian civilians to work in areas under V-weapon bombardment. In Liège, the Belgian government offered civil servants a form of "hostile fire" pay and in Antwerp municipal authorities offered a 25 percent pay differential for personnel working in the dock area. The additional pay worked but it also led to disputes because it was paid only in certain zones or areas, and the V-weapons were so inaccurate that many were bound to stray outside the designated zones, causing additional workers to demand the higher pay rates.

As the Germans increased the rate of fire for both V-weapons, the casualty rate in the city climbed. There was at least one incident per week in which at least thirty people were killed by a single bomb in October. In November it climbed to 1.5 of these per week and in December the rate of serious incidents climbed to nearly 2 per week.

On December 16, the Cinema Rex in downtown Antwerp was crowded with soldiers, sailors, civilians and merchant marine crews seeking some relaxation from the tension of living under the bombardment, when a V-2 scored a direct hit on the theater. Five hundred sixty-seven people were killed and 291 seriously injured. It was the worst single V-weapon disaster of the entire war. Numerous units were called in to help remove the bodies and treat the few survivors. Among these were the 350th Dispensary and the 358th Engineer General Service Regiment that had already suffered casualties from V-weapon hits in the port. It took five days to recover all the bodies, and after the incident all the theaters in Antwerp were shut down and large public gatherings prohibited. By the time the German bombardment ended in March 1945, 3,752 civilians had been killed and 6,072 severely injured.

Even before the V-weapons began taking their toll, the U.S. Army's Operations Division in Washington began to have serious doubts about relying so heavily on Antwerp. With the restrictions placed on ammunition entering Antwerp, plans were made to activate Ghent as a "stand-by" port. In January 1945, Ghent was opened under joint American and British control. Since it had been used by the Germans only for barge traffic, the port had to be dredged and many facilities repaired and rehabilitated. The 1080th Dredging Crew aboard the U.S. Army hopper *W.L. Marshall* were veterans of dredging along the Scheldt and had had several doors blown off the dredge by near-misses from V-1s and V-2s. The U.S. 17th Port was assigned to Ghent, and on January 23 the Liberty Ship *Hannis Taylor* berthed in the port and began unloading. Ghent rapidly increased in volume and brought in the ammunition that the authorities declined to bring into Antwerp.

For the entire period that Antwerp was under bombardment, the ship discharge rate was roughly a third less than that originally planned. The planned monthly discharge rates were lowered to 496,000 tons in January 1945; 504,000 in February; and 551,025 in March.[33] The port was unable to achieve even these modest goals.

Antwerp was not the only Allied logistical target on the Continent put under bombardment by the Germans. The situation on the Western Front in November 1944 did not allow Germany the luxury of using the V-weapons exclusively to bombard Antwerp and London. The acute shortage of German artillery on the front demanded that Wachtel's units be used to support the battle. They were first used to fire at Liège, which was a U.S. Army supply, rail and communications center.

General Hans Krebs requested of OB West that the V-1 be used to support Heeresgruppe B (Army Group B) in order to provide some relief to the army group. Von Rundstedt's headquarters then ordered

5th Flak Division to fire on Liège even at the expense of the campaign against Antwerp. Wachtel accordingly ordered six launchers in the Netherlands to fire with one of his usual exhortations to provide "relief to our army comrades who are involved in very fierce fights. I therefore demand non-stop firing from all technically-serviceable sites against the enemy supply center at Liege."[34]

The U.S. 708th Railway Grand Division, which had its headquarters in the main railway station in Liège, was about to become intimately familiar with the V-1. "On 20 November in the early afternoon, the sky suddenly cleared and exposed the sun for a few minutes. Operations at Ans, Renory and Kinkempois Yard and Guillemins were routine. At 1525 hours the sound of an approaching V-1 was scarcely noticed except by a few who chanced a casual skyward glance endeavoring to spot the flaming robot in its trajectory over the city. Heretofore an occasional V-1 had pathed the sky always carrying its guttural '6X6-like roar' out of the sound of hearing. But the sound of this V-1 grew louder and louder and finally it stopped altogether. In an instant its explosion rocked Guillemins valley. Some said it was an accident. But five minutes later there was a repetition; two more had fallen on Liege. The first robomb siege of Liege was on. The activity intensified by the hour and by the next day V-1s fell with severe regularity."

A tabulation from November 22 to 30 indicated that "331 robombs fell and detonated in the almost immediate vicinity of the Liege (Guillemins) railroad station. Several hits caused damage (none of which was unrepairable) to railroad installations, including track damage, damage to the switch control tower and damage to the bridge leading the roundhouse at Guillemins. There was considerable damage to headquarters building."[35] Glass in numerous buildings was shattered and the troops began sleeping in shelters.

On November 22, several V-1s also hit the city of Liège. In one particularly tragic incident, a descending flying bomb ricocheted off the top of a trolley and hit the upper floors of a girls' school, killing 36 and injuring many more. The 708th RGD set up a warning system of personnel who listened for the sound of approaching flying bombs. No building or facility was safe. Two days after a V-1 hit the girls' school one hit the 15th General Hospital, killing 12 and injuring 15. The following day, a V-1 exploded in the underpass at the rear of the

Guillemins engine shop, damaging the track and the bridge. Trains were delayed for four hours.

The "first siege of Liège," as it was called by the men of the 708th RGD, ended on November 30 at 1630 hours. The second began on December 15 when the Germans began their counteroffensive in the Ardennes. In addition, Luftwaffe bombers made an unwelcome appearance. The railyards were under constant bombardment. On December 17, a V-1 hit the Quartermaster fuel depot in Liège and blew up 400,000 gallons of gasoline.[36] At 6:10 A.M. on December 21, a V-1 hit freight cars in Guillemins Station, about 150 yards from the 708th's headquarters. It demolished or damaged 14 cars and set fire to at least six more. Since some of the burning cars held mail from home, everyone assisted in unloading the precious cargo before it was consumed. The day after Christmas, the 28th General Hospital took a hit from a V-1. Ironically, the only person killed was a German POW, but many of the front-line troops who were patients at the hospital asked to return to duty because they felt they were just sitting ducks in Liège.

On December 27, Company B of the 740th Railway Battalion suffered eight killed and 20 injured when a V-1 struck its boarding cars on Renory Siding in Kinkempois Rail Yard. Some of the men were in the boarding cars because the houses in which they were staying had been damaged by a V-1. In the midst of all the turmoil two officers from an AAA battalion arrived to confirm they had shot down a V-1. The reaction of the men of the 740th can only be imagined.

Flying bombs, V-2 rockets and Luftwaffe bombs and strafing continued into the new year. On January 2, a V-2 hit a hospital train at Liège, demolishing three cars, damaging five more and shattering all the glass in another train. Another problem caused by both the V-weapons and the bombing by conventional aircraft was the frequent cutting of railroad signals. Without an efficient signaling system, it is impossible to run a modern railroad, and the railroaders of the 2nd Military Railway Service and their Belgian workers found themselves constantly repairing lines to signals as well as telephone lines to keep the trains operating safely. On January 11, 1945, a V-1 hit in the Kinkempois Yard, tearing up 75 feet of track and making a crater twelve feet deep. Both main tracks were out all day.

Liège continued to suffer from the German V-weapons until they stopped all together. Major A.G. Gregory of the 708th Railway Grand

Division lived through it. He wrote:

> Mere words are highly inadequate to portray the terror and
> noise and death which all occur at the height of battle or
> bombing. In the two robomb sieges of Liege more than a thou-
> sand V-bombs fell and detonated in the city.
>   Nothing was untouched—every aspect of life suffered.
> With great loss of life and untold human misery, civilian men,
> women and children and Allied military personnel were
> caught in the city of terror. Civilian and army hospitals, stores,
> dwellings, telephone offices, theaters and railroad yards all
> suffered direct hits. The V-1s, traveling at high speed and with
> terrifying noise, would suddenly, from a great height, cut off
> and dive into the city.[37]

By the end of the campaign against Liège, 92 soldiers had been
killed and 336 wounded. There were 1,158 civilian casualties and 97
percent of the 82,700 dwellings in the Province of Liège were damaged
or destroyed in this concentrated attack.[38] In March 1945, the Chief
of Transportation received the following report from the city. "Most
of the damage to supplies, transport equipment, and Transportation
Corps personnel was from V1 and V2 bombs in the vicinity of
Liege."[39]

The V-weapons not only affected ports and railroads but also
highway traffic. Roads were blocked and bridges were damaged.
Wherever the drivers went within range of the weapons, they were in
danger. One driver who lived through a V-2 explosion reported:

> I had a double explosion rocket [typical of the V-2 breaking
> apart in the air] knock me off my truck. I was standing on the
> fender just getting ready to get in the cab when it went off. It
> was about a hundred yards away and killed a lot of civilians.
> You could see wood and everything flying high and in the air.
> They took me to an aid station but I didn't stay there long. As
> long as you don't get caught in the ring of concussion of the
> bombs you are OK. One person can be two hundred yards
> away and get killed, another the same distance away on the
> other side will be safe. The rockets have not interfered with

our operations except sometimes when we had to divert our route. But they are a continuous nervous strain.[40]

Fortunately for the Allies, the Germans had no idea of the kind of damage they were doing in Antwerp and Liège. There was no intelligence network and no aerial photo reconnaissance.

Despite the inherent inaccuracy of both the V-1 and V-2, Hitler's decision to concentrate the continental weapons on Antwerp and Liège was essentially the correct one. From the end of November 1944 to the end of March 1945, the Germans were able to limit the amount of supplies brought into the port—particularly ammunition—in the face of huge Allied air superiority, thereby forcing the Allies to expend additional resources to accomplish the same task and forcing them to open an additional port at Ghent. The only saving grace for Antwerp was the fact that the cargo it discharged created space in Cherbourg and Le Havre for the additional ammunition the two ports had to handle. The 13th and 5th Major Ports and the civilian workers at Antwerp continued to discharge cargo under appalling conditions, but the discharge rates reached neither the planned level nor the lower revised rate until the V-weapons campaign was nearly over. By limiting Allied logistical activities in Antwerp and Liège, the German V-weapons demonstrated they could go a long way to compensate for the lack of a viable bomber force, although it was an effort for a war that had already been lost.

11

The Final Vengeance

By January 1, 1945, the German Ardennes Offensive had run its course and the Allies prepared for the long-awaited push to the Rhine. In the air, the Allies were predominant except for an occasional raid by the Luftwaffe in areas where weather restricted Allied aircraft. The Germans preferred to husband their strength for air battles over the Reich, where the dwindling German fighter force fought with tenacity. Used to operating in France and Belgium with near-impunity, the Allied air forces on the Continent thus received a rude shock when they were caught on the ground by a massive German low-level attack by nearly 1,000 fighter bombers on the crisp, cold morning of New Year's Day.

Operation "Bodenplatte," involving eleven German fighter wings, hit Allied airfields at Asch, Deuma, Eindhoven, Evere, Giltze-Rijn, Grimbergen, Heesch, Le Culot, Maldegem, Melsbroke, Metz, Ophoven, St-Denis, St-Trod, Ursel, Woensdrecht and Vokel. In a matter of minutes the Allies lost over 300 aircraft. The RAF recorded 144 aircraft destroyed and 84 seriously damaged. The USAAF acknowledged 134 planes lost and 62 damaged beyond repair. In addition, 70 Allied aircraft were shot down during the battle. Luftwaffe losses were also heavy. Over 300 Luftwaffe fighters were shot down, including 85 lost to their own flak.[1] Operation Bodenplatte has been depicted as an attack designed to neutralize Allied air power poised to oppose the massive German armored assault through the Ardennes, but the decision to launch the strike when the battle had already been lost by the Germans has never been satisfactorily explained.

The raid was initially planned to destroy Allied tactical air units in the way of the German advance once it crossed the Meuse (Maas) River and headed for Antwerp. As such it had to be carefully timed to hit Allied targets at the exact moment they would be crowded with enemy fighters and fighter bombers. The weather was clear enough for the raid on December 18, but the Germans chose not to strike because their armored spearheads were still far from the Meuse. The Luftwaffe also had the opportunity to launch the raid from December 23 to 27, but the conditions requiring the strike never came. Advancing German armor never reached the Meuse and the barrier the airfields posed was never challenged. After December 28, weather closed in again and it remained overcast and snowy until New Year's Eve, when the signal to launch Operation Bodenplatte was transmitted.

Luftwaffe fighter group commanders were stunned. The weather conditions for January 1 were certainly good, but the Battle of the Ardennes was all but over and it was obvious to everyone that the Germans had lost. With the survivors of the offensive losing ground as they attempted to carry out Hitler's absurd no-retreat order, there was no need to launch a strike against Allied airfields across the Meuse. Indeed, the situation called for a further husbanding of air resources. Every pilot and plane that could be spared was needed to combat the huge armadas of Allied bombers that ranged over the Reich. The explanation that the raid provided air cover to the Wehrmacht during its retreat from the Ardennes cannot be substantiated. Hitler ordered no ground be given up and only pulled two SS divisions out of the battle for refit. When the weather cleared, "Jabos" as the Germans called the Allied tactical fighter bombers, were out in force. Between December 16, 1944 and January 1, 1945, the Allies flew 16,628 tactical air sorties in support of the Ardennes campaign. However, the majority of those missions were flown by the IX Tactical Air Force, which supported U.S. combat units. The British accounted for 1,099 sorties during the period, but only 371 of those were attacks on battlefield targets.[2]

The Luftwaffe was not certain of the exact organization of the two Allied tactical air forces, but having just abandoned the airfields in France, Belgium and Holland to advancing Allied ground troops, they knew exactly where those fields were. The Germans also had a good idea of where the dividing line between the two Allied air forces was.

During Bodenplatte, the only U.S. airfield attacked was the Ninth Tactical Air Force base at Metz. All of the other airfields belonged to the British 2nd TAC.[3] Therefore, the overwhelming force of Bodenplatte was not directed against the airfields that provided support to U.S. forces in the Bulge, but against the British. Considering previous explanations of Bodenplatte, this is the reverse of what it should have been. It is even more puzzling considering that "Operation Wirbelwind" (Whirlwind), the attack on the U.S. Seventh Army, was also underway and definitely needed air support.

The explanation that Bodenplatte was a spoiling attack to prevent the British from launching a new offensive is unlikely. The terrain facing the British was a flat, wet bog, the type of ground for which the Germans had arranged a defense in depth and had made the Allies pay dearly every step of the way; in addition, the German soldier on defense had learned very early to get along without Luftwaffe support. As it was, the British would not begin their major offensive, "Veritable," until February. In January 1945, the Germans were not in the habit of stirring up hornets' nests unless they had the resources.

The few German units who directly benefited from Operation Bodenplatte were the V-1 and V-2 launching units in Holland and western Germany. The British 2nd TAC airfields struck on the morning of January 1, 1945 were precisely the fields from which hundreds of tactical sorties flew daily looking for V-1 and, to a lesser extent, V-2 launch sites. In September, October and November 1944, 2nd TAC flew approximately 10,000 sorties against suspected V-sites. Little damage was done because the Germans kept constantly on the move and superb camouflage had become a matter of survival. The result of Bodenplatte was an immediate lessening of pressure against Wachtel's troops from the air and a resultant increase in the rate of firing of both V-1s and V-2s that lasted into early February.

Operation Bodenplatte had other consequences. The strength of the British Second Tactical Air Force was reduced by approximately 40 percent and it did not fully recover until the end of January. Allied authorities immediately downplayed the results of the raid and most accounts indicate that the losses were made up in a week, but the record shows otherwise. Compared to the Germans, the Allies had an embarrassment of riches, but 500 fighter bombers was a considerable number of aircraft and the Allies did not have that many in reserve.

Such was the importance of keeping up pressure on the V-sites that some of the losses were made up by transferring P-51 Mustang fighters from Eighth Air Force Fighter Command to British 2nd TAC. The transfer created a shortage of escorting fighters which limited the number of deep penetrations Eighth bombers made into Germany for several weeks.

Allied air commanders on the Continent also changed their tactics. Until Bodenplatte, the Luftwaffe seldom showed itself over the battlefield on the Western Front and Allied airmen operated with impunity. Security was lax and air cover for the airfields nonexistent. Bodenplatte gave the Allied air commanders the same type of disagreeable surprise the Ardennes Offensive gave to the ground commanders. Suddenly they were unwilling to discount the offensive capabilities of the Luftwaffe and changed their tactics. Standing patrols over Allied bases were strengthened. Security precautions, antiaircraft guns and night fighters were all redeployed to cover the forward airfields. The improved defensive arrangements also reduced the offensive punch of the Allied tactical air forces for several weeks.

With the collapse of the Ardennes offensive, Nazi Germany was left with few military options, but Hitler, undaunted by the forces arrayed against him, ordered his troops to fight on. He was loyally supported by Martin Bormann, Propaganda Minister Goebbels and Himmler, the head of the SS. Goering, once again addicted to drugs, had limited influence when he bestirred himself. Few of the leaders of the Third Reich were aware of the seriousness of the situation. Albert Speer was one of these and he realized that German industry, with its shrinking resources, had to be streamlined to cope with the situation. He also thought he could use the situation to regain some of the influence he had lost to Himmler after the attempt on Hitler's life in July 1944.

In early December, Dr. Waldemar Petersen, the head of the Entwicklungskommission für Fernschiessen (the commission Hitler had created to oversee long-range bombardment), suffered a stroke, leaving the organization leaderless. At Speer's direction, Oberst Friedrich Geist, the head of the office development group in the Armament Minister's Technical Office, approached Dornberger and offered him the post vacated by Petersen. Dornberger emphatically declined, with understandable bitterness: "Only a year before it had been declared impossible for me, as an Army Officer, to be granted ministerial powers in connection with my A-4 program and to give orders to organizations within the Ministry of Munitions. Now, as they no longer knew how to proceed, I was to pull their irons out of the fire. Since the problem had become insoluble, it was passed to me. I declined."[4]

Von Braun was asked to convince the general to accept the post but Dornberger would not budge. When Dornberger complained that time was of the essence and the commission was too large and cumbersome to accomplish anything in a short time, von Braun then suggested that the commission be disbanded and Dornberger form a working group with a few dedicated engineers and scientists. With a small group of talented people, Dornberger could use his position at the Heereswaffenamt to push those projects he deemed worthwhile. Dornberger liked the idea of directing a group composed of "men of action," as he termed them, rather than a committee of bureaucrats. Later in the month he made the proposal to Geist, who forwarded it to Speer, who approved it. "Arbeitsstab Dornberger" (Working Staff Dornberger) was established as a part of the Development Department of the Ministry of Munitions on January 12, 1945. The focus of the staff was breaking Allied air supremacy.

Kammler was, by now, too powerful for Speer. On January 26, 1945, the SS-Obergruppenführer assumed command of 5th Flak Division so that he controlled both the V-1 and V-2. His new organization was known as Armeekorps der Vergeltung (Corps of Vengeance) with its headquarters located at Haaksbergen in Holland. Since Kammler was now a corps commander he was not satisfied with having mere V-2 Abteilungen (battalions) to command and insisted on regiments. Artillerie Abteilung 485 became Artillerie-Regiment zu Vergeltung 902; Artillerie Abteilung 836 became Artillerie-Regiment zu Vergeltung 901; and SS Werfer Batterie 500 became SS Werfer Abteilung 500. It is not clear whether Kammler planned to expand the units or whether the change was just made to feed his ego, because the units received no additional firing crews or equipment. The corps did receive additional units to support its size and function. Added were several antiaircraft batteries, an engineer battalion, a supply battalion, three security battalions and some medical personnel.

The following day "Arbeitsstab Dornberger" held its first meeting, but Kammler was determined to control even this. An OKW teletype message of January 31 confirmed Kammler's appointment as commander of both V-1 and V-2 units and transferred all of the Luftwaffe personnel to the Waffen SS. In the long run, most of this part of the order was ignored and 5th Flak Division personnel remained in the Luftwaffe. However, the officers were required to join the Waffen SS and this was something that Oberst Eugen Walter, the acting commander of 5th Flak Division, much to his credit, refused to do. Walter was forced to step aside and Oberst Max Wachtel replaced Eugen Walter as commander of the division. Not yet satisfied with his power, Kammler went to Goering and had the Reichsmarschall appoint him "Special Commissioner for Breaking the Air Terror."

On February 6, 1945, Dornberger became part of Kammler's technical staff. This time no signatures were needed. What Kammler wanted, he got. The double assignment was approved by General Leeb, head of the Heereswaffenamt. There was little else he could do. The SS had succeeded in gaining control of all aspects of the V-weapons from development to production to deployment.

Outside the ruling circle of the Nazi Party, Hans Kammler was now probably the most powerful man in the Third Reich. Dornberger saw that as both Speer's and Kammler's deputy he had several advantages. Through Speer's Ministry of Munitions he could direct civilian agencies, and through Kammler he could direct military ones. Yet Dornberger was too shrewd not to understand that time was running out. He later wrote, "It was too late. The problem was now insoluble. I felt morally certain that we only had a few months left and that nothing we did could affect the issue decisively."[5] All projects that could not be completed by autumn 1945 were to be scrapped. Later in January, Kammler discontinued "Rheintochter" and "Enzian," two air defense weapons, and on February 6 he canceled "Rheinbote," a multi-stage rocket that was already in production. It had a 45-pound warhead and a range of 100 miles, but showed little promise due to its lack of accuracy. Under prevailing conditions it was of little use. An additional problem with "Rheinbote" was that it was launched from a modified Meilerwagen and was causing an added drain on ground support equipment that was desperately needed by the V-2 launch crews.

Internecine strife continued in the upper levels in the government while the firing crews of 5th Flak division adjusted to the tactical situation and attempted to make life in Antwerp and Liège as miserable as possible for the Allies. The problems with the V-1 continued. An analysis of 5,097 flying bombs launched in the period from October 21 to December 31, 1944 showed that 20 percent of the bombs had crashed prematurely. The failures were attributed to the following:

Control Equipment — 50%
Airframe with equipment — 32%
Catapult — 10%
Ground Equipment — 5%
Propulsion unit — 3% [6]

Unlike the report of July 1944, there is no category for human error. This seems pretty far-fetched since the launch crews were weary and short-handed and is probably an attempt by the 5th Flak Division to blame all its troubles on technical deficiencies. On January 2, 1945, a conference concerning the V-1 was held in Berlin. Oberst Walter, who was still the acting commander of the 5th Flak Division, gave a lecture concerning the technical faults of the flying bomb to the attendees, who included General von Axthelm. Management and quality control remained a major problem, especially with the V-1. By the end of December circle runners had killed 22 German citizens and injured 228. Property damage consisted of 24 houses destroyed and 101 damaged.[7] Circle runners also disrupted traffic and ruined crops. The "Terror of the Eifel" was living up to its name.

Mechanical failures continued to plague the V-1 and simple modifications were not checked. There was also a disconnect between producers and users. In the closing weeks of 1944, new steam generators for the catapults were delivered without operating instructions. At the end of the year, some flying bombs arrived with de-icer equipment that was defective. Soon, the units were ordered not to fire them. Other defects were noted and orders not to fire the affected weapons were also issued. The "no fire" orders came from design staffs responsible for the modifications or defects, not from a central controlling agency. Walter was understandably angry and wrote, "I would be grateful if the [5th Flak] division could be informed which departments and personnel are entitled to order such stoppages. It cannot be true, as it obviously has been the case up to now, that any officer or engineer who notices a fault, arbitrarily orders stoppages."[8] If this weren't bad enough news, Walter also announced that the United States had begun copying the V-1 and urged that developmental work continue in order to keep ahead of the Americans.

Wachtel continued to complain that the V-1 should not be used as a military weapon but as a weapon of political importance (a terror weapon). Nevertheless, by Hitler's order, the flying bombs and rockets were concentrated on London, Antwerp and Liège. He also gave a lecture concerning the failures of the flying bomb, but this was to the launch crews. On January 8 he told them that he had received news of more damage to German life and property from circle runners and stated, "[A]nother projectile from the sites of the third detachment has crashed onto German territory. The result was the devastation of dwellings and the death of five German women and men."[9] He went on to explain that the V-1 failures were terrifying to German civilians in the Ruhr area. Bombing by the Allies was quite enough and they didn't need the added terror of malfunctioning flying bombs.

The fact that Wachtel took the time to admonish his launch crews demonstrates there was more to the circle runners and premature crashes than equipment failure. This was nowhere near the end of the problem. While Walter lectured in Berlin and Wachtel admonished the firing crews, 124 V-1s crashed in the operational area of Heeresgruppe H in the period January 1 to January 12, 1945, killing 4 German soldiers and wounding another 60. The new year also brought bad news concerning resources. The monthly allocation of fuel to the firing units in 5th Flak Division had been approximately 35,800 gallons of gasoline and 31,300 gallons of diesel.[10] In January the allocations for both were cut to less than 15,000 gallons of each. At the same time, the daily allocation of flying bombs was cut from 160 to 100.

Along with poor quality control, problems with dispersion remained critical. Hitting a target like London was not a problem if the flying bomb worked correctly, but Antwerp was a completely different matter. The primary target was the port, a military target, which was much smaller than a city. Since there was no possible way to make the Fi 103 more accurate, the obvious answer to cutting the dispersion was to shorten the range. The code name for this operation was "Mülleimer" (Trash Can). On January 4, Headquarters Flak Regiment 155(W) decided to establish three firing sites in the vicinity of Rotterdam, roughly 56 miles from Antwerp and half the range of the launchers in the Eifel. The launchers were constructed in the simplest way possible and concealed in large buildings. One was in a storage shed at a port and another was in a sugar factory.

On January 22, the regiment reported to higher headquarters that the launchers in the Rotterdam area would be ready in three days and that they would have 300 flying bombs to fire by January 30. Firing due south also meant that the V-1s would be approaching Antwerp from a new direction and would cause the defenses to move again. The January 22 report concluded: "The enemy defense, as identified by observation in the approach area from the Dutch operational zone in front of the target Antwerp, shall be split up and disturbed."

The regiment was better than its word. On January 27, the new sites opened fire on Antwerp. Concealed from Allied photo reconnaissance, they merely had to open the doors to fire a flying bomb, but it could not have been pleasant for the crews. Not only was there the noise, but the fumes from the catapult and the pulse jet engine. On January 31, the 3rd Battalion of the Flak Regiment was ordered to move to sites east of the Rhine that had been prepared the previous month under the code name "Oktoberfest." However, on February 5, Kammler informed Wachtel that a modified flying bomb, the Fi 103 F-1, which had an increased range, was ready for deployment against London.

The F-1 was little different than its predecessors except that it had a 271-gallon fuel tank compared to the Fi 103 B-1's 182-gallon tank. It also had a payload that contained 1,169 pounds of explosive instead of the 1,830-pound payload in the earlier versions. The modifications gave it a flight time of 43 minutes instead of 30, more than enough to reach England from Holland. The Fi 103 F-1 was no more accurate that the previous prototypes but the new version, no doubt, pleased Wachtel, who was convinced that the V-1 was a political weapon rather than a military one and that firing on London would have a devastating effect on the British. Fortunately for the British, the new V-1 would not be available to the launch crews for another few weeks.

At the end of February one of the most objectionable aspects of Fi 103 development was brought to an end. The Reichenberg program was a plan to use manned flying bombs in suicide attacks on critical targets. One of the originators of the idea was test-pilot Hanna Reitsch, who had piloted the original manned Fi 103 to discover the cause of the crashes during the first catapult launches. Her rationale for the proposal was that a few idealistic pilots sacrificing their lives on important targets such as power stations and battleships would save countless others at the front. Her vision of idealists was not shared by Himmler, who suggested using "people who were tired of life, and sick persons and criminals [whoever he regarded as such] as 'Selbstopfer-Piloten' [SO-Piloten, or self-sacrifice pilots]."[11] In November 1943, a board of scientists and engineers had indicated that the concept was feasible, but the Luftwaffe's Erhard Milch was opposed to the idea. Not letting the matter drop, Hanna Reisch went directly to Hitler, who agreed to let development of the weapon continue, but reserved the right to decide whether or not it would be deployed.

The Fi 103 was initially rejected as unsuitable and experiments went forward with a Messerschmitt Me 328, which was designed as a single-sortie escort fighter. It was supposed to have a pulse jet beneath each wing, but the vibration proved to be too much. Other experiments were made with an Fw-190 fighter carrying a huge bomb. The idea was that the pilot would bail out as soon as he directed the aircraft at the target. With a large bomb load the Fw-190 was so heavy that it was extremely vulnerable to enemy fighters. Apparently it was Otto Skorzeny, Hitler's favorite commando, who recommended the Fi 103 and the flying bomb was then adopted. In the meantime the Luftwaffe activated KG 200 with the appellation "Leonidas Staffel"— after the Spartan king who, with his sacred band, died defending the pass at Thermopylae against the Persians.

Flight tests of the suicide missile began in the summer of 1944 and the program and the aircraft acquired the code name "Reichenberg," with the production version known as Reichenberg IV. The aircraft was supposed to be carried to the vicinity of the target by an He-111 bomber. The cockpit occupied the space normally reserved for the two spherical compressed air tanks and had a plywood seat with basic controls and an arming switch. Some provision was made for the pilot to exit the aircraft, but in order to escape the pilot had to stand up in front of the air intake of a pulse jet traveling at close to 400 mph in a steep dive, making the chances for survival nil. Pilots were accepted and trained with the aircraft. It was planned to send some of the pilots against industrial targets in Russia and Brigadeführer Walter

Schellenberg of SS Intelligence had already compiled a list of them. When Oberstleutnant Werner Baumbach assumed command of KG 200 in October 1944, he viewed the entire operation with misgivings and did nothing to support it. With the help of his friend Speer, Baumbach got an audience with Hitler and convinced the Führer to cancel the project. By this means there was no way Himmler could resurrect it. On February 24, 1945, all training was canceled for lack of fuel. Roughly 173 piloted Fi 103s were produced and none were used.

In January 1945, Peenemünde, always a bit removed from events going on elsewhere, was becoming more and more aware of the approach of the Red Army. Daily, thousands of refugees could be seen moving west to escape the Soviet juggernaut. The stories told by the refugees of rape and murder had a ring of truth, though they failed to add that the Russians were paying the Germans back in kind for depridations in their own homeland. Shortages were rampant in not just large industrial items but also small, everyday items. Clothing was rationed to a shirt or a topcoat a year and shoes were impossible to find. Worn soles could not be repaired unless one could find a worn-out industrial drive belt and someone to do the work. Some of the workers began to carry sidearms while others were training with the local Volkssturm, or home guard. The staff of Electromechanical Industries had also been considerably reduced. There were only 4,225 employees. Of these, the A-4 got the lion's share with 1,940. Wasserfall employed 1,220; A-4b had 270 assigned; and Taifun a mere 135. The remaining 660 were administrative personnel.[12]

While some of the work on the V-2 had to do with improving components and guidance systems, the pressing issues were a need for increasing the range of the rocket and making it easier to manufacture. One of the difficulties that arose was that experimental rockets had to come from the production lines at Mittelwerk, which was something Kammler opposed. "For him [Kammler] the only important thing was the number of operational shots. He wanted to report as many as possible to higher authority, and whether they were effective seemed for the moment to be a matter of indifference. At this time we were in constant fear that further development and experimentation would be stopped altogether."[13]

The demand for increased range made it necessary for the staff at Peenemünde to resurrect the concept of a winged rocket, an idea that had been shelved in 1943 due to lack of labor and resources. Some wind tunnel research had been done in the spring of 1940 to determine the proper shape of the supersonic wings and tail fins, but little else. In September 1944, the original material was hastily assembled and a series of tests scheduled. At first the engineers planned to construct a subscale A-7—an A-5 with wings—but that idea was rejected as impractical. While a winged missile offered greater range with a glide at the end of its trajectory, it also presented a number of control problems, not the least of which was the effect of wind on the large wing surfaces. Instead of building a new rocket, von Braun decided to add the wings to an existing A-4, christening it the A-4b, which was commonly known as the "bastard." Larger jet vanes were inserted in the nozzle for added control. While he was accused of creating the A-4b to keep the original A-4 team together, von Braun was also responding to Kammler's demand for immediate results.

The first test launch of the A-4b was made on December 27, 1944. The rocket crashed almost immediately as a result of a roll that began at take-off. The A-4 controls were unable to cope with the additional air resistance created by the wings. The next launches were little better. On January 18, 1945, the controls failed when the rocket was about 100 feet off the launch pad. Shortly after, another failed due to a leak in an alcohol tank that had developed before launch. On January 24 came the first qualified success. Dornberger wrote:

> The rocket, climbing vertically, reached a peak height of near-
> ly 50 miles at a maximum speed of 2,700 miles per hour. This
> rocket powered aircraft, with a wing area of about 145 square
> feet, broke the sound barrier without trouble. It flew with sta-
> bility and steered automatically at both subsonic and super-
> sonic speeds. On the descending part of the trajectory, soon
> after the rocket leveled out at the upper limit of the atmos-
> phere and began to glide, a wing broke. On the whole the
> result was eminently satisfactory and more than fulfilled our
> expectations.[14]

The experiment may have filled Dornberger's expectations, but it was the swan song of Peenemünde.

A number of ideas were put forward and quickly rejected as

impractical. Among these was the proposal to put A-4 rockets in a semi-submersible pod to be towed behind a U-boat. When the U-boat reached the launch point, the pod was partially flooded so the rocket in the pod would stand upright just beneath the surface. The launch crew would then transfer to the pod and fuel and launch the missile. The plan wasn't clear on the storage of hydrogen peroxide, sodium permanganate and alcohol in the cramped submarine, much less how it was to transport four-plus tons of liquid oxygen. Kammler also wanted Dornberger to look into firing V-2s from a train. Because the A-4 was designed to replace the railroad gun, it was natural for Heereswaffenamt to consider that mode of transportation from the outset. By the end of 1942, prototypes of railway cars with launchers had already been made available for testing at Peenemünde's Test Stand VII. The idea was to prepare the rocket in a tunnel, then push the car with the elevating mechanism and the firing table to the tunnel entrance. The crew was then to clamp the firing table to the rails and the rocket would be placed on it with a boom. From there the rocket was to be fueled and fired in a procedure not unlike that for the motorized units.

Dornberger was irritated with Kammler's suggestion. "Our growing air inferiority in the West and the greater mobility of the motorized units had caused us to suspend this work, but now at the end of 1944, Kammler demanded its resumption. I had no idea why. Exhaustive tests were carried out at Peenemünde in the last months of the year. I could not believe that there was any point to the work in view of the air situation and I went about it rather half-heartedly. What I had expected happened. In January 1945, after much work had been done, the whole thing was abandoned."[15]

On January 31, at Kammler's order, von Braun alerted the engineers and staff that important defense projects were to be relocated to central Germany and that they would soon be moving. The news caused quite a stir, but no one was really surprised. General Rossmann, the military commander of the installation, had urged everyone to remain calm, but the soldiers of the Northern Experimental Command were already training with antitank weapons in anticipation of a Russian attack. Priorities for the move were: A-4; Taifun; A-4b; and Wasserfall. Each of the committees had to choose who would move first.

On February 2, the effort received added emphasis when a rumor that the Russians had attacked Eberswalde, a town northeast of Berlin, swept through Peenemünde. Twenty-four hours later, the news was found to be untrue, but it hastened the movement process considerably. At this time a number of draft deferments for Peenemünde workers were canceled and this, too, added to the haste. On February 3, von Braun held an organizational meeting described by Dieter Huzel as the "last and biggest relocation meeting."[16] In all, 4,325 people, civilian and military, not counting families, were scheduled to go in six groups. There was hardly enough transportation, but authorities at Peenemünde had managed to hold on to a number of rail cars that were on sidings in the area. Motor vehicles were in short supply, as was gasoline, and mule and horse carts were used to transport everything from furniture to documents to the railhead. Some barges were also available and these were loaded with furniture so they could be towed along the coast. The launch crews at the test stands were ordered to remain in place for the time being. The group at Peenemünde used every bit of influence it could to expedite the move.

Von Braun used his SS rank when he signed orders to move, and the officials at Peenemünde took advantage of a fortuitous misprint. Some stationery for Dornberger's headquarters had arrived with the letters VzbV instead of BzbV. Erich Nimwegen, an administrative employee known for his ability to obtain difficult-to-find material, was a somewhat shady character. Nimwegen saw the opportunity immediately and the misprint suddenly became "Vorhaben zur besonderen Verwendung" (Project for Special Duty). This was, according to Nimwegen, "a top secret agency, not to be interfered with by anyone save Himmler himself. Soon VzbV signs began to appear in letters several feet high on boxes, trucks and cars. Indeed it provided complete protection against any interference."[17]

One crucial part of Peenemünde was ready to move. In September 1944, Paul Storch, the head of Electromechanische Werke, had ordered the assembly and preparation for shipment of the principal records of the facility. The new headquarters could not support test firings, so Dr. Kurt Debus, the last chief of Test Stand VII, was assigned by von Braun to take a mobile launching suite to Cuxhaven and continue flight testing from there.

The exact destination of the Peenemünde staff was, at first, in doubt. Plans to move the rocket research center had surfaced as soon as the British bombed it in August 1943. One of the original proposals made by the SS was to move the project to a safer underground facility codenamed "Zement" (Cement); it was in Austria about 60 miles east of Salzburg. Von Braun opposed the idea because the move would be too disruptive and wrote a memorandum against the concept in October 1943. By this time activities in Peenemünde had been dispersed to a remarkable degree. The valve and materials testing laboratory was moved to an airfield at Anklam and Hermann's supersonic wind tunnel was in the process of moving to Bavaria. Production was moving to Mittelwerk. A major question, never satisfactorily answered, was where test firings were to take place. In 1944, the tunnels at Zement remained to be finished, but Speer put an end to any speculation of using Zement for A-4. In August a refinery moved into the "A" tunnels of Zement and in December the "B" tunnels were turned over to aircraft production. Shortly after the February 3 meeting, von Braun left to survey the new location. He returned on February 27 with the news that everyone was moving to Bleicherode, a town east of Nordhausen.

Like their counterparts with the V-1, the V-2 launch crews continued to experience quality control problems with their missiles. The one bright spot in the news was that the failure rates for V-2 were declining. A report dated January 8 was the result of a study of 900 rockets that had been delivered to the launch sites as of December 31, 1944; 605 (67.2 percent) had been launched. Of these, 40 (6.6 percent) malfunctioned after leaving the launch pad.[18] This amounted to an overall rejection or failure rate of 37.2 percent of the rockets delivered from Nordhausen from the beginning of the offensive. November was a particularly bad month and a considerable number of rockets were rejected for bad trim motors and rudder servos. The figures for December 1944 for both Gruppe Nord and Gruppe Süd showed a marked improvement. Of 625 rockets delivered to the launch sites 87, a mere 12.3 percent, were rejected by the crews. Of the 538 launched, 44 (7 percent) malfunctioned in the air. The new failure rate was somewhat less that 21 percent.

A major problem found by an inspection team that visited the units from January 4 to 8, 1945, was training and doctrinal material. Some instructional material was printed so badly that it was illegible.

Documentation for new equipment had arrived four weeks after the equipment itself. Although not as numerous as flying bomb incidents, malfunctioning V-2s could wreak havoc on friend as well as foe. A V-2 launched on New Year's Eve in Holland fell back onto a German barracks, killing and wounding dozens of soldiers. Also, roving Allied aircraft continued to keep the launch crews on the move. Strafing by Allied aircraft was so frequent that the Germans dug foxholes all along the Rijks Straatweg, the road that led north from The Hague to Wassnaar. The foxholes were for the use of anyone, German or Dutch, who happened to be on the road. In one place there was even a sign informing passers-by of the danger of strafing attacks and indicating that foxholes were on the left of the road. However frequent the Allies' air attacks, however, they did little to stop the launches. On January 26, the day of its redesignation, Artillerie-Regiment z. V. 902 launched a record 17 rockets against England.

This was extremely unwelcome news for the British. The number of rockets hitting English soil had slackened during the Battle of the Bulge. From the 20th to the 27th of December only 6 rockets fell on London. Now, once the Germans were pushed back from their deep penetration into the American lines, the V-2s were back in force. British authorities were extremely frustrated by their inability to stop them and spent considerable effort in trying to find ways to at least neutralize them. Bomber Command refused to be diverted from its bombing of German cities and Air Defence Great Britain was left to its own resources to counter the V-2s coming from Holland.

In December, fighter bombers of Air Defence Great Britain flew nearly 400 sorties over The Hague, dropping more than forty tons of bombs. All targets were at least 250 yards from the dwellings of Dutch inhabitants, but bombing in World War II carried no guarantee and there were invariably Dutch casualties. At one point, Hill's aircraft were able to bomb a block of apartments housing some of Kammler's rocket troops. German casualties were light but the damage forced them to vacate the place. Thereafter, the rate of fire slackened thanks to the Germans' need to support the Ardennes Offensive; but ADGB understandably thought its own efforts were responsible. One pro-posal put forward by Air Marshal Hill's staff that was accepted by 2nd TAF was bombing liquid oxygen factories in Holland. On January 22, fighter bombers of 2nd TAF attacked one of the factories. Considering the Germans' need for liquid oxygen—which was critical—the British attack either failed to cause much damage or the factory really had nothing to do with liquid oxygen, because there was no slackening in the German rate of fire. A continuing concern of the authorities in London was the fear that a V-2 might penetrate one of the subway tunnels that ran beneath the Thames River. On January 26, they asked Eisenhower to sanction precision attacks by light bombers against rocket targets, but these would have accomplished little.

In mid-February, a defective flying bomb landed near Antwerp and was immediately subjected to extensive analysis. The bomb was different from those studied previously in that the nose cone was made of wood instead of metal. Initially, this was thought to be a cost-cutting measure, but Allied intelligence quickly pieced together the puzzle that the wooden nose was no accident but rather a deliberate weight-saving measure designed to increase the V-1's range. British scientists realized that the lighter, longer-range V-1 was capable of again hitting London from the launch sites in Holland and the information was passed to Air Defence Great Britain to again prepare to meet the flying bombs. The alarm was taken very seriously.

Air Marshal Hill and General Pile immediately met to realign the defenses. The gun batteries between Sheppy and Orfordness were reinforced and six squadrons of Mustang fighters were immediately assigned to daylight patrols. Three squadrons were positioned in front of the guns along the coast and three more were positioned behind the guns in front of London. Three squadrons of Meteor jets were also reassigned to bases between the guns and London. These jets, because of their high fuel consumption and limited time in the air, were placed on short-notice alert, and would take off once incoming V-1s where detected. Two squadrons of Mosquitos and a Tempest squadron were assigned as defenders against night launches.[19] Aerial reconnaissance was once again directed into the areas where potential sites might be located, and on February 26 these aircraft had identified three sites that were aligned on London. The British Tactical Air Forces, which had by now recovered from the New Year's Day strike, augmented by fighters from Air Defence Great Britain, were immediately assigned to destroy the sites.

Typhoons of No. 83 Squadron, 2nd TAF, attacked the three launch sites on March 2. Although extensive damage was caused to the area, the ramps were not damaged and that evening Colonel Wachtel and his crews managed to shoot seven V-1s at the British capital. Five were destroyed shortly after launch by antiaircraft guns and one was shot down by fighters over the North Sea. The final V-1 hit Bermondsey.[20] Ten more V-1s were launched at London that afternoon. The antiaircraft guns claimed four, patrolling aircraft got four and two hit London. After this initial burst, the launchings fell off as the Germans brought more bombs forward and repaired damage to launchers. The Allies intensified their patrols, and attacks on suspected sites increased during the next several days, but these did not hit any of the launchers or stop the flow of V-1s to the sites. On the morning of March 5, the V-1 crews began another bombardment. Over the next 23 days, Wachtel's men fired 275 flying bombs at London. Many of the bombs were shot down by antiaircraft guns and the fighters accounted for several score more. Only a few flying bombs reached England and still fewer London. The last flying bomb to reach London fell on March 28, 1945.

In February, the V-1 launch crews of the 1st Battalion of Flak Regiment 155(W), and one battery each of the Second and Third Battalions, stepped up their efforts against Antwerp. In the period February 11–20, 1945, they succeeded in launching 981 flying bombs—an impressive average of more than 98 per day—and one day saw a peak of 160. At the new shorter ranges, U.S. commanders in the Antwerp area considered the flying bombs fired from the Rotterdam sites to be 25 percent more accurate than those fired on Antwerp from elsewhere. The batteries not involved in the assault on Antwerp were preparing to fire the new flying bomb against England. They were originally scheduled to occupy the sites east of the Rhine, but these had been overrun by the Allies. They moved, instead, to two firing sites near The Hague at Vlaardingen and Ypenburg and one near Delft, and began firing against London on March 9. The first day, 49 Fi 103 F-1s were fired and 5 crashed prematurely.[21] The rate of fire was subsequently reduced to find out what was wrong.

Two days later, Kammler told Wachtel that deployment of units to fire against London was of the highest priority. He also promised that the supply situation with regard to the Fi 103 F-1 would improve shortly. On March 12, Major Heinrich Steinhoff assumed command of Flak Regiment 155(W) while Wachtel took command of the 5th

Flak Division. By March 20, the regiment had launched 116 improved V-1s at London. During the latter part of March, however, Allied aircraft scored a significant success when they destroyed the launch sites at Ypenburg and Vlaardingen.

The new center of operations for the staff from Peenemünde was the town of Bleicherode, a small community about 10 miles west of Nordhausen. It was supposed to be a scientific and engineering cooperative called the "Entwicklungsgemeinschaft Mittelbau" (roughly, the Central German Development Cooperative). Firms like the Henschel and Dornier aircraft companies and Ruhr Steel were represented there, as was General von Glydenfeldt, who had been in charge of the V-1 project and was now BzbV-Luft, Dornberger's Luftwaffe counterpart. But that's as far as it went. Dieter Huzel, who had been in charge of Test Stand VII until he became von Braun's technical assistant in autumn 1944, was one of the last to leave Peenemünde. Departing by car on March 13, he arrived in Bleicherode on the evening of March 15. What he found was not encouraging: "Extremely primitive headquarters had been set up in a former agricultural school. There was not much sense of order."[22]

It was impossible to take a large and complex organization like the development center at Peenemünde, move it 200 miles and expect it to function as if nothing had happened. Much of the office equipment, especially that loaded onto barges, had disappeared. The worst part was the morale of the scientists and engineers. They all knew the end was near and most of them just went through the motions of doing their jobs. Many of them were scattered among the local villages, totally removed from the center of what little work was actually being accomplished. After spending the night on the floor of a restaurant ballroom, Huzel found himself lodging in a train that had been used to house firing crews at Blizna. After getting in touch with as many key people as he could find, Huzel went to visit von Braun in the hospital. The leader of the project had been spending long hours on the road and both he and his driver had fallen asleep. His car had swerved off the road and von Braun ended up with a badly broken arm in a huge cast.

Von Braun was in good spirits, however, and told Huzel that the authorities had promised them adequate office space and facilities.

Huzel took von Braun at his word, but no one else did. The situation remained chaotic until March 21, when von Braun left the hospital. His offices had been prepared in the administration building of the local power plant and he had been afforded excellent quarters, but there was nothing he could do to get any of the projects back on track.

Meanwhile, Kammler's V-2 launch crews continued to bombard Allied cities. In February, SS Werfer-Abteiling 500 continued to launch its V-2s at Antwerp, while the other units of Gruppe Nord launched against London. By this time most of the missiles were equipped with the automatic fuel cut-off instead of the radio-controlled one. Enemy planes searched everywhere for the launchers, but strict camouflage discipline was maintained and they weren't found. Supply shortages began to plague the firing units as they did other units of the German armed forces. The most severe shortage was liquid oxygen. Dornberger explained,

> Oxygen also became a restricting factor after the big underground liquefaction plants at Liège and Wittringen in the Saar had been overrun. We reckoned roughly 9 tons of oxygen, which was a day's output for one machine, to one firing. Only about 5 tons remained after the oxygen had been transferred from the factory storage tanks to the railway tank cars of 48-ton capacity, thence to the 5- to 8-ton road tankers, thence to the rocket, where there was loss in standing time before launching. Thus of every 9 tons produced some 5 tons reached the rocket, which needed 4.96 tons. In the big railway cars the loss was 92 gallons in 24 hours, and in the rocket before launching 4.5 pounds per minute. On the other hand the amount of oxygen available to us in Germany, including what came to us as a by-product of the hydrogen works, did not exceed the output of thirty to thirty-five generators. We therefore had available twenty-eight to thirty rockets per day for military operations and five to seven for test shots and acceptance tests of rocket motors."[23]

The result of the shortage was that from March 3 to March 13, Artillerie Regiment 901 was unable to fire a single rocket due to the lack of "A-Stoff."

Meanwhile, the British leadership was extremely frustrated with its inability to keep V-2s from hitting London. The fighter bomber attacks against the V-2 launch sites in The Hague were doing nothing to stem the number of launches against the British capital. The attacks on supposed liquid oxygen manufacturing sites had not worked. The only option was to attack the Haagsche Bosch in the hope that some of the launch crews and their equipment would be caught in the attack. The Haagsche Bosch, the wooded terrain from which many of the firings were taking place, was only about a mile long and half a mile wide, situated in the middle of a heavily populated area. It was so small that only a precision bombing attack could hit it without causing excessive civilian casualties. Nevertheless, the British leadership felt it had to do something and the attack was worth the risk.

After negotiations with the Dutch underground, a raid was mounted with 56 medium bombers; it took place on March 3. It was an overcast day and the aircraft dropped 69 tons of bombs from an altitude of 12,000 feet. A heavy crosswind and murderous German flak caused the bombers to drop 500 yards wide of the target. Many of the bombs came down in an inhabited section south of the wood. Hundreds of civilians were killed instantly, fires erupted and many others burned to death. The German authorities, who knew the underground had approved the attack, refused to let the local fire departments fight the fires in order to teach the Dutch a lesson.[24]

The botched raid on The Hague did nothing to stop the V-2s. At 11:00 A.M. on Thursday, March 8, a V-2 fired by Gruppe Nord hit the Central Market in Smithfield. The market, which dealt in meat and fish, had just received a shipment of unrationed fish. There was a long line of prospective buyers outside the market when the rocket hit in the northwest corner of a narrow brick building and demolished it. All the buildings within a quarter of a mile were severely damaged and every structure on 29 adjoining streets was damaged. It took several days to extricate the dead and injured, and the final count was 115 dead and 123 badly wounded.[25] Nevertheless, time was running out for the Germans.

The day before the Smithfield Market incident, the Americans captured the Ludendorff Railway Bridge at Remagen and the Germans thereafter made every effort to destroy it. On March 17, SS Werfer-Abteiling 500 fired 11 rockets at the bridge from firing sites near

Nijverdal-Hellendorn, 130 miles away. One rocket landed 40 miles short of the target but the others landed remarkably close to the bridge. The closest hit landed in the backyard of the house of Herman Lange and his wife at about 9:30 A.M. Only three hundred yards from the bridge, the house was used to billet American soldiers. Three of them were killed instantly and fifteen were wounded in the explosion. Several farm animals simply disappeared. At 12:20 P.M., another V-2 hit the command post of the 1159 Engineer Combat Group, killing another three men and wounding thirty-one. Other V-2s landed in the river. At 3:00 that afternoon the bridge, which had been damaged by explosives, collapsed.[26] The V-2s were neither the direct cause, nor were they the straw that broke the camel's back, but the near-misses with one-ton warheads certainly didn't help. It was also evidence that the V-2 was definitely improving. Fortunately for the people in London and Antwerp, the V-2 launch positions in Holland were now becoming untenable.

Kammler, unwilling to believe the Third Reich was coming to an end, did everything he could to hold his command together. Again we must rely on Dornberger as an eyewitness. He told how Kammler "dashed to and fro between the Dutch and Rheinland fronts and Thuringia and Berlin. He was on the move day and night. Conferences were called for one o'clock in the morning somewhere in the Harz Mountains, or we would meet at midnight somewhere on the Autobahn and, after a brief exchange of views, drive back to work again. We were prey to terrific nervous tension. Irritable and over-worked as we were, we didn't mince words. Kammler, if he got impatient and wanted to drive on, would wake the slumbering officers of his suite with a burst from his tommy gun. 'No need for them to sleep! I can't either!'"[27]

Kammler also believed that his corps with its weapons could prevent the collapse of the Third Reich and turn the scales in favor of Germany. Trains carrying flying bombs and rockets continued to pour into Holland. When the Dutch Resistance blew up the tracks of the rail supply line to The Hague and the local commander didn't have the troops to protect it, Kammler brought in reserves from Germany to secure the line and keep it clear. He used the innovative measure of infrared devices so his truck drivers could drive safely at night.[28] No matter how frantic his efforts, however, Kammler couldn't possibly stem the tide of the Allied advance. With the Allies firmly across the Rhine by the end of March, the Germans could no longer maintain their troops in Holland and the order to retreat was given on March 27, 1945.

The final rocket against London was fired from Schoeppingen on that date by Lehr und Versuchs Batterie 444. It landed between Court Road and Kynaston Road in Orpington, fifteen miles from the city's center. Twenty-three people were seriously injured and Mrs. Ivy Millichamp was killed, the last fatality in England during World War II. The last V-2 to strike Antwerp hit on March 28, causing 27 casualties. The V-1 launch crews hung on a little longer. The last flying bomb to get through the protective barrier of Air Defence Great Britain hit Datchworth near Hatfield at approximately 9:00 A.M. An hour later, another was brought down by antiaircraft fire near Iwade, and at 12:43 the final flying bomb to approach the British Isles was shot down by Pile's gunners off Orfordness. The catapult at Delft continued to fire at Antwerp until March 30 and the last V-1 to land in that city struck on that date. By April 1, all of Kammler's troops were in full retreat.

Although there were plans to deploy some of the V-1 and V-2 firing units against the advancing Russians, there does not appear to be any record of a V-1 or V-2 fired on the Eastern Front. On April 3, 1945, Hitler ordered all shipments of explosives to the Mittlewerk in Nordhausen discontinued. The Americans were approaching rapidly, and before they could overrun the area the inmates of Camp Dora were shipped to Bergen-Belsen Concentration Camp (on April 4). Prisoners in outlying camps were rounded up and executed. In one case over a thousand were herded into a building which was then set on fire. The SS guards shot those who tried to escape the flames.

When the U.S. 3rd Armored Division captured Nordhausen on April 11, all they found was a thousand prisoners too sick to walk and on the verge of starvation. The lack of V-weapons did not deter Kammler in his insane rush to single-handedly turn the tide against the Allies. On April 8, many of his troops were converted to infantry and moved east. Meilerwagens, launch pads and Strabo cranes were either destroyed or abandoned in place, as were stored rockets and flying bombs. The V-weapon campaign was over.

On April 1, 1945, Kammler gave the order for 500 people, consisting of von Braun and nearly all the key operatives in the various guided missile programs, to leave Bleicherode. According to one account, Kammler instructed von Braun, "You will select five hundred of your key men and have them ready to embark on my special train tomorrow. No families will be permitted. I'm sending you where you can continue your important work without fear of being overrun."[29] If Kammler actually made the statement, he was obviously lying. The work could not be continued without scientific notes and equipment with which to experiment. Without it there could be no pretense at re-establishing the offices. If anyone had any doubts about what was happening, von Braun made it perfectly clear when he instructed that no equipment was to be taken. They were simply fleeing from the Allies to an unknown destination. There were vague rumors of a National Redoubt in the Bavarian Alps, but whether it really existed no one knew.

Von Braun ordered the classified material to be assembled and transported to some out-of-the-way place and hidden for later use. Huzel was selected to be the one to carry out that task. For the purpose, he was given three 3-ton trucks and a safe conduct pass. He set up a schedule and went to the existing offices to pick up the documents. The Aft End and Rudder Design Department had already departed the area, but left a locked blueprint cabinet weighing nearly a ton. It took ten men to get it onto one of the trailers. Then Huzel departed with the trucks, two of which were pulling $2^{1}/_{2}$-ton trailers. Fortunately for them it was raining as they left, which meant they would not attract the attention of roving Allied aircraft. They headed for the Harz Mountains, where Huzel eventually hid the documents in a mine shaft near the small town of Dörnten. By the time he returned to Bleicherode everyone was gone, and he used the trucks to make an unauthorized trip to Berlin to rescue his fiancé. He eventually rejoined von Braun at Oberammergau.

In the meantime, the hand-picked 500 moved 270 miles from Bleicherode to the picturesque Bavarian town famous for its Easter pageant. They were not housed in the town but in a barbed-wire enclosure guarded by SS troops. Admittedly the accommodations were comfortable and the scenery spectacular, but the barbed wire led to speculation that Kammler had assembled the 500 either as a bargaining chip for dealing with the Allies or to make sure that none of them would fall into the hands of the Allies alive. Shortly after their arrival at Oberammergau, Kammler left to continue his attempts to stem the tide with his few rocket troops turned infantry. In the final days of the Third Reich, Hitler appointed Kammler "The Führer's Plenipotentiary for Jet Aircraft"—an absurd title considering there was barely enough fuel to keep four or five of them flying at any one time. Kammler eventually reached Prague, where it was reported he had himself shot by his own adjutant to avoid capture by Czech partisans. Like Hitler and Himmler, he escaped a well-deserved fate at the end of the hangman's rope.

Kammler's absence was a boon to von Braun and the others. With the Reich collapsing and without Kammler around to issue orders, the SS commander at Oberammergau was jittery and unsure of himself. Von Braun convinced him that the 500 should be dispersed in case of an Allied air attack; otherwise the entire project might be wiped out. The SS officer dithered and protested that he didn't have any transportation. Von Braun assured him this was no problem since he had ordered about twenty of his drivers to bring their cars from Bleicherode. The SS officer agreed after von Braun turned over to him a sedan with plenty of gasoline. The deal was made and the SS escorted the engineers and scientists in small groups to the surrounding villages. Well-stocked Wehrmacht warehouses were packed with food waiting for units that would never partake of it. Using their VzbV signs and passes, the Peenemünde group was able to obtain an ample supply for everyone, including their SS watchdogs. Von Braun, however, was not in good health. He had not rested his arm and shoulder properly and it was causing him a great deal of pain. He went to a hospital noted for its treatment of ski injuries, where the chief surgeon immediately removed the cast, re-broke the first fracture and confined von Braun to bed.

The stay in the hospital turned out to be a nerve-wracking experience as Allied planes daily bombed the area and several bombs hit nearby buildings. And even here there was to be no rest. Von Braun had just learned that the French Army was only an hour away when a Wehrmacht soldier with a Red Cross armband walked into his room. The man had been sent by Dornberger to rescue him. The surgeon put a cast on von Braun and in a short time he was driven to Dornberger's refuge at a resort hotel at Oberjoch, where Dornberger had managed to gather two dozen of Peenemünde's top men, including Dieter Huzel and von Braun's brother, Magnus. The group finally surrendered to American troops on May 2, 1945. Wachtel surrendered what was left of his 5th Flak Division on May 4. Hostilities in Europe ceased on May 8, 1945.

The victors engaged in a frantic race to find as much material and information on the V-1 and V-2 as they could. The Americans had already purloined the V-1 for their own and renamed it the JB-2. They were ready to bombard Japan with it but the Japanese surrendered before it could be used. The V-2 had one last performance in Europe. In October, German crews including Debus and Huzel, under the supervision of the British, fired three V-2s into the North Sea from Cuxhaven in what was known as "Operation Backfire." The expertise of the engineers and scientists was no longer needed in their native country, but the United States was more than willing to pay them to continue their research. The first guided missile war in history was over; however, others were to follow.

12

The Reckoning

In their short operational life, the V-weapons accomplished a great deal. In the air they forced the Allies to divert thousands of aircraft and hundreds of thousands of tons of bombs in an unsuccessful attempt to stop them. On the ground the Allies committed over 2,500 antiaircraft guns, more than two hundred of the world's most advanced radar sets and over a quarter of a million men and women to protect London and Antwerp. Operationally, the V-sites in France were a major objective of the Allied armies in Normandy. Field Marshal Montgomery was compelled to include neutralization of the V-sites in Holland as part of his plan to seize a bridge over the Rhine, and his ill-conceived attack failed. The V-weapon assault on the Port of Antwerp curtailed the port's activities and forced the Allies to open the Port of Ghent.

On the strategic level, no other German weapon prompted the formation of a cabinet-level organization like the Crossbow Committee. From the first launchings of the V-1 on June 12, 1944 until the last one fell on Antwerp on March 30, 1945, V-1 and V-2 launch crews kept up a steady rain of deadly missiles on Allied targets until ground troops overran their launching sites. In spite of the impressive performance of the flying bomb and the rocket, however, the Germans never fully understood what they had created. They failed to use them to their full potential, and the byzantine nature of their political-military system delayed their deployment far more than did Allied countermeasures.

Given the nature of war as it was understood by European general staffs in the 1930s, the decision of the German Armaments Ministry to develop a long-range rocket to replace the railway gun was practical and realistic. No corps or army commander would have objected to a mobile weapon capable of hitting enemy targets deep in rear areas with a one-ton warhead. What the Heereswaffenamt couldn't know when it started the project was how long and difficult the development process would be.

The perseverance of Dornberger and von Braun was noteworthy, even though their brainchild was technically flawed. The guidance system was a compromise because Kreiselgeräte was unable to mass-produce the Sg 66 due to the demand for instruments from other services. The A-4 was not designed with mass production in mind, and a weakness in the design itself caused many of the early A-4s to break up high above the target. Much of this could have been prevented, or easily corrected, had there been a pilot production facility, but Hitler, in one of his many shortsighted decisions, refused to sanction one. The lack of a production facility also meant there were no rockets available to fire under simulated combat conditions prior to release for full mass production. As a result, the problems with airbursts and leaking fuel systems did not appear until crew training was underway at Blizna.

The requirement to assemble every experimental rocket by hand meant that thousands of small but necessary modifications had to be made, noted and reported to the engineers responsible for the working drawings, and they were months behind in their work. When von Braun announced in September 1943 that the A-4 was complete, he meant complete from an engineering standpoint. It was not in fact ready for mass production and much work remained to be done. Even after mass production began, there were serious design flaws that required thousands of modifications to correct.

The SS must take much of the blame for the situation. The move from Peenemünde to Mittelwerk to satisfy Heinrich Himmler's lust for power in the Third Reich was a major blow to the project at a critical time in the A-4's development. With neither plans, jigs, dies, tools, patterns or blue prints, the Mittelwerk began building rockets, and only one in eight left the launch pad. In their haste to seize the A-4 for the SS, Himmler and his lieutenant, Hans Kammler, failed to create a production plant that could build a complete missile, and after assembly the rockets still had to be shipped to Berlin for the installation of electrical components. Thus, it took eleven months to deploy the rocket for combat operations after it was "complete." Dornberger and the engineers at Peenemünde and Mittelwerk needed five months to correct the defects discovered at the proving ground at Blizna. Therefore, the remaining six-month delay can be charged directly to the failure to build the pilot production plant and to meddling by the SS.

The Fi 103, like its stablemate, suffered from a fitful developmental process. Unlike the A-4, it was created not to fill a particular need but to compete with the A-4 for prestige within the Nazi hierarchy. The design was assembled and tested without proper evaluation of the individual components. Airframes that worked well when dropped from aircraft were unable to stand the g forces of a catapult launch. Sensitivity over prestige prevented Luftwaffe engineers from taking advantage of more than six years of Army experience in guidance systems. The result was a guidance system that worked only well enough to hit a city, even at short range. Production of the Fi 103 was plagued by poor quality control until the end of its operational life. How much time could have been saved had the developers of Fi 103 taken a more reasoned approach or took advantage of Army experience with the A-4 is open to speculation, but the time lost between November 1943 and February 1944, when no Fi 103s left the assembly line, is certainly quantifiable. The scrapping of 2,000 Fi 103 airframes in November 1943 because of bad welding, at a time when launch crews desperately needed training missiles, was another major blunder.

Throughout its operational life there was little effort to improve or enhance the Fi 103. Once it went into mass production, malfunctioning flying bombs proceeded to plague the firing crews (sometimes killing them). The relatively simple modification of lightening the warhead, adding fuel and increasing the revolutions on the counter didn't appear until the war was nearly over. The guidance system was never improved. This stands in sharp contrast to the A-4, which improved throughout the war in both reliability and accuracy. The decision to deploy the Fi 103 in large concrete sites was an error that worked to the Germans' advantage only after they decided to abandon them. The subsequent massive Allied expenditure of bombs on the sites became a fortuitous development, albeit one the Germans hadn't intended.

On the plus side for the V-1 and V-2, the German system of transportation and supply for both weapons worked exceptionally well even in the face of Allied air superiority. After the concrete site system envisioned by Hitler was abandoned, the Germans did an excellent job of keeping their launch units supplied with both flying bombs and rockets. They were extremely adaptable in adjusting to new conditions, and at every stage of the campaign managed to keep one step ahead of the Allies. The Fi 103 was stored in tunnels and caves in France to avoid the concrete supply sites originally constructed. After St-Leu-d'Esserent and Nucourt were hit by RAF "Tallboy" bombs, the weapons were dispersed across the countryside and never again were the Allies able to attack a single V-weapon storage area. The A-4, more sensitive to open storage than its stablemate, was fired straight from the factory—a system that worked well. The Germans handled the transportation of both weapons with great skill, using rail and truck transport at night. There were inevitable shortages of supplies, such as liquid oxygen for the A-4 in November 1944 and March 1945 and fuel for the Fi 103 in January 1945. However, shortages did not affect the V-weapons as badly as they affected the rest of the German armed forces.

Hitler resolved to strike at London with the Fi 103 in order to retaliate for the Allied bombing of German cities. On the surface the decision does not make good military sense, and for that reason it is often listed as one of Hitler's blunders. As proof, critics point to Eisenhower's assertion: "I feel sure that if he [the German] had succeeded in using these weapons over a six-month period, and particularly if he had made the Portsmouth–Southampton area one of his principle targets, Overlord might have been written off."[1] This is certainly a significant statement with regard to the effectiveness of both weapons and is a reflection of the damage they did to Antwerp, but the Channel ports were not a good target for the Fi 103. The ports were only in effective range of the sites in the Cotentin Peninsula. For the other sites, the Channel ports were at extreme range, and many of the Fi 103s fired at them from the distant sites missed completely.

London, on the other hand, was a large target. It was easy to hit and one of the Allies' most sensitive areas. In a practical sense it was the nerve center of the Allied war effort, the home of the British government, a large manufacturing center, a large headquarters and military center and, emotionally, it was the city that stood up to the Nazi Blitz in 1940. More important, London was a major population center and no nation can afford to have its citizens indiscriminately slaughtered. Thus, for all the wrong reasons, Hitler selected the one target that the Allies were bound to commit tremendous resources to defend. If Southampton had been targeted, the Allies might have moved their installations elsewhere; but London could not be relocated. Even before the first Fi 103 hit the city, the Allies expended thousands of sorties and tens of thousands of tons of bombs on the large sites and the ski sites to pre-empt the flying bomb offensive. Hitler was not wrong when he said with satisfaction that every bomb that landed on the suspected sites in France was one less dropped on Germany.

Even after the end of the first flying bomb campaign in September 1944, Air Defence Great Britain had to deal with the air-launched flying bombs and to attack the A-4 sites in Holland—a tremendous expenditure of resources. Hitler's selection of Antwerp and Liège on the Continent was made for more practical reasons and this was one phase of the campaign where the success of the V-weapons can be quantified. The reduction of the discharge rate of a major port by a third was no small achievement and was worth the German effort.

Much has been made of the V-weapons' lack of accuracy, but the criticism can only be clearly evaluated by comparing, for example, the V-weapons to America's use of the Norden bombsight in its program of "daylight precision bombing." The bombsight wasn't all that precise but it was much more accurate than everyone else's. By January 1944, German bomber crews on the Western Front were so poorly trained that they were lucky if they could fly in formation and find the right city, never mind bomb a particular factory. "Operation Steinbock" amply demonstrated their lack of skill. British accuracy was not much better. Early in the war they could barely get within five miles of the target, especially at night. In August 1943, a large number of the bombers in "Operation Hydra" all but missed Peenemünde.

Later in the war, when the Germans were launching V-2s at London from The Hague, the RAF avoided bombing the area because they were afraid of the number of Dutch civilian casualties that might result. In 1945, when the British felt compelled to retaliate against the German rocket crews in the Haagsche Bosch, the bombing was inaccurate and their worst fears realized when a large number of Dutch civilians were killed and injured.

In some ways the randomness of the V-weapons worked to the Germans' advantage. It required a broad belt of guns and balloons to defend London and a wide dispersal of resources, including civil defense. During the course of the V-1 campaign against the British capital, from June to September 1944, V-1s hit 176 factories, 146 public utilities (power lines, gas mains, etc.), 141 railroad bridges, lines and yards and 57 military installations. In Antwerp, the defense could be more concentrated because the range from launcher to target was shorter. The constant change of launch areas forced the defenses to move frequently. In Antwerp and Liège, like in London, numerous transportation and storage targets were consistently hit. In 1944 and 1945 the V-weapons were a far better investment for the Germans than conventional bombers.

Throughout the life of the V-weapons there was little positive German leadership in the upper reaches of command. In the A-4's development process Walter Dornberger and Wernher von Braun provided the leadership and expertise to keep the project on track. Although he disassociated himself from the A-4 after the war, Albert Speer took the matter directly to Hitler so that the project could continue. Once the war began, there was little support or guidance from Heereswaffenamt, OKH or OKW with regard to the weapon's deployment.

In the leadership category, the Fi 103 was even worse off than the A-4. Fritz Gosslau, who first led the way to pilotless aircraft, did not provide the Fi 103 program with the firm direction that von Braun and Dornberger provided to the A-4, and no else stepped forward to assume the role. Even Luftwaffe engineers like Rudolph Bree avoided responsibility for the project. Erhard Milch may have believed that the Fi 103 was decisive, but as the Luftwaffe's second in command he did little more than give it lip service. Commander of the Luftwaffe's anti-aircraft toops Walther von Axthelm tried to exercise leadership but was too far down the chain of command to have any real influence. Luftwaffe chief Herman Goering, of course, spent most of the latter half of the war coping with substance-abuse problems or concerned with personal indulgences.

During the V-weapons' short life, the SS were little more than parasites. They took the A-4—a weapon they could not develop themselves—and forced the inventors to operate it under SS control. Their utter contempt for the scientific and engineering skill that went into the A-4 was aptly demonstrated when Himmler had von Braun arrested in March 1944. It is difficult to gauge the thought processes of the

Reichsführer-SS, but in this case he no doubt believed he could bully someone else to handle the developmental end of the project. As an engineer, Kammler was certainly more astute than his superior. He recognized that little could be done without Dornberger's and von Braun's expertise and chose to use them rather than discard them. Control by the SS added nothing to the value of V-weapons development or deployment.

The areas that clearly suffered from the lack of German leadership were the coordination of weapon launches and the conduct of the guided missile campaign. From the start, the Germans tried to do too much with the resources at hand and there was no attempt to adjust the number of units firing on each target to gain as much benefit as possible for the Reich. There was no endeavor to coordinate both weapons and no effort to coordinate the V-weapons with conventional bomber or fighter bomber attacks. More concentration on the port of Antwerp, the most important logistical target on the Continent, might have resulted in a further decline in the port's capabilities, including the Allies' ability to clear the port. The LXV Armeekorps, which was theoretically a joint headquarters, never even tried to coordinate a major strike in combination with conventional bombers in order to decisively damage the port and its clearance facilities.

The 5th Flak Division certainly did everything in its power to get maximum results from the V-1 by shortening the range and by launching low-flying bombs from various different directions in an attempt to outflank the Antwerp defenses. But the effort wasn't reinforced. A "Bodenplatte"-type operation was still within the capability of the Luftwaffe in late fall 1944. Once Kammler took control of V-2, it became merely a matter of the number of missiles that could be launched and there was no attempt to maximize limited resources by massing on a single target for decisive results.

Early in the campaign Kammler squandered rockets on such insignificant targets as St-Quentin, and during his first months in control only 22 of his 156 rockets were fired at London. Had the commander been anyone but Kammler, he would have been relieved of duty. Even so, Hitler had to re-emphasize that London was the primary target. When Kammler took over 5th Flak Division and combined both V-weapons into the "Armeekorps der Vergeltung," he also failed to coordinate the V-weapons with the Luftwaffe. As long as

"The Vengeance Corps" fired rockets and flying bombs in large numbers, the Führer and the SS were happy. Although Kammler was energetic, he was totally unaware of the potential of either of the weapons under his command and wanted them merely for the power they represented within the Nazi hierarchy. His handling of them added nothing to the effort, and any chance of causing more damage to either of the three major city targets was frittered away.

Both Kammler and Max Wachtel were delighted to draw resources from Antwerp to fire at London, but by that time the campaign had but few days to run and it didn't matter. The A-4 launches were divided between London and Antwerp, an even split between Gruppe Nord and Gruppe Süd. Here again there was no attempt to find out which was of greater benefit to the Reich. All the German agents in London had been turned, but the Germans had the Arado 234 jet reconnaissance aircraft, which the Allies could not intercept. However, the Arado was never employed to gather information that might have made the V-weapons more effective. There appear to have been some agents left in Belgium, but these provided no intelligence with regard to where the missiles were hitting. In summary, what the Germans achieved—and it was considerable—was more by accident than design.

Allied reaction to the existence of the A-4 was hesitant at first but, thanks to Dr. R.V. Jones, the British intelligence effort followed a logical course that resulted in the discovery of both weapons and their capabilities. The bureaucratic in-fighting and turf battles typical of large government organizations did not prevent the British from constructing a fairly adequate picture of the weapons and their potential. The stubborn refusal of British scientists to admit that the Germans had succeeded in building a liquid-fueled rocket did much to confuse the issue. Nevertheless, British officials recognized the threat. Churchill deserves much of the credit because he was not swayed by Lord Cherwell's closed-minded attitude toward the rocket.

The bombing of Peenemünde in August 1943 was a timely move and the forty aircraft lost were arguably an acceptable trade-off for the life of Dr. Thiel alone. After his death, no one of his caliber was available to redesign the engine to make it easier to mass-produce. The Allies' failure to follow up with a second raid was a major blunder and it allowed the Germans to disperse their resources. In late 1943, the decision to bomb the large sites and ski sites was essentially the correct one. When the photo interpreters of the CIU spotted the sites under construction in France, Churchill and his cabinet took the threat from the flying bombs very seriously and the air campaign to neutralize them began.

Over the next few months, the Eighth and Ninth U.S. Air Forces and RAF Bomber Command wrecked all of the concrete sites and prevented the Germans from using them for anything other than storage. Unfortunately, the Allies underestimated the Germans' ability to adjust to an unfavorable situation and the enemy was allowed to proceed with the construction of the "modified" sites. In what can only be called poor judgment, Allied air commanders declined to attack the modified sites because they offered a slim chance of successful destruction, and the Germans were allowed to launch the V-1s with little air opposition in the beginning. Even after the start of the V-1 campaign, the Eighth Air force and RAF Bomber Command avoided attacking the V-1 launching sites because such missions interfered with their strategic bombing program. Their claim that the sensitive industries supporting the V-1 would come under attack as a matter of course was nonsense. The raids against Peenemünde in 1944 were never made in overwhelming strength; as a result, that installation continued to function until it was endangered by the advancing Russians. Throughout, the strategic air commanders showed themselves particularly unwilling to become involved in Crossbow. What's more, after they were compelled to participate, air force leaders exaggerated the effects of their air strikes against the V-1.

Allied attempts to stop the V-2 by air attack on production, supply and transportation facilities were totally unsuccessful. The destruction of the Zeppelin and RAX factories in 1943 were fortunate occurrences rather than deliberate acts. The claim by Air Marshal Sir Arthur Harris that the battle against the V-weapons was won long before the first V-1 was fired[2] is simply not correct. In the end, the Allies committed 68,913 sorties that dropped 122,133 tons of bombs on Crossbow targets without a great deal to show for it.

The conduct of the defense of London by Air Vice Marshal Roderic Hill and Lt. General Sir Frederick Pile has to be reckoned one of the bright spots in the Allied effort to counter the V-weapons. Acting with considerable initiative and dispatch, Hill configured the defenses to provide the best possible chance of bringing down incoming flying bombs without regard to the sensitivities of the members of his own branch of service. While the defenses did an excellent job of preventing a great number of V-1s from hitting London, they were never able to halt them. Therefore, Pile's contention that the defenses "defeated" the flying bomb is not true. The only thing that stopped the V-1 was the occupation of its launch sites by Allied ground troops. The defense of Antwerp was also admirably conducted and required more operational flexibility than the defense of London. Like the defenses in England, however, and despite the lavish commitment of resources, the Allies in Belgium were unable to completely stop the V-1.

The V-2, of course, was essentially unstoppable once in the air. The only recorded instance of a V-2 being shot down was by a B-24 of the 34th Bomb Group. The rocket passed through the group's formation at 10,000 feet and was hit by a burst of machine-gun fire, causing it to crash to earth.[3] Except for that single incident, the V-2s could not be dealt with once they left the launch pad.

Since the V-2 could not be seen or heard before it struck the target, it has been overshadowed by its stablemate. There are no dramatic photographs of the V-2 cutting out over London and there was no breathtaking wait while those below listened for the engine to stop. The V-2 arrived unheralded, leaving death and destruction in its wake. Likewise, it was not as quixotic as the V-1. There are no stories of it plowing down a street, glancing off a bunker or being tipped by a Spitfire's wing. It came straight down. The insensitive fuse that the Germans were forced to use because of the airburst problem made it ideal in urban areas. The V-2 could penetrate a building and detonate after going through several floors.

Despite overwhelming evidence that the V-weapons were highly effective once their developmental problems had been overcome, there has grown since World War II a body of literature which asserts that the weapons were failures because they either failed to win the war for the Nazis or were not cost effective. Typical of the former is the statement by Basil Collier in his *Battle of the V-Weapons*: "They brought Germany no direct strategic gain in the shape of positions won or armies or fleets defeated. . . . Perhaps the only satisfactory answer to these questions [whether the decision to field the V-weapons was correct] is that Hitler lost the war and committed suicide."[4] A similar conclusion was voiced in Gregory Kennedy's *Vengeance Weapon 2: The V-2 Guided Missile*: "After all, England was not terrorized into surrender as Hitler hoped, and the effect on the flow of supplies through Antwerp and Liège was negligible, leading one to the conclusion that the V-2 failed as a weapon of war."[5]

Both statements neglect Market Garden and the interdiction of the port of Antwerp, and declare that the weapons were failures because they didn't win the war. No other weapon in World War II has been held to this impossible standard. Neither the aircraft carrier nor the B-29 won the war single-handedly but they are regarded as extremely effective weapons. On the German side, the Fw 190 fighter and the Panther tank were both considered excellent weapons even though that nation lost the war. Therefore, the conclusion that the V-weapons were failures because they didn't win the war does not objectively assess the weapons' contribution to the German effort.

Some use a cost-effectiveness approach to prove the V-weapons were failures; and the V-2 is the most frequent target of this accusation. An argument often repeated is that the entire tonnage delivered by the V-2 in 1944–45 was not equal to the tonnage dropped by a single Allied thousand-plane raid in the closing month of the war. This is the same argument put forward by Dr. R.V. Jones to Churchill during the meeting of July 18, 1944, when he tried to mollify the prime minister by minimizing the potential destructiveness of the rocket. Today, as in 1944, the statement is true but irrelevant. In defending London against the V-2, it didn't matter how many bombs the Allies dropped on the Third Reich if they couldn't prevent the Germans from killing the citizens of London and destroying their homes. The weapon was able to hit the target and the Allies were unable to intercept it. For that reason alone the V-2 was effective.

Another argument states that, even aside from the rocket's destructive power, Peenemünde and the A-4 project were simply too expensive. This was most recently brought up in Michael Neufeld's *Rockets and the Reich*, which asserts that the Peenemünde project was a military boondoggle because it cost four times as much as the Manhattan Project, the United States' program to develop the atomic bomb. Since both projects had different missions and objectives, and had nothing to do with each other, the comparison is meaningless. Conventional aircraft likewise had very high development costs. The difference between them and the A-4 is that they had established factories and engineering infrastructures that had been built up over decades. The A-4 was new technology that had to start from scratch, making it initially more expensive than machines already in production. Although the V-1 was inexpensive, it has also been criticized for not being cost effective because of the lack of damage it caused. The HERO study, "Observations on Defense Against the V-1 Missile, A Report Prepared for Sandia Laboratories," claimed the V-1 did only $10,000 damage to the port of Antwerp. Aside from the actual damage in Antwerp, which in fact far exceeded this amount, and the thousands of killed and wounded in that city, the cost of the Allied defenses arrayed against the V-1 itself dwarfs this dollar assessment.

Another criticism of the V-weapons was that in building them the Germans diverted valuable resources that could have been used for fighters. Williamson Murray in *Luftwaffe: Strategy for Defeat* states, "The distortion in military production as a result of demands for the V-1 and V-2 retaliation weapons was enormous. . . . the industrial effort and resources expended for these weapons in the last year and a half of the war alone equaled the production of 24,000 fighter aircraft. . . . Thus, just in terms of the retaliatory weapons policy, the distortion that the bombing achieved in the German war effort was of real consequence to the war's outcome."[6]

Unlike the Allies, the Germans had no strategic bomber force. The disastrous consequences of Goering's decision to cancel the heavy bomber program in 1938 were not evident until 1942, when the majority of the German medium bomber force was being consumed on the Russian Front and in the Mediterranean. By late 1943, the Allied bombing raids on France and Germany had reached massive proportions and the Germans needed a way to strike back. The idea of building nothing but fighter aircraft to defend the Reich is an armchair theory that ignores the reality of the German strategic position in the air war. That the German Luftwaffe was in a slow decline was not obvious to the German leadership in 1942. It was still a powerful force that maintained air superiority over the Russian Front, and even a year later the fighter arm was capable of inflicting heavy losses on the Americans by day and RAF Bomber Command at night. From the German point of view, then, the question was not how to fight a purely defensive war in the air over the Reich but how to strike back at their enemies in England. Since there were no heavy four-engine bombers, the alternative was to use guided missiles. The Army's A-4 was already under development and the Luftwaffe had to find a way to compete with it.

As the war progressed, the Luftwaffe faced a far more effective Soviet Air Force as well as having to carry on a two-front war in the Mediterranean and in Western Europe. As it suffered an ever-higher attrition rate in experienced pilots, it was unable to replace them due to an inadequate training base. The higher proportion of novice pilots also led to higher accident rates in the air and on the ground. Beginning with the air battles of 1943, the Luftwaffe's problem was not in the supply of aircraft but in the supply of pilots. Later, lack of fuel became the air arm's biggest problem. The pool of operational single-engine fighters available to the Luftwaffe on June 1, 1944 was 472,[7] but, according to Williamson Murray, "By mid-summer, as fighter production reached its wartime high, the Germans were approaching the situation where the hundreds of aircraft their industry turned out had neither fuel to fly nor pilots. Pilot training schools were already shutting down for lack of fuel."[8]

There was already a glut of aircraft for which there were no pilots. Most of the bomber force was obsolete and the survivability of aircraft and crews was no more than a few missions over England. Once the shortage of fighter pilots became evident, many bomber pilots were forcibly transferred to fighters, which was not always the best policy. Another self-defeating move was the use of unemployed ground crews and maintenance personnel to fill Luftwaffe combat divisions for the ground war. For the sake of beefing up the numbers of troops at the front, the Germans needlessly sacrificed skilled mechanics instead of retraining them to repair more modern aircraft. This created an additional strain on the Luftwaffe maintenance base. In the final analysis, the V-1 and V-2 did not use up resources that would have best been used for additional fighters. The fighters were already there. All the planes needed was maintenance, pilots and fuel.

Once the Allies had achieved air superiority over the Continent, it was already too late for Germany to develop a modern, long-range bomber force. Even if German industry had been able to produce significant numbers of four-engine aircraft, in the face of the USAAF and Bomber Command, the large airfields necessary for deployment would

have been vulnerable and impossible to hide. The Germans were able
to answer this dilemma with the V-weapons, which leads to another,
though difficult to quantify, aspect of their deployment: the missiles'
affect on German morale.

By mid-1944, not even Propaganda Minister Goebbels could conceal the fact that the Third Reich was losing the war. If German citizens were to sustain their faith in victory, and thus continued support
of the Nazi regime, revolutionary new weapons were required to
redress the imbalance in military fortunes caused by superior Allied
resources. When the flying bombs began wreaking havoc on London,
followed by the even more futuristic rocket, their successful offensive,
combined with the implication that more "wonder weapons" were
still to come, allowed the German public to keep their hopes alive. As
the Japanese would discover to their dismay in August 1945, new
weapons that could force the immediate surrender of a great power
were, in fact, possible. It is to mankind's benefit that German scientists
and engineers did not concentrate on splitting the atom; however, the
emergence of the V-weapons must have suggested to the German public that such decisive breakthroughs were conceivable.

To a degree, critics of the V-weapons, both in terms of cost-effectiveness and allocation of resources, benefit from the knowledge that
the war ended less than a year after the missiles' initial deployment. It
is true that Hitler, upon prioritizing development of the Fi 103 and A-
4, didn't envision their launch sites being overrun by Allied troops
beginning in June 1944. In addition to the weapons' quantifiable performance, however, one must judge their value in terms of their potential if the ground war had gone differently. The most obvious scenario
is to consider if the Normandy invasion had failed. (Allied success on
D-Day was by no means guaranteed; a German intelligence coup that
revealed the invasion fleet's destination might by itself have altered the
outcome.) Without Allied ground troops in northern Europe in 1944,
the strategic air war would then have appeared as a striking contrast:
on the Allied side, vast bomber fleets that lost hundreds of men a
week, and were enormously expensive to maintain in terms of maintenance, munitions and personnel; on the German side, robot missiles
with presumably ever-increasing range, accuracy and destructive
power. The Allies would have continued to pay for their strategic
bombing campaign with the lives of their aircrew; the Germans would

have profited from the work at Peenemünde by being able to attack Britain at little human cost to themselves. Although, despite their short operational life, the V-weapons had a major impact on the war, critics of the missiles should also consider the potential advantage the Germans had gained if, through unforeseen circumstances, the Allies had not otherwise been successful in World War II's climactic battles.

Those who approach the operational record of the V-weapons from the point of view of the postwar scientific community tend to find their criticisms encouraged. After the war, Allied scientists had little inclination to praise the achievements of their counterparts in Nazi Germany. The Germans, once in custody, and particularly while the Nuremberg Trials were in progress, were even more reticent. Indeed, since most of the surviving German scientists and engineers soon found themselves working for the Allies, it became impolitic to take pride in the revolutionary weapon system they had created, which had been used as a means of terror against Allied civilians. If there is any such thing as a happy ending to the history of the V-weapons, it is that Wernher von Braun and his associates, once enlisted by the Americans, were able to return to their original dream of putting men on the moon. This was accomplished in 1969. In 1944, von Braun had been arrested by the SS largely because he had been overheard discussing the topic of space travel with his fellow scientists instead of how to attack London.

Over half a century has elapsed since the V-weapons claimed their final victims, but the lessons they taught remain unlearned. In the West, air power was the mighty sword that brought the Third Reich to its knees, and the guided missile was the weapon of the defeated enemy. The Western powers did not ignore the guided missile, but saw it instead as a useful adjunct to air power, not a major weapon in its own right. Only after nuclear weapons became available and the stand-off between the Soviet Union and the United States began was the ability of the guided missile to get through to the target fully appreciated in the West. In the United States the guided missile was seen only as a vehicle for carrying nuclear weapons, and many systems had no conventional capability. The missile race began with each side trying to get the most "bang for the buck," but the backbone of Western defense remained the manned bomber. This is not surprising.

Most Western nations had large air forces, and careers are made in cockpits, not missile silos.

The Soviets, who operated for most of World War II without air superiority, saw a distinct advantage in guided missiles, even those with conventional warheads, and created a branch of strategic rocket troops. Had another conventional war occurred in Europe, hundreds of mobile launchers would have been available to fire at NATO political and military targets, drawing off innumerable NATO aircraft to deal with the threat.

In 1990–91, a repeat of the V-weapons campaign of World War II was played out on a smaller scale in the Gulf War. When the army of Iraqi dictator Saddam Hussein occupied Kuwait and refused to leave, the United States and its allies mounted a major campaign to eject the Iraqis from that country. The allied coalition immediately gained air supremacy and bombed Iraqi military positions. The only long-range weapon in the Iraqi arsenal, and the only one capable of replying to allied air superiority, was the Scud—little more than a modified V-2. Because it was obsolete, it was, for all intents and purposes, ignored by U.S. military planners and no attempt was made to destroy them in the first air missions. Later, when the Iraqis began launching the Scud, the coalition was embarrassed because it did not have an effective defense against it. The Patriot Missile System, which the United States fielded in Saudi Arabia and Israel, initially had a difficult time with the Scud because it was so crude and had a tendency to wobble and break up at extreme range. "Because the missiles, in effect, created their own decoys, tactical control officers at each firing battery had to learn the art of picking out the heavier warheads as they fell away from the missile debris."[9]

Despite eleven software improvements to give the Patriot the capability to shoot down ballistic missiles, contractors had to make further refinements so it could shoot down the Scud. By targeting politically sensitive targets such as Tel Aviv and Bahrain, and the cities in Saudi Arabia, the Iraqis forced the coalition to divert considerable resources to counter the Scud. At the end of the war, operational Scud launchers were still in the field while all of Iraq's missiles had either been launched or destroyed.

The U.S. Army "estimated that the Iraqis had fired eighty-six Scuds, eleven of which were aimed at Israel, prior to the deployment of Patriots. Of the remaining seventy-five, forty-seven were considered threatening and Patriots engaged forty-five of them. Other studies gave different success rates, one estimating that Patriots destroyed 89 percent of the missiles aimed at Saudi Arabia and 44 percent of the Scuds targeted on Israel."[10] Despite talk of success rates, there was still a human cost. On January 22, 1991, a Scud penetrated the Patriot defenses at Tel Aviv. Three people died of heart attacks and a hundred were forced from their homes. On February 25, a Scud hit a warehouse in Al Khubar near Dhahran that had been converted to a transient billet. The explosion killed 28 U.S. soldiers and wounded another 97, the worst single loss of U.S. military personnel in the war. Why the troops weren't in shelters has never been satisfactorily explained. This was the last Scud incident in the war, and while it was much smaller than a great number of incidents in 1944–45 it was no less tragic.

Like the V-weapons, the Scud caused a great loss in productivity because of the fear it might carry chemical weapons. United States support troops had to don protective masks and clothing for each Scud alert. The Scud did not cause a great deal of physical damage, but the campaign that surrounded it closely followed the pattern of the V-weapons campaign. The terror, and urgent defense measures, induced by robot bombs can have an effect out of all proportion to their destructive power. While U.S. "smart bombs" are able to hit a single smokestack on a designated building, the very unpredictability of V-type weapons only adds to their psychological impact. These missiles have, indeed, become a counter air supremacy weapon. Even if the West does not recognize this fact, other nations have, and the technology is readily available to those who want it. As of this writing, North Korea possesses a modified Scud capable of hitting Tokyo.

The Scud is only one descendant of the V-weapons. Today, there are literally hundreds of them, from the Exocet to the Trident, deployed across the world. We live in their shadow and they will not go away.

Chapter Notes

CHAPTER ONE
1. Ley, Willy, *Rockets, Missiles and Space Travel*, New York, The Viking Press, 1953 p. 68.
2. Congreve, Colonel Sir William, *Details of the Rocket System*, London, J. Whiting, 1814, Facsimile ed. by R.A. Printing Press, Ltd., Conclusion, page unnumbered.
3. Jobé, Joseph, ed., Guns, *An Illustrated History of Artillery*, Greenwich, CT, New York Graphic Society, 1971, p. 136.
4. Dupuy, R. Ernest and Dupuy, Trevor N., *The Encyclopedia of Military History from 3500 B.C. to the Present*, Revised Edition, New York, Harper & Row Publishers, 1970, p. 978.
5. Werrell, Kenneth P., *The Evolution of the Cruise Missile*, 1985, p. 8.
6. Ibid., p. 8.

CHAPTER TWO
1. Ley, Willy, *Rockets, Missiles and Space Travel*, New York, The Viking Press, 1953, p. 128.
2. Ibid., p. 130.
3. Ibid., p. 133.
4. Ibid., p. 134.
5. Dornberger, Walter, *V-2*, New York, Ballantine Books, 1954, p. 28.
6. Dupuy, R. Ernest and Dupuy, Trevor, N., *The Encyclopedia of Military History from 3500 B.C. to the Present*, Revised Edition, New York, Harper & Row Publishers, 1970, p. 978.
7. Neufeld, Michael J., *The Rocket and The Reich: Peenemünde and the Coming of the Ballistic Missile Era*, New York, The Free Press, 1995, p. 9.
8. Kosar, Franz, *A Pocket History of Light Field Guns*, London, Ian Allen, 1974, p. 97 & p. 122.
9. Bergaust, Erik, *Wernher von Braun*, Washington, DC, National Space Institute, 1976, p. 37.
10. Neufeld, *The Rocket and The Reich*, p. 22.
11. Dornberger, *V-2*, p. 31.

12. Ibid., p. 42.
13. Ibid., p. 57.
14. Ibid., p. 51.

CHAPTER THREE
1. Speer, Albert, *Inside the Third Reich, Memoirs by Albert Speer,* London, Weidenfeld and Nicolson, 1970, p. 230.
2. Cooper, Matthew, *The German Army 1933–1945: Its Political and Military Failure,* New York, Stein and Day, 1974, p. 127.
3. Rich, Norman, *Hitler's War Aims: Ideology, the Nazi State, and the Course of Expansion,* New York, W. W. Norton & Company, Inc., 1973, p. 65.
4. Cooper, *The German Army 1933–1945,* p. 163.
5. Dornberger, Walter, *V-2,* New York, Ballantine Books, 1954, p. 45.
6. Ibid., p. 46.
7. Ibid., p. 56.
8. Ibid., p. 67.
9. Speer, *Inside the Third Reich,* p. 208.
10. Hölsken, Dieter, *V-Missiles of the Third Reich: The V-1 and V-2,* Sturbridge, MA, Monogram Aviation Publications, 1994, p. 29.
11. Speer, *Inside the Third Reich,* p. 366.
12. Hölsken, *V-Missiles of the Third Reich,* p. 45.
13. Gregory P. Kennedy, *Vengeance Weapon 2: The V-2 Guided Missile,* Washington, DC, The Smithsonian Institution Press, 1983, p. 30.
14. Speer, *Inside the Third Reich,* p. 308.
15. Dornberger, *V-2,* p. 79.
16. Ibid., p. 82.
17. Michael J. Neufeld, *The Rocket and The Reich: Peenemünde and the Coming of the Ballistic Missile Era,* New York, The Free Press, 1995, p. 181.
18. Ibid., p. 94.
19. Ibid., p. 176.

CHAPTER FOUR
1. Suchenwirth, Richard, *Command and Leadership in the German Air Force,* Maxwell AFB, AL, USAF Historical Division, Aerospace Studies Institute, Air University, 1969, p. 17.
2. Ibid., p. 36.
3. Ibid., p. 158.
4. Hölsken, Dieter, *V-Missiles of the Third Reich: The V-1 and V-2,* Sturbridge, MA, Monogram Aviation Publications, 1994, p. 46.
5. Ibid.
6. Ibid.
7. Benecke, Th., Quick, A.W., *History of German Guided Missiles Development,* Brunswick, GE, Verlag E. Appelhans & Co., 1957, p. 401.
8. Ibid.
9. Gosslau in *History of German Guided Missiles* gives the date as April 30,

1941.
10. Hölsken, *V-Missiles of the Third Reich*, p. 50.
11. Ibid., p. 55.
12. Ibid., p. 57.
13. Benecke, Th., Quick, A.W., *History of German Guided Missiles*, p 70.
14. Ibid., p. 76.
15. Joachim Engelman, *V-2, Dawn of the Rocket Age*, Schiffer Military History Vol. 26, Westchester, PA, Schiffer Publishing Ltd., 1990, p. 4.
16. Hölsken, *V-Missiles of the Third Reich*, p. 84.
17. Ibid.
18. Ibid., p. 89.
19. Ibid.
20. Irving, David, *The Rise and Fall of the Luftwaffe: The Life of Field Marshal Erhard Milch*, Boston Little, Brown and Company, 1973, p. 231.
21. Ibid.
22. Hölsken, *V-Missiles of the Third Reich*, p. 111.
23. Ibid., p. 123.
24. Irving, *The Rise and Fall of the Luftwaffe*, p. 266.
25. Hölsken, *V-Missiles of the Third Reich*, p. 124.

CHAPTER FIVE
1. Hinsley, F.H., *British Intelligence in the Second World War: Its Influence on Strategy and Operations*, Volume One, New York, Cambridge University Press, 1979, p. 509.
2. Hinsley, *British Intelligence*, Volume Three (1984), p. 360.
3. Ibid., p. 362.
4. Jones, R.V., *The Wizard War: British Scientific Intelligence, 1939–1945*, New York, Coward, McCann & Geoghegan, Inc., 1978, p. 333.
5. Hinsley, *British Intelligence*, Volume Three, p. 364.
6. Jones, *The Wizard War*, p. 335.
7. Babington-Smith, Constance, *Air Spy: The Story of Photo Intelligence in World War II*, New York, Harper & Brothers Publishers, 1957, p. 207.
8. Jones, *The Wizard War*, p. 337.
9. Ibid., p. 340.
10. Hinsley, *British Intelligence* Volume Three, p. 372.
11. Jones, *The Wizard War*, p. 343.
12. Craven, Wesley Frank and Cate, James Lea, *The Army Air Forces in World War II*, Volume Three, *Europe: Argument to V-E Day, January 1944 to May 1945*, Chicago, University of Chicago Press, 1951, p. 90.
13. Ibid.
14. Ley, Willy, *Rockets, Missiles and Space Travel*, New York, The Viking Press, 1953, p. 214.
15. Hinsley, *British Intelligence* Volume Three, p. 380.
16. Ibid., p. 382.
17. Ibid., p. 386.

18. Ibid.
19. Jones, *The Wizard War*, p. 351.
20. Hinsley, *British Intelligence* Volume Three, p. 393.
21. Ibid., p. 592.
22. Ibid., p. 395.
23. Ibid., p. 394.
24. Irving, David, *The Mare's Nest*, London, William Kimber, 1964, p. 153.
25. Ibid., p. 154.
26. Ibid., p. 155.
27. Hinsley, *British Intelligence* Volume Three, p. 397.
28. Ibid., p. 401.
29. Babington-Smith, *Air Spy*, p. 223.
30. Hinsley, *British Intelligence* Volume Three, p. 403.
31. Jones, *The Wizard War*, p. 362.
32. Hinsley, *British Intelligence* Volume Three, p. 407.
33. Ibid., p. 399fn.
34. Collier, Basil, *The Battle of the V-Weapons, 1944–1945*, New York, William Morrow & Company, 1965, p. 56.
35. Hinsley, *British Intelligence* Volume Three, p. 413.
36. Jones, *The Wizard War*, p. 353, and Gardiner, Robert, ed dir, Conway's *All the World's Fighting Ships 1922–1946*, London, Conway Maritime Press, 1992 reprint of 1980 ed., p. 15.

CHAPTER SIX
1. Dieter Hölsken, *V-Missiles of the Third Reich: The V-1 and V-2*, Sturbridge, MA, Monogram Aviation Publications, 1994, p. 173.
2. Ibid.
3. Ibid., p. 174.
4. David Irving, *The Mare's Nest*, London, William Kimber, 1964, p. 161.
5. Ibid., p. 181.
6. Ibid.
7. Hölsken, *V-Missiles of the Third Reich*, p. 132.
8. Ibid.
9. Wesley Frank Craven, and James Lea Cate, *The Army Air Forces in World War II*, Volume Three, *Europe: Argument to V-E Day, January 1944 to May 1945*, Chicago, University of Chicago Press, 195, p. 102fn.
10. Irving, *The Mare's Nest*, p. 190.
11. Ibid., p. 195.
12. Hölsken, *V-Missiles of the Third Reich*, p. 180.
13. Ibid., p. 136.
14. Irving, *The Mare's Nest*, p. 195.
15. Hölsken, *V-Missiles of the Third Reich*, p. 180.
16. Erik Bergaust, *Wernher von Braun*, Washington, DC, National Space Institute, 1976, p. 74.
17. Ibid.

18. Irving, *The Mare's Nest*, p. 209.
19. Hölsken, *V-Missiles of the Third Reich*, p. 138.
20. Michael J. Neufeld, *The Rocket and The Reich: Peenemünde and the Coming of the Ballistic Missile Era*, New York, The Free Press, 1995, p. 216.
21. Walter Dornberger, *V-2*, New York, Ballantine Books, 1954, p. 179.
22. Ibid.
23. Ibid.
24. Ibid., p. 180.
25. Ibid., p. 181.
26. Ibid.
27. Ibid.
28. Irving, *The Mare's Nest*, p. 199.
29. Ibid., p. 211.
30. Hölsken, *V-Missiles of the Third Reich*, p. 140.
31. Ibid.
32. Dornberger, *V-2*, p. 191.
33. Neufeld, *The Rocket and The Reich*, p. 221.
34. Dornberger, *V-2*, p. 195.
35. Ibid., p. 197.
36. Ibid.
37. Irving, *The Mare's Nest*, p. 223.
38. Ibid., p. 192.
39. Irving, *The Mare's Nest*, p. 231.
40. Ibid., p. 232.

CHAPTER SEVEN
1. R. V Jones, *The Wizard War: British Scientific Intelligence, 1939–1945*, New York, Coward, McCann & Geoghegan, Inc., 1978, p. 371.
2. Ibid.
3. F.H. Hinsley, *British Intelligence in the Second World War: Its Influence on Strategy and Operations*, Volume Three, New York, Cambridge University Press, 1984, p. 434.
4. John O. Moench, *Marauder Men*, Malia Enterprises, Florida, p. 198.
5. David Irving, *The Mare's Nest*, London, William Kimber, 1964, p. 187.
6. Jones, *The Wizard War*, p. 367.
7. Hinsley, *British Intelligence*, Volume Three, p. 417.
8. Irving, *The Mare's Nest*, p. 188.
9. Ibid.
10. Jones, *The Wizard War*, p. 374.
11. Hinsley, *British Intelligence*, Volume Three, p. 419.
12. Moench, *Marauder Men*, p. 106.
13. Ibid.
14. Wesley Frank Craven, and James Lea Cate, *The Army Air Forces in World War II*, Volume Three, *Europe: Argument to V-E Day, January 1944 to May 1945*, Chicago, University of Chicago Press, 195, p. 92.

15. Ibid. p. 96.
16. Ibid. p. 98.
17. Ibid.
18. Ibid. p. 99.
19. Ibid. p. 100.
20. Ibid. p. 101.
21. Basil Collier, *The Battle of the V-Weapons, 1944–1945*, New York, William Morrow & Company, 1965, p. 57.
22. Gen. Sir Fredeick Pile, *Ack-Ack: Britain's Defence Against Air Attack in the Second World War*, London, George G. Harrap & Co. Ltd, 1949, p. 311.
23. George Raynor Thompson, Dixie R. Harris, Pauline M. Oaks, Dulany Terrett, *The U.S. Army in World War II: The Technical Services, The Signal Corps: The Test*, Washington, D.C., Office of the Chief of Military History, Department of the Army, 1957.
24. Ibid. p. 315.
25. Collier, *The Battle of the V-Weapons*, p. 57.
26. Ibid. p. 59.
27. Hinsley, *British Intelligence*, Volume Three, p. 421.
28. Ibid. p. 435.
29. Ibid. p. 436.
30. Ibid. p. 436fn.
31. Ibid. p. 437.
32. Ibid. p. 438.
33. Moench, *Marauder Men*, p. 106.
34. Hinsley, *British Intelligence*, Volume Three, p. 422.
35. Craven, and Cate, *The Army Air forces in World War II*, Volume Three, p. 103.
36. Hinsley, *British Intelligence*, Volume Three, p. 428.
37. Constance Babington-Smith, *Air Spy: The Story of Photo Intelligence in World War II*, New York, Harper & Brothers Publishers, 1957, p. 232.
38. Sir Arthur Harris, *Bomber Offensive*, New York, MacMillan Company, 1947, p. 198.
39. Air Marshal Sir Robert Saunby, *Air Bombardment: The Story of its Development*, New York, Harper and Brothers, 1961, p. 176.
40. Hinsley, *British Intelligence*, Volume Three, Part One, p. 425.
41. Ibid.
42. Ibid. p. 426.
43. Craven, and Cate, *The Army Air Forces in World War II*, Volume Three, p. 104.
44. Ibid.
45. John Terraine, *A Time for Courage: The Royal Air Force in the European War, 1939–1945*, New York, MacMillan Company, 1985, p. 557.
46. Hinsley, *British Intelligence*, Volume Three, Part One, p. 430.
47. Craven, and Cate, *The Army Air forces in World War II*, Volume Three, p. 105.

48. Jones, *The Wizard War*, p. 417.

CHAPTER EIGHT
1. Bob Ogley, *Doodlebugs and Rockets: The Battle of the Flying Bombs*, Westerham, Kent, England, Froglets Publications, 1992, p. 28.
2. David Johnson, *V-1, V-2: Hitler's Vengeance on London*, Chelsea, MI, Scarborough House/Publishers, 1981, p. 43.
3. Richard Anthony Young, *The Flying Bomb*, New York, Sky Books Press, 1978, p. 62.
4. Johnson, *V-1, V-2*, p. 45.
5. Ibid.
6. David Irving, *The Mare's Nest*, London, William Kimber, 1964, p 234
7. Ibid., p. 235.
8. Johnson, *V-1, V-2*, p. 48.
9. R. V Jones, *The Wizard War: British Scientific Intelligence, 1939–1945*, New York, Coward, McCann & Geoghegan, Inc., 1978, p. 418.
10. Irving, *The Mare's Nest*, p. 235.
11. Ibid.
12. Basil Collier, *The Battle of the V-Weapons, 1944–1945*, New York, William Morrow & Company, 1965, p. 81.
13. Young, *The Flying Bomb*, p. 64.
14. Ibid., p. 66.
15. Ibid.
16. Ibid.
17. Dieter Hölsken, *V-Missiles of the Third Reich: The V-1 and V-2*, Sturbridge, MA, Monogram Aviation Publications, 1994, p. 287.
18. Ibid., p. 203.
19. Ogley, *Doodlebugs and Rockets*, p. 50.
20. Gen. Sir Frederick Pile, *Ack-Ack: Britain's Defence Against Air Attack in the Second World War*, London, George G. Harrap & Co. Ltd, 1949, p. 329.
21. Ibid., p. 332.
22. Ibid.
23. Ibid., p. 335.
24. Collier, *The Battle of the V-Weapons*, p. 97.
25. Pile, Ack-Ack, p. 342.
26. Wesley Frank Craven, and James Lea Cate, *The Army Air Forces in World War II*, Volume Three, *Europe: Argument to V-E Day, January 1944 to May 1945*, Chicago, University of Chicago Press, 1951, p. 531.
27. Terence H. O'Brien, *Civil Defence*, London, Her Majesty's Stationery Office, 1955, p. 660.
28. Merle Miller, *Ike the Soldier As They Knew Him*, New York, G.P. Putnam's Sons, 1987, p. 628.
29. O'Brien, *Civil Defence*, p. 655.
30. Young, *The Flying Bomb*, p. 77.
31. F.H. Hinsley, *British Intelligence in the Second World War: Its Influence*

on *Strategy and Operations*, Volume Three, Part Two, New York, Cambridge University Press, 1988, p. 540.
32. Ibid.
33. Ibid., p. 541.
34. Jones, *The Wizard War*, p. 421.
35. Ibid.
36. Irving, *The Mare's Nest*, p. 251.
37. Hölsken, *V-Missiles of the Third Reich*, p. 200.
38. Young, *The Flying Bomb*, p. 95.
39. Hölsken, *V-Missiles of the Third Reich*, p. 205.
40. Ibid., p. 205.
41. Ibid., p. 206.
42. Ibid.
43. Johnson, *V-1, V-2*, p. 115.

CHAPTER NINE
1. Walter Dornberger, *V-2*, New York, Ballantine Books, 1954, p. 228.
2. R. V. Jones, *The Wizard War: British Scientific Intelligence, 1939–1945*, New York, Coward, McCann & Geoghegan, Inc., 1978, p. 431.
3. F.H. Hinsley, *British Intelligence in the Second World War: Its Influence on Strategy and Operations*, Volume Three, New York, Cambridge University Press, 1984, p. 445.
4. Ibid., p. 447.
5. Ibid., p. 449.
6. Ibid., p. 450.
7. David Irving, *The Mare's Nest*, London, William Kimber, 1964, p. 266
8. Jozef Garlinski, *Hitler's Last Weapons, the Underground War against the V-1 and V-2*, New York, Times Books, 1978, p. 145.
9. Michael J. Neufeld, *The Rocket and The Reich: Peenemünde and the Coming of the Ballistic Missile Era*, New York, The Free Press, 1995, p. 243
10. Dornberger, *V-2*, p. 207.
11. Irving, *The Mare's Nest*, p. 283.
12. Gregory P. Kennedy, *Vengeance Weapon 2: The V-2 Guided Missile*, Washington, DC, The Smithsonian Institution Press, 1983, p. 34.
13. Dieter Hölsken, *V-Missiles of the Third Reich: The V-1 and V-2*, Sturbridge, MA, Monogram Aviation Publications, 1994, p. 220.
14. Kennedy, *Vengeance Weapon 2, The V-2 Guided Missile*, p. 43.
15. David Johnson, *V-1, V-2: Hitler's Vengeance on London*, Chelsea, MI, Scarborough House/Publishers, 1981, p. 117.
16. Norman Longmate, *Hitler's Rockets: The Story of the V-2s*, London, Hutchinson, 1985, p. 171.
17. Bernard Montgomery, *The Memoirs of Field Marshal the Viscount Montgomery of Alamein*, K.G., Cleveland, The World Publishing Company, 1958, p. 246.
18. F.H. Hinsley, *British Intelligence in the Second World War: Its Influence*

on Strategy and Operations, Volume Three, Part Two, New York, Cambridge University Press, 1988, p. 565.
19. Ibid., p. 566.
20. Hölsken, *V-Missiles of the Third Reich*, p. 221.
21. Ibid.
22. Ibid., p. 224.
23. Dornberger, *V-2*, p. 210.
24. Ibid., p. 209.
25. Ibid.
26. Irving, *The Mare's Nest*, p. 288.
27. Hölsken, *V-Missiles of the Third Reich*, p. 226.
28. Richard Anthony Young, *The Flying Bomb*, New York, Sky Books Press, 1978, p. 122.
29. Hölsken, *V-Missiles of the Third Reich*, p. 226.
30. Young, *The Flying Bomb*, p. 125.
31. Hölsken, *V-Missiles of the Third Reich*, p. 227.
32. Ibid.
33. Longmate, *Hitler's Rockets*, p. 196.
34. Ibid., p. 198.
35. Ibid., p. 210.
36. Ibid.
37. Ibid., p. 202.
38. Ibid.

CHAPTER TEN
1. Steve R. Waddell, *United States Army Logistics: The Normandy Campaign 1944*, Westport, CT, Greenwood Press, 1994, p. 134.
2. Benjamin King, Richard C. Biggs, Eric R. Criner, *Spearhead of Logistics: A History of the United States Army Transportation Corps*, Fort Eustis VA, U.S. Army Transportation Center, 1994, p. 238.
3. B.H. Liddell-Hart, *History of the Second World War*, New York, G.P. Putnam's Sons, 1970, p. 565.
4. Waddell, *United States Army Logistics*, p. 99.
5. Historical Section, Office of the Chief of Transportation, European Theater of Operations, *Historical Report of the Transportation Corps in the European Theater of Operations*, Volume V, October-November-December 1944, Part 1, Paris, Office of the Chief of Transportation E.T.O 1945, 13th and 5th Major Ports, p. 1.
6. Dwight D. Eisenhower, *Crusade in Europe*, New York, Doubleday & Company, Inc., 1948, p. 327.
7. Richard Anthony Young, *The Flying Bomb*, New York, Sky Books Press, 1978, p. 123.
8. Ibid., p. 124.
9. Norman Franks, *Battle of the Airfields*, London, Grubb St., 1994, p. 76
10. Young, *The Flying Bomb*, p. 124.

11. Garry Pape and Ronald C. Harrison, *Queen of the Midnight Skies,* West Chester PA, Schiffer Military History, 1992, p. 275.
12. Charles B. MacDonald, *The U. S. Army in World War II, The European Theater of Operations: The Siegfried Line Campaign,* Washington, D. C., Office of the Chief of Military History, 1963, p. 229.
13. Hist. Sec., Office of the Chief of Transportation, ETO, *Historical Report,* Vol. V, Part 2, p. 100.
14. Hist. Sec., Office of the Chief of Transportation, ETO, *Historical Report,* Vol. V, Part 1, p. 159.
15. Roland G. Ruppenthal, *U.S. Army in World War II, the European Theater of Operations: Logistical Support of the Armies,* Volume II, Washington, D.C., Center of Military History, 1958, p. 111.
16. Ibid., p. 113.
17. H.H. Dunham, OCofT Monograph No. 29, U.S. Army Transportation in the European Theater of Operations 1942-1945, Washington D.C., Historical Unit Office of the Chief of Transportation, Army Service Forces, 1946, p. 265.
18. Ruppenthal, *Logistical Support of the Armies,* Volume II, p. 142.
19. Hist. Sec., Office of the Chief of Transportation, ETO, *Historical Report,* Vol. V, Part 2, p. 14.
20. Ibid., p. 37.
21. Historical Section, Office of the Chief of Transportation, European Theater of Operations, *Historical Report of the Transportation Corps in the European Theater of Operations,* Volume VI, January-February-March 1945, Part 1, p. 142.
22. Dieter Hölsken, *V-Missiles of the Third Reich: The V-1 and V-2,* Sturbridge, MA, Monogram Aviation Publications, 1994, p. 298.
23. Hist. Sec., Office of the Chief of Transportation, ETO, *Historical Report,* Vol. VI, Part 3, p. 21.
24. Hist. Sec., Office of the Chief of Transportation, ETO, *Historical Report,* Vol. VI, Part 2, p. 91.
25. Ibid., Motor Transport Service, p. 21.
26. First Sergeant Albert W. Spratley, *The Port of Antwerp and the Military Rail Service, 709th Railway Grand Division,* p. 2.
27. Robert M. Browning, Jr., *U.S. Merchant Vessel War Casualties of World War II,* Annapolis, Naval Institute Press, 1996, p. 467.
28. Ruppenthal, *Logistical Support of the Armies,* Volume II, p. 114.
29. Ibid.
30. Hist. Sec., Office of the Chief of Transportation, ETO, *Historical Report,* Vol. VI, Part 2, p. 108.
31. Browning, *U.S. Merchant Vessel War Casualties of World War II,* p. 477
32. Ibid., p. 483.
33. Hist. Sec., Office of the Chief of Transportation, ETO, *Historical Report,* Vol. VI, Part 1, p. 159.
34. Hölsken, *V-Missiles of the Third Reich,* p. 231.

35. Hist. Sec., Office of the Chief of Transportation, ETO, *Historical Report,* Vol. VI, Part 2, p. 32.
36. Hugh M. Cole, *The U. S. Army in World War II, The European Theater of Operations, The Ardennes: Battle of the Bulge,* Washington, D. C., Office of the Chief of Military History, 1965, p. 667.
37. A.G. Gregory, *The Saga of the 708 Railway Grand Division,* Baltimore, The Baltimore and Ohio Railroad Company, 1947, p. 20–21.
38. Ibid., p. 17.
39. Hist. Sec., Office of the Chief of Transportation, ETO, *Historical Report,* Vol. VI, Part 2, p. 72.
40. Hist. Sec., Office of the Chief of Transportation, ETO, *Historical Report,* Vol. VI, Part 3, p. 21.

CHAPTER ELEVEN
1. Danny S. Parker, *To Win the Winter Sky,* Conshohocken, PA, Combined Books, 1994, p. 447.
2. Ibid., p. 515.
3. Norman Franks, *Battle of the Airfields,*. London, Grubb St., 1994, p. 198
4. Walter Dornberger, *V-2,* New York, Ballantine Books, 1954, p. 225.
5. Ibid., p. 226.
6. Dieter Hölsken, *V-Missiles of the Third Reich: The V-1 and V-2,* Sturbridge, MA, Monogram Aviation Publications, 1994, p. 239.
7. Ibid.
8. Ibid., p. 240.
9. Ibid.
10. Ibid.
11. Ibid., p. 254.
12. Michael J. Neufeld, *The Rocket and The Reich: Peenemünde and the Coming of the Ballistic Missile Era,* New York, The Free Press, 1995, p. 225.
13. Dornberger, *V-2,* p. 212.
14. Ibid., p. 219.
15. Ibid., p. 218.
16. Dieter K. Huzel, *Peenemünde to Canaveral,* Englewood Cliffs, N.J., Prentice Hall, Inc., 1962, p. 135.
17. Ibid., p. 139.
18. Hölsken, *V-Missiles of the Third Reich,* p. 242.
19. Richard Anthony Young, *The Flying Bomb,* New York, Sky Books Press, 1978, p. 128.
20. Ibid.
21. Hölsken, *V-Missiles of the Third Reich,* p. 247.
22. Huzel, *Peenemünde to Canaveral,* p. 145.
23. Dornberger, *V-2,* p. 212.
24. David Johnson, *V-1, V-2: Hitler's Vengeance on London,* Chelsea, MI, Scarborough House, 1981, p. 186.
25. Ibid., p. 192.

26. Alfred M. Beck, Abe Bortz, Charles W. Lynch, Linda Mayo, Ralph F. Weld, *The U. S. Army in World War II, The Technical Services, The Corps of Engineers: The War Against Germany,* Washington, D.C., Center of Military History, United States Army, 1985, p. 511 and Ken Hechler, *The Bridge at Remagen,* New York, Ballantine Books, 1957, p. 188.
27. Dornberger, *V-2,* p. 231.
28. Ibid., p. 232.
29. Erik Bergaust, *Wernher von Braun,* Washington, DC, National Space Institute, 1976, p. 91.

CHAPTER TWELVE
1. Dwight D. Eisenhower, *Crusade in Europe,* New York, Doubleday & Company, 1948, p. 260.
2. Sir Arthur Harris, *Bomber Offensive,* New York, MacMillan Company, 1947, p. 184.
3. David Johnson, *V-1, V-2: Hitler's Vengeance on London,* Chelsea, MI, Scarborough House Publishers, 1981, p. 168.
4. Basil Collier, *The Battle of the V-Weapons, 1944–1945,* New York, William Morrow & Company, 1965, p. 140.
5. Gregory P. Kennedy, *Vengeance Weapon 2: The V-2 Guided Missile,* Washington, DC, The Smithsonian Institution Press, 1983, p. 51.
6. Williamson Murray, *Strategy For Defeat: The Luftwaffe, 1933–1945,* Maxwell Air Force Base, Air University Press, 1983, p. 301.
7. Ibid., p. 275.
8. Ibid.
9. Brigadier General Robert Scales, Jr., ed., *Certain Victory: The U.S. Army in the Gulf War,* Washington D.C., Office of the Chief of Staff, United States Army, 1993, p. 183.
10. Frank N. Schubert and Theresa L. Kraus, ed., *The Whirlwind War: The United States Army in Operations Desert Shield and Desert Storm,* Washington, D.C., Center of Military History, United States Army, 1995, p. 155.

Bibliography

OFFICIAL REPORTS

General Board, U.S. Forces, European Theater. *Report of the General Board, U.S. Forces, European Theater: Operation, Organization, Supply and Services of the Transportation Corps in the European Theater of Operations,* 1946.

Historical Evaluation and Research Organization (HERO). *Observations on Defense Against the V-1 Missile, A Report Prepared for Sandia Laboratories, Albuquerque, NM Under Contract No. 07-5659, June 1978,* Dunn Loring, VA, HERO, 1978.

Historical Section, Office of the Chief of Transportation, European Theater of Operations. *Historical Report of the Transportation Corps in the European Theater of Operations, Volume V, October-November–December 1944,* Parts 1, 2 and 3. Paris, Office of the Chief of Transportation E.T.O 1945.

Historical Section, Office of the Chief of Transportation, European Theater of Operations. *Historical Report of the Transportation Corps in the European Theater of Operations, Volume VI, January-February–March 1945,* Parts 1, 2 and 3. Paris, Office of the Chief of Transportation E.T.O 1945.

OFFICIAL HISTORIES

Alfred M. Beck, Abe Bortz, Charles W. Lynch, Linda Mayo, Ralph F. Weld. *The U. S. Army in World War II, The Technical Services, The Corps of Engineers: The War Against Germany,* Washington, D.C.: Center of Military History, United States Army, 1985.

Joseph Bykofsky and Harold Larson. *The U. S. Army in World War II, The Technical Services, The Transportation Corps: Operations Overseas.* Washington, D.C.: Office of the Chief of Military History, 1957.

Hugh M. Cole. *The U. S. Army in World War II, The European Theater of Operations, The Ardennes: Battle of the Bulge,* Washington, D.C.: Office of the Chief of Military History, 1965.

Hugh M. Cole. *The U. S. Army in World War II, The European Theater of*

Operations, The Lorraine Campaign. Washington, D.C.: Historical Division, Department of the Army, 1950.

Basil Collier. *The Defence of the United Kingdom*. London: Her Majesty's Stationery Office, 1957.

Wesley Frank Craven, and James Lea Cate. *The Army Air Forces in World War II, Volume Three, Europe: Argument to V-E Day, January 1944 to May 1945*. Chicago: University of Chicago Press, 1951.

H.H. Dunham. *OCofT Monograph No. 29, U.S. Army Transportation in the European Theater of Operations 1942–1945*. Washington D.C.: Historical Unit Office of the Chief of Transportation, Army Service Forces, 1946.

Gordon A. Harrison. *The U. S. Army in World War II, The European Theater of Operations, Cross Channel Attack*. Washington, D.C.: Office of the Chief of Military History, 1951.

F.H. Hinsley. *British Intelligence in the Second World War, Its Influence on Strategy and Operations*, Volume One. New York: Cambridge University Press, 1979.

F.H. Hinsley. *British Intelligence in the Second World War, Its Influence on Strategy and Operations*, Volume Two. New York: Cambridge University Press, 1981.

F.H. Hinsley. *British Intelligence in the Second World War, Its Influence on Strategy and Operations*, Volume Three. New York: Cambridge University Press, 1984.

Irving Brinton Holly, Jr.. *The U. S. Army in World War II, Special Studies, Buying Aircraft: Materiel Procurement for the Army Air Forces*. Washington, D.C.: Office of the Chief of Military History, 1964.

Benjamin King, Richard C. Biggs, Eric R. Criner. *Spearhead of Logistics, A History of the United States Army Transportation Corps*. Fort Eustis VA: U.S. Army Transportation Center, 1994.

Charles B. MacDonald. *The U. S. Army in World War II, The European Theater of Operations, The Siegfried Line Campaign*. Washington, D.C.: Office of the Chief of Military History, 1963.

Terence H. O'Brien. *Civil Defence*. London: Her Majesty's Stationery Office, 1955.

Forrest C. Pogue. *The U. S. Army in World War II, The European Theater of Operations, The Supreme Command*. Washington, D.C.: Office of the Chief of Military History, 1954.

Roland G. Ruppenthal. *U.S. Army in World War II, the European Theater of Operations, Logistical Support of the Armies, Volume II*. Washington, D.C.: Center of Military History, 1958.

George Raynor Thompson, Dixie R. Harris, Pauline M. Oaks, Dulany Terrett. *The U.S. Army in World War II, The Technical Services, The Signal Corps: The Test*. Washington, D.C.: Office of the Chief of Military History, Department of the Army, 1957.

Brigadier General Robert Scales, Jr., ed. *Certain Victory, the U.S. Army in the*

Gulf War. Washington D.C.: Office of the Chief of Staff, United States Army, 1993.

Frank N. Schubert and Theresa L. Kraus, ed. *The Whirlwind War, The United States Army in Operations Desert Shield and Desert Storm.* Washington, D.C.: Center of Military History, United States Army, 1995.

Mary H Williams. *The U. S. Army in World War II, Special Studies, Chronology, 1941-1945.* Washington, D.C.: Office of the Chief of Military History, Department of the Army, 1960.

MEMOIRS AND FIRST PERSON ACCOUNTS

Constance Babington-Smith. *Air Spy, The Story of Photo Intelligence in World War II.* New York: Harper & Brothers Publishers, 1957.

Th. Benecke, A.W. Quick. *History of German Guided Missiles Development.* Brunswick, Germany: Verlag E. Appelhans & Co., 1957.

Walter Dornberger. *V-2.* New York: Ballantine Books, 1954.

Dwight D. Eisenhower. *Crusade in Europe.* New York: Doubleday & Company, Inc., 1948.

A.G. Gregory. *The Saga of the 708 Railway Grand Division.* Baltimore: The Baltimore and Ohio Railroad Company, 1947.

Sir Arthur Harris. *Bomber Offensive.* New York: The MacMillan Company, 1947.

Dieter K. Huzel. *Peenemuende to Canaveral.* Englewood Cliffs, N.J.: Prentice Hall, Inc., 1962.

R.V. Jones: *The Wizard War, British Scientific Intelligence, 1939–1945.* New York: Coward, McCann & Geoghegan, Inc., 1978.

Field Marshal the Viscount Montgomery of Alamein. *The Memoirs of Field Marshal the Viscount Montgomery of Alamein, K.G.* Cleveland: The World Publishing Company, 1958.

Gen. Sir Frederick Pile. *Ack-Ack, Britain's Defence Against Air Attack in the Second World War.* London: George G. Harrap & Co. Ltd, 1949.

Albert Speer. *Inside the Third Reich: Memoirs by Albert Speer.* London: Weidenfeld and Nicolson, 1970.

Albert Speer. *Infiltration: How Himmler Schemed to Build an SS Industrial Empire.* New York: MacMillan Publishing Co., Inc., 1981.

BOOKS

Chief Marshal Sir Michael Armitage. *Unmanned Aircraft, Brassey's Air Power: Aircraft, Weapons Systems and Technology Series,* Volume 3. New York: Brassey's Defence Publishers, 1988.

Erik Bergaust. *Wernher von Braun.* Washington, D.C.: National Space Institute, 1976.

Shelford Bidwell, ed. *Brassey's Artillery of the World.* New York: Bonanza Books, 1977.

Robert M. Browning, Jr. *U.S. Merchant Vessel War Casualties of World War II.* Annapolis: Naval Institute Press, 1996.

Basil Collier. *The Battle of the V-Weapons, 1944–1945.* New York: William Morrow & Company, 1965.

Colonel Sir William Congreve. *Details of the Rocket System.* London: J. Whiting, 1814; Facsimile ed. by R.A. Printing Press, Ltd.

Matthew Cooper. *The German Army 1933–1945: Its Political and Military Failure.* New York: Stein and Day, 1974.

R. Ernest Dupuy and Trevor N. Dupuy. *The Encyclopedia of Military History from 3500 B.C. to the Present,* rev. ed. New York: Harper & Row Publishers, 1970.

Joachim Engelman. *V-2: Dawn of the Rocket Age.* Schiffer Military History Vol. 26. Westchester, PA: Schiffer Publishing Ltd., 1990.

Joachim Engelman. *V-1: The Flying Bomb.* Schiffer Military History Vol. 62. Westchester, PA: Schiffer Publishing Ltd., 1992.

Brian Ford. *German Secret Weapons, Blueprint for Mars.* New York: Ballantine Books, Inc., 1969.

Norman Franks. *Battle of the Airfields.* London: Grubb St., 1994.

Norman Friedman. *Desert Victory: The War for Kuwait.* Annapolis: Naval Institute Press, 1991.

T. J. Gander. *Field Rocket Equipment of the German Army 1939–1945.* London: Almark Publishing Company, 1972.

Robert Gardiner, ed dir. *Conway's All the World's Fighting Ships 1922– 1946.* London, Conway Maritime Press, 1992 reprint 1980 ed.

Jozef Garlinski. *Hitler's Last Weapons: The Underground War against the V-1 and V-2.* New York: Times Books, 1978.

William Green. *The Warplanes of the Third Reich.* New York: Doubleday and Company, 1970.

James P. Harrison. *Mastering the Sky: A History of Aviation from Ancient Times to the Present.* New York: Sarpedon, 1996.

Ken Hechler. *The Bridge at Remagen.* New York: Ballantine Books, 1957.

Dieter Hölsken. *V-Missiles of the Third Reich, The V-1 and V-2.* Sturbridge, MA: Monogram Aviation Publications, 1994.

David Irving. *The Mare's Nest.* London: William Kimber, 1964.

David Irving. *The Rise and Fall of the Luftwaffe: The Life of Field Marshal Erhard Milch.* Boston: Little, Brown and Company, 1973.

Joseph Jobe, ed. *Guns: An Illustrated History of Artillery.* Greenwich, CT: New York Graphic Society, 1971.

David Johnson. *V-1, V-2: Hitler's Vengeance on London.* Chelsea, MI: Scarborough House Publishers, 1981.

Gregory P. Kennedy. *Vengeance Weapon 2, The V-2 Guided Missile.* Washington, D.C.: The Smithsonian Institution Press, 1983.

Franz Kosar. *A Pocket History of Light Field Guns.* London: Ian Allen, 1974.

Willy Ley. *Rockets, Missiles and Space Travel.* New York: The Viking Press, 1953.

B.H. Liddell-Hart. *History of the Second World War.* New York: G.P. Putnam's Sons, 1970.

John Livingstone. *740th Railway Operating Battalion.* New York: Carlton Press, Inc, 1981.

Norman Longmate. *Hitler's Rockets: The Story of the V-2s.* London: Hutchinson, 1985.

Herbert Molloy Mason, Jr. *The Rise of the Luftwaffe, 1918–1940.* New York: The Dial Press, 1973.

Merle Miller. *Ike the Soldier As They Knew Him.* New York: G.P. Putnam's Sons, 1987.

John O. Moench. *Marauder Men.* Florida: Malia Enterprises, 1989.

Kenneth Munson. *Bombers 1914–1919, Patrol and Reconnaissance Aircraft, The Pocket Encyclopedia of World Aircraft in Color.* New York: The MacMillan Company, 1968.

Williamson Murray. *Strategy For Defeat: The Luftwaffe, 1933–1945.* Maxwell Air Force Base: Air University Press, 1983.

Williamson Murray. *Luftwaffe.* Baltimore: The Nautical and Aviation Publishing Company of America, 1985.

David Nash. *German Artillery 1914–1918.* Middlesex, England: Almark Publishing Co., 1970.

Michael J. Neufeld. *The Rocket and The Reich: Peenemünde and the Coming of the Ballistic Missile Era.* New York: The Free Press, 1995.

Bob Ogley. *Doodlebugs and Rockets: The Battle of the Flying Bombs.* Westerham, England: Froglets Publications, 1992.

Ordnance Park Corporation. *The Ordnance Manual for Use of the Officers of the United States Army, 1862.* New York: J.B. Lippincott & Co., Reprint, 1970.

Garry Pape and Ronald C. Harrison. *Queen of the Midnight Skies.* West Chester PA: Schiffer Military History, 1992.

Danny S. Parker. *To Win the Winter Sky.* Conshohocken, PA: Combined Books, 1994.

Roger Parkinson. *Blood Toil Sweat and Tears: The War History from Dunkirk to Alamein, Based on the War Cabinet Papers of 1940 to 1942.* New York: David McKay Company, 1973.

Norman Rich. *Hitler's War Aims: Ideology, the Nazi State, and the Course of Expansion.* New York: W.W. Norton & Company, 1973.

Air Marshal Sir Robert Saunby. *Air Bombardment: The Story of its Development.* New York: Harper and Brothers, 1961.

Matthias Schmidt. *Albert Speer: The End of a Myth.* New York: St. Martin's Press, 1984.

Louis L. Snyder. *Encyclopedia of the Third Reich.* New York: McGraw Hill Book Company, 1976.

Richard Suchenwirth. *Command and Leadership in the German Air Force.* Maxwell AFB: USAF Historical Division, Aerospace Studies Institute, Air University, 1969.

John Terraine. *A Time for Courage: The Royal Air Force in the European War, 1939–1945.* New York: MacMillan Publishing Company, 1985.

Steve R. Waddell. *United States Army Logistics: The Normandy Campaign 1944.* Westport, CT: Greenwood Press, 1994.

Russel F. Weigley. *Eisenhower's Lieutenants: The Campaign of France, 1944–1945.* Bloomington: University of Indiana Press, 1981.

Kenneth P. Werrell. *The Evolution of the Cruise Missile.* Maxwell AFB: Air University Press, 1985.

Chester Wilmot. *The Struggle For Europe,* 8th ed. London: Collins, 1954.

Major Bob M. Woodson. *The Story of Antwerp X.* Antwerp, Belgium: HQ Antwerp X, 1946.

Richard Anthony Young. *The Flying Bomb.* New York: Sky Books Press, 1978.

PERIODICALS

Air Defense Magazine Staff. "History of Air Defense: Antwerp V-1 Defense (1944–1945)." Fort Bliss, TX: U.S. Army Air Defense School, *Air Defense Magazine,* July–September 1976.

Major Vincent P. Di Fronzo. "Unity of Command: Countering Aircraft and Missile Threats." Fort Leslie J. McNair, Washington, D.C.: *Joint Force Quarterly,* Spring 1996.

Bryon E. Greenwald. "Scud Alert: The History, Development and Military Significance of Ballistic Missiles on Tactical Operations," in *The Land Warfare Papers.* Arlington: The Institute on Land Warfare, Association of the United States Army, October 1995.

Captain Benjamin D. King. *The First Field Artillery Guided Missile System,* in *Field Artillery Journal,* Vol. 44, No. 4. Fort Sill, OK: U.S. Army Field Artillery School, July–August 1976.

Lieutenant Colonel Albert J. Weinnig. "Radar Screening for Low-Flying Targets." Fort Monroe, VA: U.S. Army Coast Artillery School, *The Coast Artillery Journal,* March–April 1946.

Harry Woodman. *Avions-Torpilleurs, Le Prieur's Rockets, Windsock,* Vol. 10, No. 3. Berkhamstead, UK: Albatros Productions Ltd, May 1994.

Major William D. Workman, Jr. "AAA Versus the JP's." Fort Monroe, VA: U.S. Army Coast Artillery School, *The Coast Artillery Journal,* March–April 1946.

CONTEMPORARY UNIT NEWSPAPERS/ NEWSLETTERS

Public Relations Section, *The SOXOS,* Maastricht, Public Relations Section, 729th Railway Operating Battalion, 1945.

First Sergeant Albert W. Spratley, *The Port of Antwerp and the Military Rail Service,* 709th Railway Grand Division

First Sergeant Albert W. Spratley, *Highlights of History of the 709th Railway Grand Division,* 709th Railway Grand Division

Index